D0392429

DR. AXELROD'S MINI-
ATLAS
OF
FRESHWATER
AQUARIUM
FISHES
MINI-EDITION

DR. HERBERT R.
AXELROD

DR. WARREN E.
BURGESS

DR. CLIFF W.
EMMENS

NEAL PRONEK
JERRY G. WALLS
RAY HUNZIKER

Symphysodon hybrid Discus

Poecilia reticulata (Guppy)

Astyanax fasciatus mexicanus,
the Blind Cave Tetra

Photography

In addition to the photos taken by Dr. Axelrod, this book also contains many photographs by other photographers of fishes and aquarium subjects. The book is indebted to all of the people listed here . . . and to anyone else whose name might have been inadvertently omitted from the list.

Hiromitsu Akiyama
Dr. Gerald R. Allen
K. Attwood
Glen Axelrod
Dr. Hiroshi Azuma
Heiko Bleher
Pierre Brichard
Dr. Martin Brittan
Dr. Warren E. Burgess
Dr. Brooks Burr
Gerald C. Corcoran
Vojtech Elek
Jaroslav Elias
Dr. Augustin Fernandez-Yepez
Walter Foersch
Dr. Stanislav Frank
H. J. Franke
Dan Fromm
Dr. Jacques Gery
Dr. Robert J. Goldstein
Dr. Myron Gordon
Dr. Harry Grier
K. Jeno
Rodney Jonklaas
Burkhard Kahl
J. Kassanyi
S. Kochetov
R. Lawrence
Ken Lucas, Steinhart Aquarium
Gerhard Marcuse
Dr. Richard L. Mayden
Hans Mayland
Manfred Meyer

Marine Planning (Aqua Life, Japan)
Midori Shobo (Fish Magazine, Japan)
New York Zoological Society
Leo G. Nico
Aaron Norman
Dr. Joanne Norton
Anatoly Noznov
Y. W. Ong
Dr. Lawrence M. Page
Klaus Paysan
Kurt Quitschau
Hans-Joachim Richter
Mervin F. Roberts
Erhard Roloff
Andre Roth
Jorgen Scheel
Gunter Schmida
Harald Schultz
Dr. Wolfgang Staeck
Rainier Stawikowski
Glenn Y. Takeshita
Donald C. Taphorn
Edward C. Taylor
Dr. D. Terver, Nancy Aquarium
Gerald J. M. Timmerman
Dr. Bruce J. Turner
Arend van den Nieuwenhuizen
Braz Walker
Wardley Products Co.
Franz Werner
Uwe Werner
Gene Wolfsheimer
Ruda Zukal

© 1987 by T.F.H. Publications, Inc.

Distributed in the UNITED STATES by T.F.H. Publications, Inc., 211 West Sylvania Avenue, Neptune City, NJ 07753; in CANADA to the Pet Trade by H & L Pet Supplies Inc., 27 Kingston Crescent, Kitchener, Ontario N2B 2T6; Rolf C. Hagen Ltd., 3225 Sartelon Street, Montreal 382 Quebec; in CANADA to the Book Trade by Macmillan of Canada (A Division of Canada Publishing Corporation), 164 Commander Boulevard, Agincourt, Ontario M1S 3C7; in ENGLAND by T.F.H. Publications Limited, 4 Kier Park, Ascot, Berkshire SL5 7DS; in AUSTRALIA AND THE SOUTH PACIFIC by T.F.H. (Australia) Pty. Ltd., Box 149, Brookvale 2100 N.S.W., Australia; in NEW ZEALAND by Ross Haines & Son, Ltd., 18 Monmouth Street, Grey Lynn, Auckland 2 New Zealand; in SINGAPORE AND MALAYSIA by MPH Distributors (S) Pte., Ltd., 601 Sims Drive, #03/07/21, Singapore 1438; in the PHILIPPINES by Bio-Research, 5 Lippay Street, San Lorenzo Village, Makati Rizal; in SOUTH AFRICA by Multipet Pty. Ltd., 30 Turners Avenue, Durban 4001. Published by T.F.H. Publications Inc. Manufactured in the United States of America by T.F.H. Publications, Inc.

Contents

The fishes in this **Mini-Atlas** are grouped according to their systematic characteristics. Thus all the cichlids are together, all the catfishes are together, etc. In the larger **Dr. Axelrod's Atlas,** upon which this book is based, the fishes are grouped geographically.

The key to the **symbols** is found on the back cover flaps, both inside and outside, plus page 4. A discussion of the **symbols** is to be found starting on page 7.

SYMBOLS

Something new for TFH books is the use of symbols. Many previous TFH books on fishes relied extensively upon the repetitious use of words to catalogue fishes according to either their range (zoogeographic) or their ancestry (systematic). What we have attempted to do here is to use symbols which can replace words.

The captions, where possible, identify the SEX of the fishes, their FEEDING HABITS, their REPRODUCTION, AQUARIUM LIGHTING, TEMPERAMENT, AQUARIUM SET-UP, SWIMMING HABITS, the **pH of the water** which best suits them, the **hardness of the water**, their best **temperature tolerance**, how **large they grow** and the **capacity of the tank** which suits them best.

FEEDING HABITS

Dry, packaged food

Live worms, Daphnia, etc

Live fish

Vegetarian

REPRODUCTION

Egglayer

Livebearer

AQUARIUM LIGHTING

Bright with occasional sunlight

Bright, no sunlight

As dark as possible as long as fishes are visible

TEMPERAMENT

Peaceful community fish

Not recommended for beginners

AQUARIUM SET-UP

Densely planted aquarium

Rocks; no plants

Only gravel on bottom

Rocks, plants and driftwood

SWIMMING HABITS

Bottom swimmer

No special swimming level

Top swimmer

Swims in middle of water

pH = Relative acidity/alkalinity of water. Above 7.0 is alkaline. Below 7.0 is acidic.

H = Hardness of water according to German scale. The lower the number, the softer the water.

C = Temperature in degrees Centigrade.

cm = Maximum length to which the fish grows (in centimeters).

L = Capacity (in liters) of smallest aquarium in which fish may be kept.

PREFACE

There has to be a reason why any book is published; sometimes the reasons are specific. Take, for example, the book I wrote about the fishes of Lakes Malawi and Tanganyika. In the 1950's the fishes from these rift lakes of Africa were virtually unknown. When I visited the lakes and found so many beautiful cichlids, I thought I should share these beautiful fishes with the rest of the aquarium world and the book about the fishes from these lakes was published. It was very successful, going through 11 editions. More importantly, it brought fish collectors to the lakes and the poor countries of Malawi, Tanganyika, Burundi and Zaire had a source of income from the replenishable resources of their rift lakes. Naturally, this gave me a lot of satisfaction.

But many critics, rightfully so, complained that most of the photos of the original editions of that book were of "dead" fishes. While it is not true that the fishes were dead, they were placed into a special photographic tank which restrained them between two pieces of glass so the photo could be made in the available light.

. Only after the photos were taken were the fish preserved in formalin for further study. When I got back to England and America I was able to compare the fishes I had collected and photographed against the specimens in the museums which had been used as types for naming the fish, and ONLY THEN could I be sure of the identification of the fishes. Thus these fishes, though looking dead, are probably the only photographs of fishes which have been *accurately* identified.

Photographs of fishes in an aquarium can never be positively identified as to species; aquarium-bred specimens are equally difficult to be certain about. As a matter of fact, the only truly positive way to identify a fish is to photograph it, then have a scientist compare it to the type (or the description of the type), and thus confirm its identity. Many of the photographs you find in this book, perhaps even hundreds of them, may be fishes which have been positively identified in the manner described above. I have elected to use these photos, rather than more beautiful aquarium shots, because they have positive identifications. Many of the photos shown in this book are of species for which this is the only known photograph of the fish.

The main reason for this book is to help the more advanced hobbyist and dealer recognize with a fair degree of certainty the scientific names of the most popular aquarium fishes, plus many of the rarer fishes which have a good chance of being imported sooner or later.

When collecting fishes in the field, many strange things have occurred. In the early 1950's when I was searching for Neon Tetras in Brazil, I came across what I thought were "Giant Neons." Having caught them when they were young, the Cardinal Tetras, *Paracheirodon axelrodi*, looked just like regular Neon Tetras, but they kept growing and growing after I got them home. I described them as Giant Neons when I sent them to the late Dr. Leonard P. Schultz, Curator of Fishes at the U.S.N.M., Smithsonian Institution. Dr. Schultz later discovered they were a new species and subsequently named them in my honor. But, had I not "brought them back alive" and grown them in my aquarium, perhaps it might never have been named after me because someone else might have discovered they were different from the usual Neon Tetras.

Now that travelling is so relatively simple (when compared with the 1940's and 1950's when I discovered so many new species), it should be possible for many aquarists to visit faraway lands and try collecting some of their own new, rare fishes. That's another reason for this book.

Aquarists on vacation looking for native fishes in their own environment actually should take the much larger **Dr. Axelrod's Atlas** with them, but it weighs twice as much as this volume. This **Mini-Atlas** should serve to identify the genus to which most aquarium fishes belong.

If possible, make a photographic tank by using glass and the glue you can buy from your aquarium shop, and take your own photos "in the wild." It may not be as simple as you thought, but it will give you great satisfaction and will certainly make the trip "reportable" in any tropical fish hobbyist magazine, even if the fishes look "dead."

While some people object to this style of photography, it is much, much better than taking a photo of the fish in your hand; but if you break the photo tank or the fish is too large for it, then by all means photograph it in your hand or lying on a piece of wood; even hanging from a hook, if that's the way you caught it.

Many years ago I wrote a book about aquarium photography. It was not a good selling book, but it started some fine photographers into a very profitable hobby. The highlights of this book are presented for your convenience.

THE BIOLOGICAL SEXUAL SYMBOLS

Most biological books use the two familiar symbols ♀ ♂ to designate male and female. These symbols are readily recognizable by most aquarists, but do you know what their true meaning is?

The male symbol ♂ is the shield of Mars (the circle) and the "arrow" is the lance, so the symbol is the shield and lance of Mars, the great Roman God of War!

The sign for the female organism is the Mirror of Venus ♀. Venus is the Roman Goddess of Love and the most brilliant planet in our solar system. In their order of distance from our Sun, the planets are Mercury, Venus, Earth, Mars, Jupiter, Saturn, Uranus, Neptune and Pluto. Thus the Earth is "surrounded" by Venus and Mars. Many ancient tales are to be found in Latin textbooks about this God and Goddess.

FEEDING HABITS

Most fishes eat a variety of foods; it can generally be stated that most fishes prefer live foods. *Dried foods are merely a substitute for live foods.* If you want your fishes to be at their best and to have their best colors, then live foods are the way to go. Breeding aquarium fishes is greatly aided by feeding the breeders live foods as part of their conditioning.

Our symbols for "dry, packaged feed" ⚲ shows a typical package of flake or powdered food which is available at your petshop. Many fishes can live a long life with dried feeds PROVIDING they are varied. Don't feed your fishes the same food all the time; alternate brands of feed since most manufacturers tend to use the same ingredients.

Our symbol for "live worms, *Daphnia*, etc." means that the fish should be offered as much live food as possible. Your petshop may have dozens of *different* types of live foods throughout the year as the availability of many foods is seasonal. A good substitute for live foods is frozen or freeze-dried foods. The freeze-dried seem to be much better than the frozen because you are buying "water" with the frozen feeds. (The terms "feeds" and "foods" may be used interchangeably, though foods are basically meant for humans and feeds for animals.) The symbol we use for live foods is a worm ∿.

Many fishes are vegetarians, but it can be safely stated that most fish need some vegetable matter in their diet. However, certain fishes have an almost insatiable desire for vegetable matter. Those fishes which have this characteristic are identified by the symbol of an aquarium plant ⚘, which indicates they are vegetarians. It is also a warning that they will eat the plants unless special diets are offered such as lettuce and spinach leaves.

Different ways to hold a fish for photography. These are far from desirable photos, but they are better than no photos at all! Photography by Heiko Bleher in Australia.

Collecting fish while diving in Marau, South Pacific, the author photographed fishes in his photo tank even while on board a small boat. Photo (1974) by Dr. Gerald Allen. **Below:** In the Rio Calima area of Colombia, South America, the author, with Heiko Bleher, positioning a fish with a thin strip of metal in his photo tank. Photo by Dr. Martin Brittan (1973).

REPRODUCTION

There are two basic kinds of reproduction found in fishes. Those that lay eggs are called *"egglayers"* ➤. Those that have living young are called *"livebearers"* ➤. There are many types of egglayers and livebearers.

Some egglayers, such as many gouramis, make a nest of bubbles and deposit their eggs in the nest. These are sometimes referred to as "bubblenest builders." Other fishes, including some *Betta* species, many cichlids, and others, take the eggs in their mouth and brood them there. These are called "mouthbrooders." There are many egglayers that merely spray their eggs and forget about them (unless they happen to eat them!). Thus aquarium fishes are so interesting, for they represent almost every kind of animal reproduction found in Nature!

AQUARIUM LIGHTING

Most aquarium fishes are camouflaged. Their bottoms are white so, when viewed from below, they blend with the sky background. Others are blotchy and green and only show bright colors during breeding times. In order for fishes to be successfully maintained in an aquarium, their lighting requirements must be met or they will be in constant stress and die from this stress.

Our symbols for light requirements are: ○ = bright with occasional sunlight; ◑ = bright, no sunlight; ● = as dark as possible as long as fish are visible.

The great majority of aquarium fishes will do well in bright light without direct sunlight. Sunlight is usually to be avoided with aquariums since the sun not only makes algae grow uncontrollably, but it may heat the water to the point of killing the fishes.

Many fishes, especially catfishes and cichlids, like to have a place to hide, like a cave or dense vegetation. They also prefer as little light as possible, just enough light so they can see.

The symbols for these conditions are presented in the captions under each photograph. As a general rule, fishes do better with less light (intensity) than they require; too much light (intensity) is very stressful.

TEMPERAMENT

Fishes are like most other animals in the world. There are those which are peaceful and do not disturb their neighbors and those which are harmful. Peaceful or community fishes are designated with a heart ♥. These fishes can be kept together except with males of the same species. But even with these normally peaceful fishes you must exercise care since they will almost always eat other animals, fishes included, which are much smaller than themselves. Thus, while Guppies are certainly peaceful community fish, they will often eat their own babies or babies of other fishes in the same aquarium.

Probably the most dangerous of aquarium fishes are the piranhas! They not only eat other fishes but might bite your hands as well. They, and fishes which are very territorial and fight with other fishes for "living room," are designated with a skull and crossbones ☠ which is the typical "Danger" or "Pirate's" sign. It may be a bit too dramatic, but fishes which are designated with the skull and crossbones are definitely not for beginning aquarists.

AQUARIUM SETUP

There are many different kinds of aquarium set-ups. Some hobbyists make their tank like a small pool in Africa, with just stones, caves and sand. This type of tank is suitable for most African cichlids. A tank like this is marked with the following symbol which designates a tank without plants: ▣.

Cichlids also do well in completely bare tanks with just sand. Such a tank is marked with a symbol like this: ▣. It is especially suited for large cichlids which dig up everything, looking for a site upon which to deposit their spawn.

Densely planted aquariums are designated like this: ▣. These kinds of aquariums are primarily for livebearers. The plants offer the babies a place to hide away from the adults.

A typical community aquarium in which the reproduction of the fishes is secondary to the beauty of the aquarium is a tank with rocks, plants, driftwood, and such other ornaments as the hobbyist encounters and enjoys. Such an aquarium is designated like this: ▣.

SWIMMING HABITS

To balance the fishes in a community tank, it is usually desirable to have fishes which swim at different levels in the aquarium. In most cases you can ascertain this type of fish by the mouth. If the mouth opens on the bottom of the head, then it could be a bottom-dweller such as a *Corydoras*-like catfish. If the mouth opens on top of the head, it might be a top-dweller such as a killifish like an *Aphyosemion* or a livebearer like a *Poecilia*. Fishes with mouths opening in the middle, like most Characins, such as the *Paracheirodon* species, will inhabit the middle of the aquarium. Thus the swimming habits of the fish are symbolized under each photograph with the following signs: ▢ ▣ ▢ ▤.

These African fishes were photographed in 1970 in the Congo (now Zaire), Africa, at the same time the photo on page 25 was taken and in the same photo tank.

The uppermost fish, *Ctenopoma oxyrhynchum*, has a mouth which opens upwards, thus it might be expected to swim near the top of the tank. The centermost fish, *Barbodes kerstenii,* has a central mouth opening and should be a mid-water swimmer. The fish at bottom is a young *Synodontis alberti*. All of these fish were "sleeping," not dead, when photographed and brought back to America alive.

The examples given above are general. Many a livebearer whose mouth terminates on the top of the head also picks at the bottom for bits of food when it is hungry. So treat these characteristics in a general manner.

pH, HARDNESS (H) AND TEMPERATURE (C)

Besides the amount of light, there are certain characteristics of the water in which fishes are kept that are important to know. Fishes with greatly varying water needs should not be kept together!

The pH of the water is the measure of the acidity and alkalinity. A neutral pH is 7.0; when it is higher than that the water is considered to be alkaline. When it is lower, it is acid. Your local petshop has chemicals which can adjust the pH of the aquarium up or down. The caption under each photo tells you the ideal pH for that fish.

The hardness of your aquarium water is measured in degrees of hardness. Your petshop has water softeners to make your water softer and calcium blocks which make the water harder. Petshops have test kits for most water chemistry tests.

Your petshop will also have a hardness test kit. Each kit should contain instructions in the use of the kit and how to read it. Most kits use the DH scale (Deutsche Hartgrad), or German Hardness, measured in degrees. The degree of hardness in each caption is symbolized with an H.

The temperature of the water which the fishes prefer is measured in Centigrade with a C. Conversion charts from C° to F° follow in the next section.

L AND CM (SIZE OF FISH AND TANK)

The maximum size to which a fish normally grows in the aquarium is given in centimeters. Centimeters is abbreviated with the letters cm. One inch equals 2.54 cm. A chart in the next section allows you access to the conversion from inches to centimeters. Fishes can only reach their maximum growth if they are housed in a proper aquarium.

A liquid measure of about one quart equals one liter. One liter is abbreviated as 1L. Liquid measure conversion charts follow in the next section. For water, one liter equals 1,000 grams of weight equals one kilogram equals 1,000 cubic centimeters. The metric system for weight and volume is based upon water, as you can see.

Thus, if you take the inside measurements of your aquarium, preferably in centimeters (remember one inch = 2.54 centimeters), you can calculate the volume of the aquarium by multiplying the

length × width × height and that will give you cubic centimeters. Since each 1,000 cubic centimeters equals a liter of water and each liter weighs 1 kilogram (kg) which equals about 2.2 pounds, you can easily calculate the weight and volume of the water in your tank.

It will be very surprising once you have made the calculations of the capacity of the tank that it is smaller than you thought. The average aquarium, say a 20 gallon tank, is usually only 18-19 gallons in capacity! Don't think your dealer is dishonest. This practice has been going on for at least 50 years. Tanks are usually made to nest one inside the other so shipments are cheaper. The dimensions thus depend upon the "nest" of tanks to be shipped.

One U.S. gallon contains 231 cubic inches and weighs about 8⅓ pounds. The Imperial gallon contains 277.42 cubic inches and weighs 10 pounds.

LIQUID MEASURE

Metric	Approx. Apothecary
1 liter	1.04 quarts
960 cc.	1 quart
750 cc.	1-½ pints
500 cc.	1 pint
250 cc.	8 fluidounces
200 cc.	7 fluidounces
100 cc.	3-½ fluidounces
50 cc.	1-¾ fluidounces
30 cc.	1 fluidounce
15 cc.	4 fluidrachms
10 cc.	2-½ fluidrachms
8 cc.	2 fluidrachms
5 cc.	1-¼ fluidrachms
4 cc.	1 fluidrachm

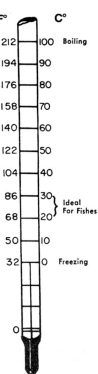

HOUSEHOLD MEASURES AND EQUIVALENTS

Household Measures	Metric Equivalent
1 teaspoonful	5 ml
1 tablespoonful	15 ml
2 tablespoonfuls	30 ml
1 wineglassful	60 ml
1 teacupful	120 ml
1 tumblerful	240 ml
1 pint	480 ml
1 quart	960 ml
1 U.S. gallon (4 quarts)	3 liter 840 ml
Imperial gallon (5 quarts)	4 liter 800 ml

AVOIRDUPOIS— METRIC WEIGHT

Ounces	Grams
1/16	1.8
1/8	3.5
1/4	7.1
1/2	14.2
1	28.4
2	56.7
3	85.0
4	113.4
5	141.7
6	170.1
7	198.4
8	226.8
9	255.1
10	283.5
11	311.9
12	340.2
13	368.5
14	396.9
15	425.2
16 (1 lb.)	453.6

AVOIRDUPOIS— METRIC WEIGHT

Pounds	Grams
1 (16 oz)	453.59
2	907.18
3	1360.78 (1.36 kg.)
4	1814.37 (1.81 kg.)
5	2267.96 (2.27 kg.)
6	2721.55 (2.72 kg.)
7	3175.15 (3.18 kg.)
8	3628.74 (3.63 kg.)
9	4082.33 (4.08 kg.)
10	4535.92 (4.54 kg.)

METRIC— AVOIRDUPOIS WEIGHT

Grams	Ounces
0.001 (1 mg.)	0.000035274
1.	0.035274
1000 (1 kg.)	35.274 (2.2046 lb.)

Above: Heiko Bleher moving the position of a fish in the photo tank as Dr. Wolfgang Tins takes photos. The tank in the back of the photo tank serves as a background.
Below: The author took this photo of two marine fish using a friend as a background. The fish are restrained.

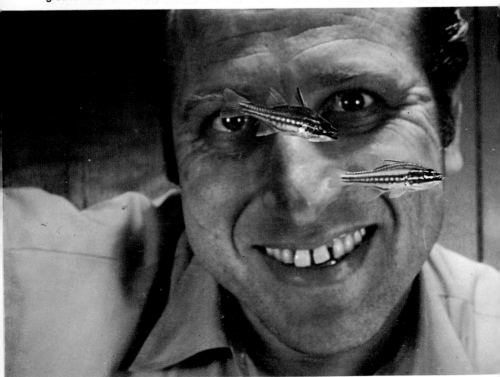

Photography for Aquarists

Since photography is the English-speaking world's number one hobby (stamp collecting is number two) and fishkeeping is number three, there is a great possibility that the home with an aquarium is also the home with a camera. It seems quite natural, then, for the fish lover to want to photograph his fishes ... and for the camera-bug to want to use the aquarium as a model.

Another important reason for me to share my knowledge of fish photography is simple ... I have written more than 50 books about fishes and hundreds of articles. Not one of them would have been a success if it were not for the beautiful photographs which adorn the pages and illustrate point after point of what I was trying to get across to the reader. With fishes going through color changes or spawning antics, it is impossible to record verbally what happens ... yet a camera records so much with just a single photograph or a series if that is possible. One of my best-selling books, **BREEDING AQUARIUM FISHES,** would have been quite impossible without photos of spawning series of more than 100 species of fishes.

Finally, to identify a fish from its scientific description, even with a drawing or photograph of the dead, preserved specimen, takes a formal education of perhaps six to eight years in a university. Using a good color photograph is nearly all that a fish-lover needs.

Once you've mastered fish photography you can submit articles to hobbyist magazines, too.

Needless to say, you need an aquarium and some fishes and plants. The fishes should be as large as possible; the aquarium should have glass which is absolutely clean and not scratched and the water must be crystal clear without debris floating in suspension. A light background of solid color is preferred. If there is no painted background the back can be covered with white paper (light blue is also very good), a white towel or anything similar of a non reflective color. By non-reflective I mean that you can't see your own image in it if you try to utilize it for a mirror. Stay away from black backgrounds until you've mastered the art.

The top of the aquarium should be open so you can shoot light into the scene from the top. You will need a minimum of one flash unit, preferably a strobe ... more preferably three strobes which are synchronized to go off at the same time that the camera shutter opens the lens.

You will also need a camera, preferably a single-lens reflex. This means that you can actually look through the lens by means of a mirror system that folds out of the way when you snap the photo. Almost any camera can take photographs of fish tanks and fishes, but the quality of the photograph and the waste of film and time will more than make up for an investment in the proper equipment.

In the jungle I do not use spot-lights, strobe lights, flash guns, model lights or a full-sized aquarium. I use a Nikon with a 55 mm Makro lens which can photograph as close as 2 inches from the subject in a 2:1 ratio (the photograph of the fish will be half as large as the fish itself). I use a small aquarium which is about 2 inches wide by 8 inches square and I drape my handkerchief over the back to act as a background and light reflector. The sun is my light . . . and there is nothing in the world better than strong sunlight for fish photography regardless of what anyone tells you (or sells you).

Of course, besides a camera you also need film. I have used almost every kind of color film and black-and-white film made. There is only one manufacturer you can depend upon for consistent quality . . . Kodak.

Kodak makes several grades of films, but the best films are Kodachrome for 35 mm color photographs (slides); Ektachrome (daylight type) for 2¼ inches square or 4 × 5 inches color films; and Tri-X for black and white photography (even though it is fast and many people will disagree with me). The use of faster color films and faster or slower monochrome films is left to the more advanced photographer. To take good photographs of fishes or anything else, stick to one camera, one lens, one color film and one black-and-white film and learn all you can about the combination. Good photographs will be a natural result of experience. But if you keep changing films and changing lenses you'll always be working out new exposures and new techniques with lighting and you'll never get down to learning how to make good photographs. Stick with what I have recommended and you'll be using what most of the successful photographers use (except for those behind the Iron Curtain who cannot get Kodak products).

LIGHTS

The best light for taking fish photographs is sunlight. Unfortunately sunlight is not always available and even if it were, it does have certain disadvantages.

I have taken thousands of color photographs of individual fishes using sunlight as the only source of light. These photographs are among the best pictures I have ever taken because this light brings out the best colors of the fish. All color films are made according to the full spectrum of sunlight. Strobe and flash lights do not have the same composition as sunlight so some colors may well be lost by using artificial light.

The disadvantages of sunlight are important. First, you normally use sunlight in the summertime. This heats up the aquarium, the camera and the photographer. Obviously, you cannot spend hours in the sunlight or the black camera case will become very hot, causing expansion of the parts and possible malfunction. Since you must have the sun coming into the aquarium over the shoulder of the photogra-

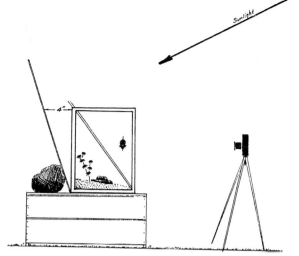

A typical jungle setup. A rock holds the background in place. The sun strikes the background and makes it light so there are no shadows from the fish cast onto the background. The position of the glass used for restraining the fish is shown before the fish is squeezed.

pher, your back will become overheated and the shadow of your head or body will often mask the photo. Since the sun is always moving in the sky, the shadow moves too, so the position of the aquarium and camera must be shifted from time to time.

I use the sun only in the jungle or on location to photograph a single fish.

If the sun is available, never use the sun two hours after sunrise or two hours before sunset. The sun when sitting low in the sky filters through too much of the dirty atmosphere of the earth and actually becomes discolored. There is such a thing as dirty sunlight, believe it or not! Photographs taken with dirty sunlight are always yellowish and lend an unreal cast of yellow to the photograph. At times I am forced to use this kind of sunlight, especially in the jungle when at 5 PM I catch a very beautiful fish that is about to die, and if I don't photograph it right then, it will be useless by the next mid-morning.

For the average aquarist, most of his photographs will be taken indoors where there is little if any sunlight available. Also, most of the photographs will be taken in the evening, so artificial light is a necessity. The only problem is: what kind of light?

I use a combination of strobe lights and regular house bulbs. The house bulbs are used as model lights which are meant only to provide enough light for focusing on the subject and for showing me how the shadows will fall upon the subject as well as the reflections the strobe will have on the glass. To do this I use special reflectors which have built in model lights which are located more or less in the same center as the strobe lights.

TAKING YOUR FIRST FISH PHOTOS

You have your camera, film, lights and all the necessary connections between the camera and lights. I assume you have an aquarium and have decided upon actually making a fish photograph. I suggest you use the technique explained later for your first photos because the fish is held more-or-less firmly in one position. It would be best if you used ice water to knock-out the fish first so you don't have complicated problems of fish and photography for your first session. Get the largest, flattest fish you can find ... and one that you don't mind losing. Stay away from round fish like rivulins (killies); try to get a *Metynnis* or even a large tetra or *Betta*. These are the easiest.

Put the fish into the photo tank and adjust it for the photo. I started in quite another way, though, that may be just as good. I pasted the picture of a fish on the front of the photo tank and did my experimental work on that. It was perfect!

Now comes the critical testing of the initial setup. Let's assume you are using two strobes. If you are using three, the top strobe is only for top lighting to get rid of shadows and to illuminate the top of the fish. Locate the camera in such a way that the plane of the film is perfectly parallel to the body of the fish. If the camera is tilted you will end up exaggerating the perspective of the fish. Locate the camera directly in front of the fish so the center of the fish is about in the center of the lens. Now focus on the fish and frame the fish in the finder so the fish fills about 80% of the frame. Now locate your light sources so that the light strikes the front glass at about a 45° angle. This ensures there will be no glare bounced back into the camera. Almost all beginners have this lighting problem though it is so simple to correct.

If for some reason you cannot locate the light sources at 45° from the front of the glass and in the same general plane as the camera, then you can easily raise the lights over the photographer's shoulder, bouncing off the glass at 45° from the top. By using model lights and viewing the subject at the same time, you can locate the lights so the reflection of the light source is not bounced back into the camera.

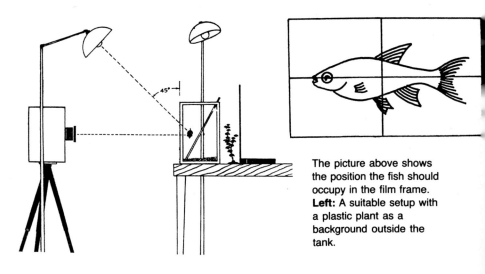

The picture above shows the position the fish should occupy in the film frame. **Left:** A suitable setup with a plastic plant as a background outside the tank.

The author with Dr. Jacques Gery in his Amazonian laboratory in Brazil. The photo tank in the author's hands is made exactly deep enough to hold a box of 35mm Kodachrome. The film is transported to the jungle in the tank and it protects the restraining glass at the same time. After the fish are photographed they are preserved for positive identification.

The main object in lighting is to *uniformly* flood the subject with light without getting reflections. This is extremely difficult to do with one source of light since it obviously must be to one side or top or bottom. Two lights coming in equally from both sides is the easiest setup to balance.

But often you only have one light . . . then what do you do? I usually solve that problem by directing my light from the front top, hitting the glass at 45° from the top, so the light source's rays are aimed directly at the center of the fish, illuminating it uniformly from mouth to tail, but highlighting the dorsal edge and leaving the belly in shadows. Because a fish is normally darker on the dorsal edge and lighter on the belly, hardly anyone realizes the fish is toplighted.

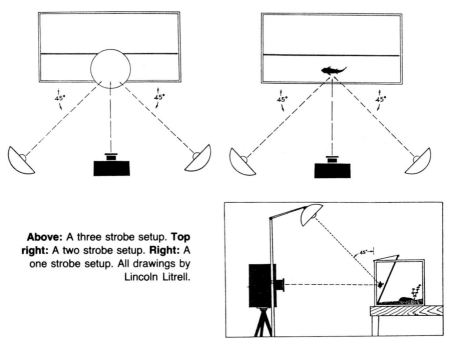

Above: A three strobe setup. **Top right:** A two strobe setup. **Right:** A one strobe setup. All drawings by Lincoln Litrell.

TAKING PICTURES IN A PHOTO TANK

You cannot go to your petshop or camera store and ask for a photo tank. They won't know what you are talking about. A photo tank is something you make yourself. I have a dozen of them in all sizes. The most convenient size is about 2 inches thick by 8 inches square. You can have a metal frame or you can glue the glass together using a silicone base cement available at all petshops. You will also need an additional pane of glass which is exactly 8 inches square. The glass should be free of bubbles and scratches and, if possible, be of photographic quality. Don't let it stop you if it isn't of photographic quality.

Also order two pieces of glass 2 inches wide and 8 inches long. This will be the two sides. The bottom piece should be about 2 x 8½ inches. Glue the larger sides to the smaller sides so the tank is actually a bit larger than 8 inches; in this way the third piece of 8 inches square glass can be used to restrain the fish.

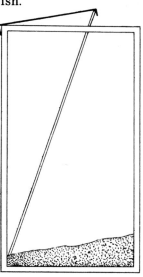

There is an art to using the restraining glass. In the diagram, the glass is set at about a 45° angle. If a thick-bodied fish is put in, it will normally swim to the bottom and jam itself in because the fish does not see the glass. You can then move the fish into position by using a thin metal band. A piece of masking tape holds the glass in position and can be used over and over again as long as it stays dry. The thinner the fish, the closer must be the restraining glass to the front glass of the photo tank.

This restraining glass should be jammed into fine sand in the bottom of the tank and angled from the bottom front to the back top. Thus, when the fish is placed into the photo tank it usually jams itself into the restraining glass and "poses." If the fish is too small you simply pull the restraining glass closer to the front glass and squeeze the fish gently between them. A piece of tape across the top will hold the restraining glass against the front glass.

I use a thin strip of metal to position the fish once it is restrained. I get the metal from steel strapping used to strap heavy bundles. I then file off the rough edges and jockey the fish into position with this simple tool. I suppose a long, dull knife blade would work as well.

The water in the photo tank should be perfectly clean without any debris floating in it. If there is debris it will reflect the light and ruin your picture. You must also have the glass perfectly clear and clean; no spots or streaks. If when you put in the water you discover air bubbles forming on the glass, simply disperse them with the same tool that you use to pose the fish (the piece of banding steel). It goes without saying that the water should be the same temperature as that in the aquarium from which the fish you want to photograph has been taken. If you actually use aquarium water (as I do) it is necessary to filter it through three layers of filter wool (made of very fine crimped Dacron) to get out all the minute particles which are being held in suspension.

If you cannot get the fish to "pose" for you by using a restraining glass you can also render them immobile by putting them to sleep with drugs (such as MS-222) or allowing them to swim in freshly opened soda water (the CO_2 acts as a narcotic). I also use ice cubes to make them immobile but this often kills the more delicate species.

Once the fish is immobilized you can pose him in the community tank by allowing him to rest on a piece of wood. You can also jam him between rocks or let him float under a leaf. Then you just go ahead, focus on him, adjust the lights and take your pictures.

The really good photographer, though, doesn't have to drug his fish or squeeze them between glass. Nor does he have to kill them. He uses his own skill as follows.

First you decide upon the area of an aquarium you wish to photograph. Then you focus on that area and set up your camera and lights in such a way that the area is in focus and lit. Then by studying the area you can ascertain where you want the fish so it will be in focus. This is almost always in front of a rock, plant leaf or piece of submerged wood. By focusing on that object and then re-focusing slightly in front of the object where the fish will be swimming, you can then be confident that the fish will be beautifully framed and in focus if you can get it into position.

Next you mark the corners of the field of view on the glass of the aquarium with a grease pencil. Now stand back and cock your camera. Hold the cable release in your hand and chase the fish with your fish poser (metal strap). When the fish gets into the area you planned as sighted by the four corner marks on the glass, just squeeze the cable release and the picture is made. Of course you will want to make quite a few exposures to be sure the fish is exactly in the position you desire. These are the best and most dramatic photos, though they often show the fish at an amusing angle which, while making the picture beautiful, makes identification of the fish from this photograph extremely difficult. Obviously the technique you use depends upon the ultimate use to which you intend putting the picture.

For really experienced photographers the marking of the glass is unnecessary and they merely focus on some object and photograph the fish when it gets near the object. I have taken so many fish photographs (more than 100,000 usable pictures) that I photograph with one eye through the lens and one eye on the fish and I actually follow the fish with the camera and shoot the camera as though it were a gun. While this is especially simple with *larger* fish in public aquariums, it is also possible with small guppies, but you need some experience, especially for closeups.

That's about all there is to fish photography except for reacting to different situations and getting the "art" of making a beautiful picture and not just having a naked fish hanging in midwater.

Pierre Brichard using the author's photo tank in what was then Leopoldville, Belgian Congo. Now the country is called Zaire. Brichard has moved his operation to Burundi. He took thousands of great pictures with this setup since he always had sun and could work outdoors. **Below:** Y. W. Ong with the author's small photo tank in Malaysia. The photo tank also makes a great viewing tank so you can see what you've caught in the net.

I use a photo tank made of four glass sides and with a metal frame. An all-glass tank would be just as good, but it wouldn't be sturdy enough for me to drag around in the jungles. In many cases I use an extra piece of restraining glass (sometimes two pieces of restraining glass so I can pose fishes in back of one another) to position the fish exactly as I want them.

In the photo tank I usually have some MS-222, which is a fish anesthetic. It puts the fish to sleep in a minute or two depending upon how much you use and the size of the fish. I then position the fish by squeezing it between the two pieces of glass and posing it with a piece of thin, flat black metal strapping. If you use more than one fish, put the thinnest fish on the bottom and the heavier fish on the top. Try to get fish about the same size or you will be forced to either squeeze the fat one too much or the distance between them will be too great to make the picture esthetic. The fish will remain immobile while you take its picture. When you place it into fresh water again, it will awaken and be perfectly normal. Sometimes you squeeze too hard and you actually squeeze the eggs or the droppings from a fish. Sometimes they bleed internally and die. I lose about two fish in a hundred this way.

While the fish are immobilized you can set up your lights and focus without any pressure of time on you. By selecting fishes of the same size you can take 100 fish photos an hour and all will be perfect once you have your lights and exposure data down pat.

For dramatic effects, drug the fish and place him in the photo tank without a restraining glass plate. Just jam him between the stiff leaves of a plant.

I place my background about 6 inches from the back of the tank. I use an ordinary piece of white typewriter paper for my light colored backgrounds and I use a piece of carbon paper for my black backgrounds. On the non-carbonized side of the carbon paper I have a nice light blue background which serves me for the in-between shades. Between the background and the back glass of the tank I usually put a rock or plastic plant, something to add glamour to the photograph. In many cases I actually place the small photo tank in front of a large aquarium so I have a natural aquarium scene for the background. This works well but there is a substantial light loss.

The skills you develop with the utilization of this technique are all *photographic* skills because it removes all of the problems of the fish. You only have photographic problems. Most beginners are overwhelmed with the fish moving in addition to the photographic problems, and that's what causes so much discouragement.

The size of the photo tank can vary with the size of the fish. It is easier to photograph small fish one inch long in a small tank three inches square. An eight-inch fish requires a twelve-inch tank or the back edges of the tank will be visible.

Family Cichlidae

Though many families of fishes are unique to a specific continent, cichlids, as fishes of the family Cichlidae are called, are found in just about every tropical to temperate area of the world, having been introduced for food purposes.

In their natural distribution, cichlids occur throughout South and Central America, except where it gets very cold or very high, with one species even making its way into Texas; over almost all of Africa, especially the Great Lakes of Africa, which probably contain more than 1,000 different cichlids; and odd places such as Madagascar, Israel, and Sri Lanka.

This section will only deal with the cichlids found in Central and South America except for the additional single species from Texas that has been variously known as *Herichthys* or *Cichlasoma cyanoguttatum*. These fishes are very popular with aquarists because they are hardy, easy to sex and breed, very colorful, interesting, and friendly, with many of them becoming tame enough to take food from their owner's fingers. (Text dealing with the cichlids of Lake Malawi and the cichlids of Lake Tanganyika accompanies those sections.)

The tribe Cichlasomini contains most of the cichlids that are *not* referred to as "dwarf cichlids;" it also does not include the large game cichlids of the genus *Cichla*. This tribe contains the genera *Cichlasoma, Petenia, Paraneetroplus, Neetroplus, Herotilapia, Uaru, Symphysodon,* and *Pterophyllum*. Another tribe, the Astronotini, contains the genera *Astronotus, Aequidens, Geophagus,* and *Acaronia* plus the dwarf cichlid genera including *Apistogramma* and *Nannacara*. The Astronotini is differentiated from the Cichlasomini by the simple character of the number of spines in the anal fin. The Astronotini have three or fewer, while the Cichlasomini have four or more. A few other very small tribes are also recognized.

Recently several ichthyologists have begun to doubt that these tribes truly reflect relationships in the American cichlids. For instance, certain forms of *Cichlasoma* are seemingly more closely related to *Aequidens* species than to other *Cichlasoma* species. The number of anal spines does allow a convenient way to group the genera, however, although it must be remembered that the resulting tribes are probably artificial and may not reflect true relationships.

THE GENUS *ASTRONOTUS*

Basically, *Astronotus* is a genus with only one species, *ocellatus*. However, the author (HRA) has collected series of *Astronotus* that are easily separable, one group from the other. One group found in central Brazil near Manaus all have several ocelli (eye spots) on their dorsal fin base. In most cases these ocelli are not bilateraly symmetrical on the fish; that is, one side of the fish may have four ocelli while the other side may have five or three. Another group found to the south around the Rio Paraguay have no ocelli in the dorsal fin but do have an ocellus on the top half of their caudal peduncle. *Astronotus* are excellent food fish and are fished for by the local people over their entire range.

The Oscar, as this fish is called, is very popular with aquarists lucky enough to have a large aquarium. A large aquarium is necessary since these fish grow to at least 350 mm in total length. They are easily spawned if given the correct conditions. The author (HRA) spawned them in shallow dirt pools in Florida. A group of Oscars, say about 20, were kept in a pool with about 200 square meters of surface and about one meter deep. The edges of the pool under the water were covered with pieces of slate laid at an angle. Daily feedings of live crayfish were given to the Oscars. Spawnings were very regular, with about one spawning per day minimum from the group. The eggs were removed and hatched artificially. Many color varieties have been developed, with the bronze, red, tiger, veiltail, ocellated, and normal varieties being the most common.

In their native habitat Oscars are found in slow-moving rivers close to the banks where there is very heavy aquatic vegetation as well as overhanging plants. They do not school but stay close to each other in their own territories. Except for the heaviness of the females, there are no apparent sexual differences.

THE GENUS *AEQUIDENS*

This is a large genus that is well distributed over tropical America from Panama to Argentina to Guyana. These fishes are small, mostly staying under 100 mm, and they are basically very timid, usually not attacking any other fish unless it is small enough to swallow in one gulp. They are very colorful, as the accompanying photographs show. For some reason they have not developed into many color varieties as have, for example, the fishes of the genera *Pterophyllum*, *Symphysodon* and *Astronotus*. One of the many species, *Aequidens portalegrensis*, was among the first tropical aquarium fishes kept as pets. This is evidenced by their appearance in old aquarium books. It was also the first cichlid spawned by the author (HRA).

The fish in this genus should be kept in as large an aquarium as possible as they are territorial when they spawn. A 40-liter aquarium is suitable for only a single pair. They usually find a smooth rock, clean it thoroughly with their mouths, then lay their eggs on the rock. At times they lay their eggs on plant leaves, sticks or even the aquarium glass. The pair usually guards the eggs, but sometimes only the male has this responsibility. Usually between 100-400 eggs are laid, and they hatch in about four days depending upon the temperature of the water. The eggs are easily hatched artificially, but in most cases the parents are to be trusted with the eggs, especially if they are well fed and left undisturbed. These fishes spawn all year long in the aquarium.

Feeding *Aequidens* is no problem as they eat everything from frozen and freeze-dried foods to live foods and such prepared foods as beef heart. They do best in temperatures ranging from 23-28°C in slightly acid water from pH 6.4-7.0.

THE GENUS *APISTOGRAMMA*

This is a large genus of small cichlids that are rather localized in their distribution. Because the genus is so large, perhaps having 65 described species by this time, some scientists have started chopping the genus into smaller units based upon very minor differences. The familiar *Apistogramma ramirezi* is now in the genus *Microgeophagus*, for example.

These small cichlids, called "dwarf cichlids" by aquarists, are extremely popular. They spawn in generally the same way that their larger brethren spawn, with the exception that many of them prefer to lay their eggs in a "secret" place rather than out in the open. Their eggs are laid on a solid base, whether it be a rock or a plant. Sexual differences in this genus are generally very apparent, with the male being much more colorful and usually with more pointed dorsal and anal fins, and with the first spines of the dorsal fin extended. Females and young males of many of these species look so much alike that they are often sold as "mixed dwarf cichlids" by fish collectors since they cannot ascertain to which species a particular female belongs. This makes it "fun" for the pet-shop that is trying to sell them, so beware. If you buy a "pair" and they don't seem to be interested in each other, then you probably have two different species. This has led to some interesting hybrids.

The eggs of many of these species are ovoid, especially those that are laid on the sides of objects rather than on the top of them. Most of their eggs are rust-brown in color, but some are white or clear. They hatch in two to five days depending upon the species and water temperature. They do best in water 22-28°C at a pH of 6.2-7.0. They do not like too much aeration or noise in their tanks. Many dwarf cichlids live very short lives and never attain their beautiful color because their tank was connected to a very noisy pump or filter or because they were in an aquarium situation with very aggressive fishes.

They eat everything, but to bring them into good condition you must offer them live foods, especially small crustaceans such as brine shrimp and *Daphnia*. A few worms now and then are also appreciated.

THE GENUS *CICHLASOMA*

This large genus ranges from Texas to Argentina, its species being found in small, slow-moving creeks and natural springs. Some of them are even found in brackish water. Including all their subgenera, there are at least 100 different fishes in this genus, and perhaps a lot more depending upon how you look at subspecies.

All of them make interesting aquarium specimens, though some are a bit large. Usually their sizes range from 100 to 300 mm, but they are friendly, interesting fishes and do well in very large tanks. Since they dig up plants and tear up the gravel beds, they are usually kept in unplanted tanks filled with rocks, driftwood and perhaps some plastic plants or aquarium gadgets that form caves and hiding places. Their spawns are usually large and are well protected by the male. Spawning usually takes place in an open area on top of a flat rock. If plants are near the chosen site the male usually tears them out. He wants lots of room around his nest to protect his fry and eggs. After hatching the fry are usually moved to previously dug pits in the sand.

The fishes of the genus *Cichlasoma*, with some exceptions, are usually easy to sex, with the males having longer and more pointed anal and dorsal fin rays and being much more colorful, especially during spawning.

These fishes are very hardy and can withstand water temperatures of 21-30°C with a pH of 6.0 to 7.5 with little difficulty. As a matter of fact, they may even be said to do better with a little salt added to their tank water to make it harder, but this is not advised for the beginner.

A single pair should be given lots of tank space, with at least 10 liters for each 3 cm of fish length per pair (that is, a pair 21 cm long should have a tank of 70 liters). All aquarium fish tanks should be covered; this is especially true of tanks containing cichlids that jump.

THE TRIBE CRENICARINI

The tribe Crenicarini contains three genera of interest to aquarists: *Crenicara*, *Batrachops*, and *Crenicichla*. The fishes of the genus *Crenicichla* are called "pike cichlids" because they are long and slender. They attack and devour other fishes, and in their natural range and habitats they travel in packs of a few dozen to attack schools of characins that occur in the same areas. They are very fast open-water fishes usually found in the clear, fast-moving waters of small creeks. They are extremely difficult to catch with a seine as they sneak under, jump over or find small holes to wriggle their slippery bodies through. They are not easy to keep successfully in an aquarium since they require lots of room and copious amounts of live fishes for food. Few have spawned in an aquarium to date, but as tanks in homes get larger and larger, more spawnings may soon be expected.

Batrachops species more or less follow the same description as the pike cichlids, but they are more rounded and have a deeper body. They are just as slime-covered, however. They are extremely difficult to catch alive except by hook and line fishing, thus they are rare.

These fishes, *Batrachops* and *Crenicichla*, often get to 300 mm or more in length. Smaller specimens are often kept in the aquarium, but they seldom live to maturity because they begin eating their tankmates.

Crenicara species, on the other hand, are the opposite of their relatives *Batrachops* and *Crenicichla*. They are small, peaceful, relatively easy to breed, and eat a normal aquarium diet. They are usually considered with the dwarf cichlids as they have all the qualities of *Apistogramma*. They rarely get larger than 125 mm.

THE *GEOPHAGUS* OR EARTHEATERS

In *Breeding Aquarium Fishes* (Book 5 in the series) is a report made by the author (HRA) on the spawning of three *Geophagus (balzani, jurupari, surinamensis)* with lots of nice color photographs. These fishes breed like few (if any) other fishes in the world. They lay their eggs, like a typical cichlid, on a flat rock that they have cleaned. Then the pair cover the rock with sand and keep it buried for two days. At that point they take the eggs into their mouths until they hatch. After hatching the young still take refuge in their mother's mouth. The mother takes care of them for three weeks, spitting them out only when she feeds.

In the aquarium these fishes are constantly digging up the bottom, chewing on the sand and taking from it whatever they are searching for. They are found throughout South America

Cichlasoma zonatum pH7.0;H10;25C;25cm;200L 〜🐟 ◑✕ 🖼 ⊡

Cichlasoma hartwegi pH7.0;H10;25C;25cm;200L 〜🐟 ◑✕ 🖼 ⊡

Cichlasoma tetracanthum pH7.2;H12;24C;25cm;200L 〜🐟 ◑♥ 🖼 ⊡

Cichlasoma synspilum pH7.3;H12;25C;30cm;250L ⌇ ➤ ◑ ♥ 🖼 ⊡

Cichlasoma maculicauda pH7.2;H12;27C;30cm;250L ⌇ ➤ ◑ ♥ 🖼 ⊡

Cichlasoma nicaraguense pH7.0;H10;27C;23cm;200L ⚲ ➤ ◑ ♥ 🖼 ⊡

Cichlasoma salvinii pH7.0;H10;24C;15cm;200L ᭡ ➤ ◑ ✕ 🖼 ⊟

Cichlasoma motaguanse pH7.0;H10;26C;22cm;200L ᭡ ➤ ◑ ✕ 🖼 ⊟

Cichlasoma managuense pH7.0;H10;25C;35cm;200L ᭡ ➤ ◑ ✕ 🖼 ⊟

Cichlasoma friedrichsthali pH7.0;H10;25C;20cm;200L ♀ 🐟 ◑ ✂ 🖼 ⊟

Cichlasoma managuense pH7.0;H10;25C;35cm;200L 〜 🐟 ◑ ✂ 🖼 ⊟

Cichlasoma dovii pH7.0;H10;24C;50cm;400L 〜 🐟 ◑ ✂ 🖼 ⊟

Cichlasoma carpintis pH7.0;H7;22C;25cm;200L 〰 🐟 ◐ ✕ 🖼 ⊟

Cichlasoma minckleyi pH7.2;H12;20C;20cm;150L 〰 🐟 ◐ ✕ 🖼 ⊟

Cichlasoma octofasciatum pH7.0;H10;24C;20cm;150L 〰 🐟 ◐ ✕ 🖼 ⊟

38

Cichlasoma coryphaenoides pH7.0;H10;26C;25cm;200L 〜〜✦ ❶ ✕ 🏞 🔲

Cichlasoma temporale pH7.0;H10;26C;30cm;250L 〜〜✦ ❶ ✕ 🏞 🔲

Cichlasoma festae pH7.0;H10;26C;30cm;250L 〜〜✦ ❶ ✕ 🏞 🔲

Cichlasoma temporale pH7.0;H10;26C;30cm;250L ～ ➤ ◑ ✖ 🖼 ▣

Cichlasoma festae pH7.0;H10;26C;30cm;250L ～ ➤ ◑ ✖ 🖼 ▣

Cichlasoma umbriferum pH6.8;H8;25C;30cm;300L ～ ➤ ◑ ✖ 🖼 ▣

Cichlasoma sajica pH6.8;H10;26C;10cm;100L 〜 🐟 ◑ ♥ 🖼 🖽

Cichlasoma hellebruni pH7.0;H8;26C;30cm;200L 〜 🐟 ◑ ✂ 🖼 🖽

Cichlasoma hellebruni pH7.0;H8;26C;30cm;200L 〜 🐟 ◑ ✂ 🖼 🖽

41

Cichlasoma sajica pH6.8;H10;26C;10cm;100L

Cichlasoma septemfasciatum var. pH7.0;H10;25C;12cm;150L

Cichlasoma spilurum pH7.0;H10;25C;18cm;200L

42

Cichlasoma psittacum pH6.8;H8;26C;15cm;200L 〰 🐟 ◐ ✖ 🖼 ▤

Cichlasoma septemfasciatum pH7.0;H10;25C;12cm;150L 〰 🐟 ◐ ♥ 🖼 ▤

Cichlasoma septemfasciatum pH7.0;H10;25C;12cm;150L 〰 🐟 ◐ ♥ 🖼 ▤

Cichlasoma labiatum pH7.0;H10;25C;38cm;250L ✎ ➤ ◐ ✄ ▨ ▤

Cichlasoma alfari pH7.0;H10;25C;20cm;200L ✎ ➤ ◐ ✄ ▨ ▤

Cichlasoma trimaculatum pH7.0;H10;25C;20cm;200L ✎ ➤ ◐ ♥ ▨ ▤

Cichlasoma altifrons pH7.0;H10;25C;20cm;150L ᔓ ⤜ ◑ ✕ ▧ ⊟

Cichlasoma alfari pH7.0;H10;25C;20cm;200L ᔓ ⤜ ◑ ✕ ▧ ⊟

Cichlasoma aff. *labiatum* pH7.0;H10;25C;20cm;200L ᔓ ⤜ ◑ ✕ ▧ ⊟

Cichlasoma citrinellum pH7.2;H12;25C;20cm;200L 〜 ➤ ◐ ♥ 🖼 ▣

Cichlasoma labiatum pH7.0;H10;25C;38cm;250L 〜 ➤ ◐ ✕ 🖼 ▣

Cichlasoma urophthalmum pH7.0;H10;26C;20cm;200L 〜 ➤ ◐ ♥ 🖼 ▣

Cichlasoma sp. pH7.0;H10;25C;20cm;200L ⌇ 🐟 ◑ ✕ 🖼 ⊟

Cichlasoma tuyrense pH7.0;H10;25C;20cm;150L ⌇ 🐟 ◑ ♥ 🖼 ⊟

Cichlasoma grammodes pH7.0;H10;25C;30cm;250L ⌇ 🐟 ◑ ✕ 🖼 ⊟   47

Cichlasoma nigrofasciatum pH7.3;H12;24C;15cm;75L 〜 ➤ ◑ ✕ ☒ ▣

Cichlasoma nigrofasciatum pH7.3;H12;24C;15cm;75L 〜 ➤ ◑ ✕ ☒ ▣

Cichlasoma nigrofasciatum pH7.3;H12;24C;15cm;75L 〜 ➤ ◑ ✕ ☒ ▣

Cichlasoma macracanthus pH7.0;H10;25C;20cm;150L ⤳ ◐ ✕ 🖼 🖾

Cichlasoma robertsoni pH7.0;H10;25C;20cm;150L ⤳ ◐ ✕ 🖼 🖾

Cichlasoma alfari pH7.0;H10;25C;20cm;200L ⤳ 🐟 ◐ ✕ 🖼 🖾

49

Cichlasoma centrarchus pH7.0;H10;26C;22cm;200L ♀ 🐟 ◑ ♥ 🏞 ⊟

Cichlasoma octofasciatum pH7.2;H12;25C;20cm;200L ∿ 🐟 ◑ ✄ 🏞 ⊟

Cichlasoma longimanus pH7.0;H8;25C;22cm;200L ∿ 🐟 ◑ ♥ 🏞 ⊟

Cichlasoma meeki pH7.0;H12;24C;12.5cm;150L ♀ ➤ ◑ ♥ ▓ ▤

Cichlasoma aureum pH7.0;H10;25C;12cm;150L ⌇ ➤ ◑ ♥ ▓ ▤

Cichlasoma bartoni pH7.0;H10;25C;22cm;200L ⌇ ➤ ◑ ♥ ▓ ▤

51

Cichlasoma severum pH7.3;H12;25C;20cm;200L ♀ ➤ ◐ ♥ 🖼 🖾

Cichlasoma severum pH7.3;H12;25C;20cm;200L ♀ ➤ ◐ ♥ 🖼 🖾

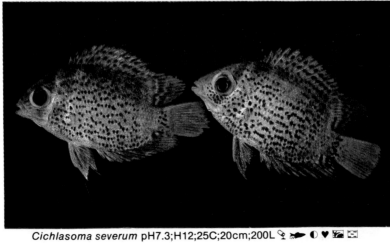

Cichlasoma severum pH7.3;H12;25C;20cm;200L ♀ ➤ ◐ ♥ 🖼 🖾

Cichlasoma severum pH7.3;H12;25C;20cm;200L ♀ ⤞ ◑ ♥ 🖼 ▣

Cichlasoma severum pH7.3;H12;25C;20cm;200L ♀ ⤞ ◑ ♥ 🖼 ▣

Cichlasoma festivum pH7.2;H10;24C;15cm;100L ∿ ⤞ ◑ ♥ 🖼 ▣

53

Petenia splendida pH7.0;H10;25C;35cm;300L

Neetroplus nematopus pH7.5;H13;25C;9cm;100L

Herotilapia multispinosa pH7.0;H10;24C;10cm;100L

Aequidens curviceps pH6.8;H8;25C;7.5cm;75L ♀ ➤ ◐ ♥ 🐟 ⊟

Aequidens dorsigerus pH7.0;H8;25C;8cm;80L ♀ ➤ ◐ ♥ 🐟 ⊟

Aequidens portalegrensis pH7.0;H8;24C;12.5cm;200L ♀ ➤ ◐ ♥ 🐟 ⊟

55

Aequidens dorsigerus pH7.0;H8;25C;8cm;80L ♀ ➤ ◑ ♥ 🖼 ⊟

Aequidens awani pH7.0;H8;24C;10cm;100L ♀ ➤ ◑ ♥ 🖼 ⊟

Aequidens itanyi pH7.3;H12;26C;14cm;100L ♀ ◑ ♥ 🖼 ⊟

Aequidens tetramerus pH7.0;H8;24C;8cm;100L ♀ ➤ ◑ ♥ 🖼 🔲

Aequidens tetramerus pH7.0;H8;24C;8cm;100L ♀ ➤ ◑ ♥ 🖼 🔲

Aequidens awani pH7.0;H8;24C;10cm;100L ♀ ➤ ◑ ♥ 🖼 🔲

57

Aequidens cf. *tetramerus* pH7.0;H8;25C;25cm;150L 〜 ➤ ◑ ✕ 🖾 ⊟

Aequidens aff. *dorsigerus* pH7.0;H8;25C;15cm;100L 〜 ➤ ◑ ✕ 🖾 ⊟

Aequidens paraguayensis pH7.0;H8;25C;15cm;100L 〜 ➤ ◑ ✕ 🖾 ⊟

Aequidens paraguayensis pH7.0;H8;25C;15cm;100L 〜 ➤ ◑ ✄ 🖼 ▣

Aequidens tetramerus pH7.0;H8;25C;25cm;150L 〜 ➤ ◑ ✄ 🖼 ▣

Aequidens pulcher pH7.0;H10;24C;20cm;150L 〜 ➤ ◑ ✄ 🖼 ▣

Aequidens vittata pH7.2;H10;25C;11cm;200L ♀ 🐟 ◐ ✕ 🖼 ⊟

Aequidens duopunctatus pH7.0;H8;24C;10cm;120L ♀ 🐟 ◐ ♥ 🖼 ⊟

Aequidens sapayensis pH7.2;H10;25C;10cm;120L ♀ 🐟 ◐ ♥ 🖼 ⊟

Aequidens synspilum pH7.0;H8;25C;15cm;100L ～🐟 ◑ ✕ 🖼 ⊟

Aequidens vittatus pH7.0;H8;25C;15cm;100L ～🐟 ◑ ✕ 🖼 ⊟

Aequidens coeruleopunctatus pH7.0;H8;25C;15cm;100L ～🐟 ◑ ✕ 🖼 ⊟

Aequidens caerulopunctatus pH7.0;H8;25C;13cm;100L ♀ ➤ ◑ ✳ 🐟 ▦

Aequidens rivulatus pH7.2;H10;25C;15cm;200L ♀ ➤ ◑ ✳ 🐟 ▦

Aequidens sp. "Gold Saum" pH7.2;H10;25C;16cm;200L ♀ ➤ ◑ ✳ 🐟 ▦

Aequidens pulcher pH7.0;H10;24C;20cm;150L ∿ ➤ ◑ ✗ 🖾 ▤

Aequidens itanyi pH7.3;H12;26C;14cm;100L ♀ ➤ ◑ ♥ 🖾 ▤

Aequidens rivulatus pH7.2;H10;25C;15cm;200L ♀ ➤ ◑ ✗ 🖾 ▤

Biotodoma cupido pH7.0;H8;26C;13cm;150L ♀ 🐟 ◑ ✕ 📷 ⊡

Geophagus gymnogenys pH7.5;H13;24C;11cm;100L ♀ 🐟 ✕ 📷 ⊡

Geophagus rhabdotus pH7.5;H12;24C;18cm;200L ♀ 🐟 ◑ ♥ 📷 ⊡

Geophagus brasiliensis pH7.3;H11;26C;18cm;125L ♀ 🐟 ◑ ♥ 🖼 ▣

Geophagus acuticeps pH7.2;H10;24C;15cm;200L ♀ 🐟 ◑ ♥ 🖼 ▣

Geophagus daemon pH7.2;H10;25C;15cm;200L ♀ 🐟 ◑ ♥ 🖼 ▣

Geophagus surinamensis pH7.0;H8;25C;24cm;300L ♀ ➤ ◑ ✕ ▨ ⊟

Geophagus brasiliensis pH7.3;H11;26C;18cm;125L ♀ ➤ ◑ ♥ ▨ ⊟

Geophagus jurupari pH7.0;H8;24C;18cm;200L ♀ ➤ ◑ ♥ ▨ ⊟

Geophagus steindachneri pH7.3;H10;25C;10cm;100L ♀ ➤ ◑ ♥ 🐟 ▤

Geophagus balzanii pH7.0;H8;24C;18cm;220L ♀ ➤ ◑ ♥ 🐟 ▤

Geophagus surinamensis pH7.0;H8;25C;24cm;300L ♀ ➤ ◑ ✘ 🐟 ▤

69

Acarichthys heckelii pH7.2;H10;25C;13cm;150L ♀ ⟶ ◑ ✕ ▨ ▣

Geophagus australis pH7.0;H12;23C;20cm;150L ♀ ⟶ ◑ ✕ ▨ ▣

Acarichthys geayi pH7.5;H12;25C;15cm;200L ♀ ⟶ ◑ ✕ ▨ ▣

Microgeophagus ramirezi pH6.8;H7;27C;5cm;40L ∿ ⇒ ◑ ♥ 🎞 ⊡

Microgeophagus ramirezi pH6.8;H7;27C;5cm;40L ∿ ⇒ ◑ ♥ 🎞 ⊡

Microgeophagus ramirezi pH6.8;H7;27C;5cm;40L ∿ ⇒ ◑ ♥ 🎞 ⊡

71

Chaetobranchus bitaeniatus pH7.2;H10;27C;12cm;100L ♀ 🐟 ◑ ♥ 🖼 ⊟

♂ *Nannacara anomala* pH7.2;H10;26C;8cm;80L 〰 🐟 ◑ ♥ 🖼 ⊟

Nannacara aureocephalus pH7.2;H10;25C;8cm;80L ♀ 🐟 ◑ ♥ 🖼 ⊟

Chaetobranchus flavescens pH7.2;H10;23C;10cm;100L 🌿 🐟 ◐ ♥ 🖼 ⊡

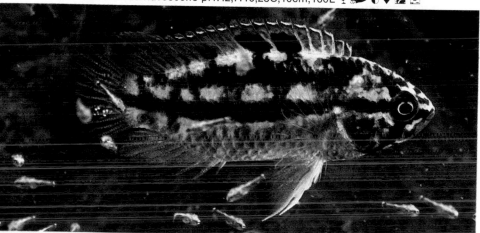

Nannacara anomala pH7.2;H10;26C;8cm;80L ∿ ◐ ♥ 🖼 ⊡

Apistogrammoides pucallpaensis pH6.8;H6;24C;6cm;50L ∿ ◐ ♥ 🖼 ⊡

73

Taeniacara candidi pH6.8;H6;25C;4cm;40L ⌇ 🐟 ◑ ♥ 🖼 ⊡

Apistogramma agassizi pH6.5;H6;24C;8cm;60L ⌇ 🐟 ◑ ♥ 🖼 ⊡

Apistogramma agassizi pH6.5;H6;24C;8cm;60L ⌇ 🐟 ◑ ♥ 🖼 ⊡

Apistogramma borelli pH6.5;H4;24C;7cm;60L 〜 🐟 ◑ ♥ 🖼 ▣

Apistogramma borelli pH6.5;H4;24C;7cm;60L 〜 ◑ ♥ 🖼 ▣

Apistogramma bitaeniata pH6.5;H4;24C;6cm;40L 〜 🐟 ◑ ♥ 🖼 ▣

♀ *Apistogramma trifasciatum* pH6.2;H3;25C;6cm;50L ∿ ➤ ◑ ♥ ▨ ▣

Apistogramma cacatuoides pH6.5;H6;26C;5cm;40L ∿ ➤ ◑ ♥ ▨ ▣

Apistogramma trifasciatum pH6.2;H3;25C;6cm;50L ∿ ➤ ◑ ♥ ▨ ▣

Apistogramma gossei pH6.5;H4;25C;6cm;40L ⌇ ➤ ◑ ♥ 🎦 ▣

Apistogramma eunotus pH6.3;H3;25C;5cm;40L ⌇ ➤ ◑ ♥ 🎦 ▣

Apistogramma macmasteri pH6.5;H4;25C;7cm;60L ⌇ ➤ ◑ ♥ 🎦 ▣

Apistogramma cacatuoides pH6.5;H6;26C;5cm;40L ⌇ ➤ ◐ ♥ 🐟 ☲

Apistogramma gibbiceps pH6.4;H5;24C;5cm;40L ⌇ ➤ ◐ ♥ 🐟 ☲

Apistogramma pertensis pH6.5;H6;25C;5cm;40L ⌇ ➤ ◐ ♥ 🐟 ☲

Apistogramma steindachneri pH6.5;H6;25C;7cm;60L ∿ ➤ ◐ ♥ 🎞 ▤

Apistogramma hippolytae pH6.5;H4;25C;6cm;50L ∿ ➤ ◐ ♥ 🎞 ▤

Apistogramma hippolytae pH6.5;H4;25C;6cm;50L ∿ ➤ ◐ ♥ 🎞 ▤

Apistogramma "Orange Fin" pH6.5;H4;24C;7cm;60L ⌇ ➤ ◑ ♥ 🎞 ⊡

♂ *Apistogramma luelingi* pH6.5;H5;25C;8cm;60L ⌇ ➤ ◑ ♥ 🎞 ⊡

♀ *Apistogramma luelingi* pH6.5;H5;25C;8cm;60L ⌇ ➤ ◑ ♥ 🎞 ⊡

Crenicara filamentosa pH7.0;H8;24C;4cm;40L ⌇ ➤ ◑ ♥ 🐟 ▭

Crenicara maculata pH7.0;H8;24C;4cm;40L ⌇ ➤ ◑ ♥ 🐟 ▭

Crenicichla wallacei pH7.0;H8;24C;25cm;100L ⌇ ➤ ◑ ✕ 🐟 ▭

Crenicara punctulata pH7.2;H10;25C;6cm;60L ⤳ 🐀 ◑ ♥ 🖼 ⊟

Crenicichla sp. pH7.0;H8;24C;25cm;100L ⤳ 🐀 ◑ ✺ 🖼 ⊟

Crenicichla geayi pH7.2;H10;24C;40cm;250L ⤳ 🐀 ◑ ✺ 🖼 ⊟

Crenicichla strigata pH7.2;H10;25C;30cm;200L ↘🐟 ◑✕ 🐟 ⊞

Crenicichla lepidota pH7.0;H8;24C;20cm;125L ↘🐟 ◑✕ 🐟 ⊞

Crenicichla sp. pH7.2;H10;25C;40cm;250L ↘🐟 ◑✕ 🐟 ⊞

Crenicichla lenticulata pH7.0;H8;25C;40cm;250L ↘ ➤ ◑ ✕ ▨ ⊟

Crenicichla saxatilis pH7.2;H10;25C;50cm;275L ↘ ◑ ✕ ▨ ⊟

Batrachops sp. pH7.3;H12;25C;50cm;400L ↘ ➤ ◑ ✕ ▨ ⊟

Cichla ocellaris pH7.0;H10;25C;75cm;400L 〜 🐟 ◑ ✖ 🏞 ⊡

Cichla temensis pH7.0;H10;25C;75cm;400L 〜 🐟 ◑ ✖ 🏞 ⊡

Cichla ocellaris pH7.0;H10;25C;75cm;400L 〜 🐟 ◑ ✖ 🏞 ⊡

Cichla temensis pH7.0;H10;25C;75cm;400L 〜 🐟 ◑ ✖ 🏞 ⊡

85

Astronotus ocellatus pH7.2;H10;26C;35cm;200L ↘ ◑ ✕ 🐟 ⊟

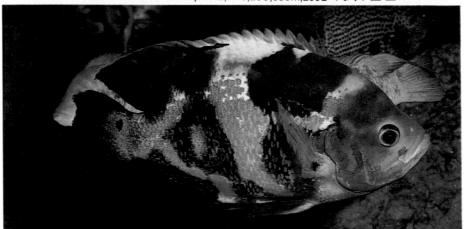

Astronotus ocellatus pH7.2H10;26C;35cm;200L ↘ ◑ ✕ 🐟 ⊟

Astronotus ocellatus pH7.2H10;26C;35cm;200L ↘ ◑ ✕ 🐟 ⊟

Astronotus ocellatus pH7.2H10;26C;35cm;200L ↘ ◑ ✕ 🎞 ▣

Astronotus ocellatus pH7.2H10;26C;35cm;200L ↘ ◑ ✕ 🎞 ▣

Astronotus ocellatus pH7.2H10;26C;35cm;200L ↘ ◑ ✕ 🎞 ▣

Uaru amphiacanthoides pH7.0;H10;26C;26cm;200L 〜 🐟 ◑ ♥ 🖼 🖽

Uaru amphiacanthoides pH7.0;H10;26C;26cm;200L 〜 🐟 ◑ ♥ 🖼 🖽

Uaru amphiacanthoides pH7.0;H10;26C;26cm;200L 〜 🐟 ◑ ♥ 🖼 🖽

The Angelfishes, *Pterophyllum*

People who have been in the aquarium hobby for enough years (more than 50 years anyway) can well remember how difficult it was to successfully spawn and raise South American angelfishes of the genus *Pterophyllum*. In the 1930's and 1940's it was the rare aquarist who could spawn these fishes, and even today no one successfully spawns on a regular basis the angelfishes imported directly from South America. The only successful breeding is now accomplished from parents that were previously spawned in the aquarium.

How Many Species of Angelfishes are There?

Basically, all the fish in a population that look alike and have certain physical characteristics in common belong to the same species (allowing, of course, for normal variation and cases of sexual dimorphism where the females and males look different). Groups of these similar populations comprise the species. Species that are closely related belong to the same genus. It is rare that every scientist who studies a given genus of fishes agrees completely with previous studies of the same genus, thus fishes' names are never stable and keep changing. Today most ichthyologists feel that there are only two valid species plus a subspecies in the genus *Pterophyllum*. These are *Pterophyllum dumerilii* (rare), *P. scalare scalare* (the common angel), and *P. s. altum* (now imported on occasion).

What Varieties of Angelfish are Available?

There are two general groups of varieties. One group comprises the varieties with different fin shapes. There are normal-finned varieties and there are long-finned varieties

Then there are the color varieties. There are a lot more color varieties than finnage varieties. We can expect many more color varieties in angelfishes than we already have, but the varieties will be limited by the genetic material already available within the genes and chromosomes of the original wild angels from which our current breeding stocks are derived. Basically, angels are black and silver and all varieties produced to date are derivatives of silver and black, or lack these colors, which produces albinos or lutinos (albino yellow body with black eyes), or are all silver with little black coloration.

Pterophyllum dumerilii pH7.0;H8;25C;10cm;80L ♀ 🐟 ◑ ♥ 🖼 🔲

Pterophyllum dumerilii pH7.0;H8;25C;10cm;80L ♀ 🐟 ◑ ♥ 🖼 🔲

Pterophyllum scalare altum pH5.9;H8;25C;13cm;100L ♀ 🐟 ◑ ♥ 🖼 🖾

Pterophyllum scalare altum pH5.9;H8;25C;13cm;100L ♀ 🐟 ◑ ♥ 🖼 🖾

Pterophyllum scalare, Silver Veiltail variety

Pterophyllum scalare, Black Veiltail variety

Pterophyllum scalare pH7.0;H8;26C;15cm;100L ♀ ⚯ ◑ ♥ 🎞 🖼

Pterophyllum scalare, Black variety

Pterophyllum scalare, Blushing Angel variety

Pterophyllum scalare, Zebra Lace variety

93

Pterophyllum scalare, Zebra variety

Pterophyllum scalare, Marble Veiltail variety

Pterophyllum scalare, Silver Veiltail variety

Pterophyllum scalare, Half-black variety

Common Brown Discus, *Symphysodon aequifasciata axelrodi*

Royal Blue Discus , *Symphysodon aequifasciata aequifasciata..*

Young Turquoise Discus.

Adult Turquoise Discus.

Symphysodon discus willischwartzi.

Young Turquoise Discus.

Symphysodon discus discus.

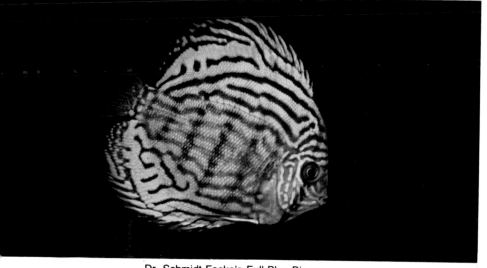

Dr. Schmidt-Focke's Full Blue Discus.

Symphysodon aequifasciata aequifasciata.

Young Schmidt-Focke Full Blue Discus.

Adult *Symphysodon aequifasciata axelrodi.*

Juvenile *Symphysodon aequifasciata.*

103

LoBue Albino Discus.

Young Turquoise and Gold Discus.

Symphysodon aequifasciata haraldi X *S. a. aequifasciata.*

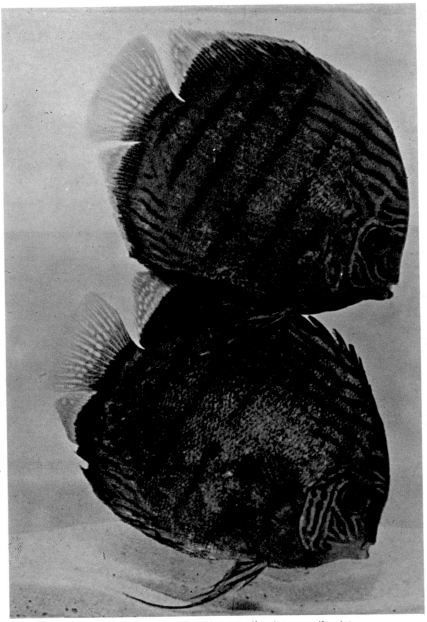

Green Discus, *Symphysodon aequifasciata aequifasciata*.

Young Turquoise/Rod Discus.

Turquoise Discus.

Blue Discus, *Symphysodon aequifasciata haraldi.*

Symphysodon aequifasciata aequifasciata.

Schmidt-Focke Turquoise Discus.

Hybrid Red Discus.

Royal Blue Discus.

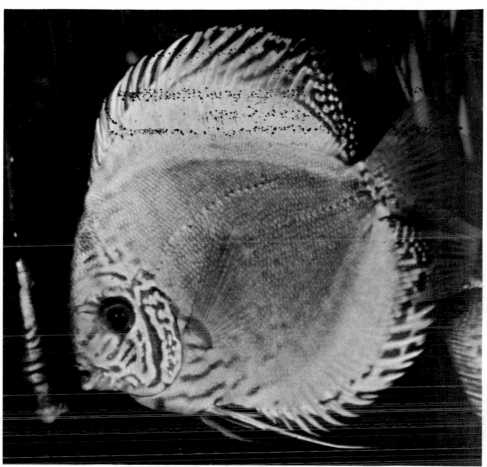

Hi-Fin Cobalt Discus.

Young Turquoise Discus.

Cichlids of Lake Malawi

The African Rift Valley contains a number of lakes that have become important to aquarists as sources of fishes of the family Cichlidae. Two of these, Lake Malawi and Lake Tanganyika, provide the bulk of the species imported. Lake Malawi has more than 250 described species (certainly with many more to come). Like Lake Tanganyika, Lake Malawi has a most unusual water chemistry: the pH is strongly alkaline, usually between 7.7 and 8.6, and the water is extremely hard.

In Malawi the cichlid fauna is divided for convenience into the *Haplochromis* species and the mbunas or rock-dwelling cichlids. Somewhere between these two groups are such genera as the peacocks, *Aulonocara* and *Trematocranus*. Although more closely related to the *Haplochromis* species, they are found among the rocks and aquarists have given them honorary mbuna status.

Most of the *Haplochromis* species are free-swimming fishes that have a rather perch-like body form with males that assume a blue coloration when in spawning condition. *Haplochromis moorii* is perhaps the most desirable species and quite a challenge to aquarists. Malawi boasts more than 100 species of *Haplochromis,* with more in the process of being discovered and described. They dazzle the aquarist mainly with blues with overtones of violet and green.

Several species of mbuna have evolved brilliant color patterns. Of these, perhaps the best known is one of the earliest imports, the zebra, *Pseudotropheus zebra*. Not far behind in beauty are *Pseudotropheus tropheops* and the two species of *Labeotropheus*. New patterns and species of mbunas are constantly being imported, but few have surpassed these original species of the hobby.

Lake Malawi cichlids are mostly easy to keep, hardy, and good spawners. They need a very alkaline pH, lots of room, and plenty of rockwork caves (especially for the mbunas). They should receive some plant material in their diet (since they feed mainly on algae in nature) but will take almost any type of prepared aquarium food.

Most Lake Malawi cichlids are mouthbrooders. The female picks up the fertilized eggs in her mouth and broods them in her buccal cavity until the fry not only hatch but are well enough developed to swim.

Haplochromis sp. pH8.2;H15;28C;20cm;150L ♀ ➤ ◐ ✕ 🎦 ⊡

Haplochromis "Electric Blue" pH8.2;H16;28C;13cm;100L ♀ ➤ ◐ ✕ 🎦 ⊡

Haplochromis fenestratus pH8.0;H15;28C;13cm;100L ♀ ➤ ◐ ✕ 🎦 ⊡

113

Haplochromis cf. *fenestratus* pH8.1;H22;28C;10cm;100L ♀ ➤ ◑ ✂ 🔒 ⊡

Haplochromis spilonotus pH8.0;H20;27C;10cm;100L ♀ ➤ ◑ ✂ 🔒 ⊡

Iaplochromis virginalis pH8.0;H20;28C;10cm;80L ♀ ➤ ◑ ✂ 🔒 ⊡

Haplochromis similis pH8.2;H20;28C;12cm;100L ♀ ➤ ◑ ✂ 🔳 ⊟

Haplochromis cf. *fenestratus* pH8.1;H22;28C;10cm;100L ♀ ➤ ◑ ✂ 🔳 ⊟

Haplochromis strigatus pH8.2;H20;28C;20cm;200L ♀ ➤ ◑ ✂ 🔳 ⊟

115

Haplochromis compressiceps pH8.0;H22;28C;26cm;300L ♀ ➤ ◑ ✕ ▣ ▣

Haplochromis cf. *labridens* pH8.1;H20;27C;12cm;100L ♀ ➤ ◑ ✕ ▣ ▣

Haplochromis cf. *taeniolatus* pH8.0;H20;28C;11cm;100L ♀ ➤ ◑ ✕ ▣ ▣

Haplochromis moorii pH8.1;H22;28C;23cm;300L ♀ 🐟 ◑ ✗ 📷 🖼

Haplochromis electra pH8.1;H21;27C;15cm;200L ♀ 🐟 ◑ ✗ 🖼 🖼

Haplochromis callipterus pH8.0;H20;27C;10cm;100L ♀ 🐟 ◑ ✗ 📷 🖼

117

Haplochromis venustus pH8.1;H22;28C;22cm;300L ♀ ➤ ◑ ✕ ▣ ▤

Haplochromis mloto pH8.1;H20;27C;10cm;100L ♀ ➤ ◑ ✕ ▣ ▤

Haplochromis cf. *euchilus* pH8.2;H20;27C;33cm;400L ♀ ➤ ◑ ✕ ▣ ▤

Haplochromis venustus pH8.1;H22;28C;22cm;300L ♀ ➤ ◑ ✕ 🔳 🖾

Haplochromis mloto pH8.1;H20;27C;10cm;100L ♀ ➤ ◑ ✕ 🔳 🖾

Haplochromis euchilus pH8.2;H20;27C;33cm;400L ♀ ➤ ◑ ✕ 🔳 🖾

Haplochromis fuscotaeniatus pH8.0;H22;28C;25cm;300L ♀ ➤ ◐ ✄ 🔳 ⊡

Haplochromis polystigma pH8.0;H22;27C;26cm;300L ♀ ➤ ◐ ✄ 🔳 ⊡

Haplochromis linni pH8.1;H21;27C;35cm;400L ♀ ➤ ◐ ✄ 🔳 ⊡

Haplochromis livingstoni pH8.0;H22;27C;30cm;400L ♀ ➤ ◑ ✕ 🔳 ⊡

Haplochromis fuscotaenlatus pH8.0;H22;28C;25cm;300L ♀ ➤ ◑ ✕ 🔳 ⊡

Haplochromis polystigma pH8.0;H22;27C;26cm;300L ♀ ➤ ◑ ✕ 🔳 ⊡

Hemitilapia oxyrhynchus pH8.2;H22;27C;20cm;200L ♀ ➤ ◑ ✕ 📷 ⊡

Petrotilapia nigra pH8.2;H20;26C;25cm;150L ♀ ➤ ◑ ✕ 📷 ⊡

Genyochromis mento pH8.2;H22;28C;12cm;100L ♀ ➤ ◑ ✕ 📷 ⊡

Chilotilapia rhodesii pH8.2;H22;28C;22cm;300L ♀ ➤ ◑ ✕ 🔳 ⊡

Cleithrochromis bowleyi pH8.0;H21;27C;16cm;150L ♀ ➤ ◑ ✕ 🔳 ⊡

Petrotilapia tridentiger pH8.1;H22;27C;12cm;100L ♀ ➤ ◑ ✕ 🔳 ⊡

Trematocranus peterdaviesi pH8.2;H21;27C;15cm;200L ♀ ➤ ◑ ✄ 📷 ⊡

Lethrinops christyi pH8.0;H20;27C;16cm;200L ♀ ➤ ◑ ✄ 📷 ⊡

Lethrinops furcicauda pH8.2;H20;28C;14cm;200L ♀ ➤ ◑ ✄ 📷 ⊡

Trematocranus sp. pH8.0;H21;27C;18cm;300L ♀ ➤ ◑ ✕ 🖻 🖼

Lethrinops aurita pH8.2;H21;27C;12cm;100L ♀ ➤ ◑ ✕ 🖻 🖼

Lethrinops furcicauda pH8.2;H20;28C;14cm;200L ♀ ➤ ◑ ✕ 🖻 🖼

125

Aulonocara nyassae pH8.1;H20;27C;16cm;200L ♀ ➤ ◑ ✕ 🔳 ⊡

Aulonocara nyassae pH8.1;H20;27C;16cm;200L ♀ ➤ ◑ ✕ 🔳 ⊡

Aulonocara sp. (Night Aulonocara) pH8.1;H21;27C;14cm;200L ♀ ➤ ◑ ✕ 🔳 ⊡

Aulonocara nyassae pH8.1;H20;27C;16cm;200L ♀ ➤ ◑ ✕ 🔳 ▣

Aulonocara nyassae pH8.1;H20;27C;16cm;200L ♀ ➤ ◑ ✕ 🔳 ▣

Aulonocara sp. (white dorsal edge) pH8.1;H20;27C;15cm;200L ♀ ➤ ◑ ✕ 🔳 ▣

Melanochromis johanni pH8.0;H21;27C;12cm;100L ♀ ➤ ◑ ✖ 📷 ⊡

Melanochromis melanopterus pH8.1;H22;27C;15cm;200L ♀ ➤ ◑ ✖ 📷 ⊡

Melanochromis perspicax pH8.1;H22;27C;13cm;100L ♀ ➤ ◑ ✖ 📷 ⊡

♀ *Melanochromis johanni* pH8.0;H21;27C;12cm;100L ♀ 🐟 ◑ ✂ 📷 🔲

♂ *Melanochromis johanni* pH8.0;H21;27C;12cm;100L ♀ 🐟 ◑ ✂ 📷 🔲

Melanochromis parallelus pH8.2;H22;28C;15cm;100L ♀ 🐟 ◑ ✂ 📷 🔲

129

Melanochromis auratus pH8.1;H22;27C;20cm;200L ♀ ➤ ◑ ✴ 🔲 ⊟

Melanochromis chipokee pH8.1;H22;27C;12cm;100L ♀ ➤ ◑ ✴ 🔲 ⊟

Melanochromis johanni pH8.0;H21;27C;12cm;100L ♀ ➤ ◑ ✴ 🔲 ⊟

Melanochromis simulans pH8.2;H22;27C;12cm;100L ♀ ➤ ◑ ✕ ▣ ▣

Melanochromis vermivorus pH8.1;H22;27C;11cm;100L ♀ ➤ ◑ ✕ ▣ ▣

Labidochromis sp. pH8.0;H21;27C;8cm;100L ♀ ➤ ◑ ✕ ▣ ▣

131

Labidochromis textilis pH8.2;H15;28C;15cm;100L ♀ ➤ ◑ ✕ 🖻 🖼

Labidochromis exasperatus pH8.2;H15;28C;15cm;100L ♀ ➤ ◑ ✕ 🖻 🖼

Labidochromis joanjohnsonae pH8.2;H15;28C;12cm;100L ♀ ➤ ◑ ✕ 🖻 🖼

Pseudotropheus novemfasciatus pH8.0;H22;27C;10cm;100L ♀ ➤ ◐ ✕ ▣ ▣

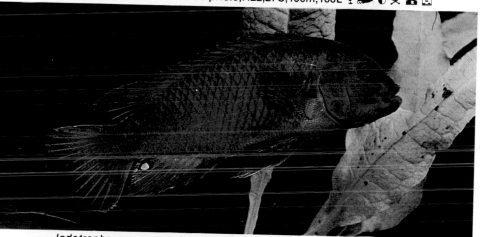

Iodotropheus sprengerae pH8.0;H22;27C;8cm;100L ♀ ➤ ◐ ✕ ▣ ▣

Gephyrochromis moorii pH8.0;H21;27C;10cm;100L ♀ ➤ ◐ ✕ ▣ ▣

Pseudotropheus tropheops pH8.2;H20;28C;10cm;100L ♀ ➤ ◑ ✕ 📷 ⊟

Pseudotropheus sp. pH8.1;H20;28C;10cm;100L ♀ ➤ ◑ ✕ 📷 ⊟

Gephyrochromis lawsi pH8.1;H20;27C;10cm;100L ♀ ➤ ◑ ✕ 📷 ⊟

Pseudotropheus tropheops pH8.2;H15;26C;20cm;100L ♀ ➤ ◑✗ ▣ ⊡

Pseudotropheus tropheops pH8.2;H15;26C;20cm;100L ♀ ➤ ◑✗ ▣ ⊡

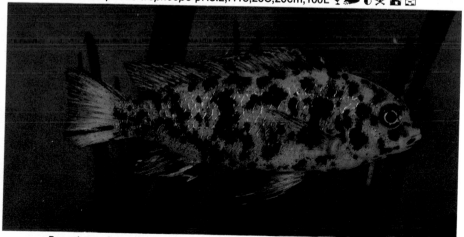

Pseudotropheus tropheops pH8.2;H15;26C;20cm;100L ♀ ➤ ◑✗ ▣ ⊡

135

Pseudotropheus tropheops pH8.2;H15;26C;20cm;100L ♀ 🐟 ◑ ✕ 📷 ⊟

Pseudotropheus tropheops pH8.2;H15;26C;20cm;100L ♀ 🐟 ◑ ✕ 📷 ⊟

Pseudotropheus tropheops pH8.2;H15;26C;20cm;100L ♀ 🐟 ◑ ✕ 📷 ⊟

Pseudotropheus elongatus pH8.0;H22;27C;10cm;100L ♀ ➤ ◐ ✕ 🖻 🖼

Pseudotropheus sp. pH8.0;H20;28C;8cm;100L ♀ ➤ ◐ ✕ 🖻 🖼

Pseudotropheus brevis pH8.0;H22;27C;10cm;100L ♀ ➤ ◐ ✕ 🖻 🖼

Pseudotropheus lanisticola pH8.1;H20;28C;9cm;100L ♀ ⇒ ◑ ✕ ▣ ▣

Pseudotropheus "eduardi" pH8.2;H21;28C;8cm;100L ♀ ⇒ ◑ ✕ ▣ ▣

Pseudotropheus sp. pH8.0;H20;27C;10cm;100L ♀ ⇒ ◑ ✕ ▣ ▣

Pseudotropheus zebra pH8.1;H22;27C;12cm;100L ♀ ➤ ◑ ✕ 🖼 ⊡

Pseudotropheus williamsi pH8.1;H22;28C;15cm;200L ♀ ➤ ◑ ✕ ‡ ⊡

Pseudotropheus lombardoi pH8.1;H22;27C;13cm;100L ♀ ➤ ◑ ✕ 🖼 ⊡

Pseudotropheus zebra pH8.1;H22;27C;12cm;100L ♀ 🐟 ◐ ✂ 📷 🔲

Pseudotropheus zebra pH8.1;H22;27C;12cm;100L ♀ 🐟 ◐ ✂ 📷 🔲

Pseudotropheus williamsi pH8.2;H20;26C;12cm;100L ♀ 🐟 ◐ ✂ 📷 🔲

Pseudotropheus zebra pH8.1;H22;27C;12cm;100L ♀ 🐟 ◑ ✂ 📷 ⊡

Pseudotropheus zebra pH8.1;H22;27C;12cm;100L ♀ 🐟 ◑ ✂ 📷 ⊡

Pseudotropheus zebra pH8.1;H22;27C;12cm;100L ♀ 🐟 ◑ ✂ 📷 ⊡

141

Pseudotropheus zebra pH8.1;H22;27C;12cm;100L ♀ ➤ ◑ ✕ 🎞 ⊡

Pseudotropheus zebra pH8.1;H22;27C;12cm;100L ♀ ➤ ◑ ✕ 🎞 ⊡

Pseudotropheus zebra pH8.1;H22;27C;12cm;100L ♀ ➤ ◑ ✕ 🎞 ⊡

142

Pseudotropheus zebra pH8.1;H22;27C;12cm;100L ♀ ➤ ◐ ✕ 🔲 ⊟

Pseudotropheus zebra pH8.1;H22;27C;12cm;100L ♀ ➤ ◐ ✕ 🔲 ⊟

Pseudotropheus zebra pH8.1;H22;27C;12cm;100L ♀ ➤ ◐ ✕ 🔲 ⊟

Pseudotropheus zebra pH8.1;H22;27C;12cm;100L ♀ ➤ ◑ ✂ 📷 ⊡

Pseudotropheus zebra pH8.1;H22;27C;12cm;100L ♀ ➤ ◑ ✂ 📷 ⊡

Pseudotropheus zebra pH8.1;H22;27C;12cm;100L ♀ ➤ ◑ ✂ 📷 ⊡

Cynotilapia sp. pH8.1;H22;28C;8cm;100L ♀ ➤ ◑ ✕ 🔲 ⛶

Cynotilapia afra pH8.0;H21;28C;8cm;100L ♀ ➤ ◑ ✕ 🔲 ⛶

Cynotilapia axelrodi pH8.1;H22;27C;8cm;100L ♀ ➤ ◑ ✕ 🔲 ⛶

145

Labeotropheus fuelleborni pH8.0;H22;28C;13cm;100L ♀ ➤ ◐ ✕ 🔲 ⊡

Labeotropheus fuelleborni pH8.0;H22;28C;13cm;100L ♀ ➤ ◐ ✕ 🔲 ⊡

Labeotropheus fuelleborni pH8.0;H22;28C;13cm;100L ♀ ➤ ◐ ✕ 🔲 ⊡

Labeotropheus fuelleborni pH8.0;H22;28C;13cm;100L ♀ ➤ ◑ ✕ 🖻 ⊡

Labeotropheus fuelleborni pH8.0;H22;28C;13cm;100L ♀ ➤ ◑ ✕ 🖻 ⊡

Labeotropheus fuelleborni pH8.0;H22;28C;13cm;100L ♀ ➤ ◑ ✕ 🖻 ⊡

147

Labeotropheus trewavasae pH8.1;H21;27C;10cm;100L ♀ ➤ ◑ ✕ 🎞 ⊟

Labeotropheus trewavasae pH8.1;H21;27C;10cm;100L ♀ ➤ ◑ ✕ 🎞 ⊟

Labeotropheus trewavasae pH8.1;H21;27C;10cm;100L ♀ ➤ ◑ ✕ 🎞 ⊟

Labeotropheus trewavasae pH8.1;H21;27C;10cm;100L ♀ 🐟 ◑ ✕ 📷 🔲

Labeotropheus trewavasae pH8.1;H21;27C;10cm;100L ♀ 🐟 ◑ ✕ 📷 🔲

Labeotropheus trewavasae pH8.1;H21;27C;10cm;100L ♀ 🐟 ◑ ✕ 📷 🔲

149

Cichlids of Lake Tanganyika

Like Lake Malawi, Lake Tanganyika is one of the African Rift Valley lakes. Also like Lake Malawi, it provides numerous species of cichlids for the aquarium hobby, with over 175 described species known so far and many more to be described. The water in Lake Tanganyika is especially hard and alkaline, with the pH averaging between 8.6 and 9.2. Although many of the species are fond of rocks, there are also many species that prefer sandy bottoms and many that are free-swimming in open water. Most of the species will take prepared aquarium foods and live foods.

In Lake Tanganyika is found the largest cichlid, *Boulengerochromis microlepis,* growing to a length of 90 cm or more. Lake Tanganyika also provides some of the smallest cichlids, species that grow no larger than 3.5 cm and live in snail shells. These shell-dwellers have become very popular in the hobby and are the current rage. Also found in Lake Tanganyika are small cichlids that act much like marine gobies and have for that reason been dubbed goby cichlids. These are members of the genera *Spathodus, Eretmodus,* and *Tanganicodus.* The most speciose genus in the lake is *Lamprologus,* its more than 40 species providing many aquarium favorites, among which are *L. brichardi, L. compressiceps, L. sexfasciatus,* and the shell-dwellers. One genus, *Julidochromis,* contains only half a dozen or so species but all have been imported and become popular in the hobby. One of the real challenges of Lake Tanganyika is the expensive *Cyphotilapia frontosa.* Although occasionally bred, there is still more demand for this spectacular fish than can be satisfied. Perhaps the leading aquarium species of Lake Tanganyika cichlid is *Tropheus moorii.* This species and its close relatives have evolved a myriad of color patterns, and new color varieties are being imported as fast as they are discovered.

Unlike the abundance of mouthbrooders in Lake Malawi, most of the cichlids imported from Lake Tanganyika are substrate spawners. These fishes, especially the *Lamprologus* species, spawn in the manner typical of most cichlids. After courtship and the cleaning of a spot on the substrate, the female lays a string of eggs and the male follows behind, fertilizing them. Once the female has become depleted, she or the male or both fish will stand guard over the eggs until the fry hatch and become free-swimming.

Julidochromis ornatus pH8.3;H21;28C;6cm;100L ♀ ➤ ◐ ✹ 📷 🖵

Julidochromis transcriptus pH8.0;H20;27C;6cm;80L ♀ ➤ ◐ ✹ 📷 🖵

Julidochromis dickfeldi pH8.0;H20;27C;10cm;100L ♀ ➤ ◐ ✹ 📷 🖵

Julidochromis transcriptus pH8.2;H20;27C;13cm;100L ♀ ➤ ◑ ✕ 🖻 ▭

Julidochromis transcriptus pH8.2;H20;27C;13cm;100L ♀ ➤ ◑ ✕ 🖻 ▭

Julidochromis marlieri pH8.2;H22;28C;13cm;100L ♀ ➤ ◑ ✕ 🖻 ▭

Julidochromis regani pH8.2;H20;27C;13cm;100L ♀ ➤ ◐ ✕ ▣ ▭

Julidochromis regani pH8.2;H20;27C;13cm;100L ♀ ➤ ◐ ✕ ▣ ▭

Chalinochromis brichardi pH8.2;H20;27C;15cm;100L ♀ ➤ ◐ ✕ ▣ ▭

153

Aulonocranus dewindti pH8.1;H19;28C;25cm;300L ♀ ➤ ❶ ✕ 🖼 🖾

Callochromis macrops pH8.2;H20;27C;15cm;200L ♀ ➤ ❶ ✕ 🖼 🖾

Chalinochromis brichardi pH8.2;H20;28C;10cm;100L ♀ ➤ ❶ ✕ 🖼 🖾

Aulonocranus dewindti pH8.0;H20;28C;12cm;100L ♀ 🐟 ◑ ✂ 📷 ⊞

Xenotilapia sima pH8.1;H21;27C;18cm;200L ♀ 🐟 ◑ ✂ 📷 ⬜

Xenotilapia flavipinnis pH8.2;H22;27C;12cm;100L ♀ 🐟 ◑ ✂ 📷 ⬜

Xenotilapia spilopterus pH8.1;H20;27C;10cm;100L ♀ 🐟 ◑ ✂ 📷 🖵

Xenotilapia flavipinnis pH8.2;H22;28C;10cm;100L ♀ 🐟 ◑ ✂ 📷 🖵

Xenotilapia ochrogenys pH8.2;H22;27C;11cm;100L ♀ 🐟 ◑ ✂ 📷 🖵

Cyphotilapia frontosa pH8.3;H22;27C;35cm;400L ♀ ➤ ◑ ✂ 🎞 ▭

Cyprichromis brieni pH8.0;H20;27C;10cm;120L ♀ ➤ ◑ ✂ 🎞 ▱

Eretmodus cyanostictus pH8.2;H21;27C;8cm;80L ♀ ➤ ◑ ✂ 🎞 ▭

157

Petrochromis polyodon pH8.2;H22;28C;10cm;100L ♀ ➤ ◐ ✂ ▣ ▣

Perissodus straeleni pH8.1;H20;28C;15cm;200L ♀ ➤ ◐ ✂ ▣ ▣

Perissodus microlepis pH8.0;H20;27C;16cm;200L ♀ ➤ ◐ ✂ ▣ ▣

Reganochromis calliurus pH8.0;H20;26C;15cm;200L ♀ ➤ ◗ ✕ 🔙 ☐

Telmatochromis caninus pH8.0;H20;28C;15cm;200L ♀ ➤ ◗ ✕ 🔙 ☐

Telmatochromis temporalis pH8.0;H20;27C;12cm;100L ♀ ➤ ◗ ✕ 🔙 ☐

159

Tropheus brichardi pH8.1;H20;27C;11cm;100L ♀ 🐟 ◑ ✕ 🎥 🖼

Tropheus duboisi pH8.0;H20;27C;9cm;100L ♀ 🐟 ◑ ✕ 🎥 🖼

Tropheus duboisi pH8.0;H20;27C;9cm;100L ♀ 🐟 ◑ ✕ 🎥 🖼

Tropheus duboisi pH8.0;H20;27C;9cm;100L ♀ ➤ ❶ ✕ ▣ ▭

Tropheus duboisi pH8.0;H20;27C;9cm;100L ♀ ➤ ❶ ✕ ▣ ▭

Tropheus moorii pH8.1;H20;27C;10cm;100L ♀ ➤ ❶ ✕ ▣ ▭

Tropheus duboisi pH8.2;H20;27C;10cm;100L ♀ 🐟 ◑ ✂ 📷 ⬜

Tropheus moorii pH8.2;H20;27C;10cm;100L ♀ 🐟 ◑ ✂ 📷 ⬜

Tropheus moorii pH8.2;H20;27C;10cm;100L ♀ 🐟 ◑ ✂ 📷 ⬜

Tropheus moorii pH8.1;H20;27C;10cm;100L ♀ ➤ ◑ ✕ 📷 ⊡

Tropheus moorii pH8.1;H20;27C;10cm;100L ♀ ➤ ◑ ✕ 📷 ⊡

Tropheus moorii pH8.1;H20;27C;10cm;100L ♀ ➤ ◑ ✕ 📷 ⊡

Tropheus moorii pH8.1;H20;27C;10cm;100L ♀ ➤ ◑ ✕ 🔲 🖂

Tropheus moorii pH8.1;H20;27C;10cm;100L ♀ ➤ ◑ ✕ 🔲 🖂

Tropheus moorii pH8.1;H20;27C;10cm;100L ♀ ➤ ◑ ✕ 🔲 🖂

Tropheus sp. (Mpulungu var.) pH8.1;H20;27C;10cm;100L ♀ 🐟 ◑✕ 📷 🖼

Tropheus moorii pH8.1;H20;27C;10cm;100L ♀ 🐟 ◑✕ 📷 🖼

Tropheus moorii kasabae pH8.0;H20;28C;10cm;100L ♀ 🐟 ◑✕ 📷 🖼

167

Cyathopharynx furcifer pH8.2;H20;26C;30cm;200L ♀ ➤ ◐ ✕ 📷 ☷

Ophthalmotilapia ventralis pH8.2;H20;26C;15cm;150L ♀ ➤ ◐ ✕ 📷 ☷

Ophthalmotilapia nasutus pH8.2;H20;26C;15cm;150L ♀ ➤ ◐ ✕ 📷 ☷

Bathybates ferox pH8.1;H21;27C;30cm;?L ♀ 🐟 ◑ ✕ 🎞 ⊡

Callochromis pleurospilus pH8.2;H20;26C;18cm;200L ♀ 🐟 ◑ ✕ 🎞 ⊡

Ophthalmotilapia ventralis pH8.2;H22;27C;30cm;400L ♀ 🐟 ◑ ✕ 🎞 ⊡

169

Haplochromis burtoni pH8.0;H20;27C;10cm;100L ♀ ➤ ◑ ✕ 🔳 🔲

Callochromis macrops melanostigma pH8.1;H20;28C;16cm;200L ♀ ➤ ◑ ✕ 🔳 🔲

Cardiopharynx schoutedeni pH8.2;H21;26C;15cm;150L ♀ ➤ ◑ ✕ 🔳 🔲

Cardiopharynx schoutedeni pH8.2;H21;26C;15cm;150L ♀ ➤ ❶ ✖ 🔲 ⊡

Haplochromis benthicola pH8.0;H20;27C;12cm;100L ♀ ➤ ❶ ✖ 🔲 ⊡

Haplotaxodon microlepis pH8.0;H20;28C;10cm;100L ♀ ➤ ❶ ✖ 🔲 ⊡

Lamprologus sp. "Magarae" pH8.0;H20;27C;6cm;40L ♀ ➤ ◑ ✂ 📷 ▭

Lamprologus callipterus pH8.1;H20;27C;18cm;200L ♀ ➤ ◑ ✂ 📷 ▭

Lamprologus compressiceps pH8.2;H20;26C;15cm;100L ♀ ➤ ◑ ✂ 📷 ▭

Lamprologus brevis pH8.0;H20;26C;6cm;40L ♀ ➤ ◑ ✕ 🖻 ⬚

Lamprologus attenuatus pH8.1;H20;27C;15cm;200L ♀ ➤ ◑ ✕ 🖻 ⬚

Lamprologus leloupi pH8.0;H20;27C;8cm;100L ♀ ➤ ◑ ✕ 🖻 ⬚

173

Lamprologus buscheri pH8.1;H20;26C;9cm;100L ♀ ➤ ◑ ✕ 📷 ⬜

Lamprologus elegans pH8.0;H20;27C;10cm;100L ♀ ➤ ◑ ✕ 📷 ⬜

Lamprologus calvus pH8.0;H21;26C;13cm;150L ♀ ➤ ◑ ✕ 📷 ⬜

Lamprologus compressiceps pH8.1;H20;26C;13cm;150L ♀ ➤ ◑ ✕ 🖻 ▢

Lamprologus compressiceps pH8.1;H20;26C;13cm;150L ♀ ➤ ◑ ✕ 🖻 ▨

Lamprologus leleupi pH8.1;H21;27C;10cm;100L ♀ ➤ ◑ ✕ 🖻 ▨

175

Lamprologus cunningtoni pH8.0;H20;27C;15cm;200L ♀ ➤ ◑ ✕ 🖻 ▭

Lamprologus fasciatus pH8.0;H20;28C;9cm;100L ♀ ➤ ◑ ✕ 🖻 ▭

Lamprologus leleupi pH8.1;H21;27C;10cm;100L ♀ ➤ ◑ ✕ 🖻 ▭

Perissodus straeleni pH8.1;H22;27C;16cm;200L ♀ ➤ ◐ ✄ 🖬 ▢

Lamprologus tretocephalus pH8.1;H20;26C;15cm;200L ♀ ➤ ◐ ✄ 🖬 ▢

Cyphotilapia frontosa pH8.2;H21;27C;32cm;400L ♀ ➤ ◐ ✄ 🖬 ▢

177

African Non-lake Cichlids

Although the current emphasis in the aquarium hobby is on the cichlids of Lakes Malawi and Tanganyika, there are numerous other African cichlids that are colorful, successful additions to the aquarium. Some of these (such as the kribs and jewels) have been popular for years, while others are just starting to appear on the market with regularity. Unlike the Lake cichlids, these species usually require less unusual water conditions, doing well in water of about neutral pH and normal hardness. They are usually content with prepared foods supplemented with feedings of brine shrimp and tubifex.

The kribs, *Pelvicachromis* species, are perhaps the most familiar of the West African small cichlids, with *P. pulcher* being available in most pet shops all year long. Other species such as *P. taeniatus* are now being imported and bred regularly, but to the delight of the aquarist all do equally well in a small tank. Although colorful enough at all times to be interesting, females in spawning condition are especially attractive, taking on a brilliant pinkish violet flush to the abdomen.

The bright red colors of the jewel cichlids, *Hemichromis bimaculatus* and relatives, have long made these fishes popular. Jewel cichlids can be quite aggressive when spawning, but their zeal does not approach that of their larger and less colorful cousin, *Hemichromis elongatus*. This species has gained a reputation as one of the more aggressive common small cichlids.

Coming in a variety of colors and shapes are the species of *Nanochromis*. They may be rather stout and hardy fishes such as *N. dimidiatus,* or more slender and delicate-looking species such as *N. parilius* and *splendens*. The male is usually more colorful than the female in this genus, but the recently introduced *N. transvestitus* has colorful females and rather plain males.

Most cichlids from western and central Africa are substrate-spawners, but the Egyptian mouthbrooders, *Pseudocrenilabrus,* are—as the common name suggests—mouthbrooders. These colorful little fishes are worth buying when you can find them.

♀ *Pseudocrenilabrus multicolor* pH7.0;H6;28C;8cm;80L ♀ 🐟 ◑ ✕ 📷 ⛶

Tylochromis polylepis pH8.0;H20;27C;14cm;200L ♀ 🐟 ◑ ✕ 📷 ⛶

Serranochromis robustus pH8.1;H20;27C;50cm;400L ♀ 🐟 ◑ ✕ 📷 ⛶

Pseudocrenilabrus philander pH7.0;H6;28C;8cm;80L ♀ 🐟 ◑ ✕ 📷 ▣

♂ *Pseudocrenilabrus multicolor* pH7.0;H6;28C;8cm;80L ♀ 🐟 ◑ ✕ 📷 ▣

Tylochromis lateralis pH8.0;H20;26C;15cm;200L ♀ 🐟 ◑ ✕ 📷 ▣

Sarotherodon leucostictus pH7.8;H20;26C;28cm;100L ♀ ➤ ◑ ✕ ▣ ▣

Sarotherodon mossambicus pH7.8;H20;27C;40cm;400L ♀ ➤ ◑ ✕ ▣ ▣

Sarotherodon mossambicus pH7.8;H20;27C;40cm;400L ♀ ➤ ◑ ✕ ▣ ▣

Sarotherodon mossambicus pH7.8;H20;27C;40cm;400L ♀ 🐟 ◐ ✖ 📷 ▦

Sarotherodon mossambicus pH7.8;H20;27C;40cm;400L ♀ 🐟 ◐ ✖ 📷 ▦

Orthochromis cf. *machodoi* pH7.8;H15;25C;6cm;80L ♀ 🐟 ◐ ✖ 📷 ▦

Sarotherodon mossambicus pH7.8;H20;27C;40cm;400L ♀ 🐟 ◐ ✕ 📷 ▱

Tilapia ovalis pH7.8;H20;26C;25cm;200L ♀ 🐟 ◐ ✕ 📷 ▱

Tilapia sp. pH7.9;H20;28C;20cm;200L ♀ 🐟 ◐ ✕ 📷 ▱

Tilapia mariae pH7.8;H18;28C;18cm;200L ♀ 🐟 ◗ ✂ 📷 ▣

Tilapia sp. pH7.8;H18;27C;17cm;200L ♀ 🐟 ◗ ✂ 📷 ▣

Tilapia nilotica pH7.9;H18;27C;15cm;200L ♀ 🐟 ◗ ✂ 📷 ▣

Steatocranus casuarius pH6.8;H5;28C;11cm;100L ♀ ➤ ◑✕ 🔳 ▣

Steatocranus mpozoensis pH7.8;H4;28C;10cm;100L ♀ ➤ ◑✕ 🔳 ▭

Teleogramma brichardi pH7.0;H4;27C;11cm;100L ♀ ➤ ◑✕ 🔳 ▭

185

Nanochromis dimidiatus pH7.0;H8;26C;8cm;100L ♀ 🐟 ◑ ✕ 📷 🖥

Nanochromis dimidiatus pH7.0;H8;26C;8cm;100L ♀ 🐟 ◑ ✕ 📷 🖥

Nanochromis splendens pH7.0;H8;26C;8cm;100L ♀ 🐟 ◑ ✕ 📷 🖥

Nanochromis dimidiatus pH7.0;H8;26C;8cm;100L ♀ ⇀ ◐ ✂ 🔲 🔲

Nanochromis splendens pH7.0;H8;26C;8cm;100L ♀ ⇀ ◐ ✂ 🔲 🔲

Nanochromis paril us pH6.8;H5;26C;8cm;100L ♀ ⇀ ◐ ✂ 🔲 🔲

187

♀ *Pelvicachromis pulcher* pH7.0;H8;26C;8cm;80L ♀ 🐟 ◐ ✕ 📷 🔄

♂ *Pelvicachromis pulcher* pH7.0;H8;26C;8cm;80L ♀ 🐟 ◐ ✕ 📷 🔄

♂ *Pelvicachromis pulcher* pH7.0;H8;26C;8cm;80L ♀ 🐟 ◐ ✕ 📷 🔄

♂ *Pelvicachromis pulcher* pH7.0;H8;26C;8cm;80L ♀ ➤ ◑ ✕ ▣ ▭

♀ *Pelvicachromis* sp. aff. *pulcher* pH7.0;H8;26C;8cm;80L ♀ ➤ ◑ ✕ ▣ ▭

♀ *Pelvicachromis* sp. aff. *pulcher* pH7.0;H8;26C;8cm;80L ♀ ➤ ◑ ✕ ▣ ▭

189

♂ *Pelvicachromis taeniatus* pH6.8;H5;26C;8cm;100L ♀ 🦐🐟 ◑✕ 📷 ▭

♀ *Pelvicachromis taeniatus* pH6.8;H5;26C;8cm;100L ♀ 🦐🐟 ◑✕ 📷 ▣

♀ *Pelvicachromis taeniatus* pH6.8;H5;26C;8cm;100L ♀ 🦐🐟 ◑✕ 📷 ▣

Pelvicachromis roloffi pH6.8;H5;27C;8cm;100L ♀ 🐟 ◑ ✕ 📷 ▭

Pelvicachromis taeniatus pH6.8;H5;26C;8cm;100L ♀ 🐟 ◑ ✕ 📷 ▭

Pelvicachromis taeniatus pH6.8;H5;26C;8cm;100L ♀ 🐟 ◑ ✕ 📷 ▭

191

Pelvicachromis subocellatus pH7.0;H8;26C;8cm;80L ♀ 🐟 ◐ ✂ 📷 ⊡

Pelvicachromis subocellatus pH7.0;H8;26C;8cm;80L ♀ 🐟 ◐ ✂ 📷 ⊡

Pelvicachromis humilis pH7.0;H8;26C;8cm;80L ♀ 🐟 ◐ ✂ 📷 ⊡

Chromidotilapia batesii pH7.8;H16;27C;8cm;100L ♀ ➤ ◑ ✂ ▣ ⊟

Chromidotilapia guentheri pH7.8;H17;27C;15cm;200L ♀ ➤ ◑ ✂ ▣ ⊟

Chromidotilapia guentheri pH7.8;H17;27C;15cm;200L ♀ ➤ ◑ ✂ ▣ ⊟

Chromidotilapia guentheri pH7.8;H17;27C;15cm;200L ♀ ⋙ ◑ ✕ ▣ ⊟

Chromidotilapia kingsleyi pH7.8;H18;27C;25cm;300L ♀ ⋙ ◑ ✕ ▣ ⊟

Thysia ansorgi pH7.8;H18;27C;10cm;100L ♀ ⋙ ◑ ✕ ▣ ⊟

196

Hemichromis cristatus pH7.5;H12;26C;15cm;200L ♀ ➤ ◐ ✕ 🖷 ▱

Hemichromis cristatus pH7.5;H12;26C;15cm;200L ♀ ➤ ◐ ✕ 🖷 ▱

Hemichromis thomasi pH7.8;H12;25C;10cm;100L ♀ ➤ ◐ ✕ 🖷 ▱

197

Hemichromis cristatus pH7.5;H12;26C;15cm;200L ♀ ➤ ◐ ✄ 🎞 ⊟

Hemichromis cristatus pH7.5;H12;26C;15cm;200L ♀ ➤ ◐ ✄ 🎞 ⊟

Hemichromis thomasi pH7.8;H12;25C;10cm;100L ♀ ➤ ◐ ✄ 🎞 ⊟

Hemichromis cristatus pH7.5;H12;26C;15cm;200L ♀ 🐟 ◐ ✂ 📷 ⛶

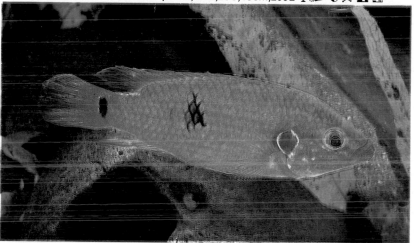

Hemichromis bimaculatus pH7.5;H12;26C;15cm;200L ♀ 🐟 ◐ ✂ 📷 ⛶

Hemichromis paynei pH7.5;H12;26C;12cm;200L ♀ 🐟 ◐ ✂ 📷 ⛶   199

Hemichromis fasciatus pH7.5;H12;27C;30cm;250L ♀ ➤ ◑ ✂ 📷 ⊡

Hemichromis elongatus pH7.5;H12;27C;14cm;200L ♀ ➤ ◑ ✂ 📷 ⊡

Hemichromis elongatus pH7.5;H12;27C;14cm;200L ♀ ➤ ◑ ✂ 📷 ⊡

Etroplus suratensis pH8.0;H20;26C;50cm;300L 〜🐟 ◑✻ 🖼 🔲

Etroplus maculatus pH8.0;H20;25C;10cm;100L ♀🐟 ◑✻ 🖼 🔲

Etroplus maculatus pH8.0;H20;25C;10cm;100L ♀🐟 ◑✻ 🖼 🔲

The Anabantoids

A large group of fishes found in southeast Asia, including the Philippines, and in almost all of Africa south of the desert, require atmospheric air in order to breathe. Not all of the fishes in this range require air from the atmosphere, and not all fishes which require air are anabantoids (such as the *Corydoras* catfishes of South America, for example). What separates the anabantoids from other fishes is the labyrinth chamber, a special organ composed of lamellae which are covered over with a special blood-soaked thin skin, enabling the fish to utilize atmospheric air. Lamellae are a series of thin plates which look very much like the underside of a mushroom cap. Engineers copied this structure for cooling and dispersing heat, as in the fins on a car radiator.

It seems that through the process of evolution certain fishes had to live in water which contained so much decaying matter, or was so algae-rich, that the oxygen available in the water was below that which was required by the fish. So that now all anabantoids MUST have atmospheric air or they will perish. I (HRA) learned this lesson on my first collecting trip to Thailand. I put a trap in the water one night, coming back the next morning to see what I had collected. Several paradisefish and some bettas were in the trap ... all dead! They had suffocated, since they could not get out of the trap and up to the surface to breathe!

While the possession of a labyrinth organ is one of the major bases for the scientific classification of the several families of fishes in the suborder Anabantoidei, our aquarium anabantoids have certain other common characteristics as well.

The families of the suborder are the Anabantidae (containing the climbing perch, *Anabas,* and the *Ctenopoma* species); the Belontiidae (containing the bettas, the paradise fish, and the croaking gouramis); the Osphronemidae (containing only one species, the "true" gourami); the Helostomidae (also containing only one species, the kissing gourami). This listing follows the scheme employed by Karel F. Liem in the early 1960's; different taxonomists take different approaches from time to time.

For the most part all of those from Asia build a bubblenest in order to keep their eggs together in a nest. The bubblenest is usually constructed by the male; after he has completed the nest, he entices a female under it to spawn. Some nests are very complex and large *(Betta, Colisa, Trichogaster)* while some are hardly recognizable *(Helostoma).* Some nests are even built underwater by some of the smaller anabantoids.

The male blows bubbles with the aid of a mucus secretion from his mouth. Once he has attracted a female and spawned with her by squeezing her body with his own as he forms a tight "U" shape, she seems to be paralyzed for a few seconds, giving the male time to gather the eggs, or in the case of species that have floating eggs, giving the eggs a chance to float up into the nest. Once the female "awakens" she usually eats any of the eggs that she finds outside the nest.

When spawning is complete, the male guards the nest, capturing any eggs or (later) any newly hatched young that escape from the nest and blowing them back into the nest.

A few species of anabantoids are even mouthbrooders (some species of *Betta*). Generally speaking, the anabantoids from southeast Asia have complex nests while those from Africa have almost non-existent nests. I have observed *Ctenopoma* spawning and was never able to detect a nest, but in several magazine articles observers of *Ctenopoma congicum* claim that a nest is built. It is very possible that fishes spawn differently under different circumstances, as I have seen some *Betta splendens* build huge nests, while others seem to be happy with just a few bubbles.

Another rather common characteristic of anabantoids is that they usually (except for the mouthbrooders) have a huge spawn. The kissing gourami, *Helostoma*, may have thousands of eggs, as do the fishes of the genus *Trichogaster* and *Colisa*. Thus, if you wish to spawn these fishes you must be prepared for a large brood. Certainly it is unthinkable to attempt to spawn and raise the family of any large anabantoid in less than a 10-gallon tank . . . and a 50-gallon tank might even be better! It is not merely a matter of crowding, because once the fish reach a certain size their labyrinth organs develop and they can live on atmospheric air; it is also a matter of fighting over food and chomping on the fins of their too-close-by brethren.

The ballet of spawning anabantoids is so beautiful and so easy to precipitate that anyone who has an aquarium and doesn't prepare a pair of Siamese fighting fish, *Betta splendens*, for spawning is missing one of the greatest thrills our hobby has to offer.

♀ *Parosphromenus deissneri* pH6.8;H5;28C;4cm;40L 〰️ 🐟 ◑ ♥ 🖼️ ▤

♂ *Parosphromenus paludicola* pH6.8;H5;28C;4cm;40L 〰️ 🐟 ◑ ♥ 🖼️ ▤

Parosphromenus nagyi pH6.8;H5;28C;4cm;40L 〰️ 🐟 ◑ ♥ 🖼️ ▤

♀ *Parosphromenus filamentosus* pH6.8;H5;28C;4cm;40L ᔓ ➤ ◑ ♥ 🖼 🗒

Parosphromenus parvulus pH6.7;H5;28C;3cm;20L ᔓ ➤ ◑ ♥ 🖼 🗒

♂ *Parosphromenus paludicola* pH6.8;H5;28C;4cm;40L ᔓ ➤ ◑ ♥ 🖼 🗒

Parosphromenus filamentosus pH6.8;H5;28C;4cm;40L ᕲ ➤ ◐ ♥ 🖼 ▤

Trichopsis schalleri pH6.8;H5;24C;6cm;80L ᕲ ➤ ◐ ♥ 🖼 ▤

Trichopsis vittatus pH7.0;H8;28C;6cm;80L ᕲ ➤ ◐ ♥ 🖼 ▤

Parosphromenus deissneri pH6.5;H4;25C;4cm;40L ⌇ 🐟 ◑ ♥ 🔳 ▤

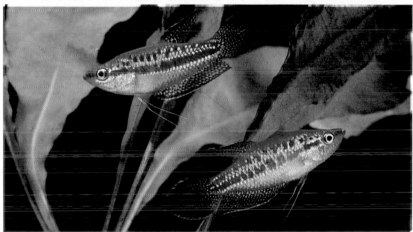

Trichopsis pumilus pH7.0;H8;27C;3cm;40L ⌇ 🐟 ◑ ♥ 🔳 ▢

Betta bellica pH7.0;H8;30C;10cm;100L ⌇ 🐟 ◑ ✳ 🔳 ▢

207

♂ *Betta pugnax* pH7.2;H10;24C;10cm;100L ∿ ⟫ ◐ ♥ 🖾 ▢

Betta pugnax pH7.2;H10;24C;10cm;100L ∿ ⟫ ◐ ♥ 🖾 ▢

Betta imbellis pH7.0;H8;26C;5cm;40L ∿ ⟫ ◐ ♥ 🖾 ▢

Betta splendens pH7.0;H8;26C;6cm;40L ♀ ➤ ◑ ♥ 📺 ▭

Betta splendens pH7.0;H8;26C;6cm;40L ♀ ➤ ◑ ♥ 📺 ▭

Betta splendens pH7.0;H8;26C;6cm;40L ♀ ➤ ◑ ♥ 📺 ▭

Betta splendens pH7.0;H8;26C;6cm;40L ♀ ➤ ◑ ♥ 🔟 ▭

Betta splendens pH7.0;H8;26C;6cm;40L ♀ ➤ ◑ ♥ 🔟 ▭

Betta splendens pH7.0;H8;26C;6cm;40L ♀ ➤ ◑ ♥ 🔟 ▭

Betta splendens pH7.0;H8;26C;6cm;40L ♀ ➤ ◑ ♥ 🖼 ▭

Betta splendens pH7.0;H8;26C;6cm;40L ♀ ➤ ◑ ♥ 🖼 ▭

Betta splendens pH7.0;H8;26C;6cm;40L ♀ ➤ ◑ ♥ 🖼 ▭

Betta macrostoma pH7.0;H8;24C;12cm;150L 〜 ➤ ◐ ♥ 🖼 ☐

Betta akarensis pH7.0;H8;27C;5cm;40L 〜 ➤ ◐ ♥ 🖼 ☐

Betta taeniata pH7.0;H8;25C;8cm;80L 〜 ➤ ◐ ♥ 🖼 ☐

212

Betta macrostoma pH7.0;H8;24C;12cm;150L ∿ ➤ ◑ ♥ 🎞 ▭

Betta edithae pH7.2;H10;24C;10cm;100L ∿ ➤ ◑ ♥ 🎞 ▭

Betta smaragdina pH7.0;H7;25C;7cm;80L ♀ ➤ ◑ ♥ 🎞 ▭

213

Macropodus concolor pH6.8;H6;24C;12cm;100L ♀ ➤ ◑ ✂ ▭

Macropodus opercularis pH7.0;H8;23C;8cm;80L ♀ ➤ ◑ ✂ 🖼 ▭

Pseudosphromenus cupanus cupanus pH6.5;H3;25C;8cm;80L ♀ ➤ ◑ ♥ 🖼 ▭

Colisa chuna pH6.7;H6;26C;6cm;80L ∿ ➤ ◑ ♥ 🖼 ☐

Colisa fasciata pH7.0;H8;26C;12cm;100L ♀ ➤ ◑ ♥ 🖼 ☐

Colisa lalia pH6.8;H7;28C;6cm;80L ♀ ➤ ◑ ♥ 🖼 ☐

215

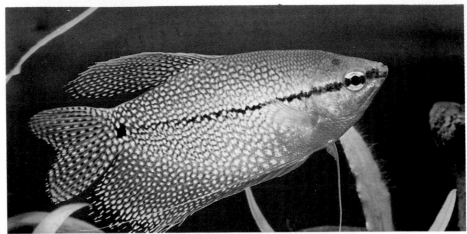

Trichogaster leeri pH7.0;H8;26C;10cm;100L ♀ ➤ ◐ ♥ 📺 ▭

Trichogaster pectoralis pH6.8;H7;26C;26cm;300L ♀ ➤ ◐ ♥ 📺 ▭

Trichogaster trichopterus pH6.8;H6;27C;15cm;200L ♀ ➤ ◐ ♥ 📺 ▭

Trichogaster microlepis pH6.8;H7;27C;15cm;200L ♀ ➤ ◑ ♥ 📺 ▭

Trichogaster trichopterus pH6.8;H6;27C;15cm;200L ♀ ➤ ◑ ♥ 📺 ▭

Trichogaster trichopterus pH6.8;H6;27C;15cm;200L ♀ ➤ ◑ ♥ 📺 ▭

Sphaerichthys osphromenoides pH6.5;H3;28C;5cm;40L ⤳ ➤ ◐ ♥ 🔄 ⊟

Sphaerichthys osphromenoides selatanensis pH6.5;H3;28C;5cm;40L ⤳ ➤ ◐ ♥ 🔄 ⊟

Sphaerichthys acrostoma pH6.5;H3;28C;5cm;40L ⤳ ➤ ◐ ♥ 🔄 ⊟

Anabas testudineus pH7.0;H8;29C;25cm;300L ♀ ➤ ◑ ✖ 🎞 ☐

Osphronemus goramy pH7.0;H8;27C;60cm;800L ♀ ➤ ◑ ♥ 🎞 ☐

Helostoma temmincki pH7.0;H10;26C;30cm;400L ♀ ➤ ◑ ♥ 🎞 ☰

219

Osphronemus goramy pH7.0;H8;27C;60cm;800L 🐟 🦐 ◑ ♥ 🖼 ☐

Helostoma temmincki pH7.0;H10;26C;30cm;400L 🐟 🦐 ◑ ♥ 🖼 ☐

Belontia signata pH7.0;H8;25C;13cm;100L 🐟 🦐 ◑ ✕ 🖼 ☐

Ctenopoma ocellatum pH6.8;H5;24C;14cm;150L ♀ ⌁ ◑ ✂ ☒ ▭

Ctenopoma acutirostre pH7.0;H8;28C;15cm;200L ♀ ⌁ ◑ ✂ ☒ ▤

Ctenopoma petherici pH6.8;H5;26C;13cm;150L ♀ ⌁ ◑ ✂ ☒ ▤

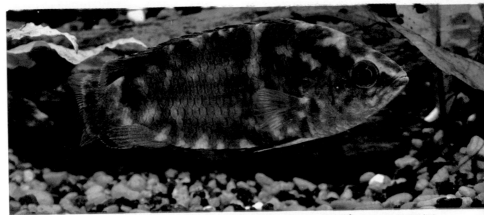

Ctenopoma cf. *argentoventer* pH7.0;H8;28C;20cm;200L ♀ 🐟 ◑ ✄ 📺 ⊟

Ctenopoma oxyrhynchum pH7.0;H8;28C;10cm;100L ♀ 🐟 ◑ ♥ 📺 ⊡

Ctenopoma maculatum pH7.0;H8;28C;20cm;200L ♀ 🐟 ◑ ✄ 📷 ⊡

Ctenopoma acutirostre pH7.0;H8;28C;15cm;200L ♀ ➤ ◐ ✖ 📺 ▱

Ctenopoma ansorge pH7.0;H8;27C;7cm;80L ♀ ➤ ◐ ♥ 🖼 ▱

Ctenopoma congicum pH7.0;H8;28C;8cm;80L ♀ ➤ ◐ ✖ 📺 ▱

Cynolebias antenori pH6.5;H7;24C;6.5cm;50L 〜 ➤ ◑ ♥ 🖼 ⊟

Cynolebias boitonei pH6.6;H6;24C;2.5cm;20L 〜 ➤ ◑ ♥ 🖼 ⊟

Cynolebias wolterstorffi pH6.8;H7;25C;10cm;60L 〜 ➤ ◑ ✖ 🐟 ⊟

Cynolebias bellotti pH7.0;H10;23C;7cm;40L 〜 🐟 ◐ ♥ 🔲 🔳

Cynolebias bellotti pH7.0;H10;23C;7cm;40L 〜 🐟 ◐ ♥ 🔲 🔳

Cynolebias minimus pH6.8;H7;25C;4cm;40L 〜 🐟 ◐ ♥ 🔲 🔳

Cynolebias adloffi pH6.8;H7;24C;5cm;40L 〜 ➤ ◑ ♥ 🔄 ⊟

Cynolebias alexandri pH7.0;H10;24C;5cm;40L 〜 ➤ ◑ ♥ 🔄 ⊟

Cynolebias nigripinnis pH6.5;H6;24C;4cm;40L 〜 ➤ ◑ ♥ 🔄 ⊟

Cynolebias whitei pH6.5;H8;23C;8cm;60L ∿ ➤ ◑ ♥ 💹 ⊟

Cynolebias dolichopterus pH6.3;H5;22C;6cm;60L ∿ ➤ ◑ ♥ 💹 ⊟

Cynolebias melanotaenia pH7.0;H10;24C;5cm;40L ∿ ➤ ◑ ♥ 💹 ⊟

229

Cynolebias whitei pH6.5;H8;23C;8cm;60L 〜 ➤ ◑ ♥ 🖼 ⊟

Cynolebias dolichopterus pH6.3;H5;22C;6cm;60L 〜 ➤ ◑ ♥ 🖼 ⊟

Cynolebias brucei pH6.8;H10;25C;3cm;40L 〜 ➤ ◑ ♥ 🖼 ⊟

Pterolebias longipinnis pH7.0;H10;20C;8cm;60L ～ ➤ ◑ ♥ 💹 ⊟

Pterolebias peruensis pH6.0;H5;21C;7cm;60L ～ ➤ ◑ ♥ 💹 ⊟

Pterolebias zonatus pH6.8;H8;22C;15cm;100L ～ ➤ ◑ ♥ 💹 ⊟

Trigonectes strigabundus pH6.7;H6;25C;6cm;60L ∿ ➤ ◑ ♥ 🌱 ⊟

Pterolebias peruensis pH6.0;H5;21C;7cm;60L ∿ ➤ ◑ ♥ 🌱 ⊟

Trigonectes balzanii pH6.5;H7;23C;7cm;60L ∿ ➤ ◑ ♥ 🌱 ⊟

Rachovia hummelincki pH6.6;H7;27C;6.5cm;60L ∿ ⟩➤ ◑ ♥ 🐛 ⊟

Rachovia maculipinnis pH6.7;H7;22C;10cm;60L ∿ ➤ ◑ ♥ 🐛 ⊟

Rachovia pyropunctata pH6.5;H7;26C;7cm;60L ∿ ➤ ◑ ♥ 🐛 ⊟

233

Rachovia brevis pH6.8;H6;27C;7.5cm;60L ∿ ➤ ◑ ♥ 💱 ▤

Rachovia brevis pH6.8;H6;27C;7.5cm;60L ∿ ➤ ◑ ♥ 💱 ▤

Austrofundulus limnaeus pH7.5;H10;**27C**;6cm;60L ∿ ➤ ◑ ♥ 💱 ▤

Austrofundulus limnaeus pH7.5;H10;27C;6cm;60L 〜 ➤ ◑ ♥ 🖾 ⊟

Cynolebias porosus pH6.8;H8;26C;15cm;100L 〜 ➤ ◑ ✕ 🖾 ⊟

Rivulus cylindraceus pH6.5;H5;25C;5cm;50L 〜 ➤ ◑ ♥ 🖾 ⊡

235

Rivulus punctatus pH6.6;H8;26C;8cm;60L ∿ ➤ ◐ ♥ 〰️ ▭

Rivulus holmiae pH6.8;H8;24C;10cm;75L ∿ ➤ ◐ ♥ 〰️ ▭

Rivulus cryptocallis pH6.5;H6;27C;6cm;60L ∿ ➤ ◐ ♥ 〰️ ▤

Rivulus magdalenae pH6.7;H8;26C;8cm;60L

Rivulus strigatus pH6.5;H8;24C;6cm;60L

Rivulus urophthalmus pH6.8;H7;24C;6cm;60L

Rivulus atratus pH6.5;H8;25C;4cm;40L ∿ ➤ ◐ ♥ 🐟 ☐

Rivulus limoncochae pH6.8;H9;25C;6cm;50L ∿ ➤ ◐ ♥ 🐟 ☐

Rivulus amphoreus pH6.6;H7;25C;7cm;60L ∿ ➤ ◐ ♥ 🐟 ☐

Rivulus beniensis pH6.5;H6;25C;5cm;40L ∿ ➤ ◑ ♥ 🖼 ▢

♂ *Rivulus agilae* pH7.0;H10;22C;5cm;50L ∿ ➤ ◑ ♥ 🖼 ▢

♀ *Rivulus agilae* pH7.0;H10;22C;5cm;50L ∿ ➤ ◑ ♥ 🖼 ▢

239

Rivulus punctatus pH6.6;H8;26C;8cm;60L 〜 ➤ ◑ ♥ ☒ ▭

Rivulus xiphidius pH6.2;H5;23C;3cm;40L 〜 ➤ ◑ ♥ ☒ ▭

Rivulus peruanus pH6.6;H8;24C;7cm;60L 〜 ➤ ◑ ♥ ☒ ▭

Cyprinodon macularius pH8.0;H14;26C;8cm;60L 〜 🐟 ◑ ♥ 🖼 ⬜

Fundulus cingulatus pH8.0;H12;24C;7cm;75L ♀ 🐟 ◑ ♥ 🖼 ⬜

Jordanella floridae pH7.5;H12;21C;5cm;75L ♀ 🐟 ◑ ♥ 🖼 ⬜

241

Fundulus chrysotus pH8.0;H14;24C;7cm;50L ♀ 🐟 ◐ ♥ 🖼 ▭

Fundulus heteroclitus pH8.0;H12;20C;12cm;60L ♀ 🐟 ◐ ♥ 🖼 ▭

Lucania goodei pH7.6;H10;15C;5cm;75L 〜 🐟 ◐ ♥ 🖼 ▭

242

Aphyosemion ogoense ottogartneri pH6.5;H3;25C;5cm;40L ∿ ➤ ◐ ♥ 🔲 ▣

Aphyosemion riggenbachi pH6.5;H3;25C;6cm;40L ∿ ➤ ◐ ♥ 🔲 ▣

Aphyosemion bitaeniatum pH6.5;H3;26C;6cm;40L ∿ ➤ ◐ ♥ 🔲 ▣

Aphyosemion bivittatum pH6.5;H3;26C;5cm;40L ⌇ ➤ ◐ ♥ 🔲 🔲

Aphyosemion bivittatum pH6.5;H3;26C;5cm;40L ⌇ ➤ ◐ ♥ 🔲 🔲

Aphyosemion loennbergi pH6.5;H3;26C;6cm;40L ⌇ ➤ ◐ ♥ 🔲 🔲

Aphyosemion gardneri mamfense pH6.5;H3;25C;7cm;40L ∿ ⟿ ◑ ♥ 🎦 ⊟

Aphyosemion gardneri clauseni pH6;H3;25C;7cm;40L ∿ ⟿ ◑ ♥ 🎦 ⊟

Aphyosemion cinnamomeum pH6.5;H3;25C;5cm;40L ∿ ⟿ ◑ ♥ 🎦 ⊟

245

Aphyosemion gardneri pH6.5;H3;25C;7cm;40L ∿ ➤ ◐ ♥ 🖼 ⊡

Aphyosemion gardneri mamfense pH6.5;H3;25C;7cm;40L ∿ ➤ ◐ ♥ 🖼 ⊡

Aphyosemion gardneri clauseni pH6;H3;25C;7cm;40L ∿ ➤ ◐ ♥ 🖼 ⊡

246

Aphyosemion roloffi pH6.5;H3;26C;5cm;40L 〜 ⟫ ◐ ♥ 🖼 ▭

Aphyosemion chaytori pH6.5;H3;26C;5cm;40L 〜 ⟫ ◐ ♥ 🖼 ▭

Aphyosemion guineense pH6.5;H3;26C;5cm;40L 〜 ⟫ ◐ ♥ 🖼 ▭

247

Aphyosemion geryi pH6.5;H3;25C;6cm;40L 〜 ➤ ◑ ♥ 💹 ⊡

Aphyosemion brueningi pH6.5;H3;26C;6cm;40L 〜 ➤ ◑ ♥ 💹 ⊡

Aphyosemion petersi pH6.5;H3;26C;5cm;40L 〜 ➤ ◑ ♥ ⊡

Aphyosemion celiae pH6.5;H3;25C;6cm;40L ∿ ➤ ◑ ♥ 🔳 🔲

Aphyosemion calliurum pH6.5;H3;26C;6cm;40L ∿ ➤ ◑ ♥ 🔳 🔲

Aphyosemion australe pH6.5;H3;25C;4cm;40L ∿ ➤ ◑ ♥ 🔳 🔲

249

Aphyosemion ahli pH6.5;H3;25C;6cm;40L 〰 ➤ ◑ ♥ 🖼 ▣

Aphyosemion calliurum pH6.5;H3;25C;6cm;40L 〰 ➤ ◑ ♥ 🖼 ▣

Aphyosemion australe pH6.5;H3;26C;6cm;40L 〰 ➤ ◑ ♥ 🖼 ▣

Aphyosemion rectogoense pH6.5;H3;25C;4cm;40L 〜 ➤ ◑ ♥ 🔯 ⊡

Aphyosemion schioetzi pH6.5;H3;25C;4cm;40L 〜 ➤ ◑ ♥ 🔯 ⊡

Aphyosemion cognatum pH6.5;H3;25C;7cm;40L 〜 ➤ ◑ ♥ 🔯 ⊡

251

Aphyosemion christyi pH6.5;H3;26C;5cm;40L 〜 🐟 ◐ ♥ 🏞 🎴

Aphyosemion gabunense boehmi pH6.5;H3;24C;6cm;40L 〜 🐟 ◐ ♥ 🏞 🎴

Aphyosemion schoutedeni pH6.5;H3;26C;5cm;40L 〜 🐟 ◐ ♥ 🏞 🎴

Aphyosemion exiguum pH6.5;H3;26C;6cm;40L ⌇ ➤ ◑ ♥ ₩ ▣

Aphyosemion bualanum pH6.5;H3;26C;6cm;40L ⌇ ➤ ◑ ♥ ₩ ▣

Aphyosemion kiyawense pH6.5;H3;25C;6cm;40L ⌇ ➤ ◑ ♥ ₩ ▣

Aphyosemion walkeri pH6.5;H3;25C;6cm;40L 〜 ➤ ◐ ♥ 🈨 ☒

Aphyosemion arnoldi pH6.5;H3;26C;6cm;40L 〜 ➤ ◐ ♥ 🈨 ☒

Aphyosemion rubrilabiale pH6.5;H3;26C;6cm;40L 〜 ➤ ◐ ♥ 🈨 ☒

Aphyosemion spurrelli pH6.5;H3;25C;6cm;40L ⤳ 🐟 ◑ ♥ 🔣 🔲

Aphyosemion filamentosum X *rubrilabiale* pH6.5;H3;25C;6cm;40L ⤳ 🐟 ◑ ♥ 🔣 🔲

Aphyosemion filamentosum-complex pH6.5;H3;25C;6cm;40L ⤳ 🐟 ◑ ♥ 🔣 🔲

255

Aphyosemion sjoestedti pH6.5;H3;26C;12cm;40L ∿ ➤ ◑ ♥ 🔛 ⊟

Aphyosemion gulare pH6.5;H3;25C;5cm;40L ∿ ➤ ◑ ♥ 🔛 ⊟

Aphyosemion cameronense pH6.5;H3;26C;6cm;40L ∿ ➤ ◑ ♥ 🔛 ⊟

Aphyosemion cameronense pH6.5;H3;26C;6cm;40L 〜 ➤ ◐ ♥ 🔲 🔲

Aphyosemion cameronense pH6.5;H3;26C;6cm;40L 〜 ➤ ◐ ♥ 🔲 🔲

Aphyosemion labarrei pH6.5;H3;26C;6cm;40L 〜 ➤ ◐ ♥ 🔲 🔲

Nothobranchius lourensi pH6.5;H3;26C;5cm;?L ⌇ ➤ ◑ ♥ Ⱳ ▤

Nothobranchius sp. (Mbeya) pH6.5;H3;26C;6cm;40L ⌇ ➤ ◑ ♥ Ⱳ ▤

260   *Nothobranchius kuhntae* pH6.5;H3;27C;6cm;40L ⌇ ➤ ◑ ♥ Ⱳ ▤

Nothobranchius janpapi pH6.5;H3;26C;6cm;40L 〰 ➤ ◑ ♥ ☒ ☒

Nothobranchius sp. (Salima) pH6.5;H3;27C;6cm;40L 〰 ➤ ◑ ♥ ☒ ☒

Nothobranchius guentheri pH6.5;H3;26C;6cm;40L 〰 ➤ ◑ ♥ ☒ ☒   261

Nothobranchius furzeri pH6.5;H3;26C;5cm;40L ∿ ➤ ◑ ♥ ☒ ⊡

Nothobranchius rachovii pH6.5;H3;26C;5cm;40L ∿ ➤ ◑ ♥ ☒ ⊡

Nothobranchius rachovii var. pH6.5;H3;26C;5cm;40L ∿ ➤ ◑ ♥ ☒ ⊡

Nothobranchius kirki pH6.5;H3;23C;5cm;40L 〜 ➤ ◑ ♥ 🔟 ▱

Nothobranchius korthausae pH6.5;H3;23C;5cm;40L 〜 ➤ ◑ ♥ 🔟 ▱

Nothobranchius kirki pH6.5;H3;23C;5cm;40L 〜 ➤ ◑ ♥ 🔟 ▱

263

Nothobranchius patrizi pH6.5;H3;26C;6cm;40L 〰 ⤚ ◑ ♥ 🆚 🖾

Nothobranchius lourense pH6.5;H3;26C;6cm;40L 〰 ⤚ ◑ ♥ 🆚 🖾

Nothobranchius melanospilus pH6.5;H3;26C;5cm;40L 〰 ⤚ ◑ ♥ 🆚 🖾

264

Nothobranchius orthonotus pH6.5;H3;25C;5cm;40L ∿ ➤ ◑ ♥ ₩ ⊡

Nothobranchius jubbi jubbi pH6.5;H3;25C;6cm;40L ∿ ➤ ◑ ♥ ₩ ⊡

Nothobranchius palmqvisti pH6.5;H3;25C;6cm;?L ∿ ➤ ◑ ♥ ₩ ⊡

Pachypanchax homalonotus pH7.0;H8;25C;7cm;80L 〜 ➤ ◑ ♥ ⱱ̲ ▭

Epiplatys chevalieri pH6.5;H5;25C;7cm;80L 〜 ➤ ◑ ♥ ⱱ̲ ▭

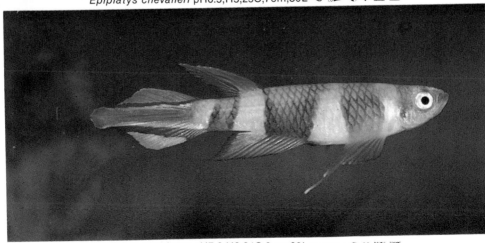

Epiplatys annulatus pH7.2;H8;24C;3cm;20L 〜 ➤ ◑ ♥ ⱱ̲ ▭

Epiplatys njalaensis pH7.0;H8;25C;6cm;40L ∿ ⮞ ◑ ♥ 🔄 ☐

Epiplatys macrostigma pH7.0;H8;24C;6cm;40L ∿ ⮞ ◑ ♥ 🔄 ☐

Epiplatys singa pH7.0;H8;24C;6cm;40L ∿ ⮞ ◑ ♥ 🔄 ☐

Pachypanchax playfairi pH7.0;H8;24C;8cm;80L ∿ ⤚ ◑ ♥ 🔙 ☐

Epiplatys huberi pH7.0;H8;26C;8cm;80L ∿ ⤚ ◑ ♥ 🔙 ☐

Epiplatys chevalieri pH7.0;H8;26C;8cm;80L ∿ ⤚ ◑ ♥ 🔙 ☐

Epiplatys sexfasciatus pH7.0;H8;25C;6cm;40L 〜 ➤ ◐ ♥ ⩊ ▭

Epiplatys dageti   pH6.8;H7;26C;6cm;40L 〜 ➤ ◐ ♥ ⩊ ▭

Epiplatys duboisi pH7.2;H9;24C;2.5cm;20L 〜 ➤ ◐ ♥ ⩊ ▭

Epiplatys bifasciatus pH7.2;H8;26C;5cm;40L ⌇ ➤ ◖ ♥ 🖾 ⊏

Epiplatys fasciolatus pH7.0;H8;25C;7cm;80L ⌇ ➤ ◖ ♥ 🖾 ⊏

Epiplatys spilargyreius pH7.0;H8;26C;6cm;40L ⌇ ➤ ◖ ♥ 🖾 ⊏

Procatopus gracilis pH7.0;H8;24C;7cm;40L 〜 ➤ ◑ ♥ ☷ ⊟

Procatopus aberrans pH6.5;H5;26C;7cm;40L 〜 ➤ ◑ ♥ ☷ ⊟

Procatopus nototaenia pH7.0;H8;25C;6cm;40L 〜 ➤ ◑ ♥ ☷ ⊟

Procatopus "Fire-tail" pH6.8;H5;24C;7cm;40L ⌇ ➤ ◐ ♥ ⱳ ⊟

Procatopus similis pH6.8;H7;25C;7cm;40L ⌇ ➤ ◐ ♥ ⱳ ⊟

Procatopus similis pH6.8;H7;25C;7cm:40L ⌇ ➤ ◐ ♥ ⱳ ⊟

Aplocheilichthys katangae pH6.8;H6;24C;5cm;40L ⌇ ➤ ◑ ♥ ☒ ▱

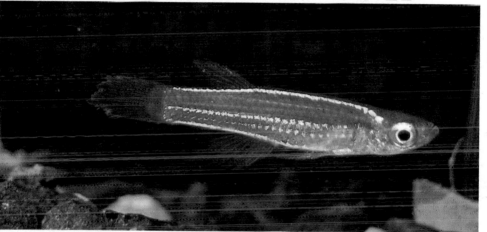

Aplocheilichthys macrophthalmus pH7.5;H10;24C;5cm;40L ⌇ ➤ ◑ ♥ ☒ ▱

Aplocheilichthys myersi pH7.0;H8;24C;3cm;20L ⌇ ➤ ◑ ♥ ☒ ▱

Aplocheilichthys sp. pH7.2;H8;25C;4cm;20L ᭨ ➤ ◐ ♥ ☒ ☰

Aplocheilichthys rancureli pH7.0;H8;24C;5cm;40L ᭨ ➤ ◐ ♥ ☒ ☰

Aplocheilichthys spilauchen pH7.2;H9;25C;4cm;20L ᭨ ➤ ◐ ♥ ☒ ☰

274

Aplocheilus blocki pH6.7;H7;25C;5cm;40L ♀ ➤ ◐ ♥ 🎞 ▭

Aplocheilus dayi pH6.8;H7;25C;9cm;100L ♀ ➤ ◐ ♥ 🎞 ▭

Aplocheilus lineatus pH6.9;H7;27C;10cm;100L ♀ ➤ ◐ ♥ 🎞 ▭

275

Oryzias celebensis pH7.0;H8;28C;4cm;40L ♀ ➤ ◐ ♥ 🖼 🖽

Oryzias javanicus pH7.0;H8;28C;4cm;40L ♀ ➤ ◐ ♥ 🖼 🖽

276   *Oryzias latipes* pH6.7;H8;27C;5cm;40L ♀ ➤ ◐ ♥ 🖼 🖽

THE CHARACOID FISHES

At one time all of the fishes that are now grouped in about fifteen different families in the suborder Characoidei were considered to be all in one family, the family Characidae. When the fishes of that family were reclassified (as done in the 1960's by Dr. Stanley Weitzman and in the 1970's by Dr. Jacques Gery), hobbyists had to begin contending with learning a bundle of new family names. No longer could they comfortably lump hundreds and hundreds of very different-looking aquarium fishes all in one family; they had to start getting familiar with new names, new relationships.

The characoids that hobbyists are most interested in now constitute six families, with the majority of them being restricted to only one family, the family Characidae, the tetras, or characins; although that family is much smaller than it once was, it's still big. The other five families contain the pencilfishes (Lebiasinidae); the piranhas and silver dollars (Serrasalmidae); the headstanders (Anostomidae); the hatchetfishes (Gasteropelicidae); the African tetras (Citharinidae). Fishes from all of these six "favorite" families are well portrayed in the following pages, but representatives of the less often encountered families also appear.

WHAT IS A CHARACOID?

A characoid is a very fish-like fish. It is usually greater in depth than in thickness and has a streamlined appearance. ALL of them have teeth and scales and NONE of them has barbels or whiskers. MANY of them have an extra fin called an adipose fin on the top, rear of their body; this fin has no spines or rays. They are not found in Europe, Asia or Australia. In the aquarium almost all the smaller tetras will eat dry foods, though they must be fed live foods if they are to really show off their beautiful colors and be brought to spawning condition.

HOW CHARACOIDS BREED

All characoids lay eggs; mostly the eggs are haphazardly sprayed wherever an interesting clump of plants are found. In nature their spawning mainly coincides with the beginning of the rainy season, but in the aquarium they spawn all year round. With but few exceptions, most of the males have longer dorsal and anal fins, and in some genera the males are more highly colored, especially during breeding time.

The best way to spawn tetras is to separate the males from the females, feed them heavily on live foods until the females grow fat and the males get more colorful, and then introduce them into a specially prepared spawning tank which has clean, aged water in which clumps of fine-leaved plants have been strategically placed. The techniques for each fish may vary slightly, but most eat their eggs almost as quickly as they lay them. Consult any of a number of good books on breeding aquarium fishes and get all the details of the particular fish in which you are interested.

CHARACOIDS IN YOUR AQUARIUM

Since characoids are basically school fishes, they do best in schools in your home aquarium. The ideal situation is a school of a single species of fish in a tank well planted around the back and sides, with plenty of free swimming room in the center.

Basically most characoids of the same size get along together fairly well if they are well fed and not crowded ... and the smallest of them, the tetras, can easily be crowded, for they are very hardy. It is not difficult to keep 200 cardinal tetras in the same heavily aerated and filtered 20-gallon aquarium, but they would not thrive. A better idea is to allow about 5 inches of fish per gallon of water; thus 100 inches of tetras would be the maximum for a 20-gallon aquarium, assuming proper aeration and filtration.

Characoids are fast eaters, so never feed them more than they will eat in three minutes. It's best to feed them several times a day, and as long as they gobble up their food in three minutes you are not overfeeding. NO FISH WILL OVEREAT; overfed tanks become polluted because the fish do not eat the food offered, and the uneaten food falls to the bottom and soon rots. No filtering system can take an endless overfeeding situation.

While characoids get along pretty well with other characoids, they usually do not get along with slow-moving fishes such as fishes with long, trailing fins like angelfish (*Pterophyllum*) or gouramis. They can be kept with other fast moving fishes like barbs, and such sedentary scavengers as most small catfish (*Corydoras* are best) but be sure the catfish have small mouths. Most catfish are nocturnal and can gobble up small tetras during the night while they are resting.

Boulengerella maculata pH7.0;H6;25C;40cm;200L ⌐ ➤ ◑ ✕ 🎞 ▤

♀ *Crenuchus spilurus* pH6.3;H6;25C;6cm;75L ⌐ ➤ ◐ ♥ 🎞 ▤

Characidium fasciatum pH6.7;H8;22C;6cm;60L ⌐ ➤ ◑ ♥ 🎞 ▭

279

Hoplerythrinus unitaeniatus pH7.0;H10;24C;50cm;250L ⌇ ⇀ ◑ ✳ ⧉ ☐

♂ *Crenuchus spilurus* pH6.3;H6;25C;6cm;75L ⌇ ⇀ ◑ ♥ ⧉ ☒

Characidium pH6.8;H9;24C;4cm;40L ⌇ ⇀ ◑ ♥ ⧉ ☐

Poecilocharax weitzmani pH6.5;H8;26C;4cm;50L ~ ➤ ◑ ♥ 🖻 ☐

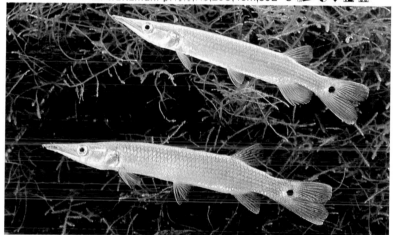

Ctenolucius hujeta pH7.0;H10;26C;25cm;100L ➤ ◑ ✕ 🖻 ☰

Hoplerythrinus unitaeniatus pH7.0;H10;24C;50cm;250L ➤ ◑ ✕ 🖻 ☐

Elachocharax junki pH6.9;H8;25C;3.1cm;40L 〜 ➤ ◑ ♥ 🖼 ▭

Nannostomus espei pH6.8;H6;26C;5cm;40L 〜 ➤ ◑ ♥ 🖼 ▤

Nannostomus beckfordi pH6.8;H6;25C;5cm;40L 〜 ➤ ◑ ♥ 🖼 ▤

Lebiasina multimaculata pH7.0;H12;28C;8cm;40L ♀ ➤ ◑ ♥ ▨ ▭

Elachocharax junki pH6.8;H10;26C;4cm;40L ⌇ ➤ ◑ ♥ ▨ ▭

Nannostomus digrammus pH6.8;H10;24C;4cm;40L ♀ ➤ ◑ ♥ ▨ ▤ 283

Elachocharax pulcher pH6.8;H10;26C;4cm;40L ⌇ ➤ ◑ ♥ 🖼 ▭

Nannostomus espei pH6.8;H6;26C;5cm;40L ⌇ ➤ ◑ ♥ 🖼 ▤

Nannostomus harrisoni pH6.8;H6;26C;6.5cm;40L ⌇ ➤ ◑ ♥ 🖼 ▤

Characidium "Gery" pH6.7;H8;23C;5.3cm;60L ᔆ ➤ ◑ ♥ 🖻 ▭

Lebiasina panamensis pH7.0;H10;27C;8.2cm;60L ᔆ ➤ ◑ ♥ 🖻 ⊡

Nannostomus harrisoni pH6.8;H6;26C;6.5cm;40L ᔆ ➤ ◑ ♥ 🖻 ⊟

285

Nannostomus eques pH6.8;H6;26C;5cm;40L 〜 🐟 ◑ ♥ 🖼 ⊟

Nannostomus trifasciatus pH6.8;H6;26C;6cm;40L 〜 🐟 ◑ ♥ 🖼 ⊟

Nannostomus bifasciatus pH6.8;H6;26C;5cm;40L 〜 🐟 ◑ ♥ 🖼 ⊟

Pyrrhulina brevis pH6.8;H6;25C;5cm;40L ∿ ➤ ◑ ♥ 🖼 ⊟

Nannostomus unifasciatus pH6.8;H7;25C;6cm;40L ∿ ➤ ◑ ♥ 🖼 ⊟

Nannostomus marginatus pH7.0;H8;26C;3cm;40L ∿ ➤ ◑ ♥ 🖼 ⊟

Copella arnoldi pH6.8;H6;27C;8.5cm;60L

Copeina guttata pH7.0;H10;24C;15cm;75L

Copella nattereri pH6.7;H8;26C;6cm;40L

Pyrrhulina sp. pH6.7;H10;22C;8cm;60L ∿ ➤ ◑ ♥ 🖼 ⊡

Leporellus vittatus pH6.0;H5;25C;12.5cm;100L ∿ ➤ ◖ ♥ 🖼 ⊡

Leporinus striatus pH7.0;H10;24C;40cm;150L ∿ ➤ ◑ ♥ 🖼 ⊡

291

Leporinus melanopleura pH7.2;H10;26C;20cm;100L ⌇ ⇀ ◑ ♥ 🖼 ▣

Schizodon fasciatum pH7.0;H10;25C;25cm;150L ⌇ ⇀ ◑ ♥ 🖼 ▣

Copella compta pH6.0;H6;25C;5.4cm;60L ⌇ ⇀ ◑ ♥ 🖼 ▣

292

Leporinus agassizi pH7.0;H10;25C;12cm;100L ⌇ ➤ ◐ ♥ 🎞 🖾

Leporinus nigrotaeniatus pH6.6;H8;26C;20cm;150L ⌇ ➤ ◐ ♥ 🎞 🖾

Copella callolepis pH6.8;H8;27C;5.4cm;60L ⌇ ➤ ◐ ♥ 🎞 🖾

Leporinus pearsoni pH6.8;H10;24C;20cm;100L ♀ ➤ ◑ ♥ 🖳 ⊟

Leporinus affinis pH7.2;H10;24C;33cm;100L ∿ ➤ ◑ ♥ 🖾 ⊟

Leporinus fasciatus pH7.0;H10;24C;30cm;100L ♀ ➤ ◑ ♥ 🖳 ⊟

Leporinus pellegrini pH6.6;H8;25C;10cm;75L ⤳ ➤ ◑ ♥ 🖼 ⊟

Leporinus octofasciatus pH7.0;H10;24C;15.6cm;100L ⤳ ➤ ◑ ♥ 🖼 ⊟

Leporinus arcus pH7.3;H10;25C;30cm;100L ⤳ ➤ ◑ ♥ 🖼 ⊟

295

Leporinus friderici pH7.0;H12;24C;20cm;100L ♀ ⮞ ◐ ♥ 💹 ▤

♀ *Leporinus* cf. *granti* pH6.2;H8;25C;15cm;100L ∿ ⮞ ◐ ♥ 🖼 ▣

Leporinus melanopleura pH6.8;H10;26C;26.5cm;100L ∿ ⮞ ◐ ♥ 🖼 ▣

Leporinus desmotes pH7.0;H12;24C;22cm;100L ♀ 🐟 ◑ ♥ 🖼 ▤

♂ *Abramites hypselonotus* pH6.8;H8;25C;12.5cm;100L ∿ 🐟 ◑ ♥ 🖼 ▤

♀ *Abramites hypselonotus* pH6.8;H8;25C;12.5cm;100L ∿ 🐟 ◑ ♥ 🖼 ▤

(juv.) *Abramites hypselonotus* pH6.8;H8;25C;12.5cm;100L ⌇ ➤ ◑ ♥ 🖼 🗔

Leporinus maculatus pH6.7;H8;26C;20cm;100L ⌇ ➤ ◑ ♥ 🖼 🗔

Leporinus melanostictus pH7.0;H10;27C;10cm;75L ⌇ ➤ ◑ ♥ 🖼 🗔

♂ *Leporinus megalepis* pH7.0;H10;26C;25cm;100L ⌇ ⇶ ◐ ♥ 🎞 ⊟

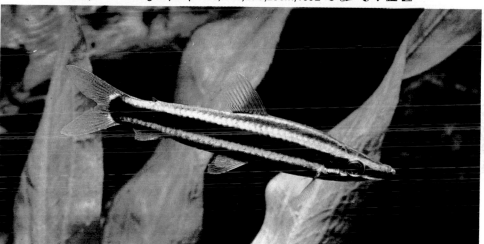

Anostomus ternetzi pH10.8,H10,24C;18cm;100L ♀ ⇶ ◐ ♥ 🎞 ⊟

Leporinus sp. pH7.0;H10;25C;25cm;150L ⌇ ⇶ ◐ ♥ 🎞 ⊟

299

Anostomus taeniatus pH6.8;H8;25C;12.5cm;75L 〜 ➤ ◑ ♥ 🖾 🖼

Leporinus sp. pH6.6;H8;26C;30cm;100L 〜 ➤ ◑ ♥ 🖾 🖼

Anostomus varius pH6.5;H8;27C;25cm;200L 〜 ➤ ◑ ♥ 🖾 🖼

Anostomus anostomus pH6.8;H8;25C;18cm;100L ⌇ ➤ ◑ ♥ 🖾 ⊟

Anostomus trimaculatus pH6.7;H8;26C;20cm;100L ⌇ ➤ ◑ ♥ 🖾 ⊟

Anostomus gracilis pH6.5;H8;28C;17.5cm;75L ⌇ ➤ ◑ ♥ 🖾 ⊟

Hemiodopsis microlepis pH7.0;H9;25C;20cm;150L ∿ ➤ ◑ ♥ 🖼 ⊟

Hemiodus unimaculatus pH6.8;H8;25C;19cm;200L ∿ ➤ ◑ ♥ 🖼 ⊟

Bivibranchia protractila pH6.8;H10;26C;30cm;100L ♀ ➤ ◑ ♥ 🖼 ▭

Hemiodopsis semitaeniatus pH6.8;H8;24C;15cm;100L ♀ ⚊ ◑ ♥ 🖼 ▭

Hemiodopsis aff. *goeldi* pH6.8;H10;22C;12cm;40L ♀ ⚊ ◑ ♥ 🖼 ▭

♀ *Hemiodopsis sterni* pH7.2;H12;25C;10cm;100L ∿ ⚊ ◑ ♥ 🖼 ▭

303

Synaptolaemus cingulatus pH6.8;H8;27C;17.5cm;150L ᴧ ➤ ❍ ♥ 🖼 ⊟

♂ *Hemiodopsis sterni* pH7.2;H12;25C;10cm;100L ᴧ ➤ ❍ ♥ 🖼 ⊡

♂ *Hemiodopsis gracilis* pH6.8;H8;24C;15cm;100L ♀ ➤ ❍ ♥ 🖼 ⊡

Sartor respectus pH6.7;H8,27C;22.5cm;200L ᔓ ➤ ◑ ♥ 🎞 ▭

Hemiodopsis immaculatus pH6.2;H6;27C;22cm;200L ᔓ ➤ ◑ ♥ 🎞 ⊟

♀ *Hemiodopsis gracilis* pH6.8;H8;24C;15cm;100L ♀ ➤ ◑ ♥ 🎞 ⊟

Parodon pongoense pH6.7;H8;27C;5cm;75L 〜 ⋗ ◑ ♥ 🖾 ⬛

Parodon affinis pH7.0;H10;18C;6.5cm;75L 〜 ⋗ ◑ ♥ 🖾 ⬛

Hemiodopsis parnaguae pH6.5;H9;27C;20cm;100L 〜 ⋗ ◑ ♥ 🖾 ⬕

Parodon piracicabae pH7.0;H10;24C;7.5cm;75L ∿ ➤ ◑ ♥ 🎞 ☐

Parodon caliensis pH7.2;H10;18C;5cm;75L ∿ ➤ ◑ ♥ 🎞 ☐

Bivibranchia bimaculata pH7.0;H10;24C;10cm;100L ∿ ➤ ◑ ♥ 🎞 ☐

Semaprochilodus theraponura pH7.3;H10;25C;35cm;150L ⚘ 🐟 ◑ ♥ 🎞 ▣

Chilodus sp. "Black-band" pH6.6;H10;26C;12cm;100L 〜 🐟 ◑ ♥ 🎞 ▣

Caenotropus maculosus pH6.5;H10;27C;12cm;100L 〜 🐟 ◑ ♥ 🎞 ▢

Semaprochilodus squamilentus pH7.0;H12;27C;25cm;200L ∿ ⏵ ◑ ♥ 🖼 ⌗

Prochilodus ortonianus pH6.7;H10;26C;25cm;400L ∿ ⏵ ◑ ♥ 🖼 ⌗

Curimata ciliata pH6.6;H10;24C;20cm;150L ∿ ⏵ ◑ ♥ 🖼 ⌗

Prochilodus nigricans pH7.0;H12;25C;30cm;350L ∿ ⬳ ◑ ♥ 🖼 ⊟

Curimata ciliata pH6.6;H10;24C;20cm;150L ∿ ⬳ ◑ ♥ 🖼 ⊟

Curimata isognatha pH6.8;H10;25C;26cm;200L ∿ ⬳ ◑ ♥ 🖼 ⊟

Chilodus sp. pH6.8;H6;26C;9cm;80L ↱ ➤ ◑ ♥ 🖼 ⊟

♂ *Curimata spilura* pH6.8;H10;25C;12.5cm;150L ♀ ➤ ◑ ♥ 🖼 ⊟

Curimata vittata pH7.0;H12;25C;25cm;250L ↲ ➤ ◑ ♥ 🖼 ⊟

311

♀ *Curimata spilura* pH6.8;H10;25C;12.5cm;150L ♀ ➤ ◑ ♥ 💹 ⊟

Curimata rhomboides pH6.7;H10;27C;25cm;250L ∿ ➤ ◑ ♥ 📷 ⊟

Potamorhina squamoralevis pH7.0;H12;24C;12cm;40L ♀ ➤ ◑ ♥ 💹 ⊟

Curimatopsis evelynae pH6.8;H10;26C;10cm;100L ⌇ ➤ ◑ ♥ 🎞 🖼

Curimatella alburna pH6.8;H10;26C;20cm;200L ⌇ ➤ ◑ ♥ 🎞 🖼

Curimata vittata pH7.0;H12;25C;25cm;250L ⌇ ➤ ◑ ♥ 🎞 🖼

Curimatopsis macrolepis pH6.8;H10;25C;20cm;200L ♀ ⭢ ◑ ♥ 🖼 ⊟

Curimata elegans pH6.7;H10;25C;25cm;200L ⌇ ⭢ ◑ ♥ 🖼 ⊟

Potamorhina latior pH6.8;H10;24C;25cm;250L ⌇ ⭢ ◑ ♥ 🖼 ⊟

Curimata spilura pH6.8;H10;25C;12.5cm;150L ♀ ⚓ ◑ ♥ 🖼 ▦

Thoracocharax stellatus pH6.8;H10;26C;7cm;40L ♀ ⚓ ◑ ♥ 🖼 ▭

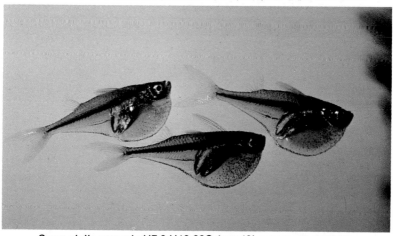

Carnegiella myersi pH7.0;H10;26C;4cm;40L ∿ ⚓ ◑ ♥ 🖼 ▭

Thoracocharax securis pH6.8;H10;25C;7.5cm;75L 〜 ➤ ◑ ♥ 🔲 🖵

Gasteropelecus sternicla pH6.4;H8;25C;6cm;50L 〜 ➤ ◑ ♥ 🔲 🖵

Carnegiella strigata pH6.5;H8;25C;8cm;75L 〜 ➤ ◑ ♥ 🔲 🖵

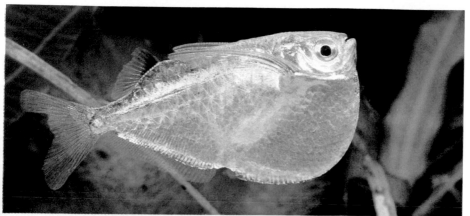

Thoracocharax stellatus pH6.8;H8;25C;8cm;75L ∿ ⋙ ◐ ♥ 𝕎 ☐

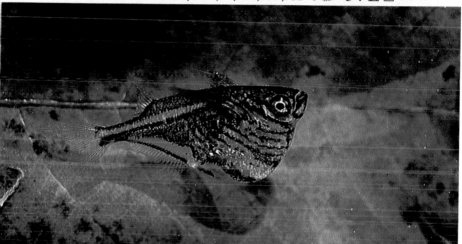

Carnegiella marthae pH6.8;H8;26C;4cm;40L ∿ ⋙ ◐ ♥ 𝕎 ☐

Mylossoma aureum pH6.6;H10;27C;25cm;200L ⚘ ⋙ ◐ ♥ 𝕎 ☐

317

Gasteropelecus sternicla pH6.4;H8;25C;6cm;50L ∿ ➤ ◑ ♥ 🖼 ⬜

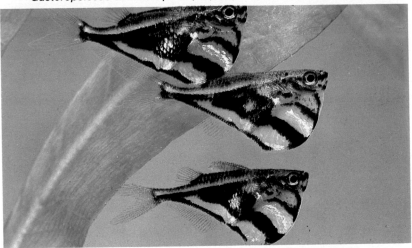

Carnegiella strigata pH6.5;H8;25C;8cm;75L ∿ ➤ ◑ ♥ 🖼 ⬜

Mylossoma duriventre pH6.8;H8;26C;23cm;200L ⌇ ➤ ◑ ♥ 🖼 ⊟

Colossoma macropomum pH7.2;H13;24C;38cm;100L ⌇ ➤ ◑ ♥ 🎴 ▤

Mylossoma paraguayensis pH7.0;H10;24C;25cm;200L ⌇ ➤ ◑ ♥ 🎴 ▤

Mylossoma aureum pH6.6;H10;27C;25cm;200L ⌇ ➤ ◑ ♥ 🎴 ▤

319

Myleus rubripinnis pH6.7;H8;26C;12cm;150L 🐟 🐠 ◐ ♥ 🖼 ▤

Myleus schomburgki pH6.5;H8;26C;22.5cm;200L 🐟 🐠 ◐ ♥ 🖼 ▤

Metynnis luna pH6.7;H10;26C;20cm;200L 〰 🐠 ◐ ♥ 🖼 ▤

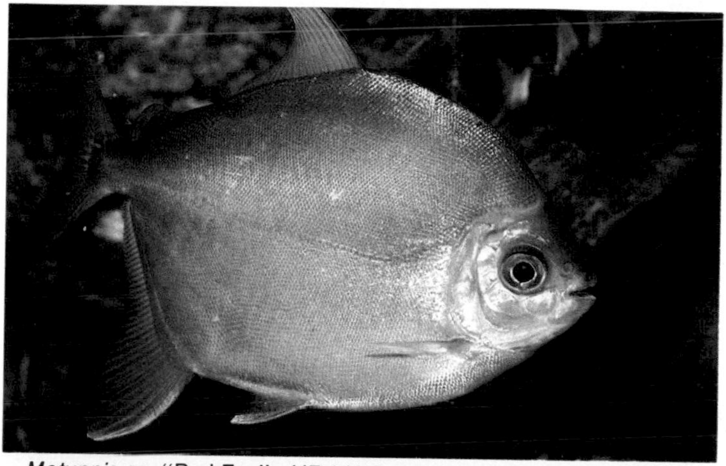

Metynnis sp. "Red Eye" pH7.1;H13;22C;16cm;75L

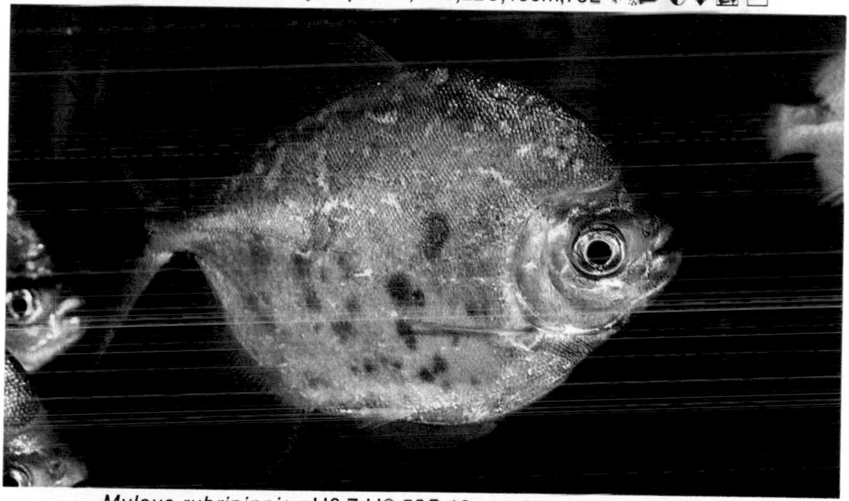

Myleus rubripinnis pH6.7;H8;26C;12cm;150L

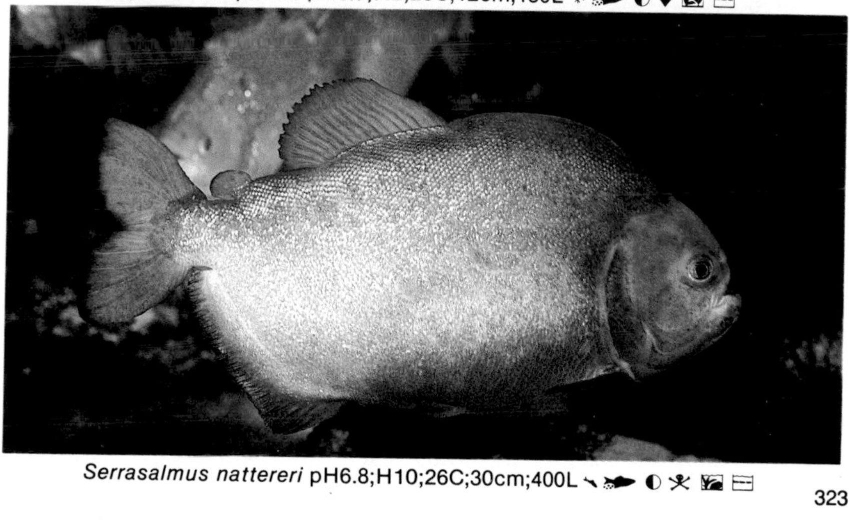

Serrasalmus nattereri pH6.8;H10;26C;30cm;400L

Myleus rubripinnis pH6.7;H8;26C;12cm;150L ⤳ 🐟 ◑ ♥ 🖼 ▤

Serrasalmus nattereri pH6.8;H10;26C;30cm;400L ⤳ 🐟 ◑ ✂ 🖼 ▤

Serrasalmus hollandi pH6.8;H8;25C;13cm;100L ⤳ 🐟 ◑ ✂ 🖼 ▤

Serrasalmus eigenmanni pH7.2;H14;26C;22cm;150L ⬐ ➤ ◑ ✕ 🐟 ⊟

Serrasalmus notatus pH6.8;H10;24C;26cm;150L ⬐ ➤ ◑ ✕ 🐟 ⊟

Serrasalmus notatus pH6.8;H10;24C;26cm;150L ⬐ ➤ ◑ ✕ 🐟 ⊟

Serrasalmus eigenmanni pH7.2;H14;26C;22cm;150L ⤆ 🐟 ◑ ✕ 🖼 ⊟

Serrasalmus sp. "Iridescent" pH6.8;H10;24C;20cm;100L ⤆ 🐟 ◑ ✕ 🖼 ⊟

Serrasalmus elongatus pH6.8;H10;28C;30cm;400L ⤆ 🐟 ◑ ✕ 🖼 ⊟

Serrasalmus gibbus pH6.6;H10;27C;30cm;400L ↘ ➤ ◑ ✕ 🖾 ☱

Serrasalmus spilopleura pH6.5;H8;27C;30cm;400L ↘ ➤ ◑ ✕ 🖾 ☱

Serrasalmus denticulatus pH6.6;H10;28C;20cm;200L ↘ ➤ ◑ ✕ 🖾 ☱

Serrasalmus sanchezi pH6.5;H8;27C;27.5cm;400L ↘ ➤ ◑ ✕ 🎞 ▤

Serrasalmus antoni pH6.5;H10;26C;17.5cm;200L ↘ ➤ ◑ ✕ 🎞 ▤

Serrasalmus striolatus pH6.6;H10;27C;20cm;200L ↘ ➤ ◑ ✕ 🎞 ▤

Serrasalmus nattereri pH6.8;H10;26C;30cm;400L ↘ ➤ ◐ ✗ 🖼 🗄

Serrasalmus manueli pH6.7;H8;27C;20cm;200L ↘ ➤ ◐ ✗ 🖼 🗄

Serrasalmus rhombeus pH6.8;H8;26C;32cm;400L ↘ ➤ ◐ ✗ 🖼 🗄

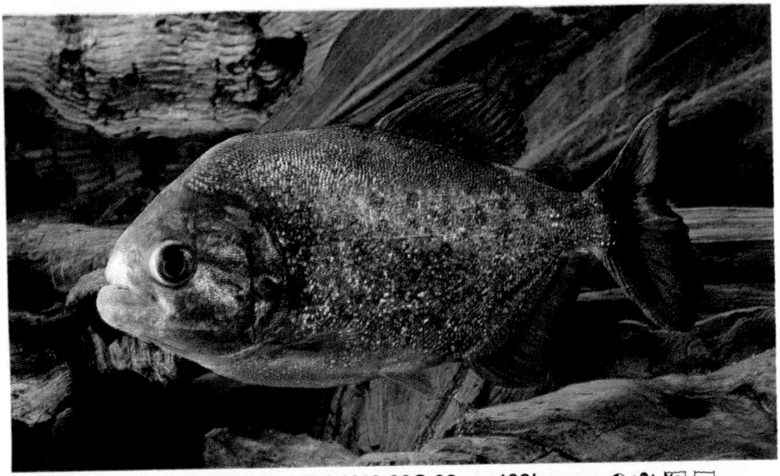

Serrasalmus nattereri pH6.8;H10;26C;30cm;400L

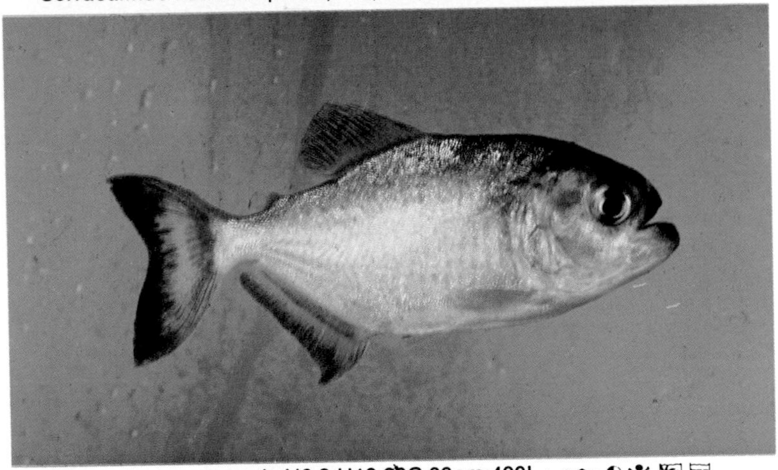

Serrasalmus nattereri pH6.8;H10;26C;30cm;400L

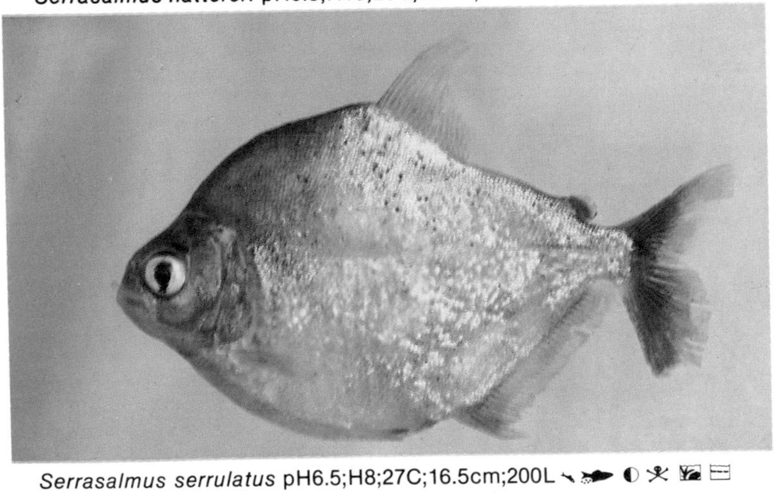

Serrasalmus serrulatus pH6.5;H8;27C;16.5cm;200L

Catoprion mento pH7.0;H20;24C;16cm;100L ⤹➤ ◑✖ 🎴 ☷

Catoprion "Bleher" pH7.0;H20;24C;16cm;100L ⤹➤ ◑✖ 🎴 ☷

Asiphonichthys condei pH6.9;H10;28C;10cm;75L ⤹➤ ◑♥ 🎴 ☒

Hydrolycus scomberoides pH6.8;H10;26C;40cm;400L ↘ 🐟 ◑ ✗ 🖼

Charax gibbosus pH7.0;H12;24C;15cm;150L ↘ 🐟 ◑ ♥ 🖼 ▤

Asiphonichthys condei pH6.9;H10;28C;10cm;75L ↘ 🐟 ◑ ♥ 🖼 ▨

Exodon paradoxus pH7.0;H10;28C;15cm;100L ⤳ 🐟 ○ ♥ 🖼 🗒

Acestrorhynchus falcatus pH7.0;H12;28C;30cm;200L ⤹ 🐟 ◐ ⚔ 🖼 🗒

Acestrorhynchus grandoculis pH7.0;H12;27C;38cm;400L ⤹ 🐟 ◐ ⚔ 🖼 🗒

333

Acestrorhynchus isalinae pH7.2;H14;23C;36cm;200L ↘ 🐟 ◑ ✖ 🖼 🗒

Brycon melanopterus pH7.2;H14;24C;18cm;75L ♀ 🐟 ◑ ♥ 🖼 🗒

Brycon cephalus pH7.2;H14;24C;18cm;75L ♀ 🐟 ◑ ♥ 🖼 🗒

Chalceus erythrurus pH6.5;H8;27C;30cm;400L ↘ ➤ ◐ ✕ ▓ ⊟

Brycon brevicauda pH6.8;H8;27C;25cm;200L ↘ ➤ ◐ ♥ ▓ ⊟

Chalceus macrolepidotus pH7.0;H12;25C;25cm;300L ↘ ➤ ◐ ♥ ▓ ⊟

Chalceus macrolepidotus pH7.0;H12;25C;25cm;300L 〜 ➤ ◑ ♥ 🖻 ⊟

Triportheus angulatus pH6.5;H8;25C;20cm;200L 〜 ➤ ◑ ♥ 🖻 ▭

(juv.) Triportheus rotundatus pH6.8;H8;27C;16.5cm;150L 〜 ➤ ◑ ♥ 🖻 ▭

Triportheus albus pH6.6;H8;26C;24cm;200L ∿ ➤ ◐ ♥ 🖼 ▭

Triportheus rotundatus pH6.8;H8;27C;16.5cm;150L ∿ ➤ ◐ ♥ 🖼 ▭

Prionobrama filigera pH6.8;H8;25C;6cm;50L ∿ ➤ ◐ ♥ 🖼 ▭

337

Aphyocharax anisitsi pH7.0;H10;24C;7.5cm;75L ⌇ ◑ ♥ 🎞 ⊟

Aphyocharax rathbuni pH7.0;H12;25C;4.5cm;50L ⌇ ➤ ◑ ♥ 🎞 ⊟

Gephyrocharax caucanus pH6.8;H8;25C;6cm;75L ⌇ ➤ ◑ ♥ 🎞 ⊟

Phenagoniates macrolepis pH6.6;H10;24C;10cm;75L 〜 ➤ ◖ ♥ 🖼 ⊟

Aphyocharax erythrurus pH7.0;H12;24C;6cm;75L ♀ ➤ ◖ ♥ 🖼 ⊟

Aphyocharax sp. "Bleher" pH6.5;H9;27C;6.3cm;75L 〜 ➤ ◖ ♥ 🖼 ⊟

Pseudocorynopoma doriae pH6.7;H8;23C;8cm;100L ♀ ➤ ◑ ♥ 🖼 🖂

Coelurichthys microlepis pH7.0;H10;22C;5.5cm;75L ∿ ➤ ◑ ♥ 🖼 🖂

Tyttocharax madeirae pH6.7;H8;26C;2cm;40L ∿ ➤ ◑ ♥ 🖼 🖂

Corynopoma riisei pH7.0;H12;25C;6cm;75L ⌇ 🐟 ◑ ♥ 🖼 ▤

Coelurichthys microlepis pH7.0;H10;22C;5.5cm;75L ⌇ 🐟 ◑ ♥ 🖼 ▤

Stethaprion erythrops pH6.6;H8;27C;8cm;75L ⚲ 🐟 ◑ ♥ 🖼 ▤

Poptella orbicularis pH6.7;H10;24C;12cm;100L ♀ 🐟 ◑ ♥ 🖼 ▭

Iguanodectes sp. pH6.8;H10;25C;6cm;60L 〜 🐟 ◑ ♥ 🖼 ▭

Boehlkea fredcochui pH6.8;H8;25C;5cm;40L 〜 🐟 ◑ ♥ 🖼 ▭

Piabucus caudomaculatus pH6.6;H10;26C;17.5cm;150L ⤳ ➤ ◑ ♥ 🖼 ⊟

Iguanodectes sp. pH6.8;H10;25C;6cm;60L ⤳ ➤ ◑ ♥ 🖼 ⊟

Carlastyanax aurocaudatus pH7.0;H12;23C;5.5cm;60L ⤳ ➤ ◑ ♥ 🖼 ⊟

Nematobrycon lacortei pH6.8;H8;26C;5cm;60L 〜 ➤ ◑ ♥ 🖼 ⊟

Nematobrycon sp. "Gery" pH6.8;H10;24C;5cm;60L 〜 ➤ ◑ ♥ 🖼 ⊟

Nematobrycon palmeri pH6.8;H8;24C;5cm;60L ♀ ➤ ◑ ♥ 🖼 ⊟

Inpalchthys kerrl pH7.0;H12;27C;5cm;60L ⌇ ⇒ ◑ ♥ 🖾 ▤

Creagrutus cochui pH6.8;H8;27C;10cm;100L ♀ ⇒ ◑ ♥ 🖾 ▤

Creagrutus beni pH6.8;H10;27C;5.2cm;60L ⌇ ⇒ ◑ ♥ 🖾 ▤

Bryconamericus loisae pH7.0;H14;24C;5cm;60L ⌇ 🐟 ◑ ♥ 🖼 ⊟

Knodus breviceps pH7.0;H10;25C;5cm;60L ⌇ 🐟 ◑ ♥ 🖼 ⊟

Pseudochalceus kyburzi pH6.7;H8;25C;8cm;75L ⌇ 🐟 ◑ ♥ 🖼 ⊟

Gymnocorymbus ternetzi pH7.0;H10;23C;8cm;75L ∿ 🐟 ◑ ♥ 🏞 ▤

Gymnocorymbus thayeri pH6.5;H8;25C;5cm;50L ∿ 🐟 ◑ ♥ 🏞 ▤

Gymnocorymbus thayeri pH6.5;H8;25C;5cm;50L ∿ 🐟 ◑ ♥ 🏞 ▤

347

Astyanax metae pH6.9;H10;26C;6cm;60L 〜 ➤ ◐ ♥ ▨ ⊟

Astyanax bimaculatus pH7.0;H12;26C;15cm;150L 〜 ➤ ◐ ♥ ▨ ⊟

Moenkhausia sp. pH6.8;H9;26C;8cm;75L 〜 ➤ ◐ ♥ ▨ ⊟

348

Astyanax fasciatus pH7.2;H12;23C;9cm;100L ↴ ➤ ◑ ♥ 🖼 ⊟

Astyanax kennedyi pH6.5;H8;27C;5cm;60L ♀ ➤ ◑ ♥ 🖼 ⊟

Astyanax abramis pH6.5;H9;27C;5cm;60L ↝ ➤ ◑ ♥ 🖼 ⊟

349

Astyanax fasciatus pH7.2;H12;23C;9cm;100L 🐟 🦐 ◑ ♥ 🖼 ☒

Astyanax fasciatus mexicanus pH7.4;H14;22C;7cm;60L ♀ 🦐 ◑ ♥ 🖼 ☒

Astyanax zonatus pH6.6;H8;27C;5cm;60L 〰 🦐 ◑ ♥ 🖼 ☒

Hyphessobrycon cf. *bifasciatus* pH6.9;H10;26C;6cm;60L 〜 ➤ ◑ ♥ 🎞 ☱

Tetragonopterus argenteus pH6.8;H10;25C;11.5cm;100L 〜 ➤ ◑ ♥ 🎞 ☱

Schultzites axelrodi pH6.7;H8;24C;10cm;100L ♀ ➤ ◑ ♥ 🎞 ☱

351

Moenkhausia oligolepis pH6.5;H8;24C;11cm;100L 〰 🐟 ◑ ♥ 🖾 🖽

Moenkhausia lepidura pH6.2;H8;27C;5.6cm;60L 〰 🐟 ◑ ♥ 🖾 🖽

Moenkhausia robertsi pH6.8;H8;27C;6cm;60L 〰 🐟 ◑ ♥ 🖾 🖽

354

Moenkhausia sanctaefilomenae pH6.8;H10;25C;7cm;75L ⌇ ➤ ◑ ♥ 🖼 ☷

Moenkhausia pittieri pH7.0;H10;26C;6cm;60L ⌇ ➤ ◑ ♥ 🖼 ☷

Moenkhausia takasei pH7.0;H10;27C;4.5cm;50L ♀ ➤ ◑ ♥ 🖼 ☷

355

Ctenobrycon spilurus pH7.0;H10;23C;8cm;100L ♀ ⏵ ◐ ♥ ▨ ▤

Bryconops affinis pH6.8;H9;27C;6.5cm;75L ◡ ⏵ ◐ ♥ ▨ ▤

Moenkhausia collettii pH6.5;H8;23C;5.5cm;60L ◡ ⏵ ◐ ♥ ▨ ▤

Hyphessobrycon bifasciatus pH6.9;H10;23C;5cm;50L ♀ 🐟 ◑ ♥ 🖼 ⊟

Hyphessobrycon minimus pH6.8;H8;27C;6.5cm;60L ♀ 🐟 ◑ ♥ 🖼 ⊟

Hyphessobrycon peruvianus pH6.8;H8;26C;5cm;50L 〜 🐟 ◑ ♥ 🖼 ⊟

Hyphessobrycon griemi pH6.8;H8;25C;4cm;50L ♀ ⇒ ◑ ♥ 🐟 ⊟

Hyphessobrycon flammeus pH6.8;H8;25C;4cm;50L ∿ ⇒ ◑ ♥ 🐟 ⊟

Hyphessobrycon loretoensis pH6.5;H8;28C;4cm;40L ♀ ⇒ ◑ ♥ 🐟 ⊟

Hyphessobrycon saizi pH6.5;H8;25C;5.3cm;60L ♀ ➤ ◐ ♥ 🖼 ▤

Hyphessobrycon herbertaxelrodi pH6.7;H8;25C;3cm;40L ♀ ➤ ◐ ♥ 🖼 ▤

Hyphessobrycon vilmae pH6.5;H8;24C;4cm;40L ♀ ➤ ◐ ♥ 🖼 ▤

Hyphessobrycon agulha pH6.6;H8;25C;5cm;60L ∿ 🐟 ◑ ♥ 🖼 ⊟

Hyphessobrycon scholzei pH6.7;H8;25C;5cm;50L ⚲ 🐟 ◑ ♥ 🖼 ⊟

Hyphessobrycon heterorhabdus pH6.5;H8;25C;5cm;60L ⚲ 🐟 ◑ ♥ 🖼 ⊟

Hyphessobrycon copelandi pH6.6;H8;27C;5cm;60L 〜 ➤ ◐ ♥ 🐛 ☷

Hyphessobrycon socolofi pH7.0;H10;26C;6cm;60L ♀ ➤ ◐ ♥ 🐛 ☷

Hyphessobrycon takasei pH6.7;H8;25C;3cm;40L 〜 ➤ ◐ ♥ 🐛 ☷

Hyphessobrycon serpae pH6.6;H7;26C;4cm;40L ♀ ⌦ ⬤ ♥ 🖼 ⊟

Hyphessobrycon erythrostigma pH6.8;H9;25C;8cm;100L ∿ ⌦ ⬤ ♥ 🖼 ⊟

Hyphessobrycon bentosi pH6.8;H8;26C;5cm;60L ♀ ⌦ ⬤ ♥ 🖼 ⊟

Hyphessobrycon sp. "Roberts Tetra" pH6.8;H12;24C;6cm;40L ♀ ⚘ ◑ ♥ 𝕎 ⊟

Hyphessobrycon sp. "Roberts Tetra" pH6.8;H8;28C;6.5cm;60L ⌇ ⚘ ◑ ♥ 𝕎 ⊟

Hemigrammus ocellifer pH7.0;H9;25C;4cm;40L ♀ ⚘ ◑ ♥ 𝕎 ⊟

Astyanax sp. "Big-Scale" pH7.0;H10;25C;6cm;60L ∿ ➥ ◐ ♥ 🖼 ▣

Hemigrammus ulreyi pH6.7;H8;25C;5cm;60L ∿ ➥ ◐ ♥ 🖼 ▤

Hemigrammus levis pH6.5;H8;28C;5cm;60L ∿ ➥ ◐ ♥ 🔱 ▤

Parapristella georgiae pH6.7;H8;28C;7.6cm;80L ♀ ➤ ◑ ♥ 🎴 ⊟

Hemigrammus erythrozonus pH6.8;H8;25C;5cm;50L ♀ ➤ ◑ ♥ 🎴 ⊟

Hemigrammus levis pH6.5;H8;28C;5cm;60L ∿ ➤ ◑ ♥ 🎴 ⊟

Hemigrammus bellottii pH6.5;H8;26C;25cm;40L ⌒ ➤ ◑ ♥ 🔙 🖿

Hemigrammus hyanuary pH7.0;H10;25C;4cm;40L ⚲ ➤ ◑ ♥ 🔙 🖿

Hemigrammus marginatus pH6.8;H8;25C;7cm;80L ⌒ ➤ ◑ ♥ 🔙 🖿

Hemigrammus pulcher pH7.0;H10;26C;5cm;60L 〜 🐟 ◑ ♥ 🔲 🎏

Hemigrammus unilineatus pH7.0;H10;26C;5cm;60L 〜 🐟 ◑ ♥ 🔲 🎏

Hemigrammus boesemani pH6.7;H8;27C;5.2cm;60L ♀ 🐟 ◑ ♥ 🔲 🎏

Hemigrammus rodwayi pH7.0;H10;0C;5cm;60L ♀ 🐟 ◑ ♥ 🖼 ⊟

Hemigrammus pulcher pH7.0;H10;26C;5cm;60L 〰 🐟 ◑ ♥ 🖼 ⊟

Hemigrammus mattei pH6.8;H9;26C;4.5cm;50L 〰 🐟 ◑ ♥ 🖼 ⊟

368

Hemigrammus rhodostomus pH7.0;H10;26C;5cm;60L ♀ ➤ ◐ ♥ 🐛 🗒

Hemigrammus caudovittatus pH6.9;H8;25C;10cm;100L ♀ ➤ ◐ ♥ 🐛 🗒

Hemigrammus coeruleus pH7.0;H10;25C;7.5cm;80L ♀ ➤ ◐ ♥ 🐛 🗒

369

Phenacogaster pectinatus pH6.5;H6;26C;5cm;60L ∿ ➤ ◑ ♥ 💹 ⊟

Hyphessobrycon bifasciatus pH6.5;H6;27C;5.2cm;60L ♀ ➤ ◑ ♥ 💹 ⊟

Petitella georgiae pH6.5;H6;24C;8cm;90L ♀ ➤ ◑ ♥ 💹 ⊟

370

Homigrammus caudovittatus pH6.9;H8;25C,10cm,100L ♀ ⟶ ◑ ♥ 🔳 🔲

Axelrodia lindeae pH6.8;H8;28C;4cm;40L ⌇ ⟶ ◑ ♥ 🔳 🔲

Hasemania nana pH6.6;H6;25C;5cm;60L ♀ ⟶ ◑ ♥ 🔳 🔲

371

Thayeria boehlkei pH7.0;H10;23C;8cm;80L ♀ 🐟 ◑ ♥ 🖾 🖯

Hemigrammus luelingi pH6.8;H10;21C;5cm;60L 〰 🐟 ◑ ♥ 🖾 🖯

Thayeria obliqua pH6.6;H6;25C;8cm;60L ♀ 🐟 ◑ ♥ 🖾 🖯

Brittanichthys axelrodi pH6.0;H6;28C;6cm;60L ⌇ 🐟 ◐ ♥ 🖼 ⊟

Megalamphodus sweglesi pH6.5;H6;25C;4cm;50L ⌇ 🐟 ◐ ♥ 🖼 ⊟

Megalamphodus megalopterus pH6.5;H6;25C;4cm;50L ♀ 🐟 ◐ ♥ 🖼 ⊟

373

Megalamphodus sp. "Rubra" pH6.2;H8;28C;4.5cm;50L ∿ ➤ ◐ ♥ 🔣 🗃

Megalamphodus sweglesi pH6.5;H6;25C;4cm;50L ∿ ➤ ◐ ♥ 🔣 🗃

Megalamphodus axelrodi pH6.5;H6;26C;3cm;40L ∿ ➤ ◐ ♥ 🔣 🗃

Paracheirodon axelrodi pH6.0;H6;22C;5cm;40L 🌱 🐟 ◐ ♥ 🖾 🗀

Paracheirodon simulans pH6.0;H6;25C;2.5cm;40L 〜 🐟 ◐ ♥ 🖾 🗀

Paracheirodon innesi pH6.8;H8;24C;4cm;40L 🌱 🐟 ◐ ♥ 🖾 🗀

375

Phoxinopsis typicus pH6.9;H8;25C;4cm;40L ∿ ⟫ ◑ ♥ 🔫 🗄

Axelrodia stigmatias pH6.9;H8;26C;5cm;50L ∿ ⟫ ◑ ♥ 🔫 🗄

Vesicatrus tegatus pH6.8;H10;21C;5cm;60L ∿ ⟫ ◑ ♥ 🔫 🗄

Hemigrammocharax multifasciatus pH6.8;H7;28C;11cm;120L ♀ ⤚ ◑ ♥ 🖼 ▭

Phago maculatus pH7.0;H10;24C;20cm;150L ⌏ ⤚ ◑ ✕ 🖼 ▱

Nannocharax fasciatus pH7.2;H8;26C;8cm;100L ⤳ ⤚ ◑ ♥ 🖼 ▱

377

Hepsetus odoe pH6.8;H6;26C;30cm;200L ⌒ ⮞ ◑ ✂ ▨ ▤

Brycinus longipinnis pH6.8;H6;25C;13cm;100L ⌒ ⮞ ◑ ♥ ▨ ▤

Micralestes stormsi pH6.6;H6;29C;11cm;?L ⚥ ⮞ ◑ ♥ ▨ ▤

Brycinus nurse pH6.8;H5;25C;25cm;200L ∿ ➤ ◐ ♥ 🖼 ⊟

Brycinus lateralis pH6.9;H7;29C;15cm;120L ∿ ➤ ◐ ♥ 🖼 ⊟

Brycinus brevis pH6.9;H7;28C;23cm;200L ∿ ➤ ◐ ♥ 🖼 ⊟

Brycinus aff. *imberi* pH6.8;H12;25C;12cm;40L ♀ ➤ ◑ ♥ 🖼 ▤

Brycinus longipinnis pH6.8;H6;25C;13cm;100L ∿ ➤ ◑ ♥ 🖼 ▤

Phenacogrammus sp. "Diamond" pH7.0;H14;26C;8cm;40L ♀ ➤ ◑ ♥ 🖼 ▤

Brycinus chaperi pH6.7;H6;25C;9cm;80L ∿ ➤ ◑ ♥ 🖼 ▣

Micralestes stormsi pH6.6;H6;29C;11cm;?L ♀ ➤ ◑ ♥ 🖼 ▣

Phenacogrammus interruptus pH6.8;H7;24C;8cm;100L ∿ ➤ ◑ ♥ 🖼 ▣

Phenacogrammus interruptus pH6.8;H7;24C;8cm;100L ∿ ➤ ◑ ♥ 🖼 ▣

♂ *Arnoldichthys spilopterus* pH7.0;H8;27C;6cm;80L ∿ ➤ ◑ ♥ 🖼 ▣

Nannocharax fasciatus pH7.2;H8;26C;8cm;100L ∿ ➤ ◑ ♥ 🖼 ▣

Phenacogrammus deheyni pH6.8;H7;28C;10cm;100L ∿ ➤ ◑ ♥ 🖼 ▣

Hemigrammopetersius intermedius pH6.5;H6;28C;10cm;100L ∿ ➤ ◑ ♥ 🖼 ▣

♀ *Arnoldichthys spilopterus* pH7.0;H8;27C;6cm;80L ∿ ➤ ◑ ♥ 🖼 ▣

383

Distichodus affinis pH6.8;H7;25C;13cm;100L ♀ ⬇ ◑ ♥ 🖼 ⊡

Citharinus citharus pH7.0;H8;30C;8cm;80L ♀ ⬇ ◑ ♥ 🖼 ⊡

Distichodus noboli pH6.8;H7;25C;10cm;100L ⌇ ⬇ ◑ ♥ 🖼 ⊡

Distichodus affinis pH6.8;H7;25C;13cm;100L ♀ ⋗ ◑ ♥ 🖼 🔲

Distichodus noboli pH6.8;H7;25C;10cm;100L ∿ ⋗ ◑ ♥ 🖼 🔲

Distichodus sexfasciatus pH7.0;H10;25C;35cm;200L ⅄ ⋗ ◑ ♥ 🖼 🔲

387

Distichodus affinis pH6.8;H7;25C;13cm;100L ♀ ⋙ ◑ ♥ 🎞 ⊟

Distichodus sexfasciatus pH7.0;H10;25C;35cm;200L ⋏ ⋙ ◑ ♥ 🎞 ⊟

388   *Distichodus decemmaculatus* pH7.0;H14;25C;8cm;40L ⋏ ⋙ ◑ ♥ 🎞 ⊟

The Catfishes

What makes a catfish a catfish? The whiskers, of course! Someone once thought that every fish which had whiskers looked like a cat and, therefore, should be called a catfish. This generalization is far from true, for while most catfishes have whiskers, not every fish with whiskers is a catfish.

The catfishes probably are the most variable group of fishes in the world. They are found almost universally where other fishes exist, and they show many adaptations that are found in almost no other fishes.

Some catfishes, such as some of those in the family Mochokidae, which ranges all over Africa except the desert, swim upside down at times (some *Synodontis*). These mochokids are very popular with aquarists even though they grow rather large, are naked in that they do not have scales, scutes, or body "armor" of any kind, and are usually very expensive, since all are imported from Africa.

For the aquarist, the most common catfishes are those from South America in the family Callichthyidae, the mailed catfishes. These are small fish which get their "mailed" name from the two rows of bony plates which overlap like the armor of one of King Arthur's knights. Most of the fishes in this family have very strong spines in their dorsal, adipose, and pectoral fins. The serration on the pectoral spines may be highly variable from species to species, especially in the genus *Corydoras*, and the author finds this characteristic extremely useful in identification.

Most callichthyids require access to the air to supplement their gills with an occasional "drink" of air which is utilized and absorbed in their lower digestive tract. *Corydoras* and *Dianema* as well as the other members of this family often swim rapidly to the surface of the water for a gulp of air.

Not all members of the family breed in the same manner. The *Corydoras*, which are exported from almost every country in South America east of the Andes Mountains, have a very elaborate spawning ritual which is still not fully understood. Basically a pair or group of *Corydoras* join in a spawning orgy. The males and females swim about one another, with the female repeatedly attacking the male's vent. It is strongly suggestive of her receiving sperm in her mouth, since further activity indicates no other contact with the male.

Once she has made a contact with the male's vent, she soon discharges a few eggs which she clasps in her ventral fins. At this time the ventral fins almost fuse into a cup which looks very much like a pair of cupped human hands. The female then swims about the tank with her eggs clasped between her ventrals looking for a suitable place to deposit her eggs. More often than not she lays the eggs on the front glass of the aquarium, but she may also choose a heater tube or a strong leaf. She seems to mouth the area upon which she will deposit her sticky eggs. It is theorized that at this time she has already spat out the sperm and merely presses the eggs into position on top of the sperm. The eggs are laid randomly in small groups all over the aquarium.

Callichthys and *Dianema* spawn much differently. They build a bubblenest under a floating log or large leaf and spawn under the nest, with the floating eggs being tended by the male. The eggs hatch in about five days, after which the male should be removed and the young raised alone.

There are many other families of catfishes of interest to aquarists. The suckermouth catfishes of the family Loricariidae are also of interest to aquarists because of the algae-eating characteristics of this family. While the Callichthyidae were characterized by two rows of bony scutes arranged laterally along the flanks, this family has three or four rows, with some even having their ventral surface covered with this same armor. *Hypostomus* (*Plecostomus*), *Loricaria*, *Farlowella*, *Otocinclus* and *Ancistrus* are just some of the loricariids which are imported regularly for aquarists from many South American countries. They are much more difficult to breed than the *Corydoras* or *Callichthys* catfishes, and no one is commercially spawning any of the loricariids.

In addition to the three catfish families discussed thus far, the order Siluriformes contains also the families Doradidae, Ageneiosidae, Plotosidae, Ictaluridae, Chacidae, Trichomycteridae, Schilbeidae, Helogeneidae, and Malapteruridae, all of which between them contain relatively few species of interest to (and available to) aquarists. Other families, in their cases containing many more species of aquarium interest, are the siluridae (which contains the popular glass catfish species *Kryptopterus*), the Clariidae (which contains the infamous walking catfish. *Clarias batrachus*); the Pimelodidae (which contains the *Pimelodus* and *Pimelodella* species as well as *Sorubim* and *Sorubimichthys*); and the Aspredinidae (containing the banjo catfishes).

Catfishes. as a rule. are very hardy and adaptable. Most are nocturnal and do best in subdued light.

Platystacus cotylephorus pH6.8;H12;25C;30cm;250L ∿ ➤ ◗ ♥ 🎞 ▭

Bunocephalus kneri pH6.8;H8;22C;10cm;100L ∿ ➤ ◗ ♥ 🎞 ▭

Bunocephalus coracoideus pH7.0;H10;23C;15cm;100L ∿ ➤ ◗ ♥ 🎞 ▭

391

Aspredo aspredo pH6.8;H12;25C;20cm;200L 〜 ➤ ◐ ♥ 🖼 ▭

Bunocephalus amaurus pH6.5;H6;22C;15cm;100L 〜 ➤ ◐ ♥ 🖼 ▭

Agmus lyriformis pH7.2;H12;21C;8cm;75L 〜 ➤ ◐ ♥ 🖼 ▭

Doras eigenmanni pH7.0;H10;25C;10cm;100L ⌇ ⤚ ◑ ♥ 🈲 ▭

Amblydoras hancocki pH7.2;H12;25C;15cm;100L ⌇ ⤚ ◑ ♥ 🏞 ▭

Agamyxis pectinifrons pH7.0;H10;25C;12cm;75L ⌇ ⤚ ◑ ♥ 🏞 ▭

Platydoras costatus pH7.0;H10;25C;20cm;100L 〰️ 🐟 ◐ ♥ 🖼️ 🖵

Platydoras costatus pH7.0;H10;25C;20cm;100L 〰️ 🐟 ◐ ♥ 🖼️ 🖵

Acanthodoras cataphractus pH6.8;H10;24C;10cm;75L 〰️ 🐟 ◐ ♥ 🖼️ 🖵

Platydoras costatus pH7.0;H10;25C;20cm;100L ⌒ ➤ ◑ ♥ ▦ ▭

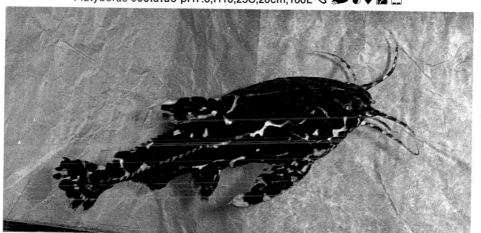

Acanthodoras cataphractus pH6.8;H10;24C;10cm;75L ⌒ ➤ ◑ ♥ ▦ ▭

Acanthodoras spinosissimus pH6.8;H10;25C;10cm;75L ⌒ ➤ ◑ ♥ ▦ ▭

Hassar notospilus pH6.8;H10;23C;7.5cm;75L 〰️ ➤ ◐ ♥ 🎞️ ▢

Trachydoras paraguayensis pH7.0;H12;20C;8cm;75L 〰️ ➤ ◐ ♥ 🎞️ ▢

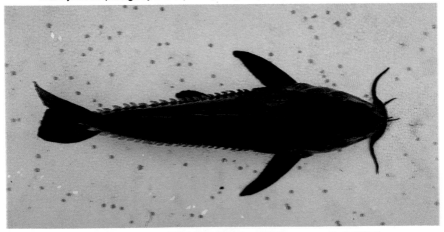

Pseudodoras niger pH7.0;H10;24C;1m;1000L 〰️ ➤ ◐ ♥ 🎞️ ▢

Parauchenipterus galeatus pH6.7;H8;24C;18cm;200L ᘁᕙ ◐ ♥ 🖼 ⊟

Auchenipterichthys thoracatus pH7.0;H12;23C;12cm;50L ♀ ᕙ ◐ ♥ 🖼 ▭

Parauchenipterus galeatus pH6.7;H8;24C;18cm;200L ᘁᕙ ◐ ♥ 🖼 ⊟

Entomocorus benjamini pH7.0;H10;25C;12cm;100L 〜 🐟 ◐ ♥ 🖼 ⊟

Trachycorystes trachycorystes pH7.0;H10;22C;11cm;100L 〜 🐟 ◐ ♥ 🖼 ⊟

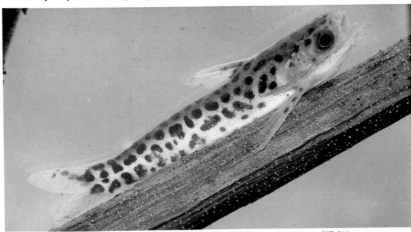

Tatia perugiae pH6.8;H8;25C;6cm;60L 〜 🐟 ◐ ♥ 🖼 ⊟

Tatia aulopygia pH6.7;H8;26C;10cm;100L ⤳ 🐟 ◑ ♥ 📷 ▱

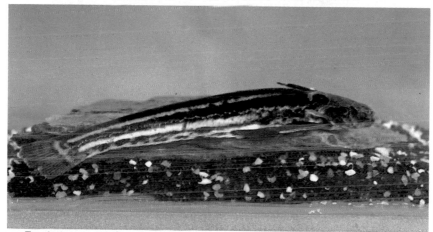

Trachelyopterichthys taeniatus pH7.2;H12;24C;20cm;75L ♀ 🐟 ◑ ♥ 📷 ▭

Auchenipterus demerarae pH6.8;H8;26C;12cm;100L ⤳ 🐟 ◑ ♥ 📷 ▱

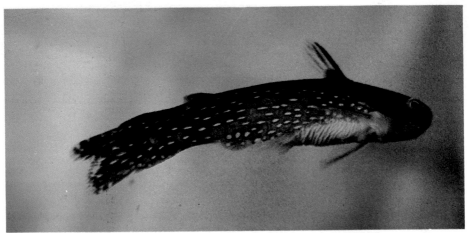

Tatia aulopygia pH6.8;H8;26C;8cm;100L ⌇ ➤ ◗ ♥ 🏞 ⊟

Pseudepapterus hasemani pH6.9;H9;26C;12cm;100L ⌇ ➤ ◗ ♥ 🏞 ⊟

Trachelyopterichthys taeniatus pH7.2;H12;24C;20cm;75L ♀ ➤ ◗ ♥ 🏞 ⊡

Liosomadoras oncinus pH5.8;H6;22C;18cm;200L 〰️ 🐟 ◑ ♥ 🖼️ ▭

Liosomadoras oncinus pH5.8;H6;22C;18cm;200L 〰️ 🐟 ◑ ♥ 🖼️ ▭

Pseudauchenipterus nodosus pH7.5;H12;22C;20cm;200L 〰️ 🐟 ◑ ♥ 🖼️ ▤

401

Liosomadoras oncinus pH5.8;H6;22C;18cm;200L 〜 ➤ ◐ ♥ 🎞 ▭

Centromochlus heckeli pH6.8;H8;26C;8cm;100L 〜 ➤ ◐ ♥ 🎞 ▤

Ageneiosus caucanus pH7.0;H10;23C;30cm;350L 〜 ➤ ◐ ✶ 🎞 ▤

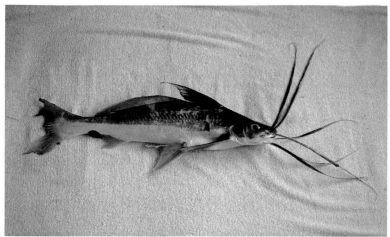

Pinirampus pirinampu pH7.0;H10;25C;1m;1000L ⌇ 🐟 ◕ ✕ 🖼 ⬚

Callophysus macropterus pH6.2;H6;26C;40cm;500L ⌇ 🐟 ◕ ✕ 🖼 ⬚

Pimelodella gracilis pH7.2;H10;22C;30cm;300L ⌇ 🐟 ◕ ♥ 🖼 ⬚

Callophysus macropterus pH6.2;H6;26C;40cm;500L ⤻ ➤ ◑ ✖ 🖼 ▭

Pimelodella gracilis pH7.2;H10;22C;30cm;300L ⤳ ➤ ◑ ♥ 🖼 ▭

Pimelodella linami pH7.2;H10;24C;12cm;200L ⤳ ➤ ◑ ♥ 🖼 ▭

Pimelodella parnahybae pH7.3;H10;24C;18cm;200L ∿ ⟆ ● ♥ 🖼 ⊡

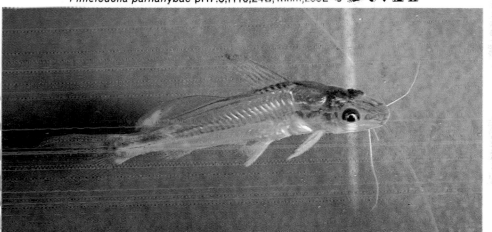

Pimelodella metae pH7.2;H10;25C;18cm;200L ∿ ⟆ ● ♥ 🖼 ⊡

Duopalatinus goeldii pH7.0;H8;25C;15cm;200L ∿ ⟆ ● ♥ 🖼 ⊡

Pimelodella dorseyi pH7.2;H12;23C;22cm;200L 〜 ➤ ◐ ♥ 🖼 ▢

Perrunichthys perruno pH6.5;H8;23C;60cm;300L 〜 ➤ ◐ ✕ 🖼 ▢

Duopalatinus barbatus pH7.2;H10;24C;18cm;200L 〜 ➤ ◐ ♥ 🖼 ▢

Pimelodus clarias pH7.0;H10;22C;30cm;300L ∿ 🐟 ◗ ♥ 🎞 ▢

Pimelodus maculatus pH7.4;H12;23C;26cm;300L ∿ 🐟 ◗ ♥ 🎞 ▢

Pimelodus maculatus pH7.4;H12;23C;26cm;300L ∿ 🐟 ◗ ♥ 🎞 ▢

407

Pimelodus albofasciatus pH7.2;H10;25C;25cm;300L ∿ ➤ ◑ ♥ 🎞 ▭

Pimelodus blochi pH7.2;H10;25C;25cm;300L ∿ ➤ ◑ ♥ 🎞 ▭

Pimelodus pictus pH7.2;H10;25C;25cm;300L ∿ ➤ ◑ ♥ 🎞 ▭

Pimelodus ornatus pH7.0;H8;25C;28cm;300L

Perrunichthys perruno pH6.5;H8;23C;60cm;300L

Merodontotus tigrinus pH7.0;H10;25C;60cm;1000L

Sorubim lima pH6.8;H8;26C;45cm;500L ⌇ ⊱ ◑ ✕ 🖼 ▭

Platystomatichthys sturio pH7.0;H10;24C;60cm;500L ⌇ ⊱ ◑ ✕ 🖼 ▭

Leiarius pictus pH7.2;H10;25C;60cm;500L ⌇ ⊱ ◑ ♥ 🖼 ▭

Phractocephalus hemioliopterus pH7.0;H8;24C;1m;1000L 〜 ➤ ◑ ✕ 🎞 🖵

Pseudoplatystoma fasciatum pH6.8;H8;26C;1m;1000L ➤ ◑ ✕ 🎞 🖵

Pseudoplatystoma fasciatum pH6.8;H8;26C;1m;1000L ➤ ◑ ✕ 🎞 🖵

411

Microglanis poecilus pH7.3;H10;25C;7cm;60L ⌇ ➤ ◗ ♥ 🎞 ▱

Pseudopimelodus albomarginatus pH6.8;H8;26C;12cm;150L ⌇ ➤ ◗ ♥ 🎞 ▱

Pseudopimelodus nigricauda pH6.8;H10;25C;10cm;100L ⌇ ➤ ◗ ♥ 🎞 ▱

Callichthys callichthys pH7.0;H8;21C;18cm;200L ⌇ 🐟 ◑ ♥ 🖼 ▭

Hoplosternum pectorale pH6.7;H8;25C;20cm;200L ⌇ 🐟 ◑ ♥ 🖼 ▭

Dianema longibarbis pH7.0;H10;24C;12cm;100L ⌇ 🐟 ◑ ♥ 🖼 ▭

413

Hoplosternum thoracatum pH6.7;H8;25C;18cm;200L 〜 ➤ ◑ ♥ 🖼 ⬜

Dianema longibarbis pH7.0;H10;24C;12cm;100L 〜 ➤ ◑ ♥ 🖼 ⬜

Dianema urostriata pH7.5;H10;24C;15cm;100L 〜 ➤ ◑ ♥ 🖼 ⬜

414

Aspidoras pauciradiatus pH6.8;H8;25C;4cm;40L ⌇ ⮞ ◑ ♥ 🖼 ⬚

Aspidoras lakoi pH6.8;H8;24C;4cm;40L ⌇ ⮞ ◑ ♥ 🖼 ⬚

Aspidoras fuscoguttatus pH6.7;H8;24C;3.5cm;40L ⌇ ⮞ ◑ ♥ 🖼 ⬚

415

Brochis splendens pH7.0;H10;20C;8cm;75L ∿ ➤ ◑ ♥ 🎞 ▭

Brochis britskii pH7.0;H12;20C;14cm;50L ♀ ➤ ◑ ♥ 🎞 ▭

Brochis multiradiatus pH7.0;H12;20C;9cm;50L ♀ ➤ ◑ ♥ 🎞 ▭

Corydoras aeneus pH7.3;H12;24C;7cm;40L ♀ 🐟 ◑ ♥ 🖼 ▭

Corydoras aeneus pH7.3;H12;24C;7cm;40L ♀ 🐟 ◑ ♥ 🖼 ▭

Corydoras aeneus pH7.3;H12;24C;7cm;40L ♀ 🐟 ◑ ♥ 🖼 ▭

417

Corydoras acutus pH6.7;H7;24C;6cm;40L 〜 ➤ ◑ ♥ 🖼 ▭

Corydoras osteocarus pH6.8;H9;25C;6cm;40L 〜 ➤ ◑ ♥ 🖼 ▭

Corydoras latus pH7.0;H12;20C;8cm;50L ♀ ➤ ◑ ♥ 🖼 ▭

Corydoras garbei pH7.0;H9;24C;4cm;40L ∿ ➤ ◑ ♥ 🖾 ▭

Corydoras semiaquilus pH7.0;H8;24C;8cm;60L ∿ ➤ ◑ ♥ 🖾 ▭

Corydoras melanotaenia pH7.0;H8;25C;6cm;40L ∿ ➤ ◑ ♥ 🖾 ▭

419

Corydoras barbatus pH6.6;H7;20C;13cm;75L 〜 ➤ ◑ ♥ 🖼 ▭

♂ *Corydoras macropterus* pH6.8;H8;21C;9cm;100L 〜 ➤ ◑ ♥ 🖼 ▭

Corydoras elegans pH7.0;H10,25C;5cm;40L 〜 ➤ ◑ ♥ 🖼 ▭

♀ Corydoras macropterus pH6.0;H0,21O,9cm, 100L ⌇ ➤ ◖ ♥ 🖼 ▭

Corydoras nanus pH7.0;H8;24C;3.5cm;40L ⌇ ➤ ◖ ♥ 🖼 ▭

Corydoras pygmaeus pH7.0;H9;24C;3cm;40L ⌇ ➤ ◖ ♥ 🖼 ▤

421

Corydoras axelrodi pH7.0;H8;24C;5cm;40L ∿ ➤ ◑ ♥ 🎞 ⬛

Corydoras habrosus pH7.0;H10;25C;3.5cm;40L ∿ ➤ ◑ ♥ 🎞 ⬛

Corydoras loxozonus pH7.0;H8;25C;5.0cm;60L ∿ ➤ ◑ ♥ 🎞 ⬛

Corydoras zygatus pH7.0;H8;25C;6cm;40L ∿ ⤜ ◐ ♥ 🎞 ▢

Corydoras treitlii pH7.0;H10;26C;8cm;60L ♀ ⤜ ◐ ♥ 🎞 ▢

Corydoras eques pH6.8;H8;24C;5.5cm;40L ∿ ⤜ ◐ ♥ 🎞 ▢

423

Corydoras rabauti pH7.3;H12;25C;6cm;60L ♀ 🐟 ◑ ♥ 🖼 ▭

Corydoras adolfoi pH7.0;H9;25C;6cm;60L ∿ 🐟 ◑ ♥ 🖼 ▭

Corydoras narcissus pH7.0;H9;24C;7cm;60L ∿ 🐟 ◑ ♥ 🖼 ▭

Corydoras elegans pH7.0;H10;25C;5cm;40L ⌇ ➤ ◖ ♥ 🎞 ⬚

Corydoras simulatus pH7.0;H8;26C;6cm;60L ⌇ ➤ ◖ ♥ 🎞 ⬚

Corydoras adolfoi pH7.0;H9;25C;6cm;60L ⌇ ➤ ◖ ♥ 🎞 ⬚

Corydoras melini pH7.0;H8;24C;6cm;60L 〜 ➤ ◑ ♥ 🖼 ▭

Corydoras metae pH7.0;H10;26C;6cm;60L ♀ ➤ ◑ ♥ 🖼 ▭

Corydoras arcuatus pH7.2;H10;25C;4.5cm;50L ♀ ➤ ◑ ♥ 🖼 ▭

Corydoras guapore pH7.0;H8;25C;4.5cm;50L ⤳ 🐟 ◐ ♥ 🎞 ▭

Corydoras panda pH7.0;H10;24C;4.5cm;50L ⤳ 🐟 ◐ ♥ 🎞 ▭

Corydoras caudimaculatus pH7.0;H9;24C;5cm;50L ♀ 🐟 ◐ ♥ 🎞 ▭

427

Corydoras gracilis pH7.0;H10;24C;2.5cm;30L ⌇ ➤ ◑ ♥ 🖼 ▭

Corydoras pastazensis pH7.0;H10;25C;6cm;60L ⌇ ➤ ◑ ♥ 🖼 ▭

Corydoras septentrionalis pH7.0;H10;24C;6cm;60L ⌇ ➤ ◑ ♥ 🖼 ▭

428

Corydoras undulatus pH7.0;H10;24C;5cm;50L ♀ ⟿ ◑ ♥ 🖼 ▭

Corydoras paleatus pH7.0;H8;24C;8cm;60L ♀ ⟿ ◑ ♥ 🖼 ▭

Corydoras ehrhardti pH7.0;H9;25C;5cm;60L ∿ ⟿ ◑ ♥ 🖼 ▭

Corydoras napoensis pH7.0;H9;25C;4cm;50L ♀ ⍤ ◐ ♥ 🖼 ▭

♀ *Corydoras paleatus* pH7.0;H8;24C;8cm;60L ♀ ⍤ ◐ ♥ 🖼 ▭

Corydoras paleatus pH7.0;H8;24C;8cm;60L ♀ ⍤ ◐ ♥ 🖼 ▭

Corydoras atropersonatus pH7.2;H9;25C;4.5cm;50L ∿ ⋙ ◑ ♥ 🎞 ⬚

Corydoras polystictus pH7.0;H8;25C;5cm;50L ∿ ⋙ ◑ ♥ 🎞 ⬚

Corydoras osteocarus pH6.8;H9;25C;6cm;40L ∿ ⋙ ◑ ♥ 🎞 ⬚

431

Corydoras nattereri pH7.0;H10;25C;8cm;60L ♀ ➤ ◑ ♥ 🎞 ▭

Corydoras xinguensis pH7.0;H8;23C;4.5cm;50L ⌇ ➤ ◑ ♥ 🎞 ▭

Corydoras sanchesi pH7.0;H8;24C;4cm;40L ⌇ ➤ ◑ ♥ 🎞 ▭

Corydoras robinae pH7.2;H10;24C;6cm;60L ∿ ➤ ◑ ♥ 🎞 ▱

Corydoras cf. *acutus* pH6.9;H8;24C;6cm;60L ∿ ➤ ◑ ♥ 🎞 ▱

Corydoras bondi pH6.8;H8;26C;5.5cm;60L ♀ ➤ ◑ ♥ 🎞 ▱

Corydoras pulcher pH7.0;H9;25C;5cm;60L ♀ ⋗ ◐ ♥ 🖼 ⬚

Corydoras osteocarus pH7.0;H12;22C;8cm;50L ♀ ⋗ ◐ ♥ 🖼 ⬚

♂ *Corydoras bondi* pH6.8;H8;26C;5.5cm;60L ♀ ⋗ ◐ ♥ 🖼 ⬚

Corydoras ambiacus pH7.2;H10;24C;6cm;60L ♀ 🐟 ◑ ♥ 🖼 ⬚

Corydoras reticulatus pH7.0;H8;25C;6cm;60L ∿ 🐟 ◑ ♥ 🖼 ⬚

Corydoras trilineatus pH7.2;H10;24C;6cm;60L ∿ 🐟 ◑ ♥ 🖼 ⬚

435

Corydoras ambiacus pH7.2;H10;24C;6cm;60L ♀ 🐟 ◑ ♥ 🖼 ▭

Corydoras sp. pH7.0;H8;25C;6cm;60L 〜 🐟 ◑ ♥ 🖼 ▭

Corydoras trilineatus pH7.2;H10;24C;6cm;60L 〜 🐟 ◑ ♥ 🖼 ▭

Corydoras melanistius pH7.2;H10;26C;8cm;60L ♀ 🐟 ◑ ♥ 📺 🖵

Corydoras delphax pH7.0;H10;24C;5.5cm;60L 〰 🐟 ◑ ♥ 📺 🖵

Corydoras sodalis pH7.3;H10;25C;5cm;50L ♀ 🐟 ◑ ♥ 📺 🖵

437

Corydoras sychri pH7.0;H8;25C;4.5cm;50L ⌇ ➤ ◑ ♥ 🖼 ▭

Corydoras melanistius pH7.2;H10;26C;8cm;60L ⚘ ➤ ◑ ♥ 🖼 ▭

Corydoras orphnopterus pH7.1;H9;24C;5cm;60L ⌇ ➤ ◑ ♥ 🖼 ▭

Corydoras ornatus pH6.8;H8;26C;5.5cm;60L ∿ 🐟 ◑ ♥ 🖼 ⬚

Corydoras evelynae pH7.2;H9;25C;5cm;50L ♀ 🐟 ◑ ♥ 🖼 ⬚

Corydoras haraldschultzi pH7.2;H10;26C;5.5cm;60L ♀ 🐟 ◑ ♥ 🖼 ⬚

Corydoras schwartzi pH7.2;H10;24C;5cm;50L ♀ ➤ ◑ ♥ 🖼 ⌷

Corydoras leucomelas pH7.0;H9;25C;6cm;60L ♀ ➤ ◑ ♥ 🖼 ⌷

Corydoras sterbai pH7.2;H9;25C;5cm;60L ᔐ ➤ ◑ ♥ 🖼 ⌷

Hypostomus plecostomus pH7.0;H10;26C;60cm;250L ⌇ ➤ ◑ ♥ ▱ ▭

Hypostomus plecostomus pH7.0;H10;26C;60cm;250L ⌇ ➤ ◑ ♥ ▱ ▭

Hypostomus plecostomus pH7.0;H10;26C;60cm;250L ⌇ ➤ ◑ ♥ ▱ ▭

441

Hypostomus punctatus pH7.2;H12;25C;30cm;200L ⌇ ➤ ◗ ♥ 🎞 ▭

Hypostomus varimaculosus pH7.0;H10;25C;15cm;200L ⌇ ➤ ◗ ♥ 🎞 ▭

Hypostomus niceferoi pH7.0;H10;26C;22cm;200L ⌇ ➤ ◗ ♥ 🎞 ▭

Hypostomus watwata pH7.0;H10;26C;28cm;200L ∿ ➤ ◗ ♥ 🎞 ⬜

Hypostomus sp. "Diagonal Bar" pH7.2;H10;25C;25cm;200L ∿ ➤ ◗ ♥ 🎞 ⬜

Hypostomus jaguribensis pH6.8;H8;26C;12cm;150L ∿ ➤ ◗ ♥ 🎞 ⬜

Cochliodon hondae pH7.0;H10;26C;26cm;200L ∿ ➤ ◑ ♥ 🎦 ⬒

Pterygoplichthys cf *gibbiceps* pH7.0;H8;25C;45cm;200L ∿ ➤ ◑ ♥ 🎦 ⬒

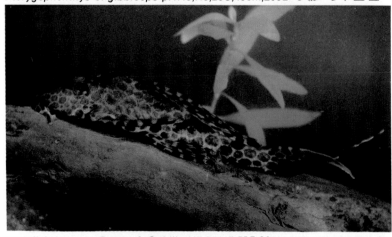

Pterygoplichthys sp. "Brown & Gold" pH7.0;H10;26C;30cm;200L ∿ ➤ ◑ ♥ 🎦 ⬒

Peckoltia vittata pH7.0;H10;24C;10cm;100L ꏹ ➤ ◑ ♥ 🖼 ▭

Peckoltia brevis pH7.0;H10;25C;10cm;100L ꏹ ➤ ◑ ♥ 🖼 ▭

Peckoltia pulcher pH7.0;H10;24C;10cm;100L ꏹ ➤ ◑ ♥ 🖼 ▭

Ancistrus hoplogenys pH7.0;H10;24C;12.5cm;100L 〜 ➤ ◐ ♥ ▨ ▭

Ancistrus hoplogenys pH7.0;H10;24C;12.5cm;100L 〜 ➤ ◐ ♥ ▨ ▭

Pseudacanthicus leopardus pH6.8;H8;25C;15cm;100L 〜 ➤ ◐ ♥ ▨ ▭

Ancistrus dolichopterus pH7.0;H10;25C;15cm;100L ⌇ 🐟 ◑ ♥ 🎞 ⬚

Ancistrus lineolatus pH6.8;H10;24C;12cm;100L ⌇ 🐟 ◑ ♥ 🎞 ⬚

Ancistrus temmincki pH7.0;H10;24C;15cm;100L ⌇ 🐟 ◑ ♥ 🎞 ⬚

Ancitrus sp. "Brown Blotch" pH7.0;H10;25C;15cm;100L

Panaque nigrolineatus pH7.0;H10;25C;38cm;200L

Panaque suttoni pH6.8;H8;24C;28cm;200L

448

Ancistrus sp. "Brown Blotch" pH7.0;H10;25C;15cm;100L ～ ➤ ◑ ♥ 🖾 ▭

Panaque nigrolineatus pH7.0;H10;25C;38cm;200L ～ ➤ ◑ ♥ 🖾 ▭

Panaque suttoni pH6.8;H8;24C;28cm;200L ～ ➤ ◑ ♥ 🖾 ▭

Panaque suttoni pH6.8;H8;24C;28cm;200L 〜🐟◑♥🖼️⬚

Parotocinclus maculicauda pH6.5;H8;23C;4.5cm;50L 🌱🐟◑♥🖼️⬚

Pterygoplichthys aff. *multiradiatus* pH7.0;H10;25C;50cm;200L 🌱🐟◑♥🖼️⬚

Panaque nigrolineatus pH7.0;H10;25C;38cm;200L ∿ ⤜ ◑ ♥ 🖼 ▭

Otocinclus affinis pH6.5;H6;26C;5cm;50L ↞ ⤜ ◑ ♥ 🖼 ▭

Farlowella acus pH6.5;H8;24C;15cm;100L ↞ ⤜ ◑ ♥ 🖼 ▭

451

Otocinclus aff. *nigracauda* pH7.0;H10;24C;4.5cm;50L 🐟 🐠 ◑ ♥ 🖼 ⬜

Otocinclus mariae pH7.0;H10;24C;4.5cm;50L 🐟 🐠 ◑ ♥ 🖼 ⬜

Otocinclus flexilis pH7.3;H10;23C;6cm;50L 🐟 🐠 ◑ ♥ 🖼 ⬜

Otocinclus affinis pH7.0;H10;25C;5cm;50L ✧ ➤ ◑ ♥ 🖼 ▭

Otocinclus aff. *nattereri* pH7.0;H10;24C;4.5cm;50L ✧ ➤ ◑ ♥ 🖼 ▭

Otocinclus mariae pH7.0;H10;24C;4.5cm;50L ✧ ➤ ◑ ♥ 🖼 ▭

Hypoptopoma gulare pH6.8;H8;24C;7cm;50L ⚘ 🐟 ◑ ♥ 🎞 🖵

Rineloricaria castroi pH6.8;H10;24C;12cm;100L ⚘ 🐟 ◑ ♥ 🎞 🖵

Rineloricaria hasemani pH7.0;H10;22C;11cm;100L ⚘ 🐟 ◑ ♥ 🎞 🖵

Hypoptopoma gulare pH6.8;H8;24C;7cm;50L ⌁ 🐟 ◑ ♥ 🖼 ▢

Rineloricaria microlepidogaster pH7.0;H10;24C;12cm;75L ⌇ 🐟 ◑ ♥ 🖼 ▢

Rineloricaria hasemani pH7.0;H10;22C;11cm;100L ⌁ 🐟 ◑ ♥ 🖼 ▢

455

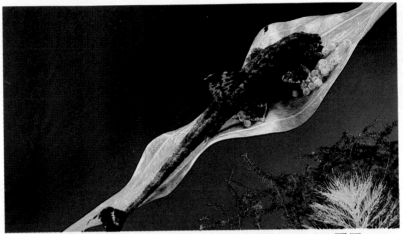

Rineloricaria castroi pH6.8;H10;24C;12cm;100L ⌇ ➤ ◐ ♥ 🎞 ▭

Rineloricaria microlepidogaster pH7.0;H10;24C;12cm;75L ⌇ ➤ ◐ ♥ 🎞 ▭

Rineloricaria lanceolata pH7.0;H10;22C;15cm;100L ⌇ ➤ ◐ ♥ 🎞 ▭

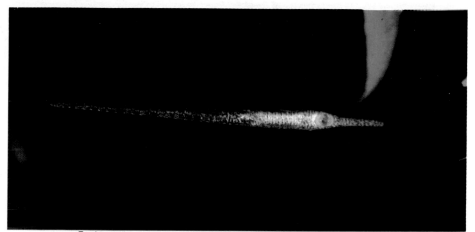

Farlowella gracilis pH7.0;H10;24C;20cm;100L ✤ 🐟 ◑ ♥ 🎞 ▭

Hemiodontichthys acipenserinus pH7.0;H10;25C;13cm;75L ∿ 🐟 ◑ ♥ 🎞 ▭

Sturisoma panamense pH7.0;H10;22C;12cm;100L ✤ 🐟 ◑ ♥ 🎞 ▭

457

Chanallabes apus pH7.2;H10;23C;30cm;200L 〜 ➤ ◑ ♥ 🖼 ⬜

Gymnallabes typus heterocercalis pH7.1;H10;27C;40cm;200L 〜 ➤ ◑ ♥ 🖼 ⬜

Gymnallabes typus typus pH7.1;H9;27C;25cm;200L ♀ ➤ ◑ ♥ 🖼 ⬜

458

Schilbe marmoratus pH7.0;H8;26C;16cm;100L 〜 ➤ ◑ ♥ 🖾 ▭

Schilbe uranoscopus pH7.3;H9;26C;30cm;200L 〜 ➤ ◑ ♥ 🖾 ▭

Schilbe mystus pH7.2;H10;27C;34cm;200L 〜 ➤ ◑ ♥ 🖾 ▭

Eutropiellus debauwi pH6.8;H7;25C;8cm;100L 〜 ➤ ◑ ♥ 🖾 ▭

Parailia occidentalis pH7.0;H8;26C;10cm;80L ♀ 🐟 ◑ ♥ 🎞 ⬜

Parailia pellucida pH7.8;H12;28C;10cm;100L ♀ 🐟 ◑ ♥ 🎞 ⬜

Parailia congica pH7.0;H8;27C;10cm;80L ⌇ 🐟 ◑ ♥ 🎞 ⬜

Eutropiellus debauwi pH6.8;H7;25C;8cm;100L ⌇ 🐟 ◑ ♥ 🎞 ⬜

Malapterurus electricus pH7.0;H8;25C;60cm;300L ✎ ➤ ◑ ✕ ▨ ▭

Amphilius atesuensis pH7.5;H10;26C;6cm;80L ♀ ➤ ◑ ♥ ▨ ▭

Phractura ansorgei pH7.0;H8;26C;5cm;40L ✎ ➤ ◑ ♥ ▨ ▭

Synodontis robertsi pH7.0;H15;28C;10cm;100L ♀ ➤● ♥ 🎞 ▱

Synodontis longirostris pH7.0;H14;27C;60cm;300L ♀ ➤● ♥ 🎞 ▱

Synodontis nigromaculatus pH7.9;H13;29C;23cm;100L ♀ ➤● ♥ 🎞 ▱

Synodontis multipunctatus pH8.0;H15;28C;17cm;100L ♀ ➤ ◑ ♥ 🎞 ▭

Synodontis petricola pH8.2;H16;27C;14cm;80L ♀ ➤ ◑ ♥ 🎞 ▭

Synodontis acanthomias pH6.9;H12;28C;40cm;300L ♀ ➤ ◑ ♥ 🎞 ▭

Synodontis polli pH8.1;H14;27C;18cm;100L ♀ ⟳ ➤ ◑ ♥ 🎞 ▭

Synodontis nigromaculatus pH7.9;H13;29C;23cm;100L ♀ ➤ ◑ ♥ 🎞 ▭

Synodontis robbianus pH7.5;H12;26C;14cm;100L ♀ ➤ ◑ ♥ 🎞 ▭

Synodontis schoutedeni pH6.9;H15;28C;14cm;150L ♀ ➤ ◑ ♥ ▓ ☐

Synodontis notatus pH7.8;H9;27C;20cm;200L ♀ ➤ ◑ ♥ ▓ ☐

Synodontis congicus pH6.6;H9;28C;15cm;100L ♀ ➤ ◑ ♥ ▓ ☐

465

Synodontis notatus pH7.8;H9;27C;20cm;200L ♀ ➤ ◐ ♥ 🎞 ▭

Synodontis decorus pH7.8;H10;28C;20cm;250L ♀ ➤ ◐ ♥ 🎞 ▭

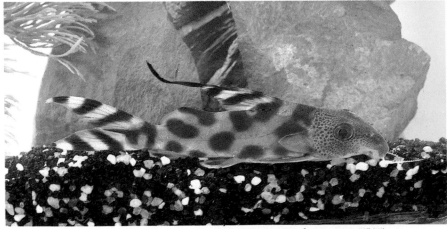

Synodontis decorus pH7.8;H10;28C;20cm;250L ♀ ➤ ◐ ♥ 🎞 ▭

Synodontis ornatipinnis pH7.0;H14;27C;30cm;300L ♀ ➤ ◐ ♥ 🎴 ▭

Synodontis flavitaeniatus pH7.3;H14;28C;15cm;100L ♀ ➤ ◐ ♥ 🎴 ▭

Synodontis pleurops pH7.0;H8;29C;25cm;300L ♀ ➤ ◐ ♥ 🎴 ▭

467

Synodontis contractus pH6.6;H9;26C;10cm;100L ♀ 🐟 ◑ ♥ 🖼 ▭

Synodontis nigriventris pH7.0;H8;27C;10cm;100L ♀ 🐟 ◑ ♥ 🖼 ▭

Synodontis angelicus pH7.1;H8;28C;30cm;200L ♀ 🐟 ◑ ♥ 🖼 ▭

Synodontis ornatipinnis pH7.0;H14;27C;30cm;

Synodontis brichardi pH7.2;H13;27C;20cm;100L

Synodontis pleurops pH7.0;H8;29C;25cm;250L

Synodontis greshoffi pH6.9;H10;28C;16cm;100L ♀ ⬤ ♥ 🎞 ☐

Synodontis nigriventis pH7.0;H8;27C;10cm;100L ♀ ⬤ ♥ 🎞 ☐

Synodontis angelicus pH7.1;H8;28C;30cm;200L ♀ ⬤ ♥ 🎞 ☐

Parauchenoglanis macrostoma pH7.2;H8;25C;30cm;100L ♀ 🐟 ◑ ♥ 📺 ⬛

Auchenoglanis occidentalis pH7.2;H9;27C;50cm;300L ⤳ 🐟 ◑ ✕ 📺 ⬛

Synodontis budgetti pH8.0;H14;28C;22cm;200L ♀ 🐟 ◑ ♥ 📺 ⬛

471

Parauchenoglanis guttatus pH7.2;H8;25C;30cm;100L ♀ ➤ ◑ ♥ 🎞 ⬜

Parauchenoglanis macrostoma pH7.2;H8;25C;25cm;80L ♀ ➤ ◑ ♥ 🎞 ⬜

Synodontis haugi pH7.2;H14;28C;25cm;200L ♀ ➤ ◑ ♥ 🎞 ⬜

472

Bagrus ubangensis pH6.6;H6;27C;30cm;200L ↘ ➤ ◑ ♥ 🎞 ▭

Chrysichthys brachynema pH9.0;H20;25C;40cm;400L ↘ ➤ ◑ ✕ 🎞 ▭

Gnathobagrus depressus pH8.5;H10;25C;20cm;200L ↘ ➤ ✕ 🎞 ▭

Phyllonemus typus pH7.6;H12;25C;8cm;60L 〜 ➤ ◑ ♥ 🖼 ▭

Lophiobagrus cyclurus pH9.0;H19;25C;10cm;80L 〜 ➤ ◑ ♥ 🖼 ▭

Chrysichthys sianenna pH9.0;H12;25C;22cm;200L 〜 ➤ ◑ ♥ 🖼 ▭

Bagrichthys hypselopterus pH7.0;H8;26C;40cm;400L ♀ ⚬ ◐ ♥ 🖼 ▭

Leiocassis siamensis pH6.8;H5;24C;16cm;200L ♀ ⚬ ◐ ♥ 🖼 ▭

Mystus tengara pH7.0;H8;25C;21cm;200L ♀ ⚬ ◐ ♥ 🖼 ▭

Platytropius siamensis pH7.0;H8;26C;25cm;300L ♀ ➤ ◐ ♥ 🖻 ▭

Kryptopterus bicirrhis pH7.1;H8;24C;10cm;100L ∿ ➤ ◐ ♥ 🖻 ▭

Ompok bimaculatus pH7.0;H8;27C;46cm;500L ∿ ➤ ◐ ♥ 🖻 ▭

THE LIVEBEARERS

Of all the aquarium fishes, those which give birth to living young are probably the most popular of all. Many millions of mollies, platies, swordtails and guppies are sold each year to beginners. There are hundreds of fish farms in Florida, Singapore, Hong Kong and Bangkok which turn out so many of these colorful, easy to keep, easy to breed fishes that several million dollars in air freight charges are spent just to get them to their respective markets.

It is interesting that the livebearers I mentioned above are all American fishes! Most originate in Mexico (the platies and swordtails), some in the United States (the mollies) and the guppy probably originated in Trinidad, though it has been so spread around that it is undoubtedly the most common wild fish to be found in Singapore at the present time.

Livebearing is not limited to the small fishes which we know in pet shops. Many of the larger fishes like rays and sharks also may give birth to living young, as may some snakes! But in most cases this livebearing capability has little comparison with mammalian livebearing. With most fishes, especially the tropical toy fishes, fertilization takes place through the modified anal fin of the male, which shoots packets of sperm into the body of the female, where internal fertilization of the eggs take place. The female then merely acts as a home for the developing eggs; she does not give the developing eggs any food, nor is her body chemistry (blood, etc.) connected with the developing fry. Once the eggs have developed sufficiently, and this usually takes about 28 days, the young are discharged and go swimming away. If she gives birth in a separate nursery tank which is heavily laden with fine-leaved plants, her young have a good chance at survival. If she releases her young in a community tank, chances are that the fry will be gobbled up by the other fishes almost as soon as they are released! Since female fishes get fatter as their eggs develop internally, it is a good idea to set up separate nursery tanks in which the female can give birth and the young can be raised.

Another important feature of livebearers from the point of view of the aquarist is that the fish are hardy and are easily bred. Then, too, as you observe your mollies, swordtails, platies and guppies, you might find an offspring that has some interesting physical characteristic which you might like to "fix" into a strain. Almost all the livebearers that are available at pet shops today are the result of mutants or sports which were observed in normal litters of fish. In nature these freaks would probably not survive, so chances of finding them are almost nil. But in the aquarium where a particular fish can be given the best of care and protection, everything is possible. Just think of the many different color varieties of swordtails and platies. Or just think of how many different kinds of guppies there are. Maybe you'll be lucky enough to find some strange freak in your own batch of babies.

In a book of this sort too much attention cannot be given to any single group of fishes, but there are plenty of books, mostly at your local pet shop (very few book stores carry specialized fish books) which cover every aquarium livebearer. Look through some of the books and if one group of fishes interests you most, study about them. Livebearers are easy . . . and they are a lot of fun.

Almost all of the livebearing species seen in aquariums belong to the family Poeciliidae, but there are a few other livebearing species from other families seen on the market from time to time. Examples would be the halfbeaks (*Dermogenys* and *Hemirhamphus*) and the goodeids (*Xenotoca, Ameca, Ilyodon,* etc.), as well as *Anableps.*

Additionally, there are many other genera within the family Poeciliidae; some of the fishes in these genera have found favor with hobbyists and are therefore included among the fishes shown in the photos accompanying this section. In this group would be the various limias (now in the genus *Poecilia* with the guppy and the mollies, but formerly in the genus *Limia*); the *Gambusia* species, which are not good aquarium fishes, unfortunately; the fishes of the genera *Girardinus* and *Brachyraphis* and *Phallichthys,* and *Phalloceros,* which are relatively small and lacking in bright colors; and the much bigger (and very dangerous) *Belonesox belizanus,* among others.

THE PLATIES
AND SWORDTAILS

For some reason the platies and swordtails have lagged behind the guppy in popularity, even though they are certainly among the most colorful of the livebearers and are almost as easy to keep as the guppy is. Perhaps it's because they're larger than the guppy, with the swordtail being a good deal larger.

There are two platy species regularly sold in the hobby: the common platy, *Xiphophorus maculatus*, and the variatus platy, *Xiphophorus variatus*. The common swordtail is *Xiphophorus helleri*.

Both the platies in the hobby have been widely hybridized with each other and with the swordtails, resulting in a total mess as far as telling which species is which. In fact, some authorities flatly state that there are no pure strains of swordtails or platies being bred commercially at this time. Even the distinction between platies as a group and swordtails as a separate group is now hazardous.

Platies and swordtails are very easy to keep and breed, and they are usually regarded as beginner fishes. Yet their extreme variability, combined with their bright colors, makes them worthy of the respect of all hobbyists, beginner and specialist alike. Without them aquaria would be much less brilliant.

The roster of swordtail and platy species, now numbering 18 nominal species, includes: *Xiphophorus alvarezi, X. andersi, X. clemenciae, X. cortezi, X. couchianus, X. evelynae, X. gordoni, X. helleri, X. kosszanderi, X. maculatus, X. milleri, X. montezumae, X. nigrensis, X. pygmaeus, X. roseni, X. signum, X. variatus,* and *X. xiphidium.* Of these 18, 7 are usually called platies: *X. couchianus, X. gordoni, X. variatus, X. evelynae, X. milleri, X. roseni,* and *X. maculatus.* The other 11 are swordtails, though several look more like platies with short swords than like typical aquarium swordtails. All of the numbers and names are subject to change as new studies are made.

Gold variegated "Mickey Mouse" platy

Gold tuxedo platy female

Gold salt and pepper platy

Gold "Mickey Mouse" hifin platy male

Gold platies, male

Gold "Mickey Mouse" platy female

481

Gold platy female

Gold platy male

Gold "Mickey Mouse" platies

Gold hifin platy female

Gold platy

Gold "Mickey Mouse" hifin platy

Gold wagtail platies, males

Bleeding heart platy male

Gold variatus platy

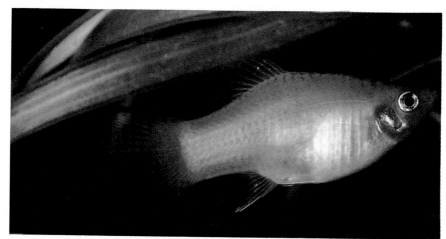

Gold platy female

Gold salt and pepper platy male

Red salt and pepper platies

485

Sunset hifin platy male

Red tuxedo hifin platy male

Red salt and pepper platy male

Red wagtail platies

Red hifin wagtail platy male

Red tuxedo wagtail platy female

Blue hifin platy female

Black variatus platy male

Black hifin variatus platy male

Sunset variatus var. male

Blue variatus platy male

Albino variatus platy

Sunset variatus platy male

Marigold variatus

Red-tailed gold variatus platy male

Red variatus male

Red-tailed black-spotted variatus

Marigold variatus platy male

Blue hifin variatus platy male

Red-tailed black-spotted variatus

Blue hifin variatus

Blue hifin variatus platy male

Sunburst platies, male right

Red hifin variatus platy male

493

Black variatus platies, male below

Red variatus platy male

Marigold variatus platy male

Xiphophorus montezumae pH7.3;H12;25C;6cm;60L ♀ 🐟 ◐ ♥ 🐌 ▣

Xiphophorus helleri pH7.3;H14;25C;13cm;60L🐟 ◐ ♥ 🐌 ▣

Green swordtail variation, male.

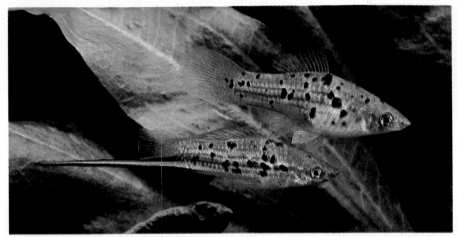

Green variegated swordtails

Green swordtail male

Green swordtail "Mickey Mouse" hybrid male

Blood red Berlin lyretail swordtail male

Brick red tuxedo swordtail male

Xiphophorus cortezi

497

Brick red wag swordtail

Red Mexican swordtails

Black Berlin swordtails

Brick red swordtail

Velvet red swordtail

Red tuxedo swordtail platy hybrid

Brick red hifin swordtail male

Blood red hifin swordtail pair

Brick red lyretail swordtail female

Brick red jet hifin swordtail male

Brick red hifin wagtail swordtails

Blood red wagtail lyretail swordtails

Brick red hifin wagtail swordtail female

Gold tuxedo hifin swordtail female

Brick red swordtail male

Piebald swordtail male

Red variegated swordtail female

Red variegated swordtails, cancerous strain

Albino swordtail male

Marigold swordtail hybrids

Marigold swordtails

Albino swordtail male

Brick red lyretail swordtails, male on right

Albino golden hifin swordtail male

Albino lyretail swordtail male

Green hifin lyretail swordtail male

Blood red hifin swordtail female

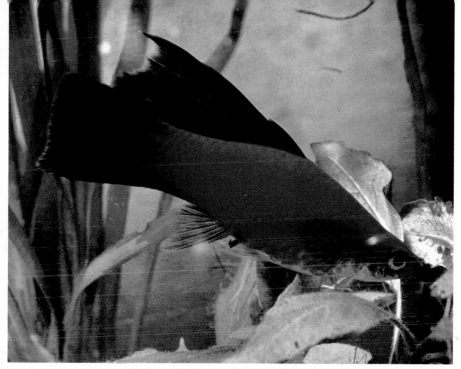

Velvet red hifin wagtail swordtail female

Brick red hifin wag-pintails

Red pineapple swordtail male

Red tuxedo swordtails

Black lyretail hi-fin swordtail

GUPPIES

Lots of books and articles have been written about guppies. Their care comes down to the best general care for all fishes: change the water as often as possible; a change of 10% of the water per day with good aged water is best. Feedings of live foods (brine shrimp is best) twice a day supplemented with a good dry food are highly recommended. Actually, guppies like to feed continuously, as they do in nature. The more often you can feed them, the better they will grow ... but never feed them more than they will eat in one minute if you feed them more than once a day. Also, if you only feed them once a day (and that is not at all recommended), feed them mainly live foods one day with dry foods the next day. Never feed more than they can clean up in three minutes.

All guppies are the same species, *Poecilia reticulata,* and require about the same basic care: water quality as close to pH 7.0 (neutral) as possible; water temperatures about 75°F.; and good strong light at least 12 hours a day (more light makes them grow faster).

People who read about or hear about a "swordtail" guppy should have some idea of what a swordtail guppy looks like, so the following pages contain photos of many different guppy types covering both color varieties and finnage varieties.

MOLLIES

The mollies (so named because they formerly were in the genus *Mollienesia*) have always enjoyed good sales in the aquarium field, even though they are not really good fishes for beginners. They are in general less hardy than the guppies, platies and swordtails and demand more from their owners by way of tank space and the provision of steady warm temperatures.

The mollies are of course closely related to the guppy, being in the same genus, but they look even more like (and are more closely related to) some of the other *Poecilia* species. There are three molly species regularly available: the sailfin molly, *Poecilia latipinna,* which ranges along the southeast coast of the United States and along the Gulf of Mexico; the Yucatan sailfin molly, *Poecilia velifera;* and the sphenops molly, *Poecilia sphenops,* which does not have the beautiful huge dorsal fin that males of the other two species possess but is easier to keep than they are.

Half-black AOC delta

Half-black blue delta

Half-black AOC delta

Half-black red deltas

Black spadetail

Black lower swordtail

Red bicolor veiltail

Blue delta

Common roundtail   Common spadetail

AOC bicolor delta flagtail   Red bicolor delta flagtail

Half-black red delta flagtail   Red veiltail
Red bicolor delta fantail   Green delta fantail

AOC bicolor delta   Red delta

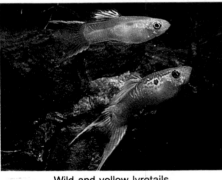

Common roundtail   Half-black pastel delta

Wild and yellow lyretails   Red delta
Varigated snakeskin delta   Yellow bannertail

Red delta fantail

Bronze veiltails

Common roundtail

Red bicolor delta

Common roundtail

Blue delta fantail

AOC bicolor delta flagtail

Red bicolor delta flagtail

513

Half-black red flagtail   Half-black blue veiltail

Purple delta flagtail   Black delta fantail

Solid delta flagtail   Black delta fantail
Purple veiltail   Half-black AOC delta

514

Red veiltail

Bronze veiltails

AOC bicolor delta

Gold snakeskin top swordtail

Bluc single swordtail

Black delta fantail

Yellow delta fantail

Lyretail

515

Yellow lyretail

Bronze common guppies

Wild single swordtail

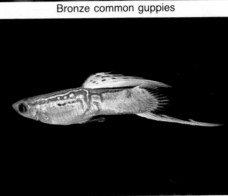

Wild single swordtail

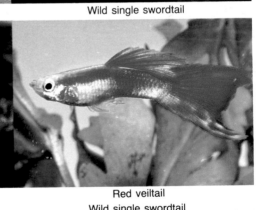

Black lower swordtail
Blue single swordtail

Red veiltail
Wild single swordtail

Wild single swordtails

Wild double swordtail

Wild double swordtail

Wild double swordtail

Yellow lyretail
Blue spadetail

Yellow lyretail
Blue crowntail

Blue-green female

Half-black AOC female

Gold flagtail female giving birth

Common male lyretail

Blue-green female

Half-black AOC female

Female yellow common roundtails

Bronze female

Poecilia latipinna (Black)

Poecilia latipinna (Marbled)

Poecilia latipinna (Balloon Molly)

519

Poecilia velifera

Poecilia latipinna (Albino)

Poecilia latipinna (Starburst)

Poecilia caucana pH7.3;H12;27C;6cm;60L ∿ ⬛ ◑ ♥ 🈂 ▣

Carlhubbsia stuarti pH7.3;H12;26C;6cm;60L ∿ ⬛ ◑ ♥ 🈂 ▣

Poecilia nigrofasciata pH7.2;H10;27C;6cm;60L ∿ ⬛ ◑ ♥ 🈂 ▣

521

Poecilia melanogaster pH7.3;H10;24C;6.5cm;60L 〜🐟 ◑ ♥ 🖾 🖾

Poecilia nigrofasciata pH7.2;H10;27C;6cm;60L 〜🐟 ◑ ♥ 🖾 🖾

Quintana atrizona pH7.2;H10;25C;3cm;40L ♀ 🐟 ◑ ♥ 🖾 🖾

Gambusia sexradiata pH7.6;H14;26C;6.5cm;80L

Poecilia melanogaster pH7.3;H10;24C;6.5cm;60L

Poecilia melanogaster pH7.3;H10;24C;6.5cm;60L

Brachyrhaphis rhabdophora pH7.2;H10;26C;5cm;50L 〜 ➤ ◐ ✕ 𝕎 ⊡

Poecilia ornata pH7.2;H10;26C;6cm;60L 〜 ➤ ♥ 𝕎 ⊡

Gambusia sp. pH7.4;H13;26C;7.5cm;60L ♀ ➤ ◐ ✕ 𝕎 ⊡

Gambusia marshi pH7.4;H15;28C;3cm;20L ♀ 🐟 ◐ ✖ 🖼 ▭

Gambusia puncticulata yucatana pH7.5;H15;27C;4cm;50L ♀ 🐟 ◐ ✖ 🖼 ▭

Poecilia melanogaster pH7.3;H10;24C;6.5cm;60L 〰 🐟 ◐ ♥ 🖼 ▭

525

Girardinus metallicus pH7.4;H14;26C;7.5cm;75L ♀ ➥ ◖ ♥ 🐌 ▭

Brachyrhaphis episcopi pH7.4;H14;27C;3cm;20L ♀ ➥ ◑ ⚔ 🐌 ▭

526   *Poecilia dominicensis* pH7.5;H12;28C;6cm;50L ♀ ➥ ◑ ⚔ 🐌 ▭

Priapichthys chocoensis pH7.2;H10;25C;4cm;40L 〜 ➤ ◑ ♥ 〰 ⊟

Priapella intermedia pH7.0;H10;25C;5cm;50L ♀ ➤ ◑ ♥ 〰 ⊟

Phallichthys pittieri pH7.3;H14;25C;10cm;75L ♀ ➤ ◑ ♥ 〰 ⊟

Priapella intermedia pH7.0;H10;25C;5cm;50L

Phallichthys amates pH7.3;H12;23C;7cm;60L

Phalloceros caudomaculatus pH7.3;H10;25C;6cm;60L

Jenynsia lineata pH7.2;H10;23C;10cm;60L 〜 ➤ ✕ ⍩ ▣

Belonesox belizanus pH7.5;H12;25C;20cm;200L 〜 ➤ ◐ ✕ ⍩ ▭

Girardinus metallicus pH7.4;H14;26C;7.5cm;75L ⚲ ➤ ◐ ♥ ⍩ ▭

529

Alfaro cultratus pH7.2;H10;27C;10cm;100L ∿ ➤ ◑ ♥ 🌳 ⊟

Belonesox belizanus pH7.5;H12;25C;20cm;200L ↘ ➤ ◑ ✕ 🌳 ☐

Girardinus metallicus pH7.4;H14;26C;7.5cm;75L ♀ ➤ ◑ ♥ 🌳 ☐

530

Ameca splendens pH7.1;H10;25C;9cm;75L ⌇ ⮞ ◑ ♥ 📺 ⊡

Ilyodon sp. "Black Band" pH7.3;H12;23C;5cm;50L ⌇ ⮞ ◑ ♥ 📺 ⊡

Allodontichthys tamazulae pH7.3;H14;27C;6cm;80L ♀ ⮞ ◑ ✻ 📺 ⊡

Ameca splendens pH7.1;H10;25C;9cm;75L ⌇ ➤ ◐ ♥ 💹 🔲

Xenoophorus captivus pH7.3;H12;23C;4.5cm;60L ♀ ➤ ◐ ♥ 💹 🔲

Xenotoca eiseni pH7.0;H10;26C;8cm;75L ⌇ ➤ ◐ ♥ 💹 🔲

Xenoophorus captivus pH7.3;H12;23C;4.5cm;60L ♀ 🐟 ◑ ♥ 🖼 🖼

Xenotoca melanosoma pH7.0;H10;26C;8cm;75L ∿ 🐟 ◑ ♥ 🖼 🖼

Xenotoca eiseni pH7.0;H10;26C;8cm;75L ∿ 🐟 ◑ ♥ 🖼 🖼

533

Ilyodon sp. "Black Band" pH7.3;H12;23C;5cm;50L ⌇ ➤ ◑ ♥ ☯ ☰

Xenotoca eiseni pH7.0;H10;26C;8cm;75L ⌇ ➤ ◑ ♥ ☯ ☰

Anableps anableps pH7.5;H14;24C;30cm;100L ⌇ ➤ ◑ ✻ ☯ ☐

534

Dermogenys pusillus pH7.5;H12;26C;7cm;80L ⬿ ➡ ◑ ✗ 𝖜 ▱

Nomorhamphus liemi pH7.5;H12;27C;10cm;100L ⬿ ➡ ✗ 𝖜 ▱

Xenentodon cancila pH7.0;H8;27C;30cm;200L ⬿ ➡ ◑ ✗ 𝖜 ▱

535

Hemirhamphodon chrysopunctatus pH7.4;H13;26C;15cm;200L ↘ ➤ ◑ ✕ ☒ ☐

Xenentodon cancila pH7.0;H8;27C;30cm;200L ↘ ➤ ◑ ✕ ☒ ☐

Nomorhamphus liemi pH7.5;H12;27C;10cm;100L ↘ ➤ ✕ ☒ ☐

BARBS AND MINNOWS—
THE CYPRINIDAE

It is sometimes hard for the hobbyist to realize that such varied fishes as the koi, barbs, goldfish, danios, rasboras, and American minnows could belong to a single family, but the large family Cyprinidae includes all these types plus many more that are seldom seen by aquarists. Although related to the catfishes and tetras, barbs lack an adipose fin. The jaws are usually weak and toothless, but there are special pharyngeal teeth located near the gills that serve to tear and grind the food. Barbels are often present at the corners of the mouth. The dorsal and anal fins are usually short and lack spines or have at best a spiny ray at the beginning of the fin. Most cyprinids are silvery to tan fishes of medium size, although many exceed two feet in length. With few exceptions, they are egg-scatterers.

As far as aquarists are concerned, cyprinids fall into two large and mostly non-overlapping groups—warm-water species and cold-water species. The cold-water species include a multitude of small to large fishes, many of which are adaptable to ornamental ponds and unheated aquaria. The most familiar cold-water species are certainly the goldfish (*Carassius auratus*) and the koi (*Cyprinus carpio*, a cultivated variety of the common carp). Both these species have adapted well to pond and large aquarium cultivation throughout the world and are now available in dozens and dozens of colors and body forms. Also popular in some areas as pond fishes are the European ide (*Leuciscus idus*) and its cultivated variety, the orfe. Other European cyprinids that are cultivated in ponds, especially in England, include the rudd (*Scardineus*), the tench (*Tinca*), and gudgeons (*Gobio*). All these fishes are natives of Europe and western Asia, and they have on the whole not done well in American ponds (the goldfish and carp excluded, of course).

The American minnows of the genera *Notropis*, *Pimephales*, and *Campostoma* are often kept in unheated aquaria, where they make interesting if not especially spectacular pets. The main problem with these little fishes is that males are only in spawning color for a few weeks—the rest of the year they are usually just silvery fishes.

Aquarists know dozens of common species of warm-water cyprinids from Africa and, especially, southern Asia. The most common are the barbs, which aquarium literature splits into three genera, *Puntius, Barbodes,* and *Capoeta.* They are very closely related to the much larger, fine-scaled barbels of Europe and cooler parts of Asia, genus *Barbus.* In fact, many ichthyologists now believe that almost all barbs—regardless of size and number of scales—should be referred to *Barbus.* There are probably as many species of barbs in Africa as in southern Asia, but few African barbs have become common in the hobby—their water requirements are often too unusual to make them community tank fishes.

The danios (*Danio* and *Brachydanio*) are brightly colored constantly-swimming little fishes with long barbels. Like the rasboras (*Rasbora* and *Parluciosoma*), there are numerous species found from India to Malaysia and adjacent areas, but only a few species are really common in the hobby. White clouds (*Tanichthys*) are perhaps the most colorful of the common cyprinids, but their very small size has prevented them from becoming as popular as they deserve. The new long-finned variety gives a "larger impression" in the aquarium and may become more popular if ever bred in quantity.

The freshwater sharks are relatively large, streamlined cyprinids belonging mostly to three genera—*Morulius* (the black shark), *Labeo* (the more common Asian and African sharks), and *Balantiocheilos* (the Bala shark). Supposedly the slender body, rather pointed head, and high dorsal fin make these attractive fishes shark-like, thus the common name. *Luciosoma,* the Apollo sharks, are often prettily colored species that come in mixed with other sharks.

We cannot hope to even mention here most of the cyprinids available to the hobby. Every shipment from Southeast Asia is likely to contain a few oddballs of uncommon genera that even specialists have trouble identifying. In fact, many advanced hobbyists consider this part of the fun of aquarium keeping, searching out the really unusual cyprinids as they come in to the wholesalers. Unfortunately, many cyprinids grow too large to spawn in the aquarium, so they never become established no matter how pretty or interesting.

Barbodes guirali pH6.8;H7;24C;10cm;60L ♀ ➤ ◑ ♥ 🎬 ▣

Barbodes camptacanthus pH6.5;H6;25C;10cm;60l ♀ ➤ ◑ ♥ 🎬 ▣

Barbodes sp. pH8.0;H12;25C;8cm;80L ♀ ➤ ◑ ♥ 🎬 ▣

539

Barbodes camptacanthus pH6.5;H6;25C;10cm;60L ♀ ➤ ◐ ♥ 🎞 ⊟

Barbodes trispilos pH6.7;H6;25C;10cm;60L ♀ ➤ ◐ ♥ 🎞 ⊟

Barbodes arcislongae pH8.0;H12;24C;12cm;100L ♀ ➤ ◐ ♥ 🎞 ⊟

Barbodes fasciolatus pH6.7;H6;25C;10cm;100L ♀ ➤ ◐ ♥ 🖼 ▣

Barbodes trevelyani pH6.8;H6;25C;8cm;80L ♀ ➤ ◐ ♥ 🖼 ▣

Barbodes macrops pH7.0;H8;24C;8cm;80L ♀ ➤ ◐ ♥ 🖼 ▣

Barbodes eutenia pH6.5;H5;26C;10cm;100L ♀ ➤ ◑ ♥ 🎦 🖃

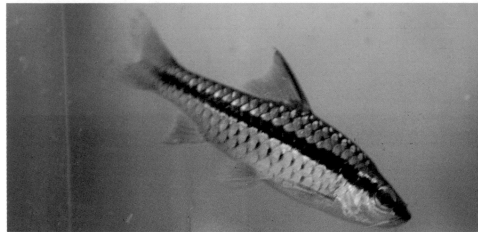

Barbodes nicholsi pH6.8;H6;25C;8cm;80L ♀ ➤ ◑ ♥ 🎦 🖃

Barbodes prionacanthus pH7.0;H8;25C;12cm;100L ♀ ➤ ◑ ♥ 🎦 🖃

Barbodes vivipara pH6.8;H7;26C;10cm;100L ♀ ➤ ◑ ♥ ▦ ▣

Barbodes vivipara pH6.8;H7;26C;10cm;100L ♀ ➤ ◑ ♥ ▦ ▣

Puntius haasianus pH6.3;H4;25C;3cm;40L ∿ ➤ ◑ ♥ ▦ ▣

543

Capoeta hulstaerti pH6.0;H2;25C;2.5cm;40L ◡ ➤ ◐ ♥ ▨ ▣

Puntius sylvaticus pH7.0;H8;26C;6cm;80L ♀ ➤ ◐ ♥ ▨ ▣

Barbodes radiatus aurantiacus pH6.8;H7;26C;10cm;100L ♀ ➤ ◐ ♥ ▨ ▣

Labeo variegatus pH7.3;H8;26C;30cm;?L ♀ ➤ ◐ ✂ ▨ ⊟

Labeo rubropunctatus pH7.5;H10;27C;50cm;400L ♀ ➤ ◐ ♥ ▨ ⊟

Labeo cylindricus pH7.2;H9;26C;70cm;500L ♀ ➤ ◐ ♥ ▨ ⊟

Opsaridium microcephalum pH7.2;H10;25C;10cm;100L ♀ 🐟 ◐ ♥ 🖼 🖃

Opsaridium chrystyi pH7.2;H10;25C;12cm;100L ♀ 🐟 ◐ ♥ 🖼 🖃

Opsaridium ubangense pH7.2;H10;25C;12cm;100L ♀ 🐟 ◐ ♥ 🖼 🖃

Raiamas ansorgii pH7.2;H10;25C;10cm;100L ♀ 🐟 ◐ ♥ 🖼 🖃

Puntius nigrofasciatus pH7.2;H5;26C;6cm;40L ♀ ➤➤ ◐ ♥ 🖼 ⊟

Puntius nigrofasciatus pH7.2;H5;26C;6cm;40L ♀ ➤➤ ◐ ♥ 🖼 ⊟

Capoeta semifasciolatus pH7.0;H5;25C;5cm;40L ♀ ➤➤ ◐ ♥ 🖼 ⊟

Puntius nigrofasciatus pH7.2;H5;26C;6cm;40L ♀ ➤ ◑ ♥ 🖼 ⊟

Capoeta semifasciolatus pH7.0;H5;25C;5cm;40L ♀ ➤ ◑ ♥ 🖼 ⊟

Puntius sachsi pH7.0;H7;26C;8cm;100L ♀ ➤ ◑ ♥ 🖼 ⊟

Capoeta semifasciolatus pH7.0;H5;25C;5cm;40L ♀ ➤ ◑ ♥ 🖼 🖻

Barbodes lateristriga pH7.2;H6;25C;20cm;200L ♀ ➤ ◑ ♥ 🖼 🖻

Capoeta tetrazona pH6.5;H3;27C;8cm;80L ♀ ➤ ◑ ♥ 🖼 🖻   549

Capoeta tetrazona pH6.5;H3;27C;8cm;80L ♀ ➤ ◐ ♥ 🎞 🖼

Capoeta tetrazona pH6.5;H3;27C;8cm;80L ♀ ➤ ◐ ♥ 🎞 🖼

Capoeta tetrazona pH6.5;H3;27C;8cm;80L ♀ ➤ ◐ ♥ 🎞 🖼

Capoeta tetrazona pH6.5;H3;27C;8cm;80L ♀ 🐟 ◑ ♥ 🎞 🖼

Capoeta tetrazona pH6.5;H3;27C;8cm;80L ♀ 🐟 ◑ ♥ 🎞 🖼

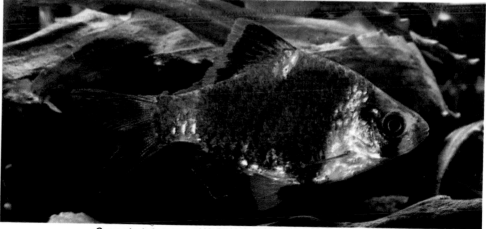

Capoeta tetrazona pH6.5;H3;27C;8cm;80L ♀ 🐟 ◑ ♥ 🎞 🖼

551

Puntius conchonius pH7;H6;26C;15cm;80L ♀ ➤ ◑ ♥ 🏞 ⊟

Puntius conchonius pH7;H6;26C;15cm;80L ♀ ➤ ◑ ♥ 🏞 ⊟

Puntius conchonius pH7;H6;26C;15cm;80L ♀ ➤ ◑ ♥ 🏞 ⊟

Puntius cummingi pH6.8;H5;27C;10cm;100L ♀ ➤ ◐ ♥ 🖼 ⬚

Puntius conchonius pH7;H6;26C;15cm;80L ♀ ➤ ◐ ♥ 🖼 ⬚

Puntius conchonius pH7;H6;26C;15cm;80L ♀ ➤ ◐ ♥ 🖼 ⬚

553

Puntius conchonius pH7;H6;26C;15cm;80L ♀ ➤ ◑ ♥ 🖼 🖾

Capoeta arulius pH6.8;H6;26C;12cm;150L ♀ ➤ ◑ ♥ 🖼 🖾

Puntius sachsi pH7.0;H7;26C;8cm;100L ♀ ➤ ◑ ♥ 🖼 🖾

Capoeta arulius pH6.8;H6;26C;12cm;150L ♀ ➤ ◑ ♥ 🖼 🖼

Capoeta titteya pH6.6;H5;28C;4cm;40L ♀ ➤ ◑ ♥ 🖼 🖼

Puntius lineatus pH6.8;H5;25C;6cm;80L ♀ ➤ ◑ ♥ 🖼 🖼

Puntius bimaculatus pH6.8;H5;26C;17cm;300L ♀ 🐟 ◑ ✕ 🎞 ▣

Puntius sp. "Odessa Barb" pH7.2;H10;24C;15cm;200L ♀ 🐟 ◑ ♥ 🎞 ▣

Puntius filamentosus pH7.0;H8;25C;13cm;150L ♀ 🐟 ◑ ♥ 🎞 ▣

Capoeta oligolepis pH7.1;H7;26C;5cm;40L ♀ ⮞ ◐ ♥ 🖼 ⊟

Puntius llneatus pH6.8;H5;25C;6cm;80L ♀ ⮞ ◐ ♥ 🖼 ⊟

Barbodes pentazona pH6.8;H4;26C;5cm;40L ♀ ⮞ ◐ ♥ 🖼 ⊟   557

Barbodes pentazona hexazona pH6.8;H4;26C;5cm;40L ♀ 🐟 ◑ ♥ 🖼 🔳

Barbodes pentazona rhomboocellatus pH6.8;H4;26C;5cm;40L ♀ 🐟 ◑ ♥ 🖼 🔳

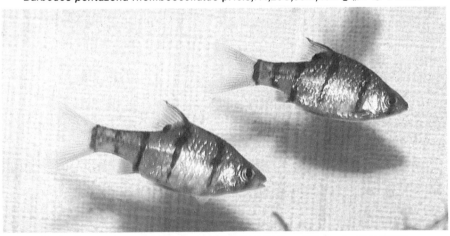

Barbodes pentazona pentazona pH6.8;H4;26C;5cm;40L ♀ 🐟 ◑ ♥ 🖼 🔳

Barbodes schwanenfeldi pH6.8;H5;25C;40cm;400L ♀ 🐟 ◑ ♥ 🖼

Barbodes lasciatus pH6.5;H5;26C;15cm;100L ♀ 🐟 ◑ ♥ 🖼 🖼

Barbodes everetti pH6.8;H6;28C;10cm;80L ♀ 🐟 ◑ ♥ 🖼 🖼

559

Barbodes schwanenfeldi pH6.8;H5;25C;40cm;400L ♀ ➤ ◑ ♥ ⊟

Barbodes daruphani pH7.0;H15;25C;15cm;150L ♀ ➤ ◑ ♥ ▦ ⊟

Barbodes everetti pH6.8;H6;28C;10cm;80L ♀ ➤ ◑ ♥ ▦ ⊟

Chela dadyburjori pH6.8;H5;27C;4cm;40L ♀ ⤙ ◑ ♥ 🎦 ⊟

Chela sp. pH7.0;H8;27C;10cm;200L ♀ ⤙ ◑ ♥ 🎦 ⊟

Chela laubuca pH6.8;H5;26C;5cm;40L ⌇ ⤙ ◑ ♥ 🎦 ⊟

561

Chela caeruleostigmata pH6.8;H5;28C;5cm;80L ♀ 🗲 ◑ ♥ 🖼 🖂

Chela laubuca pH6.8;H5;26C;5cm;40L ◡ 🗲 ◑ ♥ 🖼 🖂

Chela fasciata pH6.8;H5;26C;6cm;40L ◡ 🗲 ♥ 🖼 🖂

Esomus metallicus pH7.0;H8;25C;10cm;100L ⌇ 🐟 ◑ ♥ 🖼 ▣

Esomus danricus pH6.8;H5;24C;13cm;150L ⌇ 🐟 ◑ ♥ 🖼 ▣

Rasbora brittani pH6.6;H5;27C;5cm;40L ♀ 🐟 ◑ ♥ 🖼 ▣

Rasbora vaterifloris pH6.5;H5;25C;5cm;80L ♀ 🐟 ◑ ♥ 🖼 ▣

Rasbora borapetensis pH6.8;H6;24C;4cm;40L ♀ 🐟 ◑ ♥ 🖼 ▣

Rasbora urophthalma pH6.8;H5;26C;4cm;40L ♀ 🐟 ◑ ♥ 🖼 ▣

Rasbora pauciperforata pH7.0;H8;24C;4cm;80L ♀ ⇀ ◑ ♥ 🖼 ▣

Rasbora agilis pH7.0;H8;25C;5cm;40L ♀ ⇀ ◑ ♥ 🖼 ▣

Rasbora maculata pH6.5;H3;25C;2cm;40L ♀ ⇀ ◑ ♥ 🖼 ▣

Rasbora heteromorpha espei pH6.5;H3;26C;5cm;40L ♀ ➤ ◐ ♥ ⊟

Rasbora heteromorpha pH6.5;H3;26C;5cm;40L ♀ ➤ ◐ ♥ ▤ ⊟

Rasbora elegans pH6.8;H6;27C;13cm;200L ♀ ➤ ♥ ▤ ⊟

566

Rasbora trilineata pH6.5;H3;26C;10cm;100L ♀ 🐟 ◑ ♥ 🖼 🔲

Rasbora caudimaculata pH6.8;H5;27C;8cm;100L ♀ 🐟 ◑ ♥ 🖼 🔲

Rasbora myersi pH7.0;H8;27C;15cm;200L ♀ 🐟 ◑ ♥ 🖼 🔲

567

Rasbora trilineata pH6.5;H3;26C;10cm;100L ♀ ➤ ◐ ♥ ▧ ▤

Rasbora dorsiocellata pH7.0;H8;27C;6cm;80L ♀ ➤ ◐ ♥ ▧ ▤

Rasbora somphongsi pH6.6;H4;27C;3cm;40L ♀ ➤ ◐ ♥ ▧ ▤

Brachydanio nigrofasciatus pH7.0;H8;26C;5cm;40L ♀ 🐟 ◐ ♥ 🖼 ⊟

Brachydanio rerio pH7.0;H8;27C;5cm;40L ♀ 🐟 ◐ ♥ 🖼 ⊟

Brachydanio rerio pH7.0;H8;27C;5cm;40L ♀ 🐟 ◐ ♥ 🖼 ⊟

569

Danio malabaricus pH7.2;H8;27C;10cm;100L ♀ ⟩➤ ◑ ♥ ▣

Brachydanio albolineatus pH7.2;H8;27C;5cm;40L ♀ ⟩➤ ◑ ♥ ▤ ▣

Brachydanio kerri pH7.0;H8;26C;5cm;40L ♀ ⟩➤ ◑ ♥ ▤ ▣

Danio aequipinnatus pH7.0;H8;27C;10cm;100L ♀ ➤ ◑ ♥ 🖼 ▱

Danio malabaricus pH7.0;H8;27C;10cm;100L ♀ ➤ ◑ ♥ 🖼 ▱

Brachydanio frankei pH7.0;H8;27C;5cm;40L ♀ ➤ ◑ ♥ 🖼 ▱

Barbichthys laevis pH7.3;H8;27C;30cm;400L ♀ 🐟 ◐ ♥ 🖼 ▣

Labeo bicolor pH7.5;H10;26C;12cm;200L ♀ 🐟 ◐ ♥ 🖼 ▣

Labeo erythrurus pH7.5;H10;27C;12cm;200L ♀ 🐟 ◐ ♥ 🖼 ▣

Balantiocheilos melanopterus pH7.1;H8;26C;36cm;500L ♀ ➤ ◑ ♥ 🖼 🖭

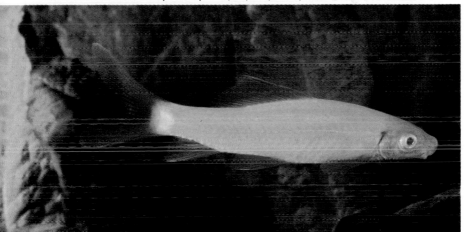

Labeo frenatus pH7.5;H10;27C;12cm;200L ♀ ➤ ◑ ♥ 🖼 🖭

Morulius chrysophekadion pH7.5;H10;27C;60cm;800L ♀ ➤ ◑ ♥ 🖼 🖭

Epalzeorhynchus kalopterus pH7.2;H10;25C;14cm;150L ♀ 🗲 ◑ ♥ 🎞 ⬜

Gyrinocheilus aymonieri pH7.3;H11;26C;13cm;150L ⚘ 🗲 ◑ ♥ 🎞 ⬜

Gyrinocheilus aymonieri pH7.3;H11;26C;13cm;150L ⚘ 🗲 ◑ ♥ 🎞 ⬜

Tanichthys albonubes pH7.2;H8;18C;4cm;40L ♀ ➤ ◑ ♥ 🖼 ⊟

Tanichthys albonubes pH7.2;H8;18C;4cm;40L ♀ ➤ ◑ ♥ 🖼 ⊟

Tanichthys albonubes pH7.2;H8;18C;4cm;40L ♀ ➤ ◑ ♥ 🖼 ⊟

Notropis welaka pH6.7;H6;20C;6.5cm;75L ⌇ ➤ ◐ ♥ ⊠ ▤

Notropis cornutus pH7.5;H12;20C;20cm;75L ⌇ ➤ ◐ ♥ ▣ ▭

Notropis atherinoides pH7.5;H12;18C;8.5cm;500L ⌇ ➤ ◐ ♥ ▭ ▤

Notropis hypselopterus pH6.5;H8;20C;8cm;75L ♀ 🐟 ○ ♥ 🖼 🗒

Notropis lutrensis pH7.5;H12;20C;7.6cm;100L ∿ 🐟 ◑ ♥ 🖼 🖼

Phoxinus erythrogaster pH8;H14;20C;8cm;50L ∿ 🐟 ○ ♥ 🖼 🗒

Leuciscus idus pH7.5;H12;18C;35cm;400L ⌇ ➤ ◑ ♥ 🖼 ⬛

Leuciscus cephalus pH7.5;H12;18C;60cm;400L ⌇ ➤ ◑ ✕ 🖼 ⬛

Chondrostoma nasus pH7.3;H10;18C;50cm;250L ⌇ ➤ ◑ ♥ 📷 ⬛

Phoxinus phoxinus pH7.0;H10;18C;12cm;100L 〜 ➤ ◐ ♥ ▦ ▣

Rhodeus sericeus pH6.8;H8;18C;9.5cm;75L 〜 ➤ ◐ ♥ ▦ ▭

Chondrostoma nasus pH7.3;H10;18C;50cm;250L ➴ ➤ ◐ ♥ ▦ ▭

579

Phoxinus phoxinus pH7.0;H10;18C;12cm;100L 〰 🐟 ◑ ♥ 🖼 ▭

Scardineus erythrophthalmus pH7.0;H10;18C;20cm;200L 〰 🐟 ◑ ♥ 🖼 ▭

Vimba vimba pH8.0;H12;16C;50cm;200L 〰 🐟 ◑ ♥ 🖼 ▭

Leucaspius delineatus pH7.0;H12;15C;10cm;50L ❀ ➤ ◐ ♥ 🖼 ⊟

Scardineus erythrophthalmus pH7.0;H10;18C;20cm;200L ∿ ➤ ◐ ♥ 🖼 ▭

Rutilus rutilus pH7.0;H12;16C;34cm;100L ❀ ➤ ◐ ♥ 🖼 ⊟

Gnathopogon chankaensis pH7.5;H12;18C;9cm;100L

Ctenopharyngodon idella pH7.5;H12;18C;1m;1000L

Carassius carassius pH7.6;H12;18C;30cm;200L

Barbus barbus pH7.0;H12;20C;80cm;200L ♀ ➤ ◐ ♥ 🖾 ⊡

Tinca tinca pH6.7;H8;18C;63cm;200L ∿ ➤ ◐ ♥ 🖾 ▭

Carassius carassius pH7.6;H12;18C;30cm;200L ∿ ➤ ◐ ♥ 🖾 ⊡

Gobio gobio pH7.0;H10;18C;15cm;100L 〜 🐟 ◐ ♥ 🖼 ▭

Tinca tinca pH6.7;H8;18C;63cm;200L 〜 🐟 ◐ ♥ 🖼 ▭

Blicca bjoerkna pH7.3;H10;18C;8cm;75L ♀ 🐟 ◐ ♥ 🖼 ▣

Rhodeus sericeus pH6.8;H8;18C;9cm;75L ⌒ ➤ ◑ ♥ 🖼 ▭

Tinca tinca pH6.7;H8;18C;63cm;200L ⌒ ➤ ◑ ♥ 🖼 ▭

Chilogobio czerskii pH7.0;H10;16C;11cm;100L ⌒ ➤ ◑ ♥ 🖼 ▭

Rhodeus ocellatus pH7.0;H10;20C;6cm;75L ∿ ➤ ◑ ♥ 🖼 ▭

Acheilognathus longipinnis pH7.3;H12;20C;8cm;75L ∿ ➤ ◑ ♥ 🖼 ▭

Rhodeus sericeus pH6.8;H8;18C;9cm;75L ∿ ➤ ◑ ♥ 🖼 ▭

Rhodeus ocellatus pH7.0;H10;20C;6cm;75L ⌁ ⍥ ◐ ♥ 🎞 ▭

Rhodeus ocellatus pH7.0;H10;20C;6cm;75L ⌁ ⍥ ◐ ♥ 🎞 ▭

Rhodeus suigensis pH7.0;H10;20C;4cm;50L ⌁ ⍥ ◐ ♥ 🎞 ▭

Tanakia tanago pH7.0;H10;20C;5cm;100L ⌇ ➤ ◑ ♥ 🖼 ▭

Acheilognathus lanceolata pH7.2;H10;20C;8cm;100L ⌇ ➤ ◑ ♥ 🖼 ▭

Acheilognathus tabira pH7.2;H10;20C;6cm;100L ⌇ ➤ ◑ ♥ 🖼 ▭

KOI,
JAPANESE COLORED CARP

Koi are highly developed forms of the common Carp (*Cyprinus carpio*) in the way that fancy-tail Guppies are highly developed forms of the common Guppy. The Koi is particularly well suited to keep in a garden pool, where its touch of brilliant colors would add a great deal of decorative effect. The Koi was produced by Japanese breeders. The results came in a great variety of color variations, and selective breeding did the rest. At the present time there are many recognized basic varieties, with the possibility of many more to come.

Because of their large size, Koi are basically pool fish and do best in an outdoor environment. They are able to withstand a wide temperature range and are undemanding as to water composition, provided that their water is richly supplied with oxygen.

The Koi illustrated here are identified according to the Japanese names for the particular variety involved. The varieties shown are only a small sampling of the many available.

FANCY GOLDFISH VARIETIES

It seems that the lessened popularity of the common Goldfish has come about as a result of the recognition on the part of hobby newcomers of the advantages the true tropical fishes have over Goldfish. However, warm-water fish tanks within the home have not greatly affected the interest in fancy Goldfish varieties. Really good Goldfish of the hard-to-get varieties are eagerly sought after and command high prices. Unfortunately, not enough hobbyists ever get a chance to see some of the fancier varieties; the excellent Goldfish photos shown here will help to make these products of patient and skillful breeding programs more familiar to everyone.

Goldfish have a wide temperature tolerance, and fish which have been kept outdoors can live under a layer of ice for quite a time. They are also kept successfully in the tropics.

Regardless of type, all Goldfish are the same species, *Carassius auratus*.

Kawari-Mono

Hikari Shiro-Utsuri

Doitsu Ogon

Asagi

Harewake-Ogon or Ogon (Platinum)

Kin Ki-Utsuri

592

Carassius auratus pH7.6;H12;19C;10cm;75L 〜 ➤ ◑ ♥ 🖼 ▦

Pearl Scale

Calico Fantail

Lionhead

Redcap, Tancho or Hon Tou

Bubble-Eye

Chinese Oranda (Hi-Cap)

Albino Oranda

Telescope Black Moor

595

OTHER FAMILIES

In addition to the families already shown and discussed, many other families of fishes contain species that appear in pet shops; some appear regularly, but some appear only sporadically. Some are especially desirable, but some are very poor candidates as aquarium species. Many of them attract attention by their oddness of appearance or habit, others by their reputations. Examples of the former would be the arowanas (*Osteoglossum, Scleropages*), stingrays (*Potamotrygon*), and elephantnoses (*Gnathonemus, Mormyrus, Marcusenius, Mormyrops, Petrocephalus,* etc.), as well as the spiny eels (*Mastacembelus*) and the butterflyfish (*Pantodon*), the polypterids (*Polypterus*), the flounders (*Achirus*), the needlefish (*Potamorraphis*), the glassfishes (*Chanda*), and the Nile perch (*Lates*), among others. An example of the latter category would be the electric eel, *Electrophorus*—fish-keeper or not, you've heard of the electric eel, and you may well have heard of the archer fish, *Toxotes*, as well.

Included in the families that contain species seen on the aquarium market with great regularity would be the puffers (*Tetraodon, Carinotetraodon, Chonerhinus*); the rainbowfishes (*Melanotaenia, Glossolepis*), the monos (*Monodactylus*), the scats (*Scatophagus*), the snakeheads (*Ophicephalus, Channa*), the loaches (*Botia, Acanthophthalmus*), and both the South American (*Gymnotus, Hypopomus, Steatogenys, Eigenmannia, Apteronotus,* etc.) and African (*Notopterus, Xenomystus*) knifefishes, and the gobies (*Brachygobius*), in addition to some of those already mentioned (such as the spiny eels and the elephantnoses).

Among those species that are less frequently seen would be the lungfishes (*Protopterus*), polypterids (*Polypterus*), the nandids (*Polycentrus, Monocirrhus*), and others. Rounding out the list of seldom-seen fishes would be *Pristigaster cayana*, a herring-family (Clupeidae) fish from South American fresh waters.

The fresh waters of the world that remain completely unexplored are dwindling in size all the time, so it is unlikely that entire new families of fishes will be discovered and brought into the aquarium hobby. Yet at the same time new discoveries are made regularly, and for many hobbyists part of the excitement of the tropical fish field is to be able to see the really new fishes that have come onto the market— whether their first acquaintance is made with them in their dealers' tanks or even in a book or magazine.

The fishes listed here often are characterized under the general title of "oddballs," in the sense that they are somehow set apart from the general run of aquarium fish families.

We might define an oddball as a fish which is unbreedable or less colorful or more aggressive than the more regular aquarium species and brought into the market in very limited quantities. Of course there are many oddballs which might not be so termed . . . and there certainly are many highly colorful and peaceful species among them.

Many of the oddballs are fishes which were, in the grand old days before World War II, almost all brought in by boat. Then a sailor could dip his nets into the nearest fresh water to the port of call in which his boat happened to be berthed at the time and, keeping everything small enough to fit into his shipboard aquarium, haul the fish back to Europe or America hoping to make some money with his rare cargo. This was a surprisingly rewarding hobby for many sailors, and it gave them something to do on the long ocean journeys. From this source quite a few brackish water species were often collected, especially from southeast Asia where scats, monodactylids and glassfish were always easy to catch, easy to keep and easy to sell. Sailors that made it to Africa often brought back colorful rivulins and annual fishes which are always to be found in small pools near busy seaports. But as fish collecting got to be a bigger and more organized business and jet aircraft, not ships, became the transportation medium of choice, sailors were replaced by professional collectors; by and large, these professional collectors have done a good job of providing the fish world with new species.

The next time you visit a pet shop and see something which might not be common, and you have an empty tank, buy it. If you can photograph it as it grows and study its habits, what it eats, how it swims, when are its periods of activity . . . then write about it in a suitable aquarium magazine. And don't forget, when it dies, preserve the corpse so you can send it to an ichthyologist and get a proper identification.

Potamotrygon hystrix pH6.7;H8;26C;122cm;400L ∿ ➡ ◑ ♥ ▭ ▭

Potamotrygon motoro pH6.7;H8;26C;100cm;400L ∿ ➡ ◑ ♥ ▭ ▭

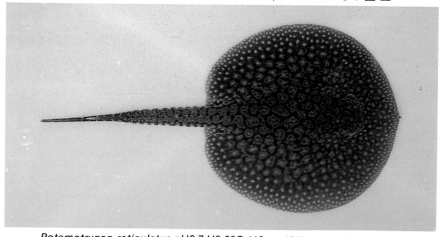

Potamotrygon reticulatus pH6.7;H8;26C;110cm;400L ∿ ➡ ◑ ♥ ▭ ▭

Potamorrhaphis guianensis pH6.8;H5;24C;80cm;400L ⬹ ➤ ◑ ✻ 🎦 ▭

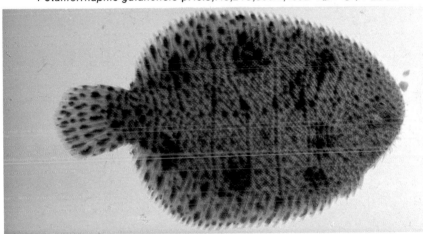

Achirus lineatus pH7.3;H11;25C;13cm;100L ⬳ ➤ ◑ ♥ ▱ ▭

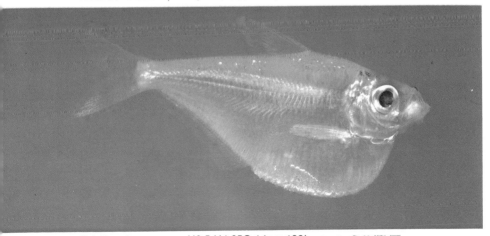

Pristigaster cayana pH6.5;H4;25C;14cm;100L ⬳ ➤ ◑ ♥ 🐚 ▭

599

Osteoglossum ferreirai pH6.5;H6;27C;40cm;200L ↘ ⭢ ◑ ✕ 📺 ▭

Osteoglossum ferreirai pH6.5;H6;27C;40cm;200L ↘ ⭢ ◑ ✕ 📺 ▭

Osteoglossum bicirrhosum pH6.7;H8;25C;60cm;400L ↘ ⭢ ◑ ✕ 📺 ▭

Osteoglossum ferreirai pH6.5;H6;27C;40cm;200L ↘ ➤ ◑ ✕ 🖼 ▭

Osteoglossum ferreirai pH6.5;H6;27C;40cm;200L ↘ ➤ ◑ ✕ 🖼 ▭

Osteoglossum bicirrhosum pH6.7;H8;25C;60cm;400L ↘ ➤ ◑ ✕ 🖼 ▭

Scleropages formosus pH7.0;H8;27C;90cm;800L ↘ 🐟 ◑ ✕ 🔲 ▭

Scleropages formosus pH7.0;H8;27C;90cm;800L ↘ 🐟 ◑ ✕ 🔲 ▭

Scleropages formosus pH7.0;H8;27C;90cm;800L ↘ 🐟 ◑ ✕ 🔲 ▭

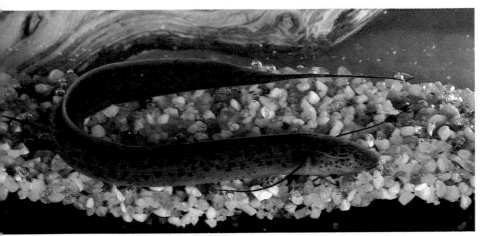

Protopterus dolloi pH7.8;H14;28C;83cm;500L ⬉ 🐟 ◐ ✕ 🖼 ▭

Protopterus aethiopicus pH7.8;H14;27C;140cm;800L ⬉ 🐟 ◐ ✕ 🖼 ▭

Protopterus annectens pH7.5;H12;26C;60cm;400L ⬉ 🐟 ◐ ✕ 🖼 ▭

603

Polypterus ornatipinnis pH7.8;H12;26C;37cm;350L ↘ ➤ ◑ ♥ 🐚 ▤

Polypterus palmas pH8.0;H14;28C;32cm;350L ↘ ➤ ◑ ♥ 🐚 ▤

Polypterus congicus pH8.1;H13;27C;70cm;400L ↘ ➤ ◑ ♥ 🐚 ▤

Gymnotus anguillaris pH7.0;H10;26C;55cm;400L ⬄ ➤ ◐ ✕ 🎞 ▭

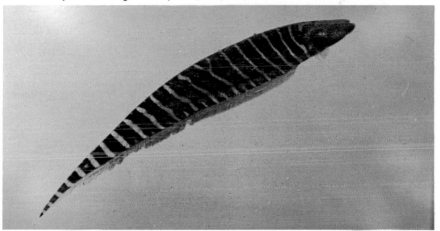

Gymnotus carapo pH6.9;H8;25C;60cm;500L ⬄ ➤ ◐ ✕ 🎞 ▭

Sternarchorhamphus muelleri pH6.8;H9;26C;50cm;500L ⬄ ➤ ◐ ✕ 🎞 ▭

Sternarchorhynchus oxyrhynchus pH6.8;H9;26C;50cm;500L ⬄ ➤ ◐ ✕ 🎞 ▭

Distocyclus conirostris pH6.5;H6;27C;20cm;200L ∿ ➤ ◑ ♥ 🔳 ▢

Hypopomus brevirostris pH7.0;H10;24C;43cm;500L ∿ ➤ ◑ ♥ 🔳 ▢

Sternopygus macrurus pH6.5;H8;26C;50cm;500L ∿ ◑ ♥ 🔳 ▢

Steatogenys duidae pH7.0;H8;27C;20cm;250L ∿ ➤ ◗ ♥ 🎞 ▭

Eigenmannia virescens pH6.9;H10;25C;45cm;500L ∿ ➤ ◗ ✗ 🎞 ▭

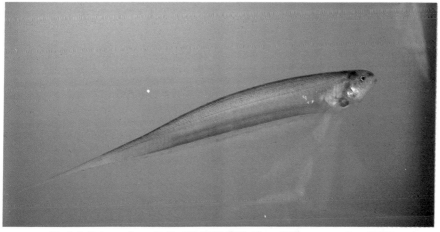

Rhabdolichops troscheli pH6.5;H6;28C;18cm;200L ∿ ➤ ◗ ♥ 🎞 ▭

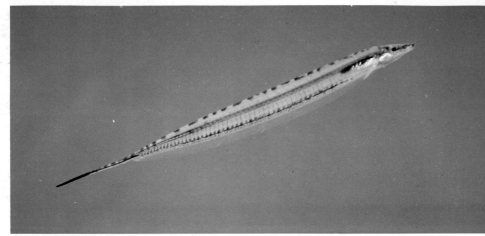

Gymnorhamphichthys rondoni pH6.7;H8;26C;15cm;200L 〜 ➤ ◑ ♥ 🎦 🖵

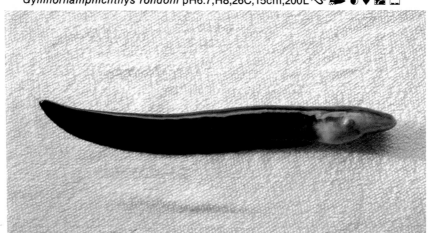

Electrophorus electricus pH6.8;H8;25C;1.8m;1000L 〜 ➤ ◑ ✕ 🎦 🖵

Apteronotus albifrons pH6.6;H7;26C;47cm;500L 〜 ➤ ◑ ♥ 🖾 🖵

Apteronotus leptorhynchus pH7.0;H9;27C;26cm;250L 〜 ➤ ◑ ♥ 🐛 ⬜

Polycentrus schomburgki pH7.0;H10;25C;10cm;100L ⬂ ➤ ◐ ✕ 🖼 ⊟

Monocirrhus polyacanthus pH6.5;H7;26C;10cm;100L 〜 ➤ ◐ ✕ 🖼 ⊟

609

Xenomystus nigri pH6.8;H6;26C;20cm;100L 〜 ➤ ◑ ♥ 🌿 ▱

Phractolaemus ansorgei pH7.0;H8;25C;16cm;80L 〜 ➤ ◑ ♥ 🌿 ▱

Pantodon buchholzi pH6.5;H3;26C;10cm;60L 〜 ➤ ◑ ♥ 🌿 ▱

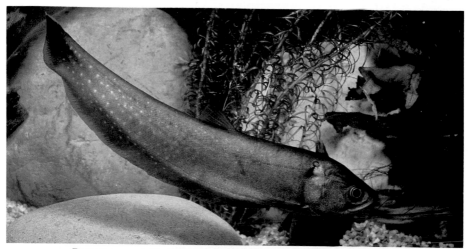

Papyrocranus afer pH6.3;H3;26C;60cm;250L ⌇ ➤ ◐ ♥ 🖼 ▭

Gnathonemus petersii pH6.8;H6;26C;23cm;100L ⌇ ➤ ◐ ♥ 🖼 ▭

Campylomormyrus cassaicus pH7.2;H10;24C;25cm;120L ⌇ ➤ ◐ ♥ 🖼 ▭

611

Pollimyrus castelnaui pH8.0;H0;24C;8cm;80L 〰 ➤ ◗ ♥ 🖼 ⬜

Campylomormyrus cassaicus pH7.2;H10;24C;25cm;120L 〰 ➤ ◗ ♥ 🖼 ⬜

Gnathonemus petersii pH6.8;H6;26C;23cm;100L 〰 ➤ ◗ ♥ 🖼 ⬜

Petrocephalus simus pH7.5;H12;28C;12cm;80L ∿ ⋙ ◑ ♥ 🖼 ▭

Pollimyrus nigripinnis pH8.1;H14;27C;11cm;80L ∿ ⋙ ◑ ♥ 🖼 ▭

Marcusensis angolensis pH8.0;H14;28C;14cm;80L ∿ ⋙ ◑ ♥ 🖼 ▭

Campylomormyrus rhynchophorus pH6.8;H10;28C;12cm;0L ⌒ ➤ ◗ ♥ 🎞 ⬜

Mormyrops engystoma pH7.0;H8;25C;35cm;200L ⌒ ➤ ◗ ♥ 🎞 ⬜

Mormyrops boulengeri pH6.9;H7;28C;35cm;200L ⌒ ➤ ◗ ♥ 🎞 ⬜

Mormyrus longirostris pH7.0;H8;29C;30cm;150L ∿ ⋙ ◖ ♥ 🎞 ☐

Brienomyrus brachyistlus pH6.8;H4;29C;8cm;80L ∿ ⋙ ◖ ♥ 🎞 ☐

Gymnarchus niloticus pH6.8;H6;25C;150cm;800L ∿ ⋙ ◖ ♥ 🎞 ☐

Channa micropeltes pH7.0;H8;26C;100cm;4000L ↘ 🐟 ◐ ✂ 🖼 ⊟

Channa striatus pH7.0;H8;27C;100cm;4000L ↘ 🐟 ◐ ✂ 🖼 ⊟

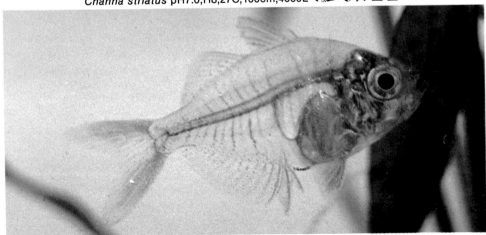

Chanda baculis pH7.5;H12;28C;5cm;40L ↝ 🐟 ◐ ♥ 🖼 ⊟

Channa argus pH7.0;H8;24C;40cm;500L ↘🐟 ◑✄ ▨ ⊡

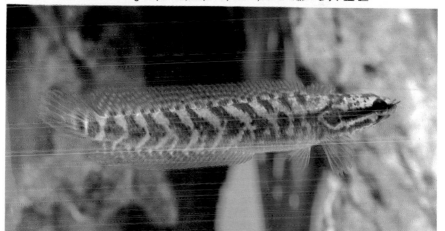

Channa striatus pH7.0;H8;27C;100cm;400L ↘🐟 ◑✄ ▨ ⊡

Chanda ranga pH7.8;H14;26C;6cm;40L ↘🐟 ◑♥ ▨ ⊡

Scatophagus argus pH7.9;H20;28C;33cm;400L ♀ ➤ ◑ ✕ 🖼 ⊡

Scatophagus tetracanthus pH7.9;H20;28C;33cm;400L ♀ ➤ ◑ ✕ 🖼 ⊡

Scatophagus argus pH7.9;H20;28C;33cm;400L ♀ ➤ ◑ ✕ 🖼 ⊡

Datnioides microlepis pH7.0;H8;26C;38cm;400L ᵔᵔ ᵔᵔ ◑ ✕ 🖼 ▣

Monodactylus argenteus pH7.2;H10;25C;23cm;250L ᵔᵔ ᵔᵔ ◑ ♥ 🖼 ▣

Toxotes jaculator pH7.5;H12;28C;15cm;200L ᵔᵔ ᵔᵔ ◑ ♥ 🖼 ▢

Badis badis badis pH7.0;H8;26C;8cm;80L ⌇ ➤ ◑ ♥ 🖼 ▭

Badis badis burmanicus pH7.0;H8;25C;6cm;80L ⌇ ➤ ◑ ♥ 🖼 ▭

Badis badis badis pH7.0;H8;26C;8cm;80L ⌇ ➤ ◑ ♥ 🖼 ▭

Sicyopterus halei pH7.3;H12;21C;15cm;200L 〜 ➤ ◑ ♥ 🖼 🖵

Parapocryptes serperaster pH7.2;H12;27C;25cm;300L 〜 ➤ ◑ ♥ 🖼 🖵

Brachygobius doriae pH7.4;H12;27C;3cm;40L 〜 ➤ ◑ ♥ 🖼 🖵

621

Stigmatogobius sadanundio pH7.2;H10;26C;9cm;100L 〜 ➤ ◑ ♥ 🖼 ▭

Awaous grammepomus pH7.5;H12;27C;15cm;200L 〜 ➤ ◑ ♥ 🖼 ▭

Periophthalmus barbarus pH7.0;H12;26C;15cm;250L 〜 ➤ ◑ ♥ 🖼 ▭

Periophthalmus papilio pH7.7;H15;27C;16cm;200L ᔓ ➤ ◑ ♥ 🖼 ▭

Periophthalmus vulgaris pH7.8;H15;28C;15cm;200L ᔓ ➤ ◑ ♥ 🖼 ▭

Periophthalmus vulgaris pH7.8;H15;28C;15cm;200L ᔓ ➤ ◑ ♥ 🖼 ▭

Lates niloticus pH7.5;H13;27C;180cm;1000L ⌐ ➤ ◑ ✕ ▨ ▣

Lates microlepis pH8.0;H17;28C;85cm;1000L ⌐ ➤ ◑ ✕ ▨ ▣

Glossogobius giuris pH7.8;H12;28C;35cm;400L ♀ ➤ ◑ ✕ ▨ ▣

624

Macrognathus siamensis pH6.7;H7;28C;25cm;200L ᔧ ➤ ◑ ♥ 🖼 🖵

Mastacembelus circumcinctus pH7.1;H8;27C;20cm;200L ᔧ ➤ ◑ ♥ 🖼 🖵

Mastacembelus "Smith" pH7.0;H8;27C;15cm;100L ᔧ ➤ ◑ ♥ 🖼 🖵

Mastacembelus armatus pH7.0;H8;26C;76cm;400L ⌇ 🐟 ◑ ♥ 🖼 ▭

Mastacembelus circumcinctus pH7.1;H8;27C;20cm;200L ⌇ 🐟 ◑ ♥ 🖼 ▭

Mastacembelus armatus pH7.0;H8;26C;76cm;400L ⌇ 🐟 ◑ ♥ 🖼 ▭

Afromastacembelus moorii pH7.5;H15;28C;16cm;100L ∿ ➤ ◑ ♥ 🖾 🖵

Afromastacembelus ophidium pH7.0;H8;27C;10cm;100L ∿ ➤ ◑ ♥ 🖾 🖵

Afromastacembelus tanganicae pH7.8;H16;28C;15cm;200L ∿ ➤ ◑ ♥ 🖾 🖵

Colomesus asellus pH7.2;H10;26C;15cm;100L ⤳ 🐟 ◖ ✕ 🖼 ⊟

♀ *Carinotetraodon somphongsi* pH7.3;H10;25C;7cm;80L ⤳ 🐟 ◖ ✕ 🖼 ⊟

Tetraodon fluviatilis pH7.0;H10;25C;12cm;100L ⤳ 🐟 ◖ ✕ 🖼 ⊟

Tetraodon leiurus brevirostre pH7.4;H10;24C;15cm;150L ⌇ ➤ ◑ ♥ 🖼 ⊟

Tetraodon palembangensis pH7.5;H12;27C;18cm;200L ⌇ ➤ ◑ ✕ 🖼 ⊟

♂ *Carinotetraodon somphongsi* pH7.3;H10;25C;7cm;80L ⌇ ➤ ◑ ✕ 🖼 ⊟

629

Chonerhinus naritus pH7.2;H10;27C;30cm;300L ♀ ➤ ◑ ✻ 🖾 ⊟

Tetraodon miurus pH7.0;H5;27C;10cm;100L ♀ ➤ ◑ ✻ 🖾 ⊟

Tetraodon schoutedeni pH7.0;H8;26C;10cm;100L ♀ ➤ ♥ ✻ 🖾 ⊟

Tetraodon mbu pH7.3;H?;28C;67cm;800L ♀ ➤ ◑ ✕ 🖼 ▤

Tetraodon schoutedeni pH7.0;H8;26C;10cm;100L ♀ ➤ ◑ ✕ 🖼 ▤

Tetraodon duboisi pH7.0;H8;28C;7cm;80L ♀ ➤ ✕ 🖼 ▤

Tetraodon miurus pH7.0;H5;27C;10cm;100L ♀ ➤ ◐ ✄ 🖾 🖾

Tetraodon lineatus pH7.4;H13;26C;15cm;200L ♀ ➤ ◐ ✄ 🖾 🖾

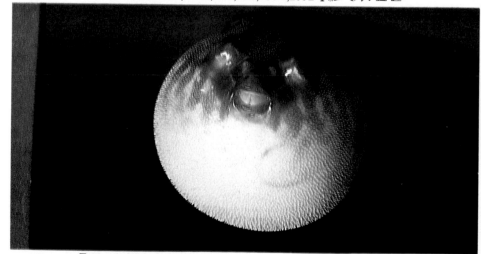

Tetraodon lineatus pH7.4;H13;26C;15cm;200L ♀ ➤ ◐ ✄ 🖾 🖾

Acanthophthalmus javanicus pH7.5;H12;28C;8cm;80L 〜 ➤ ◑ ♥ 🖼 ▭

Acanthophthalmus kuhli pH7.0;H8;28C;7cm;80L 〜 ➤ ◑ ♥ 🖼 ▭

Acanthophthalmus semicinctus pH7.0;H8;27C;8cm;80L 〜 ➤ ◑ ♥ 🖼 ▱

Acanthophthalmus myersi pH6.7;H5;28C;8cm;80L ∿ ⇒ ◑ ♥ 🎞 ▭

Acanthophthalmus shelfordi pH7.0;H8;24C;8cm;80L ∿ ⇒ ◑ ♥ 🎞 ▭

Acanthophthalmus myersi pH6.7;H5;28C;8cm;80L ∿ ⇒ ◑ ♥ 🎞 ▭

Botia dario pH6.8;H8;26C;10cm;100L ⤳ 🐟 ◑ ♥ 🖼 ▭

Botia hymenophysa pH7.0;H12;26cm;25cm;200L ⤳ 🐟 ◑ ♥ 🖼 ▭

Botia macracantha pH7.0;H8;24C;30cm;200L ⤳ 🐟 ◑ ♥ 🖼 ▭

635

Botia lecontei pH6.7;H4;26C;10cm;100L 〜 🐟 ◑ ♥ 🖼 ▭

Botia morleti pH6.8;H5;25C;10cm;100L 〜 🐟 ◑ ♥ 🖼 ▭

Botia sidthimunki pH7.5;H3;24C;4cm;40L 〜 🐟 ◑ ♥ 🖼 ▭

Botia hymenophysa pH7.0;H12;26C;25cm;200L 〜 ➤ ◑ ♥ 🎞 ▭

Botia hymenophysa pH7.0;H12;26C;25cm;200L 〜 ➤ ◑ ♥ 🎞 ▭

Lepidocephalus thermalis pH7.0;H8;25C;5cm;40L 〜 ➤ ◑ ♥ 🎞 ▭

Noemacheilus notostigma pH6.8;H5;26C;8cm;80L ᔦ ☞ ◐ ♥ ▱ ▭

Noemacheilus botia pH7.5;H8;26C;10cm;100L ᔦ ☞ ◐ ♥ ▱ ▭

Lepidocephalus thermalis pH7.0;H8;25C;5cm;40L ᔦ ☞ ◐ ♥ ▱ ▭

Lefua costata pH7.0;H10;18C;10cm;60L ∿ ➤ ◑ ♥ 🎞 ▭

Noemacheilus barbatulus pH7.8;H12;18C;12.5cm;75L ∿ ➤ ◑ ♥ 🎞 ▭

Misgurnus fossilis pH6.7;H6;18C;20cm;75L ∿ ➤ ◑ ♥ 🎞 ▭

Misgurnus anguillicaudatus pH7.0;H10;22C;20cm;50L 〜 ⟫➤ ◑ ♥ 🎞 ▭

Misgurnus anguillicaudatus pH7.0;H10;22C;20cm;50L 〜 ⟫➤ ◑ ♥ 🎞 ▭

Nemacheilus barbatulus toni pH7.0;H10;22C;22cm;50L ♀ ⟫➤ ◑ ♥ 🎞 ▭

Cobitis taenia pH7.0;H10;18C;10cm;50L ♀ ⌖ ◑ ♥ 🖼 ⬜

Lefua costata pH7.0;H10;18C;10cm;60L ⌁ ⌖ ◑ ♥ 🖼 ⬜

Nemacheilus kessleri pH7.6;H12;18C;8.5cm;75L ⌁ ⌖ ◑ ♥ 🖼 ⬜

641

Cobitis taenia pH7.0;H10;18C;10cm;50L ♀ ➤ ◑ ♥ 🎞 ⬜

Cobitis taenia pH7.0;H10;18C;10cm;50L ♀ ➤ ◑ ♥ 🎞 ⬜

Cobitis taenia pH7.0;H10;18C;10cm;50L ♀ ➤ ◑ ♥ 🎞 ⬜

Cobitis takatsuensis pH7.5;H12;20C;10cm;50L ∿ ➤ ◑ ♥ 🎞 ⬜

Acanthopsis choirorhynchus pH7.0;H8;29C;18cm;200L ∿ 🐟 ◐ ♥ 🎞

Homaloptera cf. *zollingeri* pH6.8;H5;25C;10cm;100L ∿ 🐟 ◐ ♥ 🎞 ▭

Pseudogastromyzon myersi pH6.7;H5;24C;5cm;40L ∿ 🐟 ◐ ♥ 🎞 ▭

Etheostoma pallididorsum pH7.8;H12;18C;5.1cm;60L ᭡ ➤ ◑ ♥ ▣ ▭

Etheostoma whipplei pH7.6;H10;19C;7.5cm;75L ᭡ ➤ ◑ ♥ ▭ ▭

Etheostoma radiosum pH7.8;H12;18C;7.1cm;75L ᭡ ➤ ◑ ♥ ▭ ▭

Etheostoma ditrema pH7.6;H10;19C;4.5cm;60L ᭡ ➤ ◑ ♥ ▨ ▭

Etheostoma spectabile pH7.8;H12;18C;6cm;75L 〜 ➤ ◑ ♥ ▱ ▱

Etheostoma spectabile pH7.8;H12;18C;6cm;75L 〜 ➤ ◑ ♥ ▱ ▱

Etheostoma spectabile pH7.8;H12;18C;6cm;75L 〜 ➤ ◑ ♥ ▱ ▱

Etheostoma spectabile pH7.8;H12;18C;6cm;75L 〜 ➤ ◑ ♥ ▱ ▱

Stizostedion lucioperca pH7.5;H12;18C;50cm;200L ⬐ 🐟 ◑ ✗ 🖼 ▭

Perca fluviatilis pH7.2;H10;18C;50cm;150L ⬐ 🐟 ◑ ✗ 🖼 ▭

Pungitius pungitius pH7.0;H12;15C;8cm;50L ⬐ 🐟 ◑ ♥ 🖼 ▭

Acipenser ruthenus pH7.8;H12;18C;125cm;400L 〜 ➤ ◐ ♥ ▱ ▱

Pseudoscaphirhynchus kaufmani pH7.5;H11;18C;60cm;400L 〜 ➤ ◐ ♥ ▱ ▱

Huso huso pH7.6;H12;10C;9m;1000L 〜 ◐ ♥ ▱ ▱

Oncorhynchus kisutch pH8.0;H16;14C;60cm;500L ～➘ ❶✖ 🎥 ☳

Salmo trutta pH7.5;H8;14C;50cm;500L ～➘ ❶✖ 🎥 ▭

Salvelinus fontinalis pH7.5;H8;14C;25cm;300L ～➘ ❶✖ 🎥 ▭

Lepomis megalotis pH7.5;H12;22C;20cm;200L ⚲ 🐟 ◑ ♥ 🖼 🖃

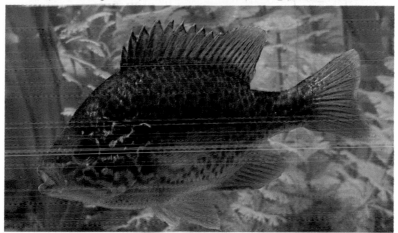

Lepomus gibbosus pH7.5;H12;22C;15cm;100L ∿ 🐟 ◑ ♥ 🖼 🖃

Lepomis gulosus pH7.5;H12;22C;25cm;250L ↘ 🐟 ◑ ✕ 🖾 🖃

Pomoxis nigromaculatus pH7.5;H12;20C;30cm;225L

Lepomis macrochirus pH7.5;H12;22C;12cm;200L

Lepomis humilis pH7.5;H12;22C;10cm;100L

Elassoma evergladei pH7.5;H8;19C;3cm;20L 〜 ➤ ◑ ♥ 🖾 ⊟

Enneacanthus gloriosus pH6.5;H6;21C;8cm;60L 〜 ➤ ◑ ♥ 🖾 ⊡

Enneacanthus chaetodon pH6.0;H4;21C;8cm;60L 〜 ➤ ◑ ♥ 🖾 ⊡

Esox americanus pH7.0;H10;20C;37cm;100L ↘🐟 ◑✕ 🖾 ▭

Esox lucius pH7.5;H8;14C;75cm;250L ↘🐟 ◑✕ 🖾 ▭

Esox lucius pH7.5;H8;14C;75cm;250L ↘🐟 ◑✕ 🖾 ▭

Macquaria colonorum pH7.2;H10;26C;60cm;800L ♀ 🦐 ◑ ♥ 🖼 🔲

Maccullochella macquariensis pH7.4;H10;21C;50cm;500L 〰 🦐 ◑ ♥ 🖼 🔲

Amniataba percoides pH7.0;H8;24C;15cm;200L ♀ 🦐 ◑ ♥ 🖼 🔲

Macquaria australasica pH7.2;H9;26C;43cm;400L ∿ ⇒ ◐ ♥ 🖼 ▣

Maccullochella macquariensis pH7.4;H10;21C;50cm;500L ∿ ⇒ ◐ ♥ 🖼 ▣

Maccullochella peeli pH7.0;H8;23C;200cm;4000L ♀ ⇒ ◐ ♥ 🖼 ▣

654

Hephaestus carbo pH7.2;H8;20C;19cm;200L ♀ ⥤ ◐ ♥ 🖼 ⛶

Leiopotherapon unicolor pH7.0;H8;23C;24cm;300L ♀ ⥤ ◐ ♥ 🖼 ⛶

Scortum barcoo pH7.0;H8;24C;30cm;400L ♀ ⥤ ◐ ♥ 🖼 ⛶

Galaxias maculatus pH7.0;H8;20C;20cm;300L ∿ ➤ ◑ ♥ 🖼 ⊡

Galaxias truttaceus pH7.0;H8;20C;20cm;300L ∿ ➤ ◑ ♥ 🖼 ⊡

Paragalaxias mesotes pH7.1;H6;19C;7cm;100L ∿ ➤ ◑ ♥ 🖼 ⊡

656

Galaxias cleaveri pH6.7;H8;19C;12cm;150L ⌇ ⇻ ◑ ♥ 🖼 ⊡

Galaxias nigrostriata pH6.8;H5;19C;7cm;100L ⌇ ⇻ ◑ ♥ 🖼 ⊡

Galaxias fuscus pH6.8;H6;20C;6cm;80L ⌇ ⇻ ◑ ♥ 🖼 ⊡

657

Galaxias tanycephalus pH7.0;H8;20C;11cm;150L ⤳ 🐟 ◑ ♥ 🖼 ▣

Galaxiella munda pH7.0;H7;19C;7cm;100L ⤳ 🐟 ◑ ♥ 🖼 ▣

Lepidogalaxias salamandroides pH7.0;H7;20C;7cm;100L ⤳ 🐟 ◑ ♥ 🖼 ▣

Glossamia sandei pH7.2;H10;26C;23cm;200L ∿ ⇒ ◑ ♥ 🖼 ▣

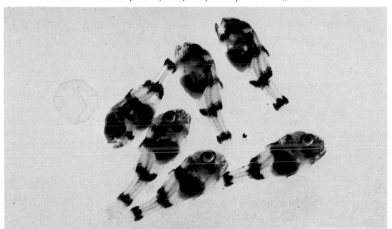

Glossamia trifasciata pH7.6;H14;26C;14cm;150L ⬏ ⇒ ◑ ♥ 🖼 ▣

Glossamia wichmanni pH7.5;H12;27C;20cm;200L ⬏ ⇒ ◑ ♥ 🖼 ▣

659

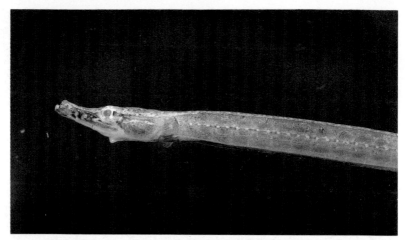

Doryichthys retzi pH8.0;H18;26C;11cm;80L ∿ ➤ ◐ ♥ 🖼 ▭

Oostethus brachyurus pH7.9;H16;28C;25cm;100L ∿ ➤ ◐ ♥ 🖼 ▭

Hippichthys spicifer pH7.6;H12;27C;17cm;100L ∿ ➤ ◐ ♥ 🖼 ▣

Chilatherina crassispinosa pH8.1;H16;28C;9cm;100L ♀ ⮞ ◑ ♥ 🖼 ▱

Chilatherina fasciata pH7.9;H16;30C;10cm;100L ♀ ⮞ ◑ ♥ 🖼 ▱

Chilatherina axelrodi pH7.8;H12;28C;9cm;100L ♀ ⮞ ◑ ♥ 🖼 ▱

661

Melanotaenia boesemani pH6.5;H5;28C;9cm;100L ♀ ➤ ◑ ♥ 🖼 ⊟

Chilatherina campsi pH7.7;H12;24C;8cm;100L ♀ ➤ ◑ ♥ 🖼 ⊟

Chilatherina campsi pH7.7;H12;24C;8cm;100L ♀ ➤ ◑ ♥ 🖼 ⊟

Glossolepis maculosus pH7.8;H12;25C;5cm;80L ♀ ➤ ◑ ♥ 🖼 ▭

Glossolepis multisquamatus pH6.7;H6;28C;12cm;150L ♀ ➤ ◑ ♥ 🖼 ▭

Glossolepis wanamensis pH7.8;H15;29C;9cm;100L ♀ ➤ ◑ ♥ 🖼 ▭

663

Glossolepis incisus pH7.2;H10;28C;12cm;150L ♀ ➤ ◑ ♥ 🖼 ▣

Melanotaenia lacustris pH7.3;H12;27C;10cm;100L ♀ ➤ ◑ ♥ 🖼 ▣

Melanotaenia coatesi pH7.2;H10;26C;9cm;100L ♀ ➤ ◑ ♥ 🖼 ▣

Melanotaenia parkinsoni pH7.7;H14;28C;11cm;150L ♀ 🐟 ◑ ♥ 🖼 ▣

Melanotaenia splendida rubrostriata pH7.0;H12;27C;12cm;150L ♀ 🐟 ◑ ♥ 🖼 ▣

Melanotaenia affinis pH7.2;H10;27C;11cm;150L ♀ 🐟 ◑ ♥ 🖼 ▣   665

Melanotaenia sexlineata pH7.1;H8;27C;7cm;100L 〜 ➤ ◐ ♥ 🎞 ⊟

Melanotaenia monticola pH7.8;H16;19C;8cm;100L ♀ ➤ ◐ ♥ 🎞 ⊟

Melanotaenia oktediensis pH7.3;H12;23C;10cm;150L ♀ ➤ ◐ ♥ 🎞 ⊟

Melanotaenia maccullochi pH7.0;H10;26C;6cm;80L ♀ 🐟 ◑ ♥ 🖼 🔲

Melanotaenia goldiei pH7.2;H13;27C;9cm;100L ♀ 🐟 ◑ ♥ 🖼 🔲

Melanotaenia herbertaxelrodi pH7.8;H14;21C;9cm;100L ♀ 🐟 ◑ ♥ 🖼 🔲

Melanotaenia goldiei pH7.2;H13;27C;9cm;100L ♀ 🦐 ◑ ♥ 🏞 ▣

Melanotaenia goldiei pH7.2;H13;27C;9cm;100L ♀ 🦐 ◑ ♥ 🏞 ▣

Melanotaenia herbertaxelrodi pH7.8;H14;21C;9cm;100L ♀ 🦐 ◑ ♥ 🏞 ▣

Melanotaenia trifasciata pH7.5;H12;28C;10cm;150L ♀ 🐟 ◐ ♥ 🖼 ⊟

Pseudomugil signifer pH7.3;H12;25C;6cm;40L 〜 🐟 ◐ ♥ 🖼 ⊟

Pseudomugil gertrudae pH7.5;H13;25C;3cm;40L 〜 🐟 ◐ ♥ 🖼 ⊟

Iriatherina werneri pH6.4;H4;28C;3cm;40L ∿ ⋟ ◑ ♥ 🖾 ⊟

Pseudomugil inconspicuus pH7.9;H16;27C;3cm;40L ∿ ⋟ ◑ ♥ 🖾 ⊟

Pseudomugil tenellus pH7.0;H8;30C;3cm;40L ∿ ⋟ ◑ ♥ 🖾 ⊟

Pseudomugil paludicola pH7.6;H14;26C;3cm;40L 〜 ➤ ◐ ♥ 🖼 🔲

Popondetta connieae pH7.7;H14;26C;5cm;40L 〜 ➤ ◐ ♥ 🖼 🔲

Popondetta furcata pH7.6;H14;25C;5cm;40L 〜 ➤ ◐ ♥ 🖼 🔲   671

Bedotia geayi pH7.4;H10;26C;7cm;100L ♀ 🐟 ◑ ✗ 🖼 ▦

Rhadinocentrus ornatus pH7.2;H10;26C;8cm;80L ♀ 🐟 ◑ ♥ 🖼 ▦

Craterocephalus stercusmuscarum pH7.2;H10;25C;7cm;100L 〜 🐟 ◑ ♥ 🖼 ▦

AQUARIUM MAINTENANCE, PLANTS, AND FISH BREEDING SECTION

DR. CLIFF W. EMMENS

Table of Contents

About the Author

D r. Cliff Emmens is both a zoologist and physiologist by profession and an aquarist as a lifelong hobby. At one time he had as many as 70 tanks of freshwater and marine fishes. He set up the first veterinary physiology department in Australia, which became a blueprint for subsequent departments in other universities, and was its chairman from 1948 to 1978, when he retired as an Emeritus Professor with the degrees of Ph.D., D.Sc., and D.V.Sc.

In the course of a long career, Cliff Emmens has been President of the Australasian Region of the International Biometric Society, the Endocrine Society of Australia, the Australian Society for Reproductive Biology, the Sydney Association of University Teachers, and the Second Asia and Oceania Congress of Endocrinology. In addition he has been on the councils of various other societies, a member of many committees, and consultant to various firms such as Mead Johnson and Syntex.

Emmens is the author of several biological and statistical texts and author or coauthor of ten books on aquarium keeping, several with Dr. Herbert R. Axelrod. His contributions to the scientific literature in the form of original research papers and chapters in textbooks exceed two hundred, while his classified papers on the techniques of bombing and their results add a further twenty or so. During World War II he travelled extensively in the North African and European theatres with the honorary rank of Wing Commander in the Royal Air Force. His awards include the Oliver Bird Medal & Prize (U.K.), the Italian Istituto Spallanzani Medal, 5 campaign and other war medals, election to the Australian Academy of Science, and an honorary Fellowship of the Australian College of Veterinary Scientists.

Photography: *In addition to the photographers listed in the front of this book as contributors of photos used in the fish catalog section, the following deserve recognition for photos used in this section: Dr. H. Frickhinger; Dr. Don Jacobs; Dr. Jorg Vierke.*

The Tank and Other Equipment

Tanks for freshwater fishes, especially tropicals,can be virtually any size you wish. However, something between 50 to 200 liters or 60 x 35 x 25 cm to 120 x 45 x 35 cm is best. A smaller tank cannot provide the plants with a good chance for their display, and a larger one becomes expensive and relatively more difficult to maintain. Since well-grown plants and aquascaping give the freshwater tank its primary attractiveness, it is worth thinking first about these aspects. The first measurement given above is the tank length, the second is its height, and the third its back-to-front dimension. In theory the wider and shallower the tank the better it is, because the air-water interface is the "lung" of the aquarium. A good water depth is attractive and necessary for a good display, and paucity of surface area can, within limits, be substituted for by aeration.

Whether the tank be all-glass or framed, careful attention must be paid to the glass and its thickness. Tanks up to 60 cm in depth and 150 cm long are often made from 6 mm plate, worse still secondhand 6 mm plate, and the risk of a burst is very great! For aquaria up to 30 cm in depth and 75 cm length, the former being the most important, thick window glass may be used (approx. 5 mm thickness), with 6 mm plate or cast glass bottom. From 30 to 45 cm in depth 9 mm plate throughout, or preferably with a 12 mm plate bottom, is needed. Above 60 cm, 12 mm or thicker glass is necessary. Pay careful attention to scratches, particularly on the long sides and bottom, and do not accept any deeply scratched secondhand glass.

Iron-framed tanks, galvanized, chromed, or not, are hardly worth having nowadays. All-glass tanks are more decorative, quite rugged as long as they are properly supported, and do not cost more. Stainless steel frames may be preferred and do add a degree of protection to the tank, but they are hard to find nowadays. They are rust-free with fresh water as long as a good grade of metal is used, but beware of the manufacturer who has used cheap material intended only for decoration or ornaments, doors, etc. Framed tanks usually have better support for the base by the presence of a rim of metal and, in any but the smallest, by subdivision of the base into two or more sections. This enables the owner to take less care regarding

Heavy aeration can be used in the aquarium that has a restricted water surface area—and it can achieve an interesting esthetic effect.

The surface on which the tank is set must be sturdy enough to hold its considerable weight, and it should be perfectly level. This tank is set too low for placement in a home housing a child as young as the little girl shown; she can too easily reach into the tank.

the supporting surface below, which can even be no more than two metal runners along the long edges, as long as the support is level and even. This is useful for banks of tanks and allows easy inspection underneath. All-glass tanks must be carefully and evenly supported below, preferably by a complete table top type of stand, with a compressible layer of 6 mm to 12 mm of plastic insulating material (styrofoam or the like). This makes up for any irregularities in the supporting surface of the tank itself and gives even support. Do not use any material that rapidly absorbs water, or sooner or later it will probably get wet and cause trouble. Tanks can also be made of plastic, which has the advantage of lightness but also has several disadvantages. Plastic scratches and it also bends, so that only fairly small aquaria carefully handled are practical. It is surprising that aluminum-framed tanks have not

become widely available, as they are light, durable, and could be made inexpensively. All in all, however, we much prefer the elegance of an unframed all-glass tank.

The tank stand may be an existing piece of furniture, if sufficiently robust, or specially designed for its purpose. Water weighs 1 kg per liter, so that a 200 liter tank plus stand and decorations, full of water, is going to weigh perhaps 300 kg—the equivalent of four average men. It will be a constant dead weight over about 0.35 sq. meters of floor surface, which may be beyond the designed strength of a wooden floor. Instances are not unknown of the room below suddenly being flooded by a ceiling collapsing (not necessarily immediately) with the deposition of shattered glass and tank contents over its floor. So take special care (if you feel it to be necessary) in the case of any tank over 90 cm in length, or at least locate it along the edge of the room, which is strongest, or over known supporting beams.

Aquaria do not have to be of the usual double-cube construction, and are often built to suit particular sites or to be decorative pieces of furniture in harmony with their surroundings. They may be used as room dividers, be built into walls, or integrated with wall units as are television sets and hi-fi units. It must always be remembered that they must be accessible, needing frequent servicing, and that provision must be made to accommodate any auxiliary equipment such as outside filters and air pumps. The latter are best placed in an adjoining cupboard or in an enclosed stand, with absolute minimal visible tubing, etc. We do not want our beautiful tank to look like a hospital casualty, with tubing and wires sticking out all over.

Placement within a room or hallway should never be over sources of heat, such as radiators, or very near to windows, which may admit too much sun or be a source of drafts. Aquarium temperatures must be as stable as possible, as small bodies of water change too rapidly in temperature for the health of the fishes if allowed to fluctuate with natural temperatures. Tanks in fully air-conditioned rooms are safe, as far as normal heating goes, but not necessarily as far as excess sunlight is concerned. This can overheat as well as over-illuminate.

A large tank is more stable in many ways than a small one. A 200-liter tank heats and cools relatively slowly, changes in water composition are slower, and thus it is less dangerous to place it near a window where direct sunlight may strike it for a few hours a day than in the case of a 50-liter tank. The latter may easily get

Decoration of the tank is purely a matter of personal taste. This colorful vista has been achieved using plastic plants alone, with no living plants.

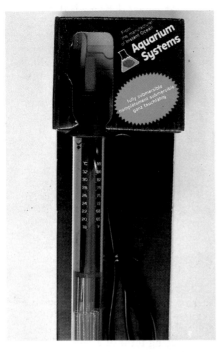

A reliable aquarium heater/thermostat combination is a requirement in all but the warmest climates.

cooked on a hot summer day. At night, a cold-water tank may even freeze over in an unheated living room, which may be harmful to all but the hardiest fishes. A larger tank is much less likely to cool down enough to do this. Adequate heating in a tropical tank takes care of the nighttime situation, but not of the effects of too much sunlight. The smaller the tank the more temptation there is to place it on a mantel shelf or a window ledge—don't!

The Tank Top

Fishes jump out of, water evaporates from, and things fall into an uncovered aquarium. So fit it out with a stout cover glass or glasses, not forgetting the need for feeding and for an inlet for airlines, electric cords, or filter stems. The cover will also protect the light and hood or reflector which will almost certainly be needed over the top of the tank. It is best countersunk 1 cm or less below the top edges of the glass or frame, by plastic or stainless steel clips, or more elegantly in an all-glass tank by cementing a rim of glass onto the inner surface of the tank. A few square cm of removable glass somewhere along the front—easiest at a corner—takes care of feeding. See that a small handle is cemented to this piece of glass. Small triangles removed from the cover glass at the back corner will allow leads and airlines to enter the tank, but a more extensive gap may have to be left for an outside filtering system. Such a cover will save a lot of cleaning of the tank top, is safer and cannot slip to one side, and ensures that nearly all splashed or evaporated water returns to the tank. It is best cut from 4 to 6 cm plate glass, no thinner or it will shatter if accidentally hit or pressed upon. Inadequate top cover arrangement is the commonest fault of readymade aquaria, so be on the lookout or be prepared to design your own.

Tanks need light, preferably from above, or fishes will swim at an angle and plants will grow sideways. Any daylight entering the tank must do so wholly or predominantly from above and behind, so that the back glass will, if left transparent, become covered by a film of green algae which forms a decoration, a protection from excessive light, and even food for some types of fishes. The main source of light should be artificial, except in specially-designed fish houses, and is provided by incandescent or fluorescent electric lighting. The appearance of ordinary incandescent lighting is preferred by some, and it is fine for plant growth. However, adequate light from incandescent bulbs may overheat a small tank, whereas fluorescent lighting is more efficient and 'colder'. If fluorescent tubes are used, there is a plethora of types available—colored, daylight, warm-white, or specially made for plant growth. Avoid the old style bluish fluorescent tube, which gives inadequate light for plant growth. Plants need predominantly the red end of the spectrum for growth, hence blue lighting is of little help. Fishes do not mind as long as they can see to feed and as long as the light is overhead. Apart from the needs of plants, the color of the lighting and its effects on the appearance of the aquarium and its contents is thus a matter of your own preferences. Sodium or halogen lamps are unsuitable for aquaria, but spot-lights can be very effective to highlight centers of interest, to encourage plant growth, or to give colored effects independent of the overall tank lighting.

Watt for watt, fluorescent lighting is about three times as efficient as incandescent lighting—hence the lower heating effect. If the light is on for about 10 hours per day, the following are the requirements of tanks of various depths, on the assumption that there are no other light sources of significance—this excludes room lighting, which is too weak to matter.

The figures in the last column, multiplied by 100, give the wattage to use assuming 10-12 hours per day of illumination and a reasonably efficient reflecting hood over the tube(s). Thus, a 20-watt tube over a 60-liter tank will be satisfactory, which is fortunate, as fluorescent tubes are usually rated at 10 watts per 30 cm. There is a complex relationship between the tank depth and lighting requirements which does not follow the inverse square law—i.e., a 480-liter tank does not need four times the lighting total of a 60-liter tank, despite its having twice the depth, because the action of reflectors and reflection within the tank means that even the bottom is better illuminated than might be expected. In addition, plants are not at the bottom of a tank, but grow upwards from it to varying degrees, and those toward the top get the same illumination whatever the depth of the aquarium.

There are, however, differences

Tank Capacity in Liters	Usual Length in cm	Usual Depth in cm	Kilowatt-hours per day
20	44	22	0.15
60	60	30	0.20
120	76	38	0.25
180	90	45	0.33
320	106	53	0.40
480	120	60	0.50

Both fluorescent and incandescent bulbs for aquarium reflectors are available in a number of wattages and color types.

in the requirements of various plants, which will be discussed in more detail later. In brief, *Crypto-coryne* and *Sagittaria* need the least light, around 100-200 lux, plants like *Cabomba* and *Myriophyllum* need more like 1000-2000 lux, and floating plants even more. In nature, these surface plants receive up to 100,000 lux in the tropics (1 lux equals the light cast by 1 watt over 1 sq. meter at a distance of 1 meter, assuming the light source to be 100% efficient).

The top light can usually be moved to different positions over the aquarium. At the front, it shows fishes to best advantage as it reflects from their sides, but in this position it tends to pull plant growth forward. A solution is to place the light toward the back routinely, and put it at the front to enjoy the aquarium when you are in the room.

Never switch the light on suddenly in a darkened room, or the fishes may panic and injure themselves. Put the room lights on first, then a few minutes later switch on the tank lights. A refinement would be a dimmer switch, so that the lights over the aquarium could be gradually switched on, but this is rarely seen. Before retiring, reverse the procedure, so that the fishes get the message that nighttime is approaching and settle down for it. Some have favorite resting places and should be given time to seek them. Try to keep to a regular rhythm of lighting, as fishes also become accustomed to this. The same goes for feeding. However, it does not seem to matter very severely if on occasion the lights are left on all night, as when one is away for a weekend. In the raising of fry, some breeders leave them on constantly to promote frequent feeding and rapid growth. In ordinary circumstances, as long as it is not for more than a few days, if the fish are to be left unattended it is best to leave the lights off, to promote quiet conditions in the absence of food. Such a period should not affect the plants significantly, but a lengthy period would see them liable to wilt and decay.

The Tropical Tank

Tropical aquaria need heating in all but the tropics themselves, and even there they may need protection from sudden drops in temperature at night or in unusual weather. The main point to remember is that few species of fish can withstand sudden big temperature changes, which do not happen in large bodies of natural waters. This particularly applies downward; a really sudden change of more than 1.5°C or an overnight swing of more than 3°C can shock or weaken fishes so that they may die or become prone to disease. Even goldfish and other coldwater species are affected, although they can stand a wide temperature range if it occurs gradually.

So the tropical tank is best fitted with a heater and a thermostat, usually combined in the one instrument. The drawback to a combined model is that if submersible it usually must be removed from the water and opened up to adjust the thermostat, disturbing the tank decor. Other models clip onto the tank in an upright position, but they in turn have the disadvantage that the thermostat sits over the heater and temperature control is not very good; also the thermostat tends to click on and off frequently and thus to wear out. Perhaps an external thermostat that clips onto the glass at one side of the tank is best; it functions perfectly well and can be made robustly of tough metal since it is not in contact with the water. Control to ±1°C is adequate; in fact, too fine a control system is a disadvantage because of frequent operation of the thermostat as mentioned above. Control is usually achieved by means of a bimetallic strip—two strips of different met-

The two basic heater types are the submergible type and the hanging type. Hanging heaters such as the one shown here are affixed to the tank in such a way that only the heating element is submerged. In dealing with any piece of electrical apparatus for aquarium use, pay close attention to the manufacturer's instructions.

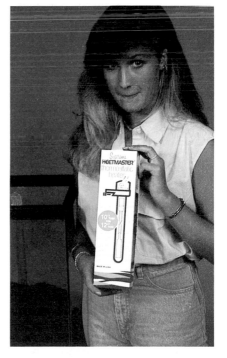

als with different coefficients of expansion fused together. Such a strip bends as the temperature changes and can be adjusted to cause electrical contacts to close at the desired temperature and so to send a current through the heater, opening again as the water heats up.

Small tanks need relatively more heat per gallon than large ones, because they have a greater radiating and conducting surface per liter. To maintain a level approximately 10°C above room temperature in a covered aquarium of 40 liters capacity requires about 1.2 watts per liter, or say a 50-watt heater on all the time. The best wattage to install thus depends on conditions—if the room is going to get really cold from time to time, make your calculations on the above basis and then add some more! In a room at 0°C a tank at

It is best to avoid putting too much heating into a tank, not only because of thermostat wear, but because a thermostat stuck in the "on" position, which occasionally happens, can cook the inhabitants if the heaters are too high in capacity. A 10°C margin is a good one to work with—safe in nearly all circumstances. The heater is normally hidden at the back of the tank, at the bottom, but not touching the glass or it may crack it. The warm water will rise to the top of the tank and circulation is thus set up with convection currents ensuring that all the water is eventually heated. However, a phenomenon

A submergible aquarium heater. Submergible heaters are easier to conceal in the aquarium.

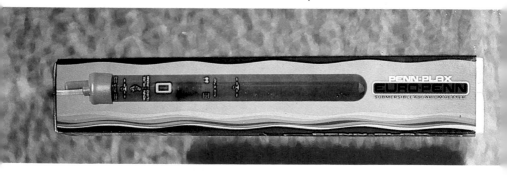

20°C needs up to 4 times (not twice) the watts per liter for a 10C rise, which would be 600 watts in a 200-liter tank if conditions remained stable. In fact, it would take a day or two of 0°C to demand such a wattage, because a 200-liter tank has a good deal of reserve heat to buffer a fall in temperature. Two 100-watt heaters in the average house would be safe unless left in winter without room heating for days on end.

called 'layering' will still occur unless the water is agitated by aeration or other means. The top of the tank will be hotter than the bottom, by perhaps as much as 3°C in a deep tank, but this does not seem to matter and the fishes can choose where they wish to be, or in the case of bottom-living species, they remain in the same somewhat cooler water. For plants it is an advantage, as they flourish better with cooler roots. Layering, after all, resembles natural conditions, when the hot tropical sun or air heats the surface of the water while the bottom is frequently much cooler.

A thermostat is a must in any tropical tank and highly desirable even in a coldwater one. It is best placed so that it measures the temperature about halfway down, but floating types that only dip down a few centimeters are very commonly used, and are unobjec-

This digital thermometer is being attached to the outside of the aquarium.

tionable as long as it is realized that they are measuring a rather higher temperature than average. An alcohol thermometer is preferable to a mercury one, because if it does get broken it will do no harm, whereas mercury is a poison. Clockface types are not always reliable and tend to fall off in time as the suction cup that usually holds them in place deteriorates. All thermometers should be checked against a standard instrument—if possible before purchasing them—as they are liable to be as much as 2°C or 3°C wrong, which is too much. Small errors can be tolerated and if necessary allowances made, but a really inaccurate instrument may be inaccurate to a different degree at different temperatures and so be very misleading and dangerous. A tropical tank is usually kept at 23°-25°C. Even a "coldwater" tank may be kept at 16°-20°C to prevent harmful falls in temperature.

Other forms of heating than a submersible heater are rarely used, but may be employed with advantage. A heating mat or cable either beneath the tank or beneath the substrate in the tank gives even heat and is unobtrusive. Its main disadvantage is that plants do not like hot "feet." In a fish room, it is common to heat the tanks by hot water pipes running below each shelf, and in such circumstances, with the pipes at least a few cm below the base of the tanks, heating is more by a blanket of hot rising air than by direct base heating.

To assist in deciding the total heating capacity needed for any particular tank, the following table gives figures for typical rectangular tanks based on the formula

$$\text{Watts per liter} = \frac{t^2 \cdot l_{60}}{100 \cdot l_x}$$

Tank Length in cm	Capacity in liters	Watts per liter	Approx. Total watts
25	4	2.4	10
30	7	2.0	14
35	11	1.7	19
40	17	1.5	26
45	24	1.3	31
50	33	1.2	40
55	45	1.1	50
60	60	1.0	60
65	72	0.9	65
70	91	0.85	77
75	114	0.80	91
80	132	0.75	99
85	160	0.70	112
90	190	0.65	124
105	303	0.60	182
120	455	0.50	228

TABLE SHOWING LIGHTING WATTAGES REQUIRED IN TANKS OF DIFFERING SIZES AND VOLUMES.

where t is the temperature difference between the tank and the surroundings (max. 10°C in the table), l is the length of a typical 60-liter tank (taken as 60 cm), and l_x is the length of the tank in question. Minor differences in tank design do not matter. Naturally, a heater of 19 or 77 watts is not going to be available, but the nearest value to the figure in the last column should be selected—preferably one higher rather than significantly lower.

Aeration

There is more misunderstanding about aeration than any other feature of aquarium management. It is often supposed, even by experienced aquarists, that the bubbles that rise from an airstone are responsible for a high proportion of the oxygen and carbon dioxide exchange that takes place. This is rarely the case, for the degree of aeration needed to accomplish this would be very considerable and the aquarium would appear to be "boiling" with very agitated water and a mass of air bubbles. Instead, it is still the surface water that maintains the major gaseous exchange with the air, and aeration, aided by heater convection in the tropical tank, keeps the surface layers turning over so that more effective exchange occurs. The best proof of this statement is that nitrogen or even carbon dioxide can be used to "aerate" a tank as effectively as air or oxygen, since the contribution of the gas used is small, while the surface turnover is what matters.

Simple aeration is achieved with one or more airstones placed usu-

Aerating devices can be hidden inside ornaments if they would otherwise detract from the appearance of the tank.

ally at the bottom of the tank, connected by plastic tubing to an air pump. The best material for such airstones is compressed small-grain ceramic or other inert material, which allows only fine bubbles to emerge. Wooden devices give very fine bubbles suitable for special purposes such as ozone treatment, but too fine for most other purposes. They do not usually continue to function satisfactorily and are best avoided in the freshwater tank. The optimum bubble size is such as to give maximum stirring action with the airstone working on its own—this is a bubble diameter of about 0.5 mm. Coarser bubbles rise to the top rapidly and carry less water upwards with them, while finer ones do not rise rapidly enough and dissipate in the water. When aeration

is maximally effective, it about doubles the air-water exchange and allows the fish population to be doubled—other things being equal.

Air pumps are available in all sorts and sizes. To service a few airstones or a small filter or two, a small vibrator-type diaphragm pump is excellent, provided it is well-made and reasonably silent. Larger pumps are available in the diaphragm range which can handle dozens of aquaria simultaneously, but these are naturally more expensive and far too high in capacity for the beginner. Piston pumps fall into the same category. Thus, for the beginner or possessor of few tanks, the diaphragm (vibrator) pump is the thing. It should be placed above the level of the water and preferably out of

Vibrator pumps are available in many different styles and degrees of pumping power.

the way, not on top of the tank, where it may cause irritating vibration of cover glasses, etc., and be a general nuisance. Control of air flow may be achieved by a device on the pump itself, or by valves governing the individual airlines leading to the airstones. The latter method is usually best, with the pump working at constant loading somewhere more or less remote from the aquarium or aquaria. Pressure gauges and storage tanks may intervene between a pump and the aquaria but are usually quite unnecessary. If a gauge is used, about 0.3kg/cm² is the maximum desirable pressure, as connections tend to blow if this is much exceeded.

Filtration

This is another topic about which we are always learning more, and there are many kinds of filters and filter materials from which to choose. Aeration and filtration are not absolutely necessary in freshwater aquaria, but, except in undisturbed, understocked tanks, they help a great deal. It pays to consider the objectives of filtration, thence how best to achieve them in the simplest manner. They are:

1. To remove unwanted gross particulate matter such as uneaten food and feces (mulm) from the water so as to keep it clear and "sweet."
2. To remove unwanted coloring matter, which gradually accumulates in the water, turning it yellow and then brown if it is not frequently changed.
3. Occasionally to remove algal or bacterial 'blooms', which cloud the water and make it opaque, green, or milky in appearance.
4. To remove invisible, colorless dissolved matter such as ammonia and nitrites that are poisonous to the fishes in all but minute amounts.
5. To maintain a suitable pH, so that the water is not too acid or too alkaline.
6. Occasionally to remove chemicals or medicines that have been added to the water to cure disease or as preventives, and which are no longer needed—these or their breakdown products may be colored and toxic if left around.

An ordinary coarse filter material such as synthetic filter floss or filter pads of various types only copes with the first item above when it is first set up or if the filter is frequently cleaned out, but as time goes on an old filter bed will start performing some of the other functions as well, particularly no. 4. This is because bacteria grow in it that convert unwanted products of fish life, such as those listed, to harmless ones—particularly nitrates—which are utilized by the plants.

The main toxic material produced by the breakdown of excreta, uneaten food, etc., is ammonia. This is converted to nitrites by bacteria such as *Nitrosomonas,* then by further bacterial action, involving *Nitrobacter,* the nitrites are converted to nitrates. Both ammonia and nitrites are harmful to fishes, even in minute amounts, and can be monitored by suitable test kits. Nitrates are relatively harmless and can be ignored unless no water changes are made or no plants are present, when even they can build up to dangerous levels. When setting up a new aquarium, it pays to measure nitrite levels for the first few weeks as a precaution against getting a buildup of ammonia and nitrites, but it is rarely necessary to worry about them in a freshwater tank later on.

Another popular filter material, activated carbon or charcoal, performs, in particular, functions 2, 4, and 6 right from the start. Fine granulated so-called gas grade charcoal has an enormous adsorptive surface on which chemicals of all descriptions may be adsorbed, and on which bacteria may also grow. These bacteria may interfere with the charcoal's main function, although a balance often seems to be achieved, with quite

Test kits make it possible to check the aquarium's water to monitor it for ammonia and nitrite content.

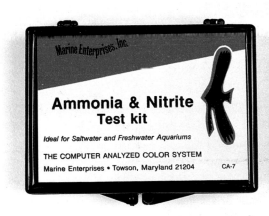

old charcoal continuing to adsorb chemicals and grow bacteria. Eventually, it will clog up and have to be replaced, but it can take up to more than half its own weight of adsorbed materials with it. When in a semi-clogged condition, both filter wools and activated charcoal extract finer and finer materials and may assist in item 3. Otherwise, this usually needs to be dealt with by other means, from a general overhaul and tightening up of cleanliness to the use of a power filter, which forces the water through a very fine capsule or material such as diatomaceous earth and extracts the algae or bacteria by mechanical means. Ion-exchange and other resins may also be used to perform similar functions to activated charcoal, in bead form, or as a mat over which the water flows rather than through it. It is claimed that such filter materials, sometimes combined with activated charcoal, can absorb practically all harmful substances with infrequent need for replacement.

It is clear from the above that most of the desirable functions of a simple filter will be performed if it is provided with a bed of fine filter floss and activated charcoal. The charcoal is usually placed between layers of floss, so that it cannot escape into the aquarium. Coarse grades of charcoal are not much use, unless large filters with a lot of carbon surface are employed, but this introduces other problems of pH disturbances and continuous leaching of toxic materials sometimes present in the coarse charcoal itself. Even if present in fine granular charcoal, they can be washed out much more readily in a preliminary washing before use in the filter. The pH of the water may be influenced by special pads that can be laid on top of the filter bed.

So far, we have been considering mechanical filtering devices, which will be described more fully further on, but mention must also be made of the undergravel filter, which uses the aquarium gravel as a filter bed and is a very efficient type of filter in certain circumstances. It is often referred to as a biological filter because its functioning depends on the growth

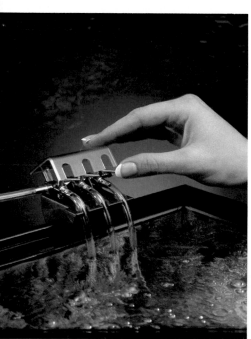

Gang valves allow the easy control of air delivered to various pieces of air-operated equipment, such as aerators and many filtration devices.

of bacteria, but we have just seen that this is true of other types of filters as well. The great power of the established undergravel filter is the large surface and volume of filter bed it offers, much greater than the average separate mechanical filter. It too will be discussed later, when we shall see that its main drawback in the freshwater tank is that it discourages plant growth and tends to acidify the water in a planted tank, yet it may be dangerous to turn it off for too long a time so as to give the plants a better chance.

An inside corner filter. Such filters are easy to operate and easily movable from tank to tank.

Types of Filters

The simplest filter is a small box that fits inside the aquarium and usually sits on the bottom in a back corner, where it is almost invisible. It has a central stem with a small airstone below it, and a slotted removable cover through which water is drawn down into the filter bed and flows up with a column of bubbles to the surface. It is thus a filter + aerator. The whole thing works because a mixture of air and water is lighter than water alone so that the water in the tank pushes through the filter bed and displaces the mixture in the central column, becoming part of the mixture itself as it does so. It is a quite efficient and cheap piece of equipment usually made of transparent plastic.

Other filters may hang inside the top of the tank, or outside the top of the tank, and are then known as "inside" or "outside" filters. An airlift conveys water into the filter on the same principle just enunciated, except that a simple injection of air into a plastic tube is used. In an inside filter, the airlift curves over at the top, the air-water mixture flows into the filter and the water passes down through the filter bed and escapes back into the tank via perforations at the base of the filter. In an outside filter the water is drawn into a tube by an airlift in the tank and so returns to the tank, while one or more siphon tubes convey water from the tank to the filter, where it passes through the filter bed (or beds) and back into the tank. If the airlift fails, the filtration stops without flooding from the tank; if the siphon tube or tubes get blocked, the filter runs dry. Either way the tank contents remain inside and are not spilled onto the floor.

An external filter may have several compartments and be quite complicated, but this is rarely any great advantage. It may even be driven by a small electric motor and filter at a considerable rate, but again this is rarely necessary except for power filtration through a capsule, for example, to clear up cloudy water. A simple airlift can turn over hundreds of liters per hour, more than is needed in most circumstances. The faster the filtration, the wider the siphon tubes need to be, and if they are very wide and there are small fishes present, or snails, it is advisable to fit guards over the intake ends. A small diaphragm pump can take care of all filter types just described; a larger one can run several aquaria at the same time.

The undergravel filter consists of a plate or plates with slots or perforations, the whole being supported about 1 cm above the bottom of the aquarium. An airlift or airstone arrangement as in a simple corner filter takes up water from below the plate, which is constantly replaced by water flowing down through the gravel. From 5 to 8 cm of gravel is an excellent filter bed which may never need complete replacement and forms an efficient biological filter. The gravel size must be such as to root down plants, allow good water flow but not the passage of large particles of food or mulm, yet it must not pass through the filter plate and clog the whole works. A rather coarse gravel of mixed com-

One of the main advantages of undergravel filters is that they are almost completely concealable within the tank and take up relatively very little needed space.

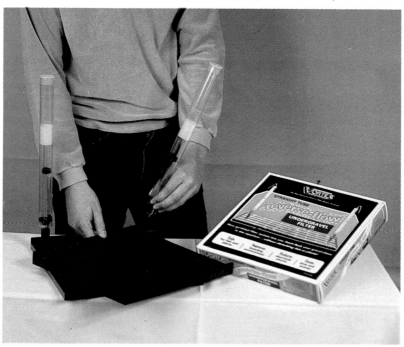

Undergravel filters can be fitted with attachments designed to make them more effective.

position, varying from about 2.5-5.0 mm, with slots in the plate of 1-2 mm is about right. As a further precaution, plastic fly-screen can be placed between the gravel and the plate. As the gravel clogs with mulm, sections can be siphoned off and replaced, but never all at once. In some versions of undergravel filters, the plate is replaced by slotted or perforated tubing which performs the same function and allows the gravel to sit right down onto the aquarium base. In any undergravel filter, it is best to have ready access to the airlift connections, so that tank arrangements are not wrecked if a blockage occurs. This can be arranged by having the air tube entering the airlift above gravel level, or better still by lowering the tube fitted with a small airstone down a wide enough airlift. This arrangement gives a very strong flow of water and is quite admirable.

Power filtration, using an electrically driven water pump, has the advantages that water can be drawn from anywhere one chooses and that the filtering equipment may be placed above, below or beside the tank, or even completely inside it. A powered undergravel filter can turn over many hundreds of liters per hour, even thousands, and is of great use in marine tanks rather than in freshwater ones. The main use of a power filter is, as mentioned above, to force water through a capsule membrane or fine material such as diatomaceous earth to remove even the finest particles—which may include infective organisms. Additives are also available to cause coagulation of fine particles in water, so that the larger agglomerates are more easily trapped in a filter. This, in conjunction with fine filtration, can really "polish" the water.

Another type of filter can be built into the tank. There may be a side or back compartment in which filter material is placed, with slots in the divider so that water can be pumped through the filter material back into the tank. The best arrangement is a dark-colored false back, so that nothing is visible in the display area except a nozzle or nozzles returning the filtered water. The concept may be enlarged, so that all equipment is placed in a series of back compartments in a necessarily

693

rather large aquarium, including aeration, heating, filtration, and any other process one chooses. A design of my own (C.W.E.), primarily developed for marine tanks where brisk water movement is needed, has water flowing through an undergravel filter into a rear heating and aerating compartment, from that into a filter, then into a pump compartment to be returned to the display area—all in a 90-cm tank. An extension of this, in a 180-cm tank, has a pump and filter at each end with a central heating and aeration compartment, with an automatic device to switch first one pump on and then the other so as to give a wave-like movement to the water in the display. The great advantage of a within-tank arrangement is safety—no hoses to leak, nothing outside the tank except the pump(s), sitting over the top or even underwater and not outside at all. The other advantages are cheapness, ease of operation, and a gadget-free display.

Filters usually come with a nominal rating—200 or 600 liters per hour, for example, but it is easy to check the actual performance by diverting the flow into a measured container, timing how long it takes to fill. Thus, a 5-liter bucket taking 1 minute to fill means 5 x 60 = 300 liters per hour. Remember to keep conditions as near as possible to operating ones when making such a test.

Gravel, Rocks, etc.
Except when used with an undergravel filter, the grain size of gravel is, within reason, immaterial, but very fine sand cakes and packs and does not allow adequate plant rooting; it also turns foul easily. Too large a gravel size allows uneaten food and other particulate matter to penetrate the bed and also go foul, but if mixed grain sizes are used, the spaces between the large grains will be sufficiently filled by smaller ones. Quite pebbly gravel looks good and may be used as long as smaller grains are present in sufficient numbers. Plants are then easy to root and will grow satisfactorily. It is living, growing plants that keep the gravel healthy; without them, or an undergravel filter, it would go foul.

Do not use calcareous gravel in a freshwater tank; crushed shells, coral sand, dolomite, or any other calcium or magnesium-containing sands will turn the water far too hard and alkaline. Instead, any neutral gravel such as well-washed river gravel or coarse sands, silica, or granite are much better and will not change the composition of the water. Lava gravel has been in vogue, as it is decorative although dark, and light in weight. However, it tends to float around too easily and is of dubious use. Even coal has been used, but may be dangerous unless of proven neutrality, such as anthracite. The same applies to decorative rocks. Avoid marble, sea shells, or coral unless you want hard and probably alkaline water—which is fine for some particular fishes, such as estuarine and brackish water species and Rift Lake cichlids, but very unsuitable for most tropicals, particularly for breeding them. Also avoid any iron-containing rocks, or any rock that is not guaranteed by your dealer to be inert in fresh water. Suitable rocks are granite, basalt, sandstone not containing iron, porphyry, or slate. It is sometimes required for show purposes to have rocks and gravel of the same nature, and not to mix say silica sand with sandstone rocks, but

Three different filter types are shown here: sponge filter (upper left); outside hanging power filter with "waterfall" effect (upper right); canister-type power filter (lower left).

this is a nicety you may choose to ignore unless aiming for a completely natural look. Do not use any plastic or other decorations or equipment that have a smell, particularly of camphor, as it, too, is likely to affect the water and may even be poisonous.

Wood, particularly driftwood, can be used to good effect in aquaria. It must be dead and have all sap leached from it or trouble can occur. Other woods such as bamboo or other canes can give very decorative if rather artificial looking scenes—it all depends on taste. Other materials that might prove toxic or would deteriorate submerged in water can be placed in a diorama at the back and/or sides of the tank. The glass separating them from it must of course

Some aquarists want plenty of movement in their aquariums over and above what is provided by the fishes, and they supply it in the form of ornaments powered by air bubbles.

Plastic plants will be featured in this girl's tank—but the inclusion of artificial plants doesn't eliminate the possibility of using living plants as well.

be kept scrupulously clean or the effect is lost. A sense of great depth to the underwater scene can be achieved by this technique. A substitute method is simply to place a suitable picture, available commercially, against the back glass. Embossed sheets are also available that give some illusion of depth.

Some aquarists like to place ornaments suggestive of ocean depths in the tank—a diver, wreck, mermaid, or cockleshell that opens and shuts as air is pumped into it are common examples. In a typical pond or river scene where foreign objects are found, these are much more likely to be an old boot or tin can, but we haven't seen anyone place models of these in the tank.

All material such as gravel,

An aquarium set up with the amount of non-natural ornamentation visible in this one would be cherished by some hobbyists and abominated by others—you pays your money and you takes your choice.

rocks, and decorations should be thoroughly washed or soaked in several changes of hot fresh water before use so as to get rid of surface dirt and readily leached components. Even so-called "washed gravel" usually needs a further washing before use. Newly collected fresh gravel is usually filthy and requires prolonged washing with a hose in small lots in a bucket. Up to 20 or 30 rinses is not unknown before the water runs off clear, and if this is not done, you may have a persistently cloudy aquarium that is very difficult to get clear.

Environmental Aquaria

The above term can be interpreted in various ways, each of which may be the basis of a tank setup. Many beautiful aquaria are de-

signed which completely ignore the congruity of their contents—the plants and fishes come from all over the world and many would never be found together in nature. If you enjoy such a tank, what does it matter? As long as the fishes are happy, or as happy as a fish can get, that is the main thing in some eyes. However, it is interesting to go for more realistic scenes, copying a natural environment as far as possible, and only putting into the tank fishes, plants, and even decorations and gravel that would be found together. Less stringent interpretations of the term could be placing together only fishes and plants that would be found in ponds, or in streams, or in bogs or brackish surroundings, irrespective of where in the world they hail from; or placing together only

The value of aquariums as contributors to the good looks of their surroundings can't rightfully be questioned; aquariums are unarguably among the most effective decorative devices available to the average householder and are increasingly being used in business offices as well. The arrangement below (deliberately skewed in the horizontal dimension) shows a freshwater and a saltwater tank set up in tandem.

fishes and plants that flourish at the same temperature, pH, or salinity—indeed, the latter is wise in any case! Another choice may be to have tanks with only gouramies, tetras, catfishes, or other closely related fishes together. Specialist breeders are particularly likely to favor such aquaria, in which fishes can be conditioned satisfactorily.

In creating strict environmental tanks, i.e., copying a particular locality, the rock or gravel may have to be simulated rather than authentic, as in substituting granite for quartz, and some of the plants may have to be as near as feasible to the natural ones—an Asian *Aponogeton* species might be substituted by one from Sri Lanka. Also, some plants now found almost everywhere were originally confined to one area but have spread (or been spread) around the world, like *Elodea canadensis*, the Canadian water weed.

The following arrangements, taken from Emmen's *How to Keep and Breed Tropical Fish*, T.F.H., revised ed. 1983, are examples:

Amazon Rivers
Roots, driftwood, and darkish rocks with coarse gravel form a suitable background in this type of aquarium, with a wealth of rooted and floating plants. Rooted plants should include the famous Amazon swords, of which there are many species ranging from giants

This tank has been set up to contain fishes representative of only one area, southeast Asia.

to dwarfs. *Cabomba, Hygrophila, Sagittaria, Eleocharis, Salvinia, Azolla,* and *Riccia* are other suitable plants. The varieties of appropriate fishes are vast. Any of the South American tetras, catfishes, pencilfishes, angels, and discus are suitable, but most of them look best in schools with few species per tank. There are various types of water, from clear to cloudy and white to deep brown (the "black" water imitated in tanks by soaking in peat moss). However, all are soft, and clear white water of pH 5.5 to 6.5 at 20° to 30°C is appropriate. Hardness should not exceed about 50 ppm (parts per million), and for breeding species such as neons, which require very soft water, less than about 15 ppm.

All of the fishes kept in this aquarium are characoids, but they're from different continents, the pencilfishes coming from South America and the Congo tetras from Africa.

Central American Hardwaters
For the keeping of most livebearing fishes (the Poeciliidae) a tank with quite hard but not necessarily very alkaline water is needed. Up to 500 ppm hardness and pH around neutral (7.0) are fine for guppies, for instance, although as we pass to swordtails, platies, and further still to mollies, an increasing pH and salinity is best. Mollies can stand full strength sea water—so too can guppies, if gradually acclimated to it.

As a planted tank is best for livebearers, and plants cannot in general stand brackish water, the livebearer tank is nicest at about 300 to 400 ppm (15-20 German degrees of hardness), mildly alkaline, say pH 7.5, so that the fishes will breed and thrive. Use root—driftwood—rock—gravel scenarios, with *Sagittaria, Cabomba, Ceratophyllum, Myriophyllum,* with perhaps some hardy floating plants to help shelter the young. Temperatures can vary from 21° to 27°C.

Malayan Streams
These streams tend to have a rocky and pebbly base, with stones of various sizes and perhaps some roots, copied in the tank by driftwood. The water is very clear, soft, and acid, pH 5.0 to 6.0, and at a temperature of 24° to 27°C, or even higher. However, the fishes are quite happy at the lower part of the range. There is a wide choice of plants suitable to the locality, in which are found *Cryptocoryne* species, *Aponogeton, Hygrophila,* and *Fontinalis.* Various loaches such as *Botia macracantha* and *B. hymenophysa, Labeo* sharks, barbs, and rasboras are native to the area—before purchasing just check that the species you have in mind are suitable.

701

African Lakes

Recent concentration of ichthyologists and others on the central African lakes has provided hundreds of new species of fishes from isolated areas in which they alone occur—particularly cichlids. Many of the lakes are large and deep, resembling inland seas, and it is only around their shores that vegetation (if any) and aquarium-type fishes are found. The lakes vary enormously in hardness and salinity and in the nature of their shores. It is thus necessary to decide on a type of locality to imitate.

Since the cichlid species are of most interest and many do not tolerate dense planting, it would be sensible to copy a rocky area with perhaps a sandy base and just a few plants. *Vallisneria* and *Cabomba* appear to grow in such localities, with fairly hard water, but a pH of 7.7 to 8.6 is important for the welfare of the fishes. Attractive species are *Melanochromis vermivorus, Pseudotropheus zebra,* and various *Haplochromis* species, which thrive at a temperature of 24° to 28°C.

Brackish Water

This aquascape is difficult to make very attractive as higher plants do not thrive in really brackish water. An imitation of a mangrove swamp would show tree roots (easily imitated with driftwood and safer than the real article) with perhaps a sparse growth of *Marsilea* or *Elodea* if the salinity were kept low. This is an instance where the fishes would form a primary attraction, and should include *Scatophagus argus,* especially the red *(rubifrons)* variety, *Monodactylus argenteus, Periophthalmus* (the mudskipper), and *Pseudomugil signifer* (the blue-eye).

These fishes are happy at an alkaline pH of 7.5 to 8.5, in hard water, which need not in fact be very salty, and at temperatures of 21° to 27°C.

Plants

The functions of plants in an aquarium are:

1. To decorate and beautify the tank. The initial impact of a well set up aquarium is the plant growth and its attractiveness, which is usually apparent before the fishes are even noticed.
2. To absorb waste products and help to keep the tank clear and healthy as they grow and multiply.
3. To provide cover for timid or shy fishes and even food for some.
4. To hide equipment such as heaters and airstones (rocks assist in this).

Strangely, plants do *not* on the average make a significant contribution to oxygenation of the aquarium. They may, in fact, contribute to a dangerous degree of oversaturation with oxygen if in direct sunlight for some time, but in dim light or darkness they utilize oxygen and give off carbon dioxide, just as do the fishes. This is why the concept of a balanced aquarium, with plants absorbing carbon dioxide produced by the fishes and producing oxygen for them, is not correct. It is true on a global scale, but not within a closed-system fish tank.

Plastic plants of suprisingly lifelike quality are becoming very popular. They certainly do not deteriorate rapidly if not properly cared for and they perform all the functions listed except number 2. This, however, is very important, even in the presence of a biologi-

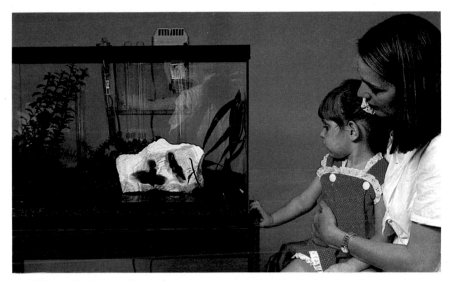

Children should be educated about a new aquarium in the home and even, to the degree that they are able, allowed to participate in setting it up. Keep in mind that small children should be supervised around the aquarium.

cal filter, and so naturally growing plants are to be strongly preferred. In a good aquarium they need frequent thinning out and pruning, and can be a source of income from which to purchase other requisites. Their healthy steady growth is an index of the health of the tank, and a great contribution to it. Any serious aquarist will value his plants and their place in the aquarium.

Other Equipment

Other than plants, there are auxiliary pieces of equipment, some of which are essential and others more in the class of luxury items. Plastic airlines are best cut as needed from a longer piece originally purchased from your dealer. Make a rough estimate of how much will be needed, depending on the position of the air pump and the amount of equipment to be included, and then add a meter or two for safety. Use soft plastic airlines; hard unyielding ones are a nuisance to handle and do not fit easily along desired routes and positions. Join the lines firmly to their connections or they may slip off under pressure, and purchase a set of gang-valves from which to lead off lines to the airstone, filter, and any other air-operated equipment. Leave a spare line available for afterthoughts or for aerating newly bought fishes in their container.

Further items that will be needed sooner or later are:

Siphon tubing—a siphon is required to remove water and mulm from the aquarium. Fit a glass or hard plastic tube of about the same depth as the tank onto about twice the length of soft rubber tub-

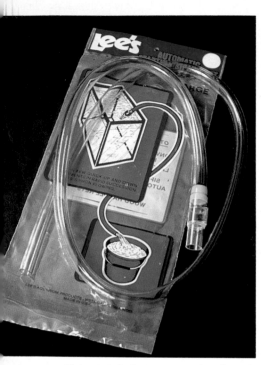

Siphoning devices are very handy gadgets for removing water from an aquarium. Never use a siphon previously used for draining petroleum products.

Dip tube—a tube much the same as the glass or hard plastic tube above, but slightly longer, that can be used to dip out individual small pieces of debris or uneaten food by placing a finger over the end and lowering it into the water, releasing the air when it is over the object concerned. Remove the finger gently, or the water will splash out from the top of the tube.

Net—at least one medium-sized net will be needed to handle fishes. For catching them out of the tank, a net of about half the back-to-front measurement is the most convenient. It should be made of soft, fine-mesh nylon or other synthetic material that will not rot and dries easily. When catching fish, two such nets make the task much easier. Also, either use a fairly dark green or brown material, which frightens the fishes much less than gleaming white, or use a white net with a dark patch at the bottom. The fish takes the patch to be a hole in the net and presto! Grand for catching in the wild, too.

Water quality testing kits will be dealt with later on. They are not a must, except perhaps for a simple pH test kit, and a nitrite test kit when first setting up.

Water changers are now available that will constantly replace part of the water in your tank with fresh tap water as long as it is in operation. This keeps the tank water fresh and saves the aquarist time and work.

ing, all about 1 cm to 2 cm in internal diameter. Rubber tubing eventually rots and has to be replaced in time, but it is much easier to handle and compress by hand than plastic tubing of the same diameter.

The use of test kits can avert potential troubles resulting from imbalances in the makeup of the aquarium water.

Airstones are inexpensive and reliable, and some help to provide interesting effects.

Dip tubes on the market today are far advanced over the old style plain glass tubes.

Setting Up the Aquarium

We shall take as an example a tank fitted with a single outside filter, an airstone, and a thermostat with separate heater, to be situated on its own stand. It will be supposed that all necessary equipment has already been purchased and that the gravel has been carefully washed and is ready for use. The fishes will be purchased later. Look under heading 7 below for prior treatment of plants.

1. Make a diagram of the proposed aquascaping of your aquarium as seen from top and front. Few of us can plant and arrange a tank satisfactorily without such an aid. It helps to study a setup you admire, not to copy it, but to use it as a guide in making your own composition. Think of where the heater and airlines will run and try to hide them completely if possible. Stick to one particular type of environment in any single tank, such as flat rocks and pebbly bottom, or submerged wood with a finer and differently colored gravel. Decals can be purchased to use as a backdrop seen through the back glass, which then has to be kept clean inside and out, or, if you prefer, the back glass may be painted blue or black on the outside. Many aquarists leave the glass as it is, particularly in all-glass aquaria where an effect like a cube of clear ice can be achieved if the water is kept sparkling clear.

2. Clean the aquarium thoroughly with water only, or if necessary to get off paint or stains, with acetone or rubbing alcohol on a rag, to be thoroughly washed off afterward. Take a careful look to see if previously unnoticed defects in the glass are present and see that the best face is in front. Clean cover glasses and all equipment in the same manner. With a framed tank, do not fill it as a test prior to use—it may spring a leak when emptied again.

3. See that the stand is steady, dead level, and exactly where you want it to be. Place any supporting material on the stand and tape it temporarily in position, so that when you put the aquarium on top of it, it does not slide about and have to be replaced. A large tank is difficult to move and requires at least two people. Lift the tank from below, not by its upper rim unless it is quite small, and see how good you are at getting your

A number of water treatment products intended to reduce or eliminate potential damage to fishes introduced into a newly set up tank are available.

The key to having an aquarium that's a good looking focus of attention instead of a murky eyesore is to get the right equipment and set it up properly, exercising a little patience as well as common sense.

Enclosing an aquarium within a furniture-style cabinet makes the tank less accessible to maintenance and can restrict viewing angles somewhat—but it can be worth it.

fingers out of the way as you lower it into position. With an all-glass tank, the recommended support will take care of any small irregularities, but with a framed tank, make sure that it does not rock and that there are no long runs without contact. If any are found (by slipping a knife blade along the long sides in particular) pack them with matchbox wood or other slightly compressible material.

4. Place the main body of gravel in position as gently as possible. This is best done with the gravel wet, which makes the task cleaner and easier and avoids air pockets later on. Slope the gravel so that it forms a shallow half-basin from back to front and side to side, several inches deep in the back corners and an inch or two deep at the center front, depend-

ing somewhat on the size of the tank. This will eventually look better and assist mulm to collect where it can most easily be seen and removed. If you wish, some flat rocks or clean pieces of brick can be placed at the back before putting the gravel in, so as to conserve gravel. If this is done, see that the depth of actual gravel is adequate for plant growth.

5. Place rocks or other decorations where desired and put the heater, thermostat, airline(s), and airstones in position. Hang the gang valves and filter (already packed ready for use) at the back or sides of the tank as preferred. Put anchoring stones or such over the heater lead (if submersed) and airlines so that at the next step they do not float up or move out of position. A submersible heater

must be so placed that it is flat on the bottom but cannot get into contact with the glass of the aquarium and is not blanketed by gravel or decorations, or it may overheat.

6. Fill the aquarium gently to the halfway level by running a hose into a small basin placed at center front, allowing this to overflow without disturbing the arrangements so far made. It is best to run the hose for a few minutes prior to this step so as to avoid using water that may be contaminated by standing in metallic pipes or in the hose itself. Running water through copper piping, as long as the latter is not newly installed, or over metallic hose connections is not dangerous.

7. The plants should have been purchased a few days prior to setting up and have been carefully washed and left for one or two days in a harmless disinfectant such as 3 ppm or 3 mg per liter of potassium permanganate. If a rush job has to be done, 15 minutes at 7.5 mg per liter is of some use, as is 15 seconds in sea water or brine at 1½ tablespoons of crude salt per liter. The very short period recommended avoids harm to the plants, which should be given a wash in fresh water before planting. Trim all plants to the desired size if necessary, including trimming the roots to 2 to 5 cm according to size. Long roots are hopeless to deal with and will die off anyway. Plant by pushing with the forefinger along a track a few cm away from the eventual site, so that the plant ends up rooted beneath the gravel where you want it. This makes a slight mess of arrangements that is easily repaired. If a plant such as a *Cryptocoryne* or the Amazon sword has a crown above the roots, do not bury it or the whole plant may decay.

The number of plants needed depends on your scheme of decoration, but a typical 90-cm (ca 180 liters) tank will need several dozen individual tall plants at the back, a dozen or two side and shorter plants, and a centerpiece, say 5 dozen plants in all. A pair of sticks with notched ends can be very useful as replanters when something floats up out of the arrangement and it is no longer possible to plant as originally intended.

At the same time as planting, push a few pinches of garden soil under the gravel at scattered places—not a lot, and not much in total, say about a teaspoon divided into 6 or 8 pinches. This is to inoc-

Living plants can flourish in an aquarium if provided with the proper nutrient base to get them started.

ulate the tank with bacteria that will later act on fish excreta and urine to start up the nitrogen cycle, about which more later. Alternatively, use some gravel from an established tank or purchase a "starter" preparation from your dealer.

8. Fill the tank to within about 2 cm from the top, or just under the top frame if a framed tank, and put everything else in place—thermometer, airlifts for filter (if not already in position), cover glasses, etc., and test out all equipment. Leave everything going if satisfactory, with the lights on for 10-14 hours per day, for several days. This will allow the water to equilibrate and plants to settle in a bit and everything to heat up when a tropical tank is being established. Check after this period that the thermometer reads between 22-25°C (approx.), preferably around 24°C, but that is not critical.

Outside hanging power filters provide excellent water movement and aeration in addition to their efficient filtration.

Stainless steel thermometers are very popular for aquarium use.

9. It is assumed that your tap water will be suitable as it is, except perhaps for the removal of chlorine gas or in its pH. The chlorine will disappear in a day or two, but the pH will possibly remain unsuitable. Some water supplies are treated with chloramine, which must be neutralized by suitable chemical treatment. Consult your dealer about this after first checking with local authorities. Do not check pH with paper strips to be dipped into the water, as these are not sufficiently sensitive and are sometimes unreliable. Relatively cheap kits in which a sample of water is mixed with a colored indicator are much better; the color developed is then compared with a chart, or much preferably with (in more expensive kits) a series of color transparencies or color tubes. A pH of around neutral (pH 7) is best, but anywhere between pH 6 and pH 8 will not harm most

Products that allow the pH of the water in a tank to be adjusted upward or downward can be of great use in areas in which the natural water supply is unsuitable for certain fishes.

fishes. For breeding or with special fishes, better control of pH and perhaps a different range may be needed, but we are not concerned with that at the moment. If the pH is not between 6 and 8, see the relevant sections later in this volume for methods of changing it and for other factors affecting water quality such as hardness and salinity.

10. After several days, you can start to introduce fishes. Don't load the tank with all it can hold in theory right away, because it can't at this early stage. It has to settle down and establish bacterial growth and plant growth, and this may take several weeks. To introduce all of the fishes at once invites the 'new tank syndrome,'

which means that in an overloaded new tank the waste products of the fishes will not be adequately dealt with by the equipment or the plants and so the fishes will poison themselves and become unduly liable to outbreaks of disease. So put in a few, preferably hardy, fishes such as some of the common livebearers, barbs, catfishes, or danios, avoiding more delicate fishes such as characins, top-minnows, angels, and expensive varieties of any sort.

Over the next few weeks, add fishes gradually up to the desired number or the limit of the aquarium capacity.

11. How to add fishes to the aquarium:

They will normally be supplied in plastic bags, with oxygen added if they have to travel far or are crowded, and should be kept in an insulated container if the outside air is cool. Ask your dealer if they are in local water and what are its pH and temperature. When you get them home, check that they are not at a very different temperature from your own tank (1° or 2°C warmer or up to 3°C cooler), and have not been at a very different pH (more than one unit). If they have been, or are, take several hours to complete the next step. If not, ½ hour may be sufficient before transferring them.

Float the bag or bags in the tank and start to change the bag water for tank water gradually, by allowing some to run into the bag and pouring a little out from time to time so as to keep the water mixing and the bag floating. When the water in the bag is mostly that from the tank, gently tip the fishes into the tank.

Main Alternative for Setting Up
This method uses an undergravel filter. Omit the outside filter in

step 5 above, and between steps 3 and 4 insert the following:

3a. Place an undergravel filter in position before putting in the gravel. In a freshwater tank, in contrast to marine tanks, it is not necessary for the filter tray to cover more than about ⅓ of the bottom, particularly in a large aquarium. The filtering capacity will still be impressive and clear water maintained with the filter going continuously. If it covers all of the bottom, it may have to be turned off for half of the time, and tends to get forgotten and is anyway bad for the filter bed. Constant undergravel filtration has a detrimental effect on the growth of at least some plants. The causes are probably that it competes with the plants for nitrogenous and other products and it bathes their roots with an unaccustomed flow of warm, oxygenated water. The plants will keep gravel sweet and clean if on their own, but they do so in a less aerobic situation than the filter provides.

It is best therefore to put the filter where fewest plant roots will be, namely in the center of the tank toward the front rather than the back. If this means an ugly stem rising toward the middle of the tank, either hide it with adequate rockwork or place the filter at an angle so that the corner with the stem is at the back and the filter forms a diamond in the tank center. When the gravel is eventually added, make sure that sufficient depth covers the filter (about 5 cm) for it to function efficiently. If you are going to have a rock centerpiece, it can sit over the filter without serious impairment to its function, but a plant centerpiece might still suffer a bit. If this is feared, place the filter to one side so that it doesn't exert its main effect right under the plant. A rea-sonable balance is all that is needed to get the best of both worlds.

Types of Plants

Most aquarium plants are rooted in the gravel, but some float freely, either in the water or on the surface. There is a large variety of plants available to the tropical aquarium keeper, but a smaller number is suitable to the coldwater tank. They are arranged so that the tallest are at the back and sides of the tank, hiding much of the equipment, while a swimming space is left toward the front of the tank with only smaller plants or gravel below it. An exception may be a large single plant as a centerpiece, or more than one in a very large aquarium.

Pieces of equipment known as power heads can be attached to undergravel filters and also to inside box filters, greatly increasing flow rate and aeration activity.

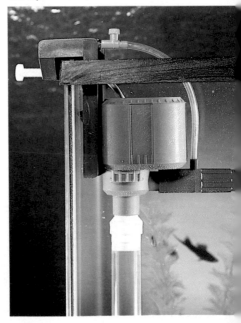

Coldwater Plants (also suitable for the tropical tank)

Grass-like varieties such as the eelgrasses *(Vallisneria)* and the arrowworts *(Sagittaria)* are available in many forms, from long, straplike plants with quite wide flat or spiral leaves to dwarf varieties 2 cm or so in height. These plants are equally at home in cold or warm water and are probably the most widely used genera. Plant the tall ones at the back of the tank. They reproduce by runners which produce new plants at frequent intervals as they traverse the aquarium, and they need frequent pruning. Their growth being rapid, they are valuable as consumers of waste material produced by the fishes.

Anacharis *(Elodea)* is a cultivated variety of *Elodea nutalli*, resembling the Canadian water weed, introduced into various other localities and rapidly becoming a pest. It grows very rapidly, putting out short privet-like leaves and roots at intervals, and may be used as a rooted plant, best in bunches, or left more or less floating in the water. Hornwort *(Ceratophyllum)* is a rather brittle but otherwise similar plant that grows quite fast and is rootless. It has much more divided leaves and forms a good refuge for young or very small fishes, and can be left floating or pushed into the gravel as though it had roots, again best in bunches.

Some of the milfoils *(Myriophyllum)*, ludwigias *(Ludwigia)*, and *Hygrophila* are adaptable to cold water. All are rooted plants of fast to reasonably fast growth, can be propagated by thrusting pieces into the gravel, and will readily strike roots and grow. They can be used for more forward planting than the eelgrasses or arrowworts, as they can be pinched back if

Elodea canadensis, generally sold under the name anacharis.

Cabomba caroliniana.

they grow too high, or they may be allowed to grow longer at the back of the tank.

Coldwater surface plants include duckweed *(Lemna)* and *Salvinia* with larger leaves, both of which reproduce profusely, particularly in bright light. They float with their roots in the water, giving shade in natural conditions, but tend to be a nuisance in the aquarium as they must frequently be skimmed off or they cut down the light to the lower layers too much. Duckweed in particular is best avoided as it is difficult to eradicate once it has been introduced; the minutest fragment will grow and soon cover the surface again.

Salvinia auriculata.

More Strictly Tropical Plants

Fanwort *(Cabomba)* will grow in cold water but flourishes beautifully in the tropical tank as a series of light green fan-like broad fronds that spread from a rapidly growing stalk. It is best planted in groups and kept to a little over aquarium depth—it will grow dozens of feet long if allowed to. *Ambulia* (sometimes called *Limnophila*) is similar in habit, purely tropical, and somewhat more spidery in appearance.

The sword plants *(Aponogeton)* and Amazon sword plants *(Echinodorus)* offer a series of magnificent tropicals that vary in size from dwarf to massive. The Amazon sword makes a fine centerpiece and multiplies freely by budding from runners on or below the surface. The *Cryptocoryne* series are similar and can be of any size depending on the species, but are slow growers and rather choosy as to water conditions. They are beautiful plants when at their best, and decaying nuisances when not.

Floating tropicals are the water sprite *(Ceratopteris)* or water lettuce, a large attractive plant rather more suited to the pond than to the aquarium, and crystalwort *(Riccia)*, which forms masses of entangled angular, narrow leaves or stems just below the water surface and is great for the protection of livebearer and other fry. Java moss *(Vesicularia)* can float or root and will fill an aquarium with an entangled mass of small-leaved growth if allowed to do so.

The Madagascar lace plant *(Aponogeton madagascariensis)* is a most attractive large plant, rather like an Amazon sword with small holes scattered throughout its leaves (hence the name), which must be kept free of algal growth to look their best. It is quite hard to grow satisfactorily, and is primarily a hardwater plant.

Algal growth, which is of course plant growth, can form an attractive addition to the tropical tank in particular, and may be allowed to coat rocks and the back and side glasses, but not higher plants and not anywhere in excess. Blue-green algae *(Oscillatoria,* etc.) smell unpleasant and are not attractive.

Fish Capacity of Tanks

An aquarium with bare rocks and gravel can support a given amount of fish life by virtue of its air-water interface exchange, as long as partial water changes are made every few days so as to keep toxic products diluted and gross mulm or uneaten food removed. A filter would increase this capacity; so would aeration. Plants make little difference, as we have seen, because they don't much affect oxygen supplies on average.

In other books, you will find inches-per-gallon rules (which don't yet seem to have become cm-per-liter), that are not very helpful because a 1 inch fish weighs 1/8th of a 2-inch fish of the same overall shape, so that it clearly uses up more like 1/8th of the oxygen and puts out a corresponding amount of carbon dioxide and other waste products. However, even this is not strictly correct, since smaller, often younger fishes are more active, are growing relatively faster, and actually fall somewhere in between length-of-fish rules and weight-of-fish rules.

The basis of calculations is therefore, as proposed by myself (C.W.E.) 30 years ago, the 6.25 cm (at that time the 2½-inch) tropical fish, which is allowed 130 cm^2 (20 square inches) of aquarium surface area. This is in line with general experience and is on the generous side, therefore allowing for growth and for mistakes in aquarium maintenance on the part of its owner. Aeration and general good practice (see later) can halve this requirement, but *only* in experienced hands. For coldwater fishes, including the general run of goldfish, multiply by 3 and allow 400 cm^2 of surface area per fish. For fancy goldfish varieties such as lionheads, bubble-eyes, and other handicapped types, allow 800 cm^2 per 6.25 cm fish. A fish is mea-

Body length in cm	No. of fishes per 1000 cm^2 of surface	Square cm per fish (approx.)
1	400	2.5
2	110	9
3	50	20
4	25	40
5	12	80
6	8	125
8	5	200
10	2	500
12	1	750
15	1	1100

Crayfish are very interesting invertebrate inhabitants for an aquarium, but they have definite drawbacks in that they'll destroy plants and kill fishes if they can.

Freshwater shrimp can be worthwhile additions to some aquariums . . . but notice what this *Macrobrachium niponensis* is eating.

The red ramshorn snail is more colorful than most other aquarium snails and makes a fine fish food.

A mystery snail, one of the Ampullaria species.

sured from snout to the base of the tail, so that this calculation does *not* include tail length.

The results of the rule for various lengths of fish have been shown. It does not matter if a fish is slim or full-bodied; slimmer fishes are usually more active and demand more oxygen. Smaller fishes are also given more oxygen—i.e., more tank surface in proportion to their weight.

Readers will see what very large differences may occur from the results of the 1-inch-per-gallon or similar rules. Many more smaller tropical fishes could be housed in, say, a 90-cm tank than this would allow, but fewer larger fishes. Most tropicals are small when purchased and can be crowded to a remarkable extent. All the same, don't be misled by the gross crowding often seen in dealers' tanks—the fishes wouldn't do well indefinitely in such conditions. The rule can be varied for air-breathing fishes such as gouramis, for obvious reasons. Twice as many could be safely housed as far as tank capacity is concerned, but other considerations such as excreta and the nitrogen cycle would prevent permanent housing under such conditions without very frequent water changes. When a tank of mixed sizes of fishes is to be set up, how do we use the rule? We must make a trial calculation along the following lines:

In a 90 x 35 cm tank, surface area 3150 cm², how would the following assortment do?

Answer—even with an assortment of 28 rather large tropicals, there is plenty of room for more; with good aeration, more than twice as many in a well-established tank in the hands of a good aquarist.

Suppose these were coldwater fishes? Then we must multiply by 3, and would find that 6150 cm² are really needed for such an assortment and therefore that even with good aeration they would soon be overcrowded and could not be expected to flourish and to grow in size.

Other Tank Inhabitants

Almost all tank inhabitants other than plants and fishes are undesirable, with the exception of snails. These are a mixed blessing, according to species. Many insects or crustaceans prey on small fishes and may carry fish diseases, others will themselves rapidly be eaten—and like mosquito larvae form a very nice addition to the diet when available. There are a few decorative exceptions, such as the great water beetle *(Hydrophilus piceus)*, which is a vegetarian and large enough to look after itself. Most other beetles and their larvae, like the dragonfly larva, feed on small fishes voraciously and can catch a fish larger than

6 neons, each 3 cm long	=	6 x 20 cm²	= 120 cm²
12 mixed barbs, each 5 cm long	=	12 x 80 cm²	= 960 cm²
4 anabantids, each 8 cm long	=	4 x 100 cm²	= 400 cm²
2 corydoras, each 6 cm long	=	2 x 125 cm²	= 250 cm²
4 angels, each 5 cm long	=	4 x 80 cm²	= 320 cm²

Total 2050 cm²

Melanoides tuberculata, a livebearing snail from Malaya.

themselves and suck its blood or chew into it. Crayfish are also an exception, but will be attacked by many of the larger fish species.

Aquarium-bred snails, free from diseases that wild-caught snails may carry, feed on algae and decaying vegetation while doing little damage to healthy plants or none at all. Very large specimens are best avoided, as an unnoticed death may seriously foul the water. A fairly recent introduction is the best of all, the Malayan snail *(Melanoides tuberculata),* a small brown-shelled conical snail that burrows in the gravel and helps to keep it sweet and healthy in the absence of an undergravel filter, or even in its presence if the filter covers only a part of the aquarium bottom. These snails may be rarely seen during the daytime, but they come up out of the gravel at night and may be culled then, as their one fault is to overpopulate the gravel. They are carnivorous as well as eating decaying vegetable matter.

More decorative snails include the ramshorns *(Planorbis corneus),* which are handsome snails growing up to 2.5 cm or so in diameter, their shells forming a flat coil, hence the name. The red variety is especially beautiful and has a semitransparent shell and a bright red body. Whelk-like snails include the Australian red snail *(Bulinus australianus),* a small bright red species, and various *Lymnaea* species, some of which are also carnivores that feed only on dead material and are harmless to other creatures. The Japanese livebearing snail *(Viviparus malleatus)* is best avoided, as it grows very large and is dangerous if it dies without prompt removal.

Beware of bivalves! These include freshwater mussels, which do not thrive in tropical tanks. They die unnoticed, and some, such as *Anodonta cygnea,* the swan mussel, not only plough up the bottom and spoil the scenery, but if allowed to propagate the female frees masses of larvae into the water that live as parasites on the fishes for several months before dropping off again.

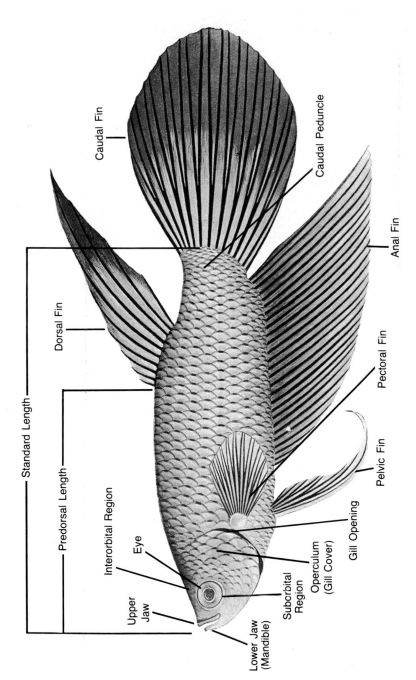

This diagram of *Betta splendens* shows the major external features of the fish.

Caudal Fin

Caudal Peduncle

Anal Fin

Dorsal Fin

Pectoral Fin

Standard Length

Predorsal Length

Pelvic Fin

Interorbital Region

Eye

Gill Opening

Upper Jaw

Operculum (Gill Cover)

Suborbital Region

Lower Jaw (Mandible)

Fish Anatomy and Physiology

The first two chapters helped you to start your aquarium and to put you on the right road to successful aquarium keeping. Now is the time to understand a little more about the peculiarities of fishes and how to keep them healthy and attractive. Fishes are vertebrates, of the most primitive class now surviving in any significant way. They are cold-blooded vertebrates animals possessing a backbone and whose body temperature remains the same as or only a very little above that of the surrounding water. The last is a property they share with the amphibians (frogs, newts, etc.) and the reptiles (snakes, crocodiles, lizards, and so forth), in contrast to the warm-blooded birds and mammals. Otherwise, they are built on the same basic plan as most other vertebrates, with fins in place of limbs, a tail, and the same bony and soft structures in general, except for gills in place of lungs. The gills serve the same purpose as lungs, and absorb oxygen from the water while donating carbon dioxide to it. They also exchange salts with the water, a function not performed by lungs.

When it comes to describing and identifying fishes, two important features are taken into primary consideration—the skin and its scales, and the fins. The other organs of the body are less visible and need dissection for a positive identification in some cases, but very often surface description, particularly if accompanied by a good drawing or photograph, best in color, is all that is needed. It is interesting that ichthyologists were in the past sometimes misled into misclassifying specimens available only as preserved, bleached specimens in bottles, when a single color picture or a glimpse of the living fish would have been enough to put them on the right track.

Skin, Scales, and Body

The skin of a fish may be naked, as in some catfishes, but it is typically provided with scales. Sometimes, as in the group of so-called "armored" catfishes, there are bony plates over most or all of the body, covered by a more or less transparent layer of skin. Scales are often counted on certain parts of the head and body as a guide to classification, but we shall not worry about such details.

The scales may be transparent or opaque. The red, white, orange, and black patterns on koi or fancy goldfish are beneath the scales and are due to color in the lower layers of skin. In other fishes, such as the guppy, pigments overlying the scales in the outer layers of the skin are predominant and are often present in contractile cells called chromatophores, which when expanded expose the colors they contain and when contracted render them invisible. The commonest chromatophore is the melanophore, containing a black or dark brown pigment, melanin. Thus, such a fish can change color dramatically, like a chameleon. Others show varying powers of the same nature, and may often darken at night and color up due to underlying pigments when the chromatophores contract by day. Iridophores (iridocytes) are cells containing crystals of guanin that gleam by reflected light and give some fishes the iridescent appear-

721

ance such as seen in Siamese fighters.

The body of the fish is predominantly composed of a lateral muscle on each side of the backbone, by which it usually swims. This muscle is divided by sheets of connective tissue into segments corresponding with the bony segments of the backbone (vertebrae), seen in cooked fish as the typical flakes. The body cavity of the fish is often small compared with this large muscle mass, and is seen to be between the pectoral fins and the front edge of the anal fin. In it lie all the internal organs, or viscera. Much of the so-called body is thus really the tail, carrying the tail fin at its extremity. The electric organs of fishes like the electric catfish or eel are modified muscle tissue. All muscles produce electric currents as they are stimulated and work, and this capacity has been grossly exaggerated in these species.

Fins

There are, in a normal fish, two pairs of fins and three unpaired fins. In some varieties, such as fancy goldfish, these may be in part suppressed or duplicated. The paired fins are the *pectoral* fins and the *pelvic* (ventral) fins, corresponding to our arms and legs respectively. The unpaired fins are the *dorsal* (back) fin, the *anal* fin, and the *caudal* (tail) fin. These are supported by *fin rays*, the count of which is frequently used as a guide to classification. In some families, the dorsal fin is split into two (or more) separate fins, the front one usually with spiny (unsegmented) rays and the hindermost one with soft (segmented) rays, in others the spiny and soft rays are present in a single fin, the spines always anterior. In some fishes, notably the characins, an adipose fin, a mere blob of fatty tissue with no rays at all, is present behind the rayed dorsal fin.

A closeup of chromatophores in the skin of a fish.

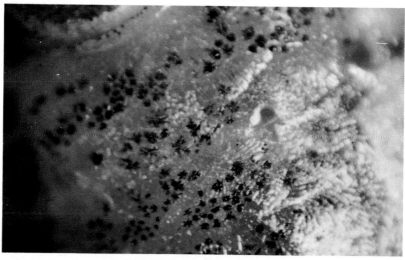

This male dwarf gourami, *Colisa lalia*, is a representative anabantoid, one of the labyrinth fishes.

Lateral Line

Another feature of fishes is the lateral line system, seen externally as a series of canals on the head and a line running from the head along the sides of the body. These canals are a series of tubes lying under the skin with pores opening through it and filled with a gummy secretion and with stiff bristles at their base. They detect vibrations and form a kind of radar-receiving network by which fishes detect what is going on around them. The inner ear is a part of the same network. Some fishes send out quite complex signals as an aid not only to detection of surrounding objects, but to the concerted action of schools of their kind.

Chemical Senses

In fishes, the senses of taste and smell are more generalized than in ourselves, and as an overall chemical sense are distributed outside and inside the body. There are nostrils, two or four in total, on each side of the head.

The Labyrinth

Some families of fishes have auxiliary breathing organs. One such is the labyrinth, present in the anabantoids (gouramis, fighting fishes, etc.). It is richly supplied with blood vessels, and the fish passes air via the mouth over these vessels, where exchange of oxygen and carbon dioxide occurs. As a result, such fishes can live in putrid water or in very crowded conditions and may be kept in small jars or pots without harm—a particularly useful trait for fighting fishes, the males of which cannot be kept together since they fight and severely damage or even kill one another.

Swim Bladder

Many fishes have an internal sac, which may or may not be connected with the gut, into which gases are secreted from the bloodstream. The primary function of this, the swim bladder, is to help to keep the overall density of the fish near that of the water in which it swims, so that it does not have to exert itself to remain at any particular level beyond a mild action of the fins. If a fish is suddenly brought up from deep water and its swim bladder is such that it cannot get rid of the expanded gases rapidly enough, it will expand, even explode, and the fish cannot be saved. It must be staged (decompressed) just like a diver if this is to be avoided.

A female *Nannacara* using her pectoral fins to fan her eggs.

Swimming and Balancing

The usual swimming motion is achieved by movements of the large body-tail muscle mass already described. Waves of contraction which result in a side to side movement (in contrast to the mammalian top to bottom movement as seen in whales or dolphins) pass down the body from head to tail and drive the fish forward. The paired and unpaired fins serve only as auxiliary control and balancing organs when this type of swimming occurs.

In slower swimming the pectoral fins, which are often transparent, may be used instead of body motion, and they alone, with the unpaired fins and tail acting as antiroll equipment, are used in balancing in the water without progression. Even rapid swimming is achieved in some of the coral fishes with pectoral fins alone.

The fins are thus the organs by which balancing and in part swimming are achieved, but their control via the spinal cord or the brain is dependent on messages received from the *inner ear*, which tells the fish about its attitude in the water, just as in ourselves; from the *eyes*, which perform a similar function; and from the *muscles*, which convey information to the brain about their own state of activity, so that a so-called feedback mechanism is always in operation by which the fish is informed about its own movements. In nature, when most illumination falls from above, the fish is helped to keep an upright position by keeping the eyes equally illuminated. If a slanting source of illumination is supplied, many species swim or hover at an angle, so that it is important that in an aquarium the brightest illumination comes from above. Not only do the fishes look odd when swimming about with a tilt, but it is said to cause permanent damage if they are subjected to such conditions for a long period.

Internal Organs

These do not differ from our own, with fishes possessing a digestive tract, liver, pancreas, spleen, etc. just as we do. Absence of lungs has already been mentioned. Many fishes have teeth, some of which may be placed in the throat rather than forward as in sharks and ourselves. Their circulatory and nervous systems are simpler editions of the higher vertebrate pattern, but their general plan and functions are the same—to circulate oxygenated blood to the body, to remove waste products, and to control body functions, respectively.

Water Temperature

The so-called coldwater fishes, particularly those commonly kept in aquaria, are usually tolerant of a wide temperature range. They should really be called temperature-tolerant fishes, or some such name, as some can stand anything between near freezing to 30°C. It is the tropical fishes that are intolerant of cold, and which with some exceptions are very unhappy below 18°-20°C and happiest at about 24°C. No fish, however, can safely be subjected to sudden temperature changes unless it comes from a very specialized environment like a tide-pool. This is in part why newly acquired specimens are treated as described earlier. Even in a fish tank, it is unwise to allow day to night swings of more than 3°C so that if on a hot summer day the water temperature rises to, say 27°C, do not let it fall below 24°C that night, but take a few days to bring it down again, if it is a coldwater tank. This shouldn't happen in a large tank, but take care with small, exposed aquaria.

The paradise fish, *Macropodus opercularis*, is very tolerant of temperature fluctuations if they occur gradually.

If tropical fishes have been badly chilled in transit (or for any other reason) it has been found better to raise them rapidly up to normal tropical temperatures than to take time for the change. Thus an *upward* temperature rise is less harmful than a *downward* one, but still best avoided *within* the normal range for the species. Fishes received at, say 12°C, should be staged to 24°C within ½ hour, mixing the tank and transit water as usual. Fishes that are in a tank at, say 17°C, because of heater failure, should not be rapidly heated because they won't have been harmed by a brief period at 17°C and should not be subjected to unnecessary stress.

The symptoms of harmful chilling are immediate and long term. Immediate results are a characteristic weaving motion called the "shimmies," like swimming without getting anywhere, and perhaps clamped fins and tail. The later effects are outbreaks of disease, most commonly of a disease called "white spot" or "ich" in freshwater tropicals and often of a rather similar disease called velvet or *Oodinium* disease. Both are discussed later. The symptoms of heat stroke are a gasping respiration, sudden plunges around the tank, or a hugging of the surface and lack of balance. These are in part related to lack of oxygen, but will occur in overheated fishes even in the presence of sufficient oxygen. The only cure is gently lowering the temperature to a reasonable zone, quiet, patience, and strong aeration.

From the above, it will be clear that acclimatization of tropicals to a permanently lower temperature is not feasible. There are some so-called tropicals that have a wide range, but the majority cannot survive low temperatures for more than short periods. Even those that can survive will not breed at low temperatures, so the continuation of the species, in the wild or in the aquarium, resides in the truly tropical fish dependent on warm water conditions.

Growth and Metabolism

The activity of a fish and its rate of growth, including the production of eggs or young if in a female, are the main factors determining its metabolic rate at normal temperatures. Both will be slowed at lower temperatures than normal for the species. The metabolic rate is the rate at which an animal uses up energy and produces heat, an increase in its own weight, or waste products. In a warmblooded animal, the metabolic rate is usually increased by cold conditions and decreased by warmth, because a good deal of the energy produced from food and oxygen intake is needed to keep up a steady body heat. In a coldblooded animal, the reverse is true, because the higher the temperature of its body the more rapidly it processes its food intake, obeying relatively simple chemical laws like a reaction in a test tube. In warmer water, therefore, up to a limit of about 28°C, fishes are hungrier, more active, and require more oxygen. As oxygen is less soluble in warm water than in cold, there comes a point where availability of oxygen is a limiting factor and then the fish slows down again.

Young fishes are growing faster than older ones, and this too will make them hungrier. They cannot eat enough at any one time to keep going for long, and thus will be stunted unless they are able to feed frequently. This means that for optimum growth and health, young fishes need plenty of space,

A cloud of fry surrounding their dwarf cichlid mother. Free-swimming fish fry require large amounts of food in relation to their size.

plenty to eat, frequent feedings, or constantly available food. This would usually have to be live food or it will go foul—except for some newer products that are alleged not to do so. However, many fishes do not respond to food restriction as do mammals. A semistarved human doesn't grow as tall or as large in skeletal size as does an adequately fed one, but he doesn't stay at, say, 60 cm tall. He grows much the same as normally, but if thin, wasted, and miserable. A semistarved fish stops growing and may become sexually mature and even breed at a fraction of the normal size for the species. Of course, if a well-grown fish is starved, it will decline and die, because it is already large and needs adequate food to maintain body weight and fitness.

An interesting example of the above was the production of a dwarf strain of seahorses which had been bred for three generations in quite small, overcrowded aquaria. The parent stock of the *Hippocampus* sp. were about 10 cm long and were bred in captivity, producing young, fed on newly hatched brine shrimp, that didn't grow to more than about 5 cm in length. These became mature and bred, and in turn produced equally small young. The main differences from the parent stock were that the dwarf offspring ate newly hatched brine shrimp throughout their lives, a great advantage for the aquarist, and produced only about 30 young per birth instead of several hundred. Presumably, if given adequate conditions and feeding, the offspring of these dwarfs would once more grow and behave normally, for their genetic makeup wouldn't have changed.

Salt and Water Balance

Although this is a book about freshwater fishes, some species can live in either fresh or salt water, while others are accustomed to brackish water, and the degree to which they can tolerate either pure fresh water or sea water varies. The tolerant fishes, such as salmon, eels, and *Scatophagus*, are *euryhaline*, while fishes that cannot tolerate much change in salinity are *stenohaline*. Most freshwater species can tolerate up to about their own blood level of salts, which is about ⅓ marine strength, at least for short periods.

It used to be thought that the blood concentration of salts resembles what was believed to have been the composition of sea water when fishes first evolved hundreds of millions of years ago, and that the blood of the fish, closely resembling our own, has remained sealed off from the external world while the seas have become saltier and saltier. This belief has been shattered by more recent evidence that the sea has been about as salty as it now is for longer than fishes have existed, and so some other reason must be found why their blood has been kept at a much lower salt concentration.

The main regulatory mechanisms for salt and water control of the blood are the gills and the kidneys. The blood composition has to be kept very steady indeed, or

Scatophagus argus, one of the euryhaline species often encountered in the tropical fish hobby.

A male (lower fish) and female *Betta splendens*, one of the species in which differences between the sexes are greatly pronounced.

illness results. The gills exchange gases with the water, oxygen and carbon dioxide mainly, and some salts are absorbed in fresh water but excreted in salt water. The kidneys excrete various waste products and also some salts, passing copious, dilute urine in fresh water, but a sparse, salty urine in marine or brackish water. The euryhaline fishes can do either; stenohaline fishes virtually only one or the other. Calcium salts have been found to facilitate this ability in many euryhaline fishes, which transfer readily either by stages or even directly from salt to fresh water or *vice versa* as long as the fresh water is hard—i.e., with calcium present in sufficient quantity. So with proper management, we can add to the freshwater tank a variety of species originating in brackish or even full-strength marine water, but we cannot necessarily mix them with freshwater species requiring soft water conditions.

Reproduction

Fishes almost always have separate sexes, but may in some in-

729

A male (lower fish, with gonopodium thrust forward) and female of a livebearing species, *Heterandria formosa*. Distinctions in size and shape between the sexes are often less obvious in other livebearing species.

stances change their sex as they grow up. This, however, is quite uncommon in freshwater fishes. Sex is determined genetically as in other vertebrates and is often accompanied by color differences, so that it is easy in many species to tell males from females just by color or shape, but in some it is bafflingly difficult. Even the fishes themselves don't always seem sure, and two female angels may spawn side by side producing, of course, infertile eggs.

The livebearing fishes, as their name suggests, produce living young and do not lay eggs. The main group of livebearers (Poeciliidae) contains the guppy, platy, molly, swordtail, and many others. The male is characteristically possessed of a *gonopodium*, a modified anal fin adapted to placing packets of spermatozoa into or near the female's genital aperture, which find their way to the eggs she contains. One contact with a male can provide the female with enough spermatozoa for several successive litters, as she can store them alive for two or three months.

The egglaying fishes—the majority of species—spawn with the male and female shedding spermatozoa and eggs more or less simultaneously, since the spermatozoa of those species examined are very short-lived, only about 60 seconds in the trout for example. The eggs usually hatch soon after fertilization, within 1-3 days, usually more quickly the higher the temperature. In some annual fishes, a much longer period of up to several months may elapse between laying and hatching, sometimes related to dry periods during which the species may be represented only by dormant eggs.

Water

Water from the tap may or may not be satisfactory for the aquarium. After standing for a period to get rid of excess chlorine, or treatment to neutralize chloramine, it will often be quite suitable. When giving instructions for starting up an aquarium, this was assumed to be the case. However, areas exist where the water is too hard or too soft, too alkaline or acid, or in other ways unsuitable for general aquarium use. Local aquarists or your dealer can often advise you on this.

Water for breeding fishes often needs special attention and the water in which fishes from which it is intended to raise young are kept is best very carefully monitored. We live in an age of pollution, but luckily tap water must be suitable for human consumption and is nowadays safer than many natural waters, even rainwater, which used to be recommended. Today, rainwater is likely to collect harmful chemicals on the way down (ex. acid rain) as well as dirt and grossly harmful amounts of toxic substances as it runs over roofs and into guttering and drainpipes. Only after a prolonged period of heavy rain is it likely to be safe. Adequate quantities of distilled or demineralized water are likely to be costly or difficult to handle, but if they are available they may form the basis of suitable tank water.

Pure rainwater, distilled water, and demineralized water are too pure for immediate use with most fishes. It is best to add some salts in approximately the proportions:

3 teaspoons (20 g) of common salt (NaCl)

1 teaspoon (7g) of magnesium sulphate ($MgSO_4$)

1 teaspoon (7g) of potassium sulphate (K_2SO_4)

per 40 liters of "pure" water.

Add one liter of this mineralized water per ten liters of aquarium water, which will give a total of about 0.008% of solids predominantly of NaCl instead of calcium salts, needed only for special purposes, as for instance the keeping of estuarine fishes.

Natural and Tank Waters

The "hardness" of natural waters springs mainly from their calcium and magnesium content and is usually expressed as "total hardness," meaning that everything is measured as though it were calcium carbonate, which is then expressed as parts per million or sometimes in German degrees of hardness (one such degree equals 18 ppm). The most important salt of calcium in water is $Ca(HCO_3)_2$ (calcium bicarbonate), followed by Ca_2SO_4 (calcium sulphate). The former is responsible for "temporary" hardness and can be precipitated by boiling, the latter is responsible for "permanent" hardness and is not precipitated, although sparingly soluble. Total hardness is the sum of the two, including corresponding magnesium salts. The pH, or alkalinity or acidity, has already been mentioned and is measured on a scale of 0 (most acid) to 14 (most alkaline), but for all practical purposes in the aquarium the range of 5 to 9 covers our interests (in extreme cases natural waters go beyond these limits but rarely contain fishes if they do so). Salinity is not often considered by freshwater aquarists, although it is very important to marine fishkeepers. The salinity of a body of water refers to its salt content in total, measured as sodium chloride, the main constituent of saline (salty) waters. It is most important to distinguish between hardness and salinity, although in the oceans they go together. Very soft water, containing almost no calcium or magnesium, may be quite saline.

The finer points of pH hardness and salinity may be appreciated from the following table:

Salt used in an aquarium to make the water more saline should not be regular table salt, which is normally iodized.

Type of water	pH	Hardness (ppm)	Salinity (ppm)
Hard tap water (e.g. London)	7.8	310	50
Soft tap water (e.g. New York)	6.7	72	58
Very soft tap water	6.4	12	47
Clean rain water	5.6	2	0
Brackish creek water	7.3	850	2700
Soft water aquarium	6.6	16	73
Community aquarium	6.9	87	245
Goby and "scat" aquarium	7.7	335	1480

The last two aquaria had had some salt or sea water added to make them as suitable as possible to the fishes they contained. It will be noticed that soft water is usually acid and hard water is usually alkaline, but it is possible to have alkaline soft water or acid hard water by purposeful manipulation or sometimes even in nature. The salt content of the water bears no relationship to its pH.

It is only when measurements are made of the three factors above that an aquarist can intelligently appreciate conditions in his tanks, although freshwater aquarists may get along without worrying about salinity, as it makes little difference to most fishes up to quite a high reading—*except* for breeding purposes, when it may be very important. Other conditions that may be measured are the ammonia, nitrite, and nitrate contents, which will be mentioned later, but in normal circumstances they are not of great importance to the freshwater aquarist, since they are automatically taken care of in a well kept tank. Similarly, with oxygen or carbon dioxide, these are difficult for the amateur to measure and not normally catered to by available kits.

Measuring and Adjusting pH

Some details have already been given for measuring pH, and com-

Some pH kits do more than just test the water; they also contain chemicals that can be used to change the pH of the water.

mercial kits are readily available. Choose the more expensive "comparator" types if you can afford them, as they are much more reliable. A suitable indicator of pH in the range of greatest interest is bromothymol (or bromthymol) blue. This is a dyestuff that is yellow at pH 6.0, changes through shades of yellow-green to green at pH 7.0, then to blue at pH 7.6, the upward limit of its useful range. The color developed when 10 drops of a 0.1% solution of bromothymol blue are added to 10 ml (2 teaspoons approx.) of water in a tube is usually compared with a standard disc of colored glasses or with comparator liquid-filled tubes. In the best equipment, these colors are viewed through a specimen of untreated tank water in case it has enough color of its own to confuse the issue. Otherwise, the aquarist is likely to get so used to knowing the appearance of various pH levels that he tends to rely on his own judgment without reference to a standard, which is not very wise.

The pH of an aquarium may need adjustment, particularly when it is first set up, or if it goes sour because of overcrowding or neglect. Permanent improvement in pH can only be attained by attention to housekeeping details, such as cleanliness and care of the pH of any new water introduced. Temporary pH changes may be made by adding chemicals to the water or by using filter media designed to maintain, usually, a neutral pH. The pH can be lowered (made more acid) by adding $small$ amounts of acid sodium phosphate (NaH_2PO_4), preferably in solution at 1% by weight (10 gm per liter), with frequent measurements of pH as mixing takes place. Remember, do not change the pH of an inhabited tank abruptly by more than about 0.5 units per day. The pH can be increased (made more alkaline) by using similar solutions of alkaline sodium phosphate (Na_2HPO_4) or sodium bicarbonate ($NaHCO_3$) in the same way.

A safer and somewhat more lasting change may be achieved with *buffer* mixtures of the two phosphates, so-called because they resist changes in pH until broken down in the aquarium—which may unfortunately happen in only a few days. Pure acid sodium phosphate has a pH in solution of about 4, and pure alkaline sodium phosphate a pH of about 9.5. Together, they give mixtures ranging between the two, with maximum buffering capacity and hence usefulness in a half-and-half mixture of pH 6.8—a useful attribute. Adjust the pH to the desired level as before, or more elegantly as follows: Take, for instance, 1 liter of aquarium water and add small quantities of whichever phosphate solution is needed until the desired pH is obtained, testing at intervals and recording the amount of phosphate solution used. Then multiply the number of liters in the aquarium by the volume of 1% phosphate solution added to your test liter and mix slowly into the aquarium. On top of this, add about 2.5 ml per liter of buffered solution of the desired pH to the tank to keep the pH level steady. These adjustments for pH should be made after all other treatments of the water have already been carried out, as they might change the pH again if they follow it.

The table below shows the pH resulting from various mixtures of the two phosphates:

A slower but more natural acidification of the water can be achieved with a peat filter, which colors the water, but the color in turn may be removed with activated charcoal or perhaps ozone treatment. This more natural method may be best when breeding is contemplated, and the resultant water seems to suit fishes that come from soft water or so-called black water regions very well. These waters have been subjected to soaking of rotting vegetation producing the same effect. The peat is the same as that supplied to gardeners; the German variety is seemingly best and softens the water at the same time as acidifying it. Shellgrit or any lime-containing material in the filter will turn it both alkaline and hard, also desirable for some types of fish.

Measuring and Adjusting Hardness
There are several different ways of measuring hardness, most of which appear to be quite satisfactory and kits for this can be readily purchased. The versenate method is a good one and available under various trade names. Hard water can be softened to a variable extent by boiling it, which removes the so-called temporary hardness, but this is not a very practical method for any but small aquaria. Hard water con-

Percentage of		Resulting
1% Na_2HPO_4	1% NaH_2PO_4	pH
10%	90%	5.9
20%	80%	6.2
30%	70%	6.4
40%	60%	6.6
50%	50%	6.8
60%	40%	7.0
70%	30%	7.2
80%	20%	7.4
90%	10%	7.7

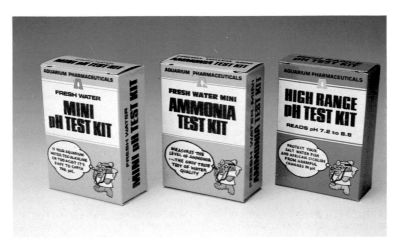

Pet dealers can give sensible advice about which types of test kits you need and how to use them properly. Test kits can vary in their usefulness according to the type of water being tested.

tains up to several hundred ppm, soft water less than one hundred (by definition), but one type of course blends gently into the other in reality.

Adjustment of hardness is achieved by various methods. If a small change is needed, simply remove some of the tank water and replace it with distilled or demineralized water, or clean rain water. In most cases it will be easier to use an ion-exchange resin, which takes up heavy metals and replaces them either with acid (not usually safe to employ) or with sodium chloride according to whether it has been charged with acid or salt originally. Combinations of two resins may be used to produce the completely demineralized water just mentioned. The amount of sodium chloride freed is usually unimportant and will not do any harm. The single resin, such as zeolite, can be recharged

and used again by passing concentrated brine through it. These resins come as tiny beads and must be placed in the filter as for activated charcoal, with a protective layer of fiber above and below them. Use only about 100-200g, as a typical resin can completely soften up to a thousand liters of hard water per kg. Water-softening pillows may also be used, but are rather slow in action.

To harden water, simply add the requisite amount of calcium chloride, best already in solution. For each ppm additional hardness required, equivalent to 1 mg per liter of calcium carbonate, 1.1 mg per liter of calcium chloride is needed. So if you wish to increase hardness from 30 ppm to 100 ppm, 77 mg per liter is needed. It is very rarely necessary to use magnesium salts, as the physiological effects of hard water are mainly due to its calcium content.

Measuring and Adjusting Salinity

In a strictly saltwater aquarium salinity is measured with a hydrometer, which floats higher in the water the denser it is, but the small amounts of salt in a freshwater tank would hardly be detectable by such an instrument. Sea water contains around 3.5% of salt, or 35,000 ppm, a very different proposition from the 10-100 ppm typical of tap water. Avoid adding more salt to an aquarium than would bring it to 300 or 400 ppm, as plants begin to be affected above that level.

The easiest way to measure salinity in fresh water is to titrate against silver nitrate, with potassium chromate as the indicator. Sodium chloride exchanges the chloride ion with silver nitrate ($AgNO_3$) and the silver chloride produced is insoluble in water and forms a white precipitate. If a dilute silver nitrate solution, say 0.1%, is run slowly into a sample of the tank water, say 100 ml, to which a few ml of indicator have been added, silver chloride will precipitate until all of the sodium chloride has been used up, when a reddish-orange precipitate of silver chromate will start to form instead. Stop at this point, read off the amount of silver salts added, which will be in direct proportion to the amount of sodium chloride (or potassium or any other soluble chloride) present. Your druggist will know how to make up suitable solutions if you show him this page and ask for his advice.

To adjust salinity is very easy. If it is to be increased, add calculated amounts of pure rock salt or chemically pure sodium chloride—*not* table salt, which contains unwanted additives and also clouds the water. One level teaspoon per 5 liters increases salinity by about 1000 ppm (0.1%),

which is usually more than needed. More accurately, calculate as for hardness above. To decrease salinity, extract the salt with an ion exchange resin in the acid phase (remembering that you will adjust pH later), or siphon off part of the water and replace it with distilled or demineralized water.

Filling a New Tank

To avoid all of the measurements and adjustments above when filling a new aquarium, it is possible to start with demineralized water and add suitable chemicals

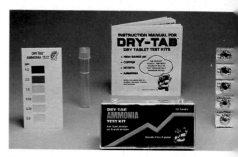

This ammonia test kit is suitable for use with either freshwater or saltwater aquariums.

straight away as described for using rain water earlier. The formula then given was not designed for a specific purpose, but with calculations from the information just supplied you can make up water to any specifications you wish. Thus, 250 liters of water to which is added 0.5 liters of an equal mixture of phosphates and five level teaspoons of rock salt will be of pH 6.8, hardness zero, and salinity 100 ppm—very good for tetras (Characidae).

The Nitrogen Cycle

Of several cycles taking place in natural waters and in the aquarium, the nitrogen cycle is the most important for the aquarist. It concerns the breakdown and eventual

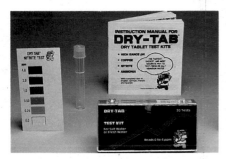

It can be important to monitor the nitrite/nitrate levels in aquaria, and relatively inexpensive kits are available to test the water.

fate of products of decomposition, from uneaten food to feces and decaying plants, all of which contain organic nitrogen—compounds of more or less complexity containing nitrogen but eventually breaking down to simple compounds. Most of this breakdown is the work of bacteria that convert the waste products to ammonia, which exists in water in part as ammonium hydroxide ("liquid ammonia"), in part as ammonium and hydroxyl ions, and in part as dissolved ammonia gas:

nia (dissolved ammonia gas) there is. This is a prime culprit, more toxic than ammonium ions or ammonium hydroxide, and not tolerated by fishes beyond a small fraction of a part per million. It is therefore essential to get rid of the ammonia, and this is done for us by the bacteria that convert ammonia to nitrous acid derivates.

Unfortunately, nitrous acid and its salts, the nitrites, are also somewhat poisonous, so we are not much better off at that stage. Other bacteria luckily bring about a further conversion of nitrites to nitrates, which are no longer very toxic and can also be readily utilized by plants. This is the nitrification stage of the nitrogen cycle, which then continues into a buildup of nitrogenous plant material which takes us back to one of the starting points of the cycle. Some plants can absorb ammonia as well, and some bacteria also carry the process further to produce free nitrogen gas, also harmless, but the main route of conversion is as described.

Kits are available for the measurement of ammonia, nitrites, and nitrates, but few are very reliable. However, some attempt at measurement when things are going wrong is better than none, and the most valuable measurement in an established tank would be of the nitrite level. Once ammonia levels have reached a certain point, bacteria will become established, especially in a tank with an

$$NH_4OH \longleftrightarrow NH_4^+ + OH^- \longleftrightarrow NH_3 + H_2O$$

| ammonium hydroxide | ammonium and hydroxyl ions | dissolved ammonia gas and water |

The higher the pH, the more the equilibrium point is pushed toward the right hand side of the equation and the more free ammo-

undergravel filter, which will rapidly convert it to nitrites, which are more likely to accumulate and cause trouble than is dissolved

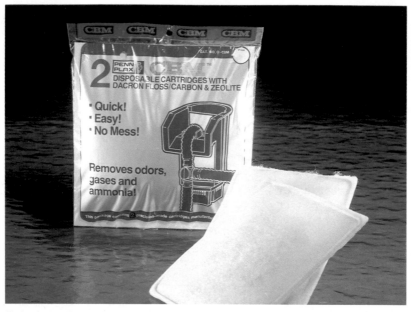

Both power filters and undergravel filters can be equipped with auxiliary filtering agents designed to be effective in removing unwanted chemical contents from the water. The cartridges shown are for a power filter.

ammonia gas. If any detectable level of nitrites exists, steps must be taken to correct the situation—water changes, less feeding, fewer fishes, and a general cleanup all help, as does better illumination for the plants, if it is felt to be needed, to increase their demand for nitrogenous material. Nitrates only matter if over about 40 ppm, which is easily detected with a standard kit, even if approximate in its reading.

In a newly set up aquarium, without an established population of bacteria to keep things in equilibrium, a phenomenon known as the "new tank syndrome" is liable to occur. Since ammonia is the first toxic product of waste material breakdown, and suitable bacteria for its conversion to nitrites may not yet be established, it is liable to build up to enormous levels relative to its toxicity, which is around 0.1 ppm. These may reach 5.0–10.0 ppm, with disastrous results. The same may occur with nitrites, because the bacterial population for their breakdown has also to be established, and as with ammonia this is not stimulated until the material on which these bacteria thrive has accumulated. So an ammonia peak may be followed by a nitrite peak, only later to die down to a steady production of nitrates and very low levels of the first two substances. In a saltwater tank this regularly occurs, because few or no plants are available to deal with the early production of ammonia or nitrites until algae may become established. In a freshwater tank, depending on circumstances, the phenomenon may be considerably modified, but few studies are available for our information. The presence of living, growing plants in the freshwater tank *may* save the day, but it may not, and weakened fishes are very likely to break out with disease at this early stage. This is why care must be taken in stocking a newly set up aquarium.

Other Cycles

A carbon dioxide cycle occurs to a limited extent in a planted tank, with plants in adequate light converting carbon dioxide to sugars and freeing oxygen into the water. The oxygen gas can be seen rising from the plant leaves as a string of bubbles in bright sunlight. However, as the plants are a detriment in poor light or in the dark, the cycle is irregular and of no permanent benefit. The water surface interchange of oxygen and carbon dioxide has already been explained and is far more important.

A phosphorus cycle also occurs, and may be stimulated if phosphate buffers are used as described above. If overused, and perhaps in combination with the excess production of nitrates, algal "blooms" may occur in the aquarium and give rise to green water, which is essentially healthy but hides the fishes and is not welcomed by the aquarist. It is dangerous to try to cure green water by cutting down the light drastically, as this may cause death of the algae and sudden severe pollution. Similarly, excess nutrients in the water may also cause gray or white cloudy water, due to bacteria, and usually occurring in the absence of strong illumination. Both types of cloudiness need careful handling. They can be cleaned up rapidly by fine filtration such as the temporary installation of a capsule-containing power filter, but are likely to return if attention is not given to the

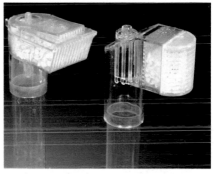

Above: Ammonia removing cartridges designed for use on undergravel filters. **Below:** cartridges attached to undergravel filter stems.

basic cause—once more, better housekeeping is needed. Adjust the lighting gradually, cut down on feeding, and have a general cleanup including a partial water change, while checking that you are not overcrowding the tank. Turn up filters temporarily, and with luck all will soon be well.

Water Changes

Despite the control over water conditions that can be managed by careful husbandry, certain waste products or pollutants are likely to accumulate in aquarium water and not be dealt with by filters or plants or even charcoal. These may be undetectable except by declining health or fertility of the fishes, so that periodic water changes are highly desirable. A nice balance must be achieved in this—too great a water change may be harmful because the fishes or other aquarium inhabitants may have become accustomed to the subtle differences between the old and new water and may not respond at all well to a sudden big change. The older aquarists used to keep their aquarium water even when cleaning up the tank and conserve it carefully for return to the tank, with the belief that the water became in some undefined way "conditioned" and better for the fishes. In the days before activated charcoal or ozone treatment it could become a rich amber color and still be prized (in a way, it was slowly producing black water, but with unwanted products as well). Such water can be tolerated by some fishes, particularly if they have grown up with it, but it is liable to be toxic for newly introduced specimens.

It is therefore standard practice to change part of the water at frequent intervals. It is best to stand the new water in a container for a day or two prior to use, with an airstone if feasible. As long as your local water is not terrible stuff, it may be safe to make small changes, with care about temperature, direct from the tap, but it is always wise to take precautions. A change of 10 to 20% once or twice a month is adequate, the extent of the change depending on how crowded the tank is and how things seem to be going. If you feed heavily, make changes toward the top of the recommended range, but do not exceed it except for a very good reason. This gradual turnover of water keeps toxic substances down to a much lower level than they might otherwise achieve, stops salts or colored waste products from accumulating unduly even if a carbon filter is not used, and often stimulates the fishes to perk up and to feed better even when there is nothing obviously wrong. Quite a small replacement of, say, 10%, will sometimes be followed by a brightening of color and more active behavior, just like opening the window of a stuffy room.

When the water is changed, advantage can be taken of the chance to clean the aquarium up a little. Siphon the water from around any dead spots in the tank, where mulm may collect and not get swept into the filter or absorbed effectively by an undergravel filter. Tip up rocks gently so that any mulm under or around them puffs out and can be siphoned away. If the surface of the gravel is getting clogged in an old aquarium, scrape the siphon inlet along it and rough it up a little, at the same time allowing a gentle flow of water so as to pick up disturbed debris. Any gravel that has been inadvertently siphoned off can be returned subsequently, but avoid much disturbance or the siphon tube will clog. When refilling, if the water is poured gently from 30 cm or so above the aquarium, it will cause bubble formation and not disturb the scenery as the flow of ingoing water is disrupted by the rising bubbles. Alternatively, pour the water onto a rock or large well-rooted plant, which will break up the downward flow and stop disturbances at the bottom of the tank, or even onto your hand, held under the water, or into a basin if there is room to place it on the bottom without crushing plants.

An automatic water changer, a piece of equipment designed to make periodic water changes in an aquarium without any effort by the hobbyist.

When the tank is partly empty take the opportunity to clean the inside of the glass and to make other adjustments. It is a less splashy procedure if there are a few cm of airspace above the water. Clean the glass with a plastic or steel wool pad, making sure that it is quite clean itself before use. The plastic can be washed and re-used, but it is best to throw the steel wool away unless you rinse it thoroughly and use it immediately for another tank—but beware of passing on infection or parasites.

Automatic water changers are available at your pet shop and are a great convenience, especially if you have several tanks.

The great variety of different packaged foods available to hobbyists today allows them to offer their fishes a multitude of different food materials in different forms—flakes, pellets, freeze-dried cubes, frozen, etc. Live foods such as brine shrimp and tubifex worms also are commonly sold in pet shops.

Foods and Feeding

Although some fishes are difficult to feed, few freshwater species pose any particular problems and will thrive as long as suitable foods are provided. We are still fairly ignorant of the finer details of food requirements of fishes, and the well-founded advice to give a mixed diet with a reasonable live food content remains best. A diet of live food alone, although imitating nature, is not always best under aquarium conditions as it is apt to be too restricted in variety and alternative foods may be refused when the sources of live food fail. There is a plethora of good canned, deep-frozen, and dried foods available, making it possible, although not necessarily desirable, to feed entirely on preserved foods of one type or another, except when dealing with very young fishes or newly-hatched fry.

Fishes are very good assimilators of food, meaning that they turn it into their own substance more efficiently than other vertebrates about which anything is known. Typical animals in the wild and we ourselves convert about 10% of our food into flesh. Domestic animals and fowls can go up to 35%, while the brown trout converts 50%. Protein requirements of fishes are therefore high—most studies have been made on coldwater species important in fish farming, but the same must be supposed to hold true for other species until we know more. Temperature is also important; salmon need 40% protein at 8°C, but 55% to gain the same weight increase at 14.5°C. Marine fishes need more protein than freshwater ones, and younger fish more than older ones, but all need

Frozen brine shrimp is just one of the many different types of frozen foods available.

plenty. Thus it is important to look at the labels on commercial foods and make sure that you purchase dry foods of not less than 45-50% protein. Frozen or live foods will naturally have less, containing so much water (70% or over), but their *dried* equivalent is what matters.

Fishes need carbohydrates and fats too, but cannot digest saturated fats (animal fats) as well as we can, and not at all in some species. Polyunsaturated fats, which are oily and occur in fishes naturally, are readily digested and should be the main fats supplied. Starch as such cannot be absorbed, but must be broken down as in ourselves to simple sugars.

The water-soluble vitamins appear to be needed and to perform much the same functions as in higher vertebrates. Something is known of the B complex vitamins—tocopherols are needed to assist fat assimilation, thiamine for carbohydrate utilization, and pyridoxine for protein intake. Some fishes cannot make vitamin

743

C as can most animals, so it is best supplied just in case. This vitamin is needed for growth, healing, and stress responses. The fat-soluble vitamin requirements are not well known, despite the fact that they are plentiful in fish liver oils. Vitamin D_3 is needed in the trout for calcium uptake, and an excess of A and D has been shown to be harmful, but it appears not to have been established that either is actually needed.

Mineral requirements are equally poorly established. A balanced intake of magnesium, calcium, and phosphorus is required in trout, in which iodine deficiency and disturbed thyroid function as a consequence has also been reported. No doubt other fishes have similar needs, but an otherwise adequate diet can fairly safely be assumed to supply them.

Manufacturers often offer foods suitable for the general run of fishes and in addition have specialized foods used for particular purposes or particular species.

Manufactured Foods

A very large choice of commercially made fish foods is available, with varieties specially designed to maintain fishes in a healthy state while others are designed to bring them into breeding condition. They are usually colored to attract the customer rather than the fishes, but this does not matter as long as the coloring matter is not harmful. They may contain attractants, such as dried blood, which stimulate feeding and are therefore of real value. Many containers specify the nature of the ingredients and the percentages of protein, fat, etc., found on analysis, and it is perhaps advisable to restrict purchases to those that do. The average good fish food contains the recommended 45 or 50% protein, although special foods for vegetable eaters will necessarily fall short of this.

Flake foods, made by drying thin layers of prepared mix over rollers, are very popular and can be used with many fishes as a staple diet, to be supplemented with occasional feeds of a different type, frozen or living, for example. Flakes float on the water, where fishes soon learn to eat them, and may also drop gently down if left uneaten for a period. A good flake does not cloud the water or cause pollution if not eaten immediately, and it does no harm if a little remains after a few minutes. However, no food should be left to accumulate for long, as it will decompose and pollute the tank in the end.

Granular dried foods can contain ingredients unsuited to making flakes and are better for the larger fishes, but in the right grain size they are still suitable for small ones. They may contain ground insects, dried *Daphnia*, fish roe, tuna flesh, meat, wheat meal,

Watching their fishes eat is one of the pleasures of owning tropical fishes; seeing their fishes grow almost day by day because of the good care and feeding they've given them provides a great sense of satisfaction to aquarists.

745

Specialized diets are formulated by manufacturers according to both dietary requirements (vegetarian as opposed to carnivorous, for example) and size of the fishes they're intended for.

spinach, dried algae, egg, and so forth, and are varied in composition to suit predominantly carnivorous or vegetarian fishes. As with color, one suspects that the nature of the ingredients, except for predominance of animal or vegetable material, attracts the aquarist rather than his fishes, although some fishes show preferences. At least one food on the market uses color coding to indicate the nature of the food in the flake—an intelligent use of color. Powdery varieties of these foods are suitable for young livebearers at birth and for some types of fry. There is a tendency for manufacturers to offer less expensive and usually less nutritious foods for really large fishes such as carp and pond fishes in general, but their needs

are just the same as those of similar fishes except for the temperature effect noted above and their food should be as good.

Dried or freeze-dried single foods are also readily available— *Daphnia*, *Tubifex*, fairy shrimp, krill, and the old favorite "ants' eggs," which are in fact the pupae of ants and not very nutritious. Some of these foods, in particular the freeze-dried varieties, are very much appreciated by the fishes and would seem to be of good value for the money. Freeze-dried tubifex worms are a great favorite with the fishes and seem to be a good source of nutrition, likewise freeze-dried adult brine shrimp. The process of freeze-drying is stated to kill harmful bacteria, of especial importance with *Tubifex*, but this seems unlikely as freeze-drying is one method of preserving some bacterial cultures. When feeding ordinary live *Tubifex* the bacteria are present; so as long as the worms do not still have a gut full of filth it probably doesn't matter very much.

Deep-Frozen or Canned Foods

A large variety of frozen foods is also on the market, from algae and plankton to brine shrimp, other shrimps, and even small fishes. They are a valuable addition to the menu, particularly as some are sterilized by gamma irradiation. Canned foods intended for human consumption can also be used for fishes, but avoid oily foods. A very good staple diet can be constructed from such items as deep-frozen scallops, shrimp or prawns, fishes of various types, and canned crab, lobster, spinach, peas and other vegetables, after grinding or chopping to sizes suitable to the fishes in question. For the more vegetarian types can be added breakfast cereals of suitable types (not sugar-frosted however!).

Sieve and wash a mixture so as to get rid of unwanted fine particles and juices, then freeze and keep in suitable containers in the freezer compartment of a domestic refrigerator, where it will last almost indefinitely. Add the contents of an ordinary multiple vitamin capsule to each 500g of mix. Take out a day's feeding at a time by using a suitably sized ice cube or similar tray so that you do not have to thaw and refreeze more than is required. The original purchases and the contents of opened cans should be placed in small plastic bags or containers and kept frozen until further use.

Another way of dealing with preserved or canned foods originally recommended by Myron Gordon is to make dried porridge. The original mix was intended for feeding very large numbers of fishes, since he kept about 600 aquaria, and was as follows:

Beef liver	5 lb.	or	2.3 kg
Pablum or Ceravim	14 lb.	or	6.4 kg
Shrimp shell meal	6 lb.	or	2.7 kg
Shredded shrimp meat	3 lb.	or	1.4 kg
Spinach	3 lb.	or	1.4 kg

The raw beef liver is cut into 5 cm pieces and boiled for 15 minutes, then ground or chopped to a suitable size. The water in which it was boiled is used to boil up the rest of the formula, the chopped liver is returned to the mix for a further 15 minutes' boiling, and the paste is ground and kept for feeding, *or* it can be frozen and fed as a porridge. It is of course perfectly possible to make smaller quantities of Gordon's formula by dividing by 10 or any other factor.

Other Preserved or Cooked Foods
Fishes like chopped-up meat of suitable sizes, despite its un-

wanted content of saturated fats. Ham is particularly favored by Europeans as a substitute for live foods; fishes learn to like it and then avidly feed on it. Minced heart or liver is also popular, so is fish itself, but too much of any such food is inadvisable—beef heart contains a toxic factor, meats in general cause intestinal troubles if fed excessively, and raw fish, strangely, has vitamin-destroying properties. Goldfish may be fed non-oily and unspiced kitchen scraps, and so may large tropicals—again, in moderation. Many fishes will readily eat various cereals or shrimp porridge, made as for humans but with some dried shrimp included. Do not feed excessively, or it fouls the tank.

Whether it is worthwhile to prepare your own fish foods will most often depend on how much is needed. It can be very expensive to feed hundreds of fishes on purchased foods, so the keen aquarist with many tanks will tend to prepare his own. It is equally fussy and unnecessary to prepare your own foods if you only have a single aquarium, but it is still a good idea to introduce a little variety by feeding some of that breakfast cereal or egg, some of that canned salmon, or the delicious crab you had for dinner—just put a few grams aside for the fishes! Fishes also like bread—as anyone who gives some of his lunch to pond fishes knows. A few bread crumbs, especially from wholemeal bread, fed to your tropicals now and then supply bulk, vitamins, and minerals.

Live Foods
While live foods are no longer essential to reasonably successful fishkeeping, they are needed for maximum health and for success-

Asellus, a crustacean suitable for fishes big enough to swallow them.

ful breeding in many species. Young fishes in particular need frequent feeding with live foods as their growth tends to be poor without them. Pet shops usually keep adequate supplies, from cultured worms of various small species to freshly caught *Tubifex, Daphnia,* or other crustaceans. Newly hatched brine shrimp are invaluable for large fry and fishes up to the size of neon tetras, but fishes above this size need either a lot of newly hatched brine shrimp or may unfortunately ignore them. It is possible to culture one's own microworms, white worms, Grindal worms, and earthworms, but *not* tubifex worms.

These various species of live foods and others are discussed below.

Earthworms

These are culturable, but unless you keep many tanks it is easiest to dig for them or buy them. They are very good fish food and can be chopped up for the smaller fishes, and even shredded or made into worm puree with instruments specially designed for the purpose. These grind the worms to a paste—grand for fry, but distasteful for the sensitive aquarist. The worms can be killed by dropping them

Bloodworms, the larvae of the insect *Chironomus.*

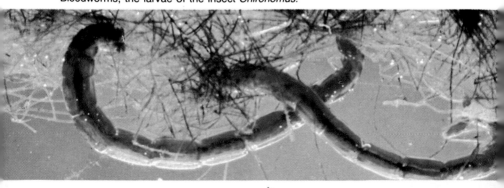

into boiling water, but the fishes don't seem to relish them so much as fresh worms. Earthworms can be bought but may not be easy to get in some areas. If so, they store quite happily in leaf mold, slightly dampened. In an emergency they can be coaxed from the lawn by pouring a solution of 15 mg per liter of potassium permanganate onto it, after which they will emerge if present.

The yellow, smelly dung worm is to be avoided.

Mosquito and Other Larvae

All kinds of insect larvae are fine food, and if caught in ponds they will live in the aquarium almost indefinitely until eaten. Be careful, however, to avoid collecting the larvae of predaceous species such as the dragonfly or water beetles, which can kill small fishes. Luckily, they are usually at the bottom of the pond, whereas the safe larvae are usually at the top. Mosquitos of various species lay egg-rafts on the surface of the water, small sooty-looking clumps of several hundred tiny eggs per raft that hatch as a swarm of tiny surface-clinging "wrigglers" that grow up to about 0.8 cm long in the course of the next 8 or 9 days and turn into pupae that can also be eaten by large fishes. The pupae are comma-shaped, and both larvae and pupae are air breathers. When disturbed they wriggle down into the water, but soon collect again at the surface, tail-up. Found best in smelly, stagnant ponds or puddles, these larvae can be collected with a fine net, washed clean and sorted for size with domestic sieves, and stored in covered vessels until use. Pupae of course do not last for long and will hatch out into annoying mosquitos, so feed them first to the fishes. Refrigeration keeps

Mosquito larvae, a good food in any form.

Three different insect larvae can be seen here: bloodworms (red), mosquito larvae (darkest), glassworm (lightest).

749

them longer and retains more of the nourishment, which is otherwise used up by the starved larvae unless they are fed on decaying vegetable matter. If caught from bodies of water with no fishes present, there is little risk of disease from such larvae.

Chironomus, the bloodworm midge whose larvae are found in similar conditions, is another fine food for medium to large fishes. The parents are gnats, and the larvae are surprisingly large when fully grown. They are blood-red, hence the name. They live deeper in the water than mosquito larvae and are harder to collect cleanly; also they are less frequently found. Whereas the larvae discussed above are found only in mild to warm weather, *Chaoborus,* like a bloodless *Chironomus* in appearance, is a cold-weather species. It is known as the glassworm, but neither it nor *Chironomus* are worms; they are insect larvae.

Land-living larvae are not usually a serious proposition, except that the mealworm is another very welcome change for large fishes. It is the larva of a beetle. Maggots of various types are also much appreciated and can be cultivated, as for instance the blowfly maggot, if you care to do so. This is done by placing some flies in an enclosed vessel with pieces of meat, when the females will lay their eggs. This is best done outside!

Crustaceans
Small crustaceans may also be collected from ponds and form an equally valuable source of live

Live daphnia and other small crustaceans shown after having been collected from a pond; insect larvae also appear in the collection.

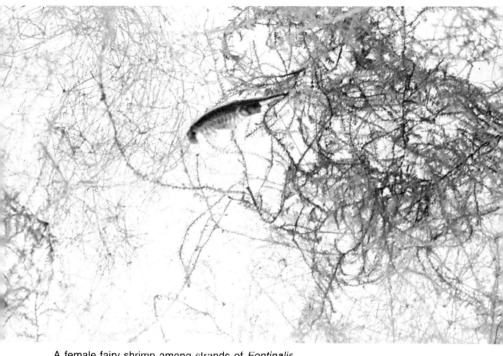

A female fairy shrimp among strands of *Fontinalis*.

food. *Daphnia pulex*, the water flea, is the commonest. It swarms in warmer weather in outdoor pools and may be cultivated and fed on liver powder, dried blood, or similar protein-rich powders. Baby foods are a possibility also. *Daphnia* occur in clouds in the water and may be netted out in quantity with any luck They can be green, red, or yellowish in color according to strain and food; the green ones are full of the algae they have eaten. All that is needed is a good wash and cool storage. Transportation is sometimes a problem if many are collected. This can be solved by laying the fleas onto flat trays of cheesecloth or similar material kept soaking wet. Colonies of *Daphnia* can be started from dried *Daphnia*, although not freeze-dried *Daphnia*,

as the winter eggs laid towards the end of the season survive drying up as they do in nature, and hatch in the spring.

Daphnia are perhaps the easiest live food to cultivate except for some of the small whiteworm species. They only need room, and cannot be raised successfully in small tanks. A temperature of about 15°C is best, not too warm, as the flea tends to die off above about 21°C. An old tank or tub of at least 100 cm in length or a pool of larger size and about 60 cm deep is ideal. If outdoors, feed with dried liver, blood, or sheep manure 2 or 3 times a week and, if feasible, supply aeration. If indoors, confine feeding to yeast or wheat flour to achieve a less smelly mix. The adults give birth to live young, a process that is fascinating to watch under a low-power microscope.

No other small crustacean is of much importance as a live food, and the ubiquitous *Cyclops* should be avoided. It is not a very acceptable food as far as the fishes are concerned and can become a pest in the aquarium, being suspected of feeding on fish eggs in addition. *Moina, Diaptomus,* and some other small crustaceans can be collected on occasion and are equally easy to cultivate. They are not so palatable to all fishes, but most will eat them. The larger, shrimp-like *Gammarus* and *Asellus* species are more acceptable when they can be found. Both can be cultivated much as for *Daphnia.* They occur in streams as well as ponds and can be netted from water weeds and the roots of floating or border plants. They are coldwater breeders but may of course be fed to tropical fishes. *Hyalella,* commoner in the U.S. than Europe, will live and breed in warmer waters. The brine shrimp, a most important article of diet, will be dealt with in the next section.

Brine shrimp *(Artemia salina)* live in very saline water, such as the Great Salt Lake in Utah, and has the very useful attribute that its eggs can withstand drying for several years. The eggs are often collected from salt-pans where the commercial evaporation of sea water is taking place. They are dried if necessary, sifted, and packed for long term storage under vacuum, but are available from retailers in small or large amounts in bottled form. Although they should be used within a few years of collection for maximum hatching, I (C.W.E.) recently discovered a quart tin of them that had been overlooked for at least 15 years, and obtained excellent hatches in ordinary sea water.

The eggs are very small and form a fine brownish powder that is measured out for hatching in quite small quantities. The smallest pinch contains hundreds of eggs that hatch out in sea water or an equivalent mix, although the adult requires a much denser brine. There are two methods of hatching, both of which can be achieved using a salt solution made from 35 gm (a little under 2 heaped tablespoons) of common salt per liter of tap water, which is approximately the same strength as sea water (a 3½ per cent solution). A temperature between 21-26°C is best; below 21°C they hatch very slowly and below 18°C they may not hatch at all.

If limited amounts of newly-hatched shrimp are required (the so-called nauplii, or first larval form) advantage is taken of the fact that the eggs float on water. *Method 1.* Take a shallow pan, such as a photographer's developing tray, and use not more than one half teaspoon of eggs per 4 liters of salt water. Pour them carefully onto the surface of the water and spread as evenly as possible—the eggs will do this for themselves if not dumped carelessly onto the water, when they may in part sink and in part clump up. Cover and leave for 1-2 days at 21°C or over during which time they should hatch out. The empty egg shells that are not wanted remain on the surface while the nauplii swarm down into the water. If there is much difference in illumination, they will collect at the brightest part, but may suffocate themselves if too crowded for too long.

When the shrimp are to be harvested, dip a flexible siphon tube below the surface of the water and start it up—running it either into a collecting vessel or over a very

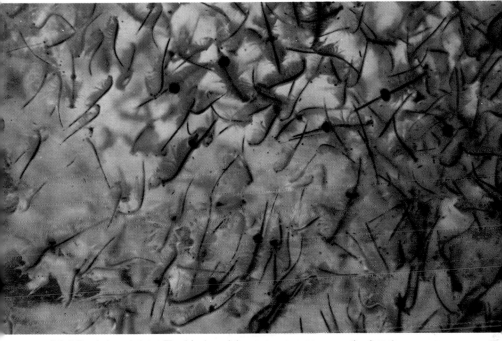
Adult live brine shrimp. The black nodules are egg masses on the females.

fine cloth, to catch the shrimp free of salt water. With careful manipulation, practically all the shrimp can be collected free of eggs, and if screened off onto a cloth as suggested, can be washed carefully with a little fresh water and fed into the aquarium, where they will live for a long enough period in fresh water to be consumed—but do not feed in excess. The salt water can be re-used several times before discarding it.

If large amounts of shrimp are needed, hatching in flat trays may become tedious. The second method uses aeration in deeper vessels.

Method 2. Take one or more 4-liter or larger containers, preferably glass or plastic bottles, and leave about 1 liter of air-space at the top. Introduce an airstone giving as fine bubbles as possible and put in twice the quantity of eggs per liter as in Method 1, if desired. Turn up the aeration very briskly so that the water is boiling in appearance and the eggs are whirled around constantly After the same hatching period as above, turn off the aerator and let things settle for 10-15 minutes. Some egg shells will float, and some may remain at the bottom, while the body of the water will be substantially free of egg shells and contain the shrimp. These are then siphoned off and treated as before.

Newly hatched brine shrimp will live in salt water for a few days without feeding, but they die eventually if not fed. If you wish, they can be raised, even to the adult stage, in a brine consisting of 80 gm of common salt (NaCl), 15 gm of Epsom salts ($MgSO_4$), and 8 gm of baking soda ($NaHCO_3$) per liter of tap water. This brine has about twice the concentration of the hatching solution or of sea water and is much more alkaline. The young shrimp, which normally feed on algae and bacteria, can be raised on baker's yeast, just a pinch or two per liter at first, well stirred into the brine and kept suspended by brisk aeration. Do not overcrowd, especially if you intend to grow them up to the adult stage—a hundred per liter is enough. However, thousands can be raised to a larger size for a week or two if they are to be used sooner. Feed more yeast when the cloudy suspension clears and cover to prevent too much evaporation if in a tank.

At 20-27°C the shrimp will take about 6-8 weeks to attain maturity, when they are about 1 cm long. They will then breed, laying eggs that, if not dried out, hatch rapidly and can provide a continuous culture once the process has been started. However, do not expect too much unless you are prepared to culture on a really large scale and need adult sizes for feeding.

Bottles of suspended shell-less brine shrimp eggs are obtainable, although at a relatively greater cost than for the usual product. Each drop of suspension, well shaken, contains 1000-2000 eggs, so that a small vial can hold a million eggs quite readily. Hatching is as

Brine shrimp hatchery kits containing brine shrimp eggs, salt and related equipment can be purchased at many pet shops.

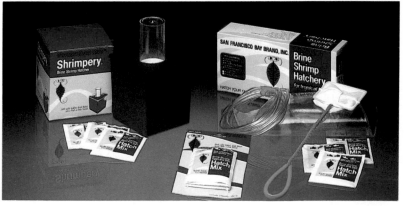

above, without the trouble of separating shrimp from shells. The real convenience of these eggs is that they can be fed directly into the marine aquarium.

The directions above refer primarily to San Francisco brine shrimp—some other varieties need extra ingredients to hatch and grow, notably those from Utah. The container usually provides the necessary information about such eggs, and special salt mixes can be obtained that suit them.

Tubifex

There are many species of *Tubifex* and *Limnodrilus* that are all sold under the name of tubifex worms (more correctly, tubificid worms). They are red to brown (sometimes very dark brown) worms, with a length of 2-10 cm or even more, according to species. They are excellent fish food. Some fishes will only start to eat when offered them, others may be hard to wean from them. The worms live in filth and must be carefully cleaned before use. They come from slowly moving polluted waters, where they have constructed tubes into which they retire on being disturbed. It is the tail end that waves in the water, absorbing whatever oxygen it can get amidst the pollution. When present in any quantity worth collecting, the worms can be dug or grabbed out with a minimum of muck, but some will always be present. Placed in a bucket, they will gradually come up to the top for air, and can be harvested over the course of the next few hours or a day or so, according to their concentration. If they are very thick, place a thin layer of fine sand over the mass and give it a water drip so as to clean and aerate the worms at the same time. If left too long without some air, they will die amidst potent odors.

Wash the worms as they are removed from the bucket and keep them under a dripping water supply until clean—no smell, no cloudy water, no muck entangled with the worms, and no dead worms to remain. They will collect into solid bunches which must be

Live tubifex worms. The worms shown are healthy and have good color; avoid worms that form a reddish-gray sludge.

White worms in their culture medium.

broken up periodically as they die at the center and recommence pollution. After a day or two the gut will have emptied and the worms will be clean enough to feed to the fishes. An alternate method of storing clean worms is in closed vessels or plastic bags in the refrigerator (not frozen). Wash them briskly before use however they have been kept, best in a very fine sieve or, with care, in a container. Unless you are very enthusiastic or have many fishes to feed, it is much easier to buy clean worms from a dealer. Remember, however, that they must be clean, and don't assume this to be the case. They may need further washing before use.

Excess tubifex feeding can lead to the establishment of colonies in the aquarium, where they may be hard to eradicate. Various bottom-living fishes like loaches or armored catfishes *(Corydoras* species) can do the job, but may not clean out everything satisfactorily.

However, as long as not too many worms become established, they may be an asset rather than otherwise, but a heavy population looks out of place and is a potential danger since it may die off and cause severe trouble. It also uses up too much oxygen and may interfere with undergravel filters.

White Worms
These are related to tubifex and are small round worms about 2.5 cm long found in damp places such as beneath dust bins, flower pots, and anywhere there is darkness, moisture, and decaying matter. The common cultivated variety is *Enchytraeus albidus* and has been cultured for very many years. Starter colonies can be purchased or begged from a friend. The best method of cultivation is in wooden or plastic boxes with soil enriched by adding milk and oatmeal, bread crumbs, mashed potatoes, and many other suitable porridge-like

foods. Do not over-enrich, but place small pockets of wet food in the soil and renew every few days. Cover tightly in contact with the soil and store in a cool place in the dark; a glass cover is best, further shaded if necessary by an opaque cover on top. Exposure to the light enables you to see the state of affairs under the glass or after removing the top cover. Worms will breed in and around the food pockets and collect on the cover, especially if it is glass. If trouble is found in harvesting worms, put small amounts of medium plus worms onto a rather hot surface, when the worms will come to the top.

Grindal Worms
A somewhat smaller worm, about 1.5 cm long, also an *Enchytraeus* species, has been named after its original discoverer, Mrs. Morten Grindal. It likes a hotter environment and can be cultivated at 21-24°C by similar techniques, preferably using peat instead of soil. It is a more rapid grower, due to the higher temperature, and suitable for small species of fish. Altogether it is an excellent food.

Microworms
These are nematodes (much smaller than *Enchytraeus*) of the genus *Anguillula*, which contains the vinegar "eel," paste worm, and many soil-living species. The commonly cultivated variety may be *A. silusiae*, from the soil. The maximum length is about 2.5 mm, and it bears living young, multiplying with great speed when in favorable circumstances. It is an important food for young fishes, but of limited interest to larger fishes, many of which ignore microworms. The young are naturally very small, smaller than newly hatched brine shrimp, and for this reason are suitable for feeding newborn fry of many species.

Culture is accomplished in shallow vessels with about 0.5 cm of any good cooked oatmeal or wheatmeal or other quick-cooking

Microworms, eagerly accepted by small fishes.

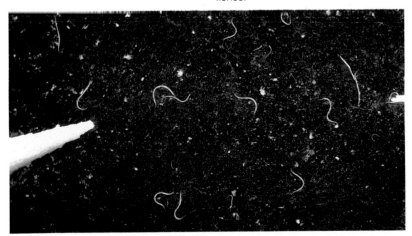

Fruit flies; these are not the wingless variety.

breakfast cereal. Cook without salt and preferably with milk. Cool, and then inoculate with a little baker's yeast and microworm culture. Place small pieces of water-soaked wood crisscrossed in tiers so that they emerge above the food and sit over it two or three layers deep, and the worms will crawl up onto them, as they may also do on the sides of the container. Do not leave the culture uncovered, but keep it in the dark and preferably quite warm—up to 27°C. It is easier to maintain a series of cultures rather than to feed existing ones, so new cultures should be set up each week so as to have a constant supply of worms. The worms can withstand desiccation and can be scraped off and stored for use in airtight (thus wormtight!) tubes. A

dried-up culture can be restarted just by wetting it.

All the worms mentioned above may be purchased from dealers, with food if needed, and with instructions for their cultivation.

Fruitflies

The famous fly of geneticists, *Drosophila melanogaster*, exists as a wingless mutation that makes good fish food. Culture is easy, usually in milk bottles with wide tops and cotton wool plugs in the neck. To prepare a culture, bottles should be sterilized by boiling and dried inverted, then sterile cotton-wool plugs are placed in the necks. Sterile cotton-wool is easily purchased. One overripe banana per bottle is skinned, mashed or blended in a machine, sieved if necessary, and to the result is added 75 ml of water and ¼ teaspoon of nutrient agar per banana. This is boiled over a slow heat, constantly stirred, and when it is boiling ¼ teaspoon of mold inhibitor (available from many biological supply houses) is stirred in. Stirring is continued for 3 minutes, then about 2.5 cm of the liquid is poured into each bottle with care to touch nothing inside the bottle and to replace the plug as rapidly as possible. A small fan of sterile paper towelling is also placed in each bottle so that it reaches from a little below the plug to the bottom.

After everything has cooled down, a pinch of any variety of yeast is added and a few flies put in. Keep the bottles warm, about 24°C is excellent, and the flies will mate and lay their eggs, which will then produce larvae in about a week. These crawl up the paper fans when ready—about 2 weeks from the start—and flies emerge after pupation. Excellent for small reptiles and amphibians as well as for fishes, the flies are just shaken from the bottle as needed, and each bottle will produce more than one generation before a new start is needed.

Feeding Fishes

Coldwater fishes have appetites depending on temperature. If not kept warm in winter, they need feeding only twice or three times weekly, but in summer they catch up to their tropical brethren and need feeding several times a day, preferably, but at least once a day. Small fishes in warm weather cannot eat enough at a single feeding to tide them adequately over 24 hours. In such circumstances, live food in mild excess, of a type which will live on in the aquarium, is very useful. Tubifex can be placed in special feeders that allow individual worms to filter through gradually; mosquito larvae or daphnia can be fed in excess so that some remain to be eaten later. There are also special porridge-like mixtures that can be cooked in small quantities and placed in lumps in the aquarium with alleged safety, to be chewed away for several hours. Some flakes do not pollute the water if not grossly overfed and can form a supply of food available for some time after feeding. However, great care should be taken about pollution and the safety of such procedures should be carefully watched in your own tanks.

Otherwise, the old rule applicable to all other types of food should never be forgotten:

Feed only enough prepared food at one time so that practically ALL of it is consumed within five minutes.

Then siphon off any that remains!

Even the use of undergravel filters does not alter this rule, they merely make for somewhat greater safety if by chance it is broken.

When an aquarist is really experienced, he can feed adequately but not excessively without having to watch the results. But in gaining experience he should watch what

This male guppy is approaching a worm feeder designed to be used for holding tubifex worms so that they can be released slowly to the waiting fishes; the feeder shown is holding live bloodworms, however, instead of tubifex worms.

is going on, particularly with dried or prepared foods. It is also a great advantage, however experienced he may be, at least fairly frequently to watch the fishes eat to see that each one is getting his share and eating it so as to pick up the early signs of anything going wrong. Dry food should also be fed rather slowly and sparingly, as many varieties swell up and should not be offered rapidly in large quantities such that the food could swell up in the stomach and cause distress. This is another reason for feeding little and often rather than dumping a lot of food in at once. It is possible to soak the food before offering it to the fishes, but many fishes do not feed so readily if this is done and appear to prefer the nuttier or dryer flakes or granules. As a guide, a tropical fish of average size, say 5 cm long excluding the tail, will do well at 24°C on twice daily feeding of 10 mg dry weight per feed, which means that each fish consumes 140 mg per week, or 14 gm per 100 fishes—not very much, but enough for normal maintenance.

What to do when away from home is always a problem. Substitute feeders usually overfeed, so if you arrange for a friend to come in and feed the fishes and he is not a fellow aquarist of good experience, make up packets of food to be given strictly one at a time to each tank. Automatic feeders are available; although rather expensive they may be the solution with tanks containing really precious specimens. If you are only away for a short time, even up to a week, it may be safer to let the fishes go hungry. Coldwater fishes could take two weeks of starvation in other than hot weather, but unluckily most of us are more likely to be away during the summer than at other times. Well fed fishes will not suffer permanently from such a period of starvation, but they must have been well looked after prior to it, not kept at a poor level of nutrition. Some will get a certain amount of food from the plants or from encrusting algae on the back, sides, or contents of the tank, although this will not help the carnivores. Leaving the lights on will tend to increase this growth, but unfortunately also to increase fish activity. However, plants need light, and so it is best either to leave the lights permanently on, or purchase a timer switch if away for a week or more, or get someone in to feed and switch lighting on and off.

The Fishes

This chapter forms a brief introduction to those fishes of interest to the freshwater aquarist. It helps to know something about the classification of fishes and to appreciate where those normally kept in small aquaria fit into the scheme. The following, therefore, outlines the main groups of fishes important to aquarists, with easy-to-keep (thus recommended) species noted.

The majority of freshwater aquarium fishes belong to a very few families—Characidae, Cyprinidae, Cobitidae, Callichthyidae, Cyprinodontidae, Cichlidae, Poeciliidae, and Anabantidae—except for the last two, a curious conjunction of families beginning with the letter "C." Those of most interest to the beginner are listed below, preference being given to colorful, easily kept species.

Family Pantodontidae

This is represented by a single species, *Pantodon buchholzi*, the butterfly fish, and is completely unrelated to the marine butterflyfishes, of which there are many species (family Chaetodontidae). An attractive fish looking rather like a flying fish and best kept on its own.

Family Mormyridae

Several genera of fishes are included, some with elongated snouts giving rise to the common name of elephant-nosed fishes.

Pantodon buchholzi, the freshwater butterflyfish, doesn't always accept food readily.

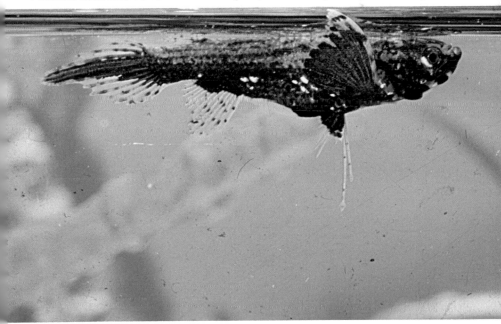

Notopterus chitala, a knife fish from Asia.

Xenomystus nigri, an African knife fish.

Apteronotus albifrons, another gymnotid knife fish . . . and one of the most popular.

Eigenmannia virescens, one of the South American knife fishes of the family Gymnotidae.

Gnathonemus petersi, among the most commonly seen of the elephantnose fishes.

Campylomormyrus tamandua, a mormyrid species occasionally in good supply.

Campylomormyrus tamandua, or worm-jawed mormyrid from the Congo, is a typical example from the hundreds of species in Africa, few of which are yet familiar to us. They are rather delicate fishes, best kept on their own.

Family Notopteridae
A family with few aquarium species, of which the best-known is *Xenomystus nigri*, the African knife fish, so-called because of its body shape and long anal fin that joins the tail fin ventrally.

Characidae and Related Families (Suborder Characoidei)
This is an enormous group compared with those listed above, not only in fishes suitable for the aquarium, but overall. Mostly represented in South America and Africa, the characoids must approach 2,000 species, many small and colorful, making excellent aquarium inmates. They are characterized by normally having an adipose fin, which is, as its name suggests, a small knob of fat adjacent to the tail and on top of the body. Another common feature is the characin hooks on the anal fins of males.

Many characoid species have been bred in captivity for many generations and are beginning to show the polymorphism characteristic of domesticated animals of all kinds. This means that generations of partial or even complete inbreeding have encouraged the appearance of mutant strains, such as albinos and long-finned varieties, which only survive under the aquarist's care and selection. Man himself is polymorphic in a mild way, with different skin, eye, and hair colors for example, but for extreme polymorphism think of varieties of the dog or of the goldfish.

The beauty of this group of cardinal tetras, *Paracheirodon axelrodi*, makes it clear why they're popular.

The bleeding heart tetra, *Hyphessobrycon erythrostigma*.

The oddly shaped hatchetfishes are popular characoids; shown is *Gasteropelecus maculatus*.

Anostomus anostomus, one of the headstanding characoids.

Most characoids are peaceful and very suitable for community tanks, yet the fearsome piranhas belong to this group. They almost all prefer soft, acid water, particularly for breeding, and may gradually decline in unsuitable hard or alkaline water. Many are hardy enough to withstand most community tank conditions, where livebearers, tetras, catfishes, etc. are expected to live together harmoniously, but water conditions should be kept neutral and not too hard for success with such a tank.

Some old and tested favorites among the hardier species are *Gymnocorymbus ternetzi*, the black tetra; *Hemigrammus ocellifer*, the head and tail lights; *H. rhodostomus*, the rummy-nosed tetra; and of course *Paracheirodon innesi*, the neon tetra, sold by the millions. *Paracheirodon axelrodi*, the cardinal tetra, is not so very old as an aquarium fish, but is mentioned in connection with *P. innesi* because of their similarity in appearance and breeding requirements—very soft acid water. *Aphyocharax anisitsi*, the bloodfin, is another old favorite, but peculiar in that it likes hard and alkaline water, even for breeding.

A fairly small family of characoids with a few rather large fishes as aquarium representatives is the Anostomidae. These used to be included in the family Characidae. *Anostomus anostomus*, the striped headstander, was the first known species of the genus, all of which are characterized by a head-down stance which is quite natural to them. *Leporinus fasciatus*, the banded leporinus, is the most popular of a genus with a more normal posture. These are all South American fishes.

Family Cyprinidae

This is a large family of fishes, but with fewer aquarium species. The general run of barbs *(Barbodes, Capoeta,* or *Puntius* species) come from the Old World, mainly India and further east, the rasboras from Sumatra, Malaysia, and Borneo, with a few from India and Sri Lanka, while the danios have a similar range. The barbs were gathered together under the genus *Barbus* until recently, but have

Gymnocorymbus ternetzi, the black tetra.

The fish in the foreground is a male black ruby barb, *Puntius nigrofasciatus*, in breeding colors.

Brachydanio albolineatus, the delicately colored pearl danio.

now been split up mainly into the genera above. They comprise many old favorites, in fact relatively few new barbs are being discovered. They are excellent aquarium fishes, many are easily bred, colorful, and peaceful, and at worst do a little fin nipping.

Tried and tested species include *Puntius conchonius*, the rosy barb; *P. nigrofasciatus*, the black ruby barb; *P. sachsi*, the golden barb and *Barbodes everetti*, the clown barb. The group of vertically striped barbs, oddly not all in the same genus, is often a source of confusion to aquarists. *Barbodes pentazona hexazona*, *B. pentazona pentazona*, *Capoeta tetrazona partipentazona*, and *C. tetrazona tetrazona*, as their names suggest, grade from six to four stripes in the order mentioned, but can be identified using care, although even dealers seem to get confused on occasion. *C. tetrazona*, the tiger barb, is the most colorful and pop-

ular. *C. titteya*, the cherry barb, is the last that will be mentioned of this group, and is a little beauty. Even when not in breeding condition, the males glow rather than just show color. The black ruby barb is its nearest rival in this regard. The barbs are another group of fishes that have been so inbred that long-finned, albino, and other mutants are available.

The rasboras (genus *Rasbora*) are in general small and delicate fishes, not necessarily hard to keep, but usually difficult to breed. They are peaceful, and in contrast to the barbs, which tend to nibble plants, leave them alone. *Rasbora heteromorpha*, the harlequin fish, is an old favorite, breeding in nature in schools, but breedable in aquaria even in pairs. *R. pauciperforata*, the red-line rasbora, and *R. trilineata*, the scissortail, are equally popular. The latter has been known for a hundred years, but was not imported to Eu-

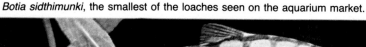

Botia sidthimunki, the smallest of the loaches seen on the aquarium market.

Rasbora maculata, the smallest of the rasboras.

Labiobarbus festiva, a flashy cyprinid species.

Botia modesta, a desirable loach species not always in good supply.

rope until 1932.

The danios are not represented by many species, but practically all are splendid fishes, hardy and easy to breed. They are all slim-bodied schooling fishes that roam actively about the aquarium. *Brachydanio rerio*, the zebra danio, is the best known, being hardy and able to stand cool water down to 15°C or so. *B. albolineatus*, the pearl danio, is another attractive species, and so is *Danio aequipinnatus*, the giant danio, giant meaning 10 cm as opposed to the 5-6 cm of the others.

Family Cobitidae

The loaches and botias are mostly bottom-living fishes, those of aquarium interest coming mainly

from Malaysia, Indonesia, and other parts of the Far East, although the family is widespread. They are good scavengers, but need feeding in addition. *Acanthophthalmus kuhlii*, the coolie loach, is exported by the millions, together with its close relatives *A. myersi* and *A. semicinctus*. *A. myersi* has full vertical bands, the others have only half-bands that do not extend over the abdomen.

Botia hymenophysa, the banded loach, *B. macracantha*, the clown loach, and *B. morletti* (formerly *B. horae*), Hora's loach, are popular species, the clown loach being particularly attractive, with bright red fins and an orange body with wide vertical black stripes. It looks best in groups which swim around together.

Danio aequipinnatus, the giant danio.

The mochokid catfish *Synodontis angelicus*, not often seen but always appreciated.

Family Mochokidae

This family was originally famous for the first-kept member of the genus *Synodontis*, *S. nigriventis*, the upside-down catfish, which swims consistently the wrong way up. It is otherwise not a very attractive fish. Other members of the genus are much nicer, but usually swim normally. *S. angelicus*, the polkadot catfish, is a beauty but unfortunately rare and nocturnal. These fishes come from Africa.

Family Callichthydae

This is a family of small, heavily armored catfishes, outstandingly containing the genus *Corydoras*, of which there are many aquarium species. They come from South America and Trinidad. Their overlying body armor gives them a hard, stony feel; it must be difficult to eat a *Corydoras*. The first popular fish of the genus was *C. aeneus*, the bronze corydoras, found all over South America. It is

Synodontis nigriventris, the upside-down catfish . . . here swimming in normal belly-down orientation.

Corydoras rabauti, more colorful than most other *Corydoras* species.

Otocinclus vestitus, much smaller than most of the other loricariid catfishes.

an excellent fish but not showy and has tended to be displaced by others over recent years. These include *C. arcuatus*, the skunk corydoras with a black stripe along its back, *C. julii*, the leopard corydoras, and *C. nattereri*, the blue or Natterer's corydoras. *C. hastatus*, the pygmy corydoras, differs from the rest in swimming up into the water column most of the time and in its small size of about 3 cm—the others typically reach about 6-7 cm.

Family Loricariidae
A relatively small family as far as aquarium interest goes, but containing a diversity of "uglies"—odd individual species—all from South America. Some grow large in the wild, but aquarium specimens obtained young tend to stay small and even breed as relative midgets.

The oddities include *Hypostomus plecostomus*, the sucker catfish, known to Linnaeus in 1766 and essentially an algae eater; *Rinelori-*caria parva, the whiptailed catfish, a much smaller "ugly"; and *Otocinclus arnoldi*, Arnold's sucker catfish, which only grows to about 5 cm and is a favorite that is often confused with *O. affinis*, a more difficult fish to keep. All the above are good algae clearers.

Family Cyprinodontidae
Cyprinodontidae includes the killifishes, close relatives of the poeciliid livebearers. In fact, the two families have recently been merged and their species redistributed among 9 to 14 newly formed families. Aquarists still use a broad family Cyprinodontidae for egglaying killifishes and a family Pocciliidae for the livebearers.

The aphyosemions are a genus of beautiful fishes with many available species, many of which have been hybridized and also inbred to produce special strains. Often grouped together as panchaxes, they are characterized by laying eggs that are usually adher-

A pair (male above) of *Aplocheilus lineatus*, an Asiatic killifish.

Two males and a female *Aphyosemion australe*, one of the most easily obtainable of the killifishes.

A male of the African killifish species *Aphyosemion cognatum*.

ent to plants. Some may take weeks or months to hatch and may be dried without dying. *Aphyosemion australe,* the lyretail panchax, is one of the most beautiful and relatively hardy species, with a lyretail in the male. Rivalling it is *A. bivittatum,* the two-striped aphyosemion, with color varieties (now often considered full species) that are even more striking. *A. calliurum* also exists in several color varieties and has several subspecific names, with the males the more decorative (as is usual). All the above are from Africa.

Aplocheilus lineatus, the striped panchax, is a member of a less colorful genus, but still a beauty, from India and Sri Lanka. The next genus, *Cynolebias,* takes us across the Atlantic to South America, and of it *Cynolebias bellotti,* the Argentine pearl fish, is the most

famous. These fishes are annuals, living in water holes that dry out completely in the dry season, so that at times no adults exist—only eggs. These hatch when the rains return.

Family Poeciliidae
The livebearers include some of the most popular and easy-to-breed species—guppies, platies, swordtails, and mollies.

Poecilia reticulata, the guppy, from Trinidad and northern South America, is undoubtedly the most widely kept livebearer, many varieties of which have been cultivated in decades of tank breeding. *Xiphophorus helleri,* the swordtail, from Mexico to Guatemala, like the guppy, has many colorful cultivated varieties. However, the original green male swordtail has a magnificent sword, better than in

Male *Nothobranchius palmquisti*, an African annual killifish.

Male *Cynolebias bellottii*, a South American annual killifish.

most more colorful cultivated strains. The female has no sword. Cultivated red, speckled, long-finned, and other varieties have been selected in part by inbreeding and in part by crossing with *X. maculatus,* the platy, and selecting from the offspring. The platy is similar in many ways to the swordtail, lacking a sword however. As usual with popular and easily bred fishes that have been around for a long time, it exists in many colors and finnages.

The mollies are a very popular group, so-called because their generic name used to be *Mollienesia. Poecilia latipinna,* the sailfin molly, comes in a variety of colors, from jet black to greenish gray, with a magnificent dorsal fin in the male, much influenced in development by environmental conditions. *P. sphenops,* the common molly, is a short-finned but attractive fish also coming in a variety of colors and forms. *P. latipinna* is from the southeastern U.S. to the Yucatan, and need brackish, alkaline water and a vegetable diet; *P. sphenops* is a more tropical Mexican and Central American species. Mollies can be adapted to full sea water and form a nice addition to a marine tank.

Family Toxotidae
This family is mentioned because of its famous species, *Toxotes jaculator,* the archer fish, from India to the Philippines. It can shoot drops of water at insects or other prey above water level with astounding accuracy. A brackish water fish in nature.

A black male *Poecilia sphenops* of the lyretail form.

Toxotes chatareus, one of the interesting but difficult-to-keep toxotid species.

Family Scatophagidae

Another limited, brackish water family with the capacity to adapt to alkaline fresh water or sea water. *Scatophagus argus*, the spotted scat, has a very colorful cousin, *S. argus* var. *rubrifrons*, the tiger scat. They come from coastal Indo-Pacific waters and appear to breed in estuaries. *Selenotoca multifasciata*, the silver scat, is another attractive fish, hardy as long as it has hard alkaline water.

Family Cichlidae

The cichlid fishes are very popular, showy, and many are rather large and often pugnacious, although there are dwarf and peaceful species. Many new species have been described from the lakes of Africa, previously almost unexplored commercially. Some of these are beautiful, polymorphic species, but can hardly be classed yet as old and tested favorites. The most popular of the cichlids is undoubtedly the angelfish, followed by the discus fishes. The latter were very expensive until recently, but tank-bred young are now relatively cheap.

Pterophyllum scalare, from South America, is the common angel. It has been bred in the aquarium for many years and now comes in black, golden, lace, veiltail, and other varieties. As with cichlids in general, the parents look after the young.

Pelvicachromis pulcher, the kribensis, is an African species but not from the Rift Lakes area.

Symphysodon discus, the red discus, is the original discus from the Rio Negro, a very much showier fish than the brown discus, *S. aequifasciata axelrodi*, imported in large numbers from the 1930's onwards. Other varieties of *S. aequifasciata* include the blue and the green discus, beautiful fish now well established as breeding stock. Few were bred until it was discovered that the young feed at first from the skin secretions of their parents.

Among the more normally "fish"-shaped cichlids must be mentioned the blue acara, *Aequidens pulcher*, aggressive but beautiful, and *Hemichromis "bimaculatus"*, the jewel cichlid (actually a complex of several species), even more aggressive but so beautiful that many still keep it. More peaceful are *Cichlasoma festivum*,

The brown discus, *Symphysodon aequifasciata axelrodi,* is the least colorful of the discusfishes but beautiful nonetheless.

Geophagus balzanii, a South American cichlid that follows a modified mouthbrooding spawning pattern.

Herotilapia multispinosa, the rainbow cichlid, a fish that is brilliantly colorful during the spawning period.

the flag cichlid, *Cichlasoma meeki*, the firemouth, and *Etroplus maculatus*, the orange chromide and the only cichlid genus from India and Sri Lanka. All are fine fishes.

We pass now to the very popular dwarf species, many of which are beautiful, peaceful species. Some are easy to breed also. They are mostly confined to the genera *Apistogramma* and *Nannacara*, large at 7 cm. *Apistogramma agassizi*, Agassiz's dwarf cichlid, quite variable in color, *Microgeophagus ramirezi*, the butterfly cichlid or ram, and *Nannacara anomala*, the golden dwarf cichlid, are examples of attractive, peaceful and breedable South American species. *Pelvicachromis pulcher*, the kribensis (because it used to be called *Pelmatochromis kribensis*) is usually classified as a dwarf, but is no longer and is a peaceful and beautiful fish and, in contrast, an Old World fish from West Africa.

Anabantidae and Related Families

This is the last group on our list, the labyrinth fishes, which have an air-sac in the gill region in which air gulped in at the water surface can be stored, making the fishes relatively independent of oxygen from the water itself. Most build bubblenests from a sticky saliva-like secretion that make the young, usually guarded by the male, also able to survive in foul conditions until they later develop their labyrinths.

Macropodus opercularis, the paradise fish, was one of the first exotic fishes kept, as it can stand cold water. From the Far East, it unfortunately has a nasty temper, even towards its own species. A more acceptable but still pugnacious fish is *Betta splendens*, the Siamese fighting fish. The short-finned wild type males have been bred into splendiferous long-finned types of almost any color

A pair (male is upper fish) of blue gouramis, *Trichogaster trichopterus*, showing a partial "Cosby gourami" color pattern.

A male pearl gourami, *Trichogaster leeri*, under vegetation that he'll incorporate into his bubblenest.

The dwarf gourami, *Colisa lalia*, is definitely to be recommended to beginning aquarists.

The paradise fish, *Macropodus opercularis*, has been kept by aquarists probably longer than any other anabantoid. Shown is the wild form; an albino variety is even more commonly seen.

demanded. Females remain short-finned, but colorful, and do not fight.

Turning to peaceful species, we have *Colisa lalia*, the dwarf gourami, a 5-cm gem, the male having an enameled appearance with blue and red vertical stripes. Another is *Helostoma temmincki*, the green (or pink depending upon the variety) kissing gourami, famous for its habit of kissing each other, purpose uncertain. *Trichogaster leeri*, the pearl gourami, has a beauty hard to explain without seeing it—just silver, violet, and black with lacy fins and tail, while *T. trichopterus*, the blue or three-spot gourami, is another very attractive, peaceful fish that has been inbred to produce many color varieties, with the added talent of an appetite for *Hydra*, a small freshwater polyp that feeds on fry.

The Health of Fishes

Fishes in the aquarium are subject to a range of diseases similar to our own, and in addition suffer from a degree of external parasitism that far exceeds anything we normally endure. A fish infected with white spot, for example, would be somewhat like a man covered in cysts several centimeters in diameter, and one with fish lice rather like a man infested with large sucking tarantulas that he cannot dislodge. No wonder they scrape themselves on the scenery.

In nature, fishes are rarely so badly infected as they become in the confined space of a tank. Typically, practically every fish caught in the wild is suffering from something, but only mildly. If it has white spot there will only be the odd cyst, and although epidemics can occur they are unusual. This is because there is normally a lot more water per fish than in the aquarium, and the likelihood of a parasite finding its host is much lower. This fact is even apparent in the fish tank itself—if you keep few fishes per tank, an infestation or infection often dies down without treatment, but the typical aquarium is too crowded to hope for this to happen. That is probably why marine aquaria can show recovery without treatment more readily—they are never as crowded as freshwater aquaria, and a disease can die down as the fish gain immunity before it kills them.

As we shall see later, some external diseases and parasites are relatively easy to recognize, while internal ones need more expert diagnosis and usually remain unrecognized in their early stages and

so prove more disastrous. In addition, experience has been gained in the successful treatment of external conditions, while internal ones are usually harder to treat, even when recognized. So we are at present largely in the state of knowing how to deal with a series of external pests, once properly diagnosed, while we don't know how to treat most of the internal ones even when we know what is wrong. This deficiency will no doubt gradually decrease as time goes on, but that's how it is at present.

We have another difficulty to face in treating aquarium fishes. It may be undesirable or even impossible for the aquarist to remove a fish or fishes from the tank in order to treat them. There may be no facilities, or it may be necessary to treat the tank itself in order to eliminate the trouble. This means that we cannot usefully employ a number of effective drugs to treat a whole tank because they kill plants or nitrifying bacteria, stain equipment, or color the water so deeply that nothing can be seen. This is why the present recommendations will rarely include the use of potassium permanganate, methylene blue and various other dyes, or most antibiotics. Sometimes they have to be used, particularly the antibiotics, but only as a last resort and by techniques that will minimize their disadvantages.

Another aspect of the treatment of disease and its diagnosis in the home aquarium is that normally the aquarist does not wish to kill fishes in order to discover what is wrong and does not, anyway, have the knowledge to diagnose ailments from smears of skin or organs or from examination of a corpse. Furthermore, he is unlikely to possess a microscope and other necessary equipment. This means that he must depend on observations of the fishes in the aquarium and can only see external symptoms. In this chapter it will therefore be assumed that that is all he can do, and that the fishes will, if possible, be treated in the tank.

When this is done, it must be recalled that activated charcoal and most resin-containing filter media will remove remedies very effectively, so filters containing them must be turned off. Undergravel filters are affected by some drugs, particularly by antibiotics, and must also be turned off as far as is feasible if high doses of these are used—but turning an undergravel filter off for longer than a few hours (exactly for how long is an open question) has its dangers, as the bacteria may start dying. So the best we can do if a drug is a danger to nitrifying bacteria is to turn undergravel filters down to a minimum or off for several hours

Bleeding heart tetras, *Hyphessobrycon erythrostigma*, badly infested with the protozoan parasite *Ichthyophthirius*, causative agent of the disease known as "ich."

at a time and then on again for an hour or two. Actually, the best we can really do is to avoid adding such a drug to the tank water at all costs—a rather difficult matter of judgement. With filters turned down or off, it is best to increase aeration to a maximum, putting in airstones if they are not already in use.

The following table lists various symptoms visible to the aquarist. The physical symptoms are most important in helping to decide what may be wrong, but in combination with behavioral symptoms the two may suggest an almost certain diagnosis. If the fishes are covered by white spots and are also glancing off rocks and plants it is almost certainly a case of *Ichthyophthirius* infection. If the symptoms suggest more than one possible disease, do not forget that it is often possible to give simultaneous treatments, particularly if a trial of the drugs recommended in a few liters of tank water at the dosages stipulated does not show any interaction, such as a precipitate or cloudiness.

Activated carbons and charcoals and other filtration aids can remove or greatly affect drugs put into the aquarium water.

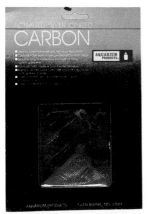

Physical Symptoms	Probable Cause(s)
Small white spots on fins or skin	*Ichthyophthirius* (white spot)
Very fine peppery coating on fins or skin, usually yellowish and moving	*Oodinium* (velvet)
Gray or white fluffy patches on skin	*Saprolegnia* or *Achlya* (fungus)
Gray or white fluffy patches around mouth	*Chondrococcus columnaris* (mouth fungus)
Pale appearance as if beneath the skin	*Plistophora* ("neon disease")
Black to red nodules beneath the skin	Metacercariae (digenetic flukes)
White to dark nodules beneath the skin	Cestoda (tapeworm larvae)
Milky cloudiness on surface of skin	*Costia, Chilodonella, Trichodina*, or even pH too extreme
Red streaks on skin or fins	Red pest (bacterial)
Destruction of tail or fins	Tail or fin rot (bacterial)
Ulcerated patches on skin	Red pest or *Ichthyosporidium*
Yellow to black nodules on skin or below it	*Ichthyosporidium*
Emaciation, hollow belly, possibly sores	Tuberculosis, *Hexamita*
Protrusion of scales, with bloated body	Dropsy (*Aeromonas*)
Protrusion of scales, often reddish, body normal	Infection of scales and skin (bacterial)
Pop-eye (exophthalmus)	Gas embolism, copper poisoning, various diseases
Cloudiness of eyes, even blindness	Toxins, severe white spot, or velvet
Holes in head, ulceration of lateral line	*Hexamita*

Physical Symptoms	Probable Cause(s)
Crustaceans on skin	*Argulus, Ergasilus*, etc.
Flukes visible on skin or gills	*Gyrodactylus*, etc.
Worms hanging from anus	Nematoda
Nodular white swellings on fins or body	Lymphocystis (a virus); *Glugea* or *Henneguya* (sporozoans)
Spinal deformity	Genetic, vitamin deficiency, calcium deficiency, tuberculosis, *Ichthyosporidium*

Behavioral Symptoms

Glancing off rocks or plants	Velvet or white spot, toxins
Fins clamped	Velvet or white spot, toxins
Sluggish movements, loss of balance	Trypanoplasma (sleeping sickness), tank too cold, possibly other diseases
Severe loss of balance, even belly up	Swim bladder disease
Gasping at surface	Oxygen deficiency, carbon dioxide excess, tank too hot, toxins
Jumping out of water, sudden dashes	pH wrong, toxins
Unusual coloration, particularly if dark	*Ichthyosporidium*, toxins

Further diagnosis is not possible without examination of smears from skin or gills or dissection of the fish and, usually, microscopic examination of the organs.

Commercial preparations of the drugs recommended below are frequently available, often in combination so as to cater for a variety of diseases. If the make-up of a remedy is not specified it is best avoided, otherwise follow the manufacturer's directions carefully as he knows (or should!) the effects of his particular drugs. Ask your dealer whether any remedy you think of using colors or clouds the water, kills plants, or has other side effects, and avoid it if it does. Luckily, some drugs such as acriflavine have a curative effect on several diseases—both velvet and fin or tail rot for example—so that uncertainty of diagnosis may lead to the choice of such a preparation as the best bet.

In the following pages we shall deal with the commoner diseases of aquarium fishes, in order roughly of the size of the infective or parasitic organism—from viruses to flukes and crustaceans.

VIRAL DISEASES

Very little is known about viral diseases in fishes, and the only outstanding one in aquarium specimens is lymphocystis. Viruses are obligatory parasites, unable to propagate outside the living cells of a host, and consisting of little more than some genes in a sheath of protein. They are minute, up to about 0.3u in diameter (u = 0.001 mm and there is usually no known treatment.

The **lymphocystis** virus causes the host cells to swell up enormously in local groups, giving rise to tumors with a granular appearance, white, and rather like spawn of some kind attached to body or fins. The disease is not usually fatal, but it is of course infectious and there is no cure. Depending on circumstances, it is usually best to destroy the infected fish. Lymphocystis is not common in freshwater tanks.

Lymphocystis in the skin of an infected fish.

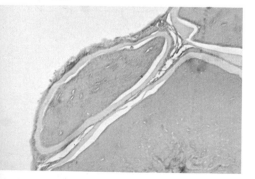

BACTERIAL DISEASES

In contrast to viruses, bacteria, which are much larger (although still microscopic in size), can usually live and multiply as free organisms and are much more susceptible to treatment. However, since there is usually neither the time nor facilities to determine for certain exactly which bacterium is the cause of any particular outbreak, the diseases caused by bacteria will be dealt with under general headings rather than by reference to the particular species of bacterium that may be causing them.

Red pest is so-called because bloody streaks occur on body, fins, or tail, which may proceed to ulceration, and in the case of the appendages, to **fin** or **tail rot**, with parts of the fins or tail actually dropping off. The fishes are infected internally and external treatment is not usually effective except in the case of a very light infection. If the fishes are not badly affected, treat the whole tank with a disinfectant, also clean it up as far as possible and feed only lightly while treatment continues. The best disinfectants for this purpose are acriflavine (trypaflavine) or monacrin (monoaminoacridine) using a 0.2% stock solution at the rate of up to 1 ml per liter. Acriflavine gives a yellow tinge to the water and monacrin a rather attractive bluish sheen, both disappearing as the drugs dissipate. Further treatments can be given every two days or so, but when a cure is effected the water should be gradually changed so as to get rid of any residual drug since prolonged treatment has been said to cause sterility (if this matters). If the fishes do not respond within a few days, particularly if conditions appear to be worsening, do not persist

A severe case of lymphocystis disease is observable on the fins of this unfortunate green terror cichlid, *Aequidens rivulatus*.

Skin cells of a sunfish attacked by lymphocystis.

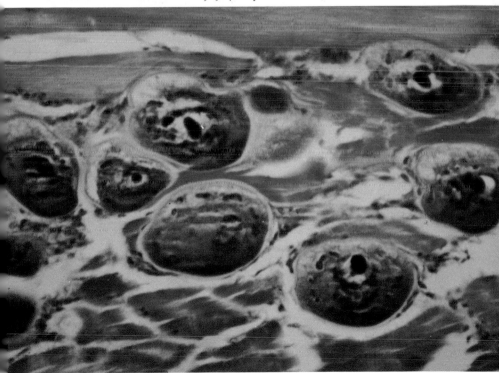

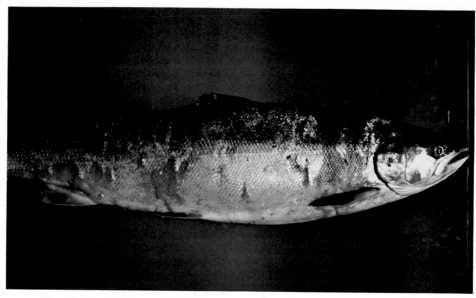

The bloody splotches are indicative of an infection by *Aeromonas liquefaciens*, shown here on a salmonid fish.

An *Aeromonas* species formed into colonies grown in a laboratory.

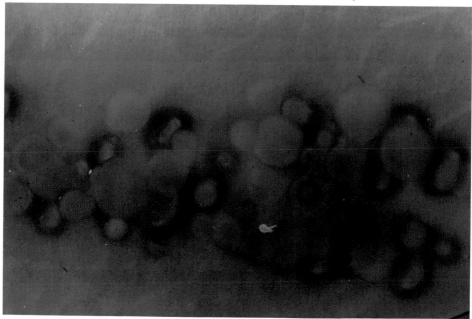

Cichlids displaying the symptoms of severe fin and tail rot.

with these drugs, but switch to the following treatment instead.

It has already been stated that general dosage of the tank with antibiotics is to be avoided. This is because of the dangers of encouraging resistant strains to develop, and also because it is best to treat internal diseases internally instead of hoping that sufficient amounts of the drug will get into the fish if it is added to the water. So, as long as the affected fishes are eating, an antibiotic is added to the food. The best food is flakes or a granular dry food, to which about 1% of the chosen antibiotic is added and carefully mixed with it so as to get an even suspension. If the fishes are kept hungry, the food will be snapped up before much of the antibiotic dissolves in the water. Twice daily feeding will give an effective dosage to the fishes in most instances, while the amount escaping into the tank will be insufficient to cause drug resistance—we hope! Thus, the amounts of typical antibiotics usually recommended—upwards of 10 mg per liter—are far in excess of the few mg of drug that will get into the water instead of being eaten. Suppose we feed 1 gm of dry food to the inhabitants of a 60-liter tank, which is quite a lot. Then if all of the 10 mg of antibiotic dissolves in the water there will still only be 0.17 mg per liter.

Antibiotics will usually be available in capsule form, 250 mg per capsule. If added to 25 gm of dry

795

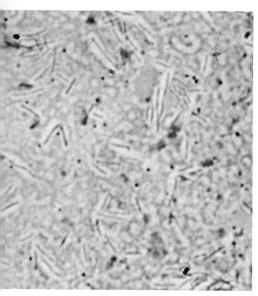

Myxobacteria from a lesion caused by the bacterial disease columnaris.

food, one capsule should suffice to treat dozens of fishes, even if treatment is continued for weeks. The average tropical fish eats around 25 mg per day of dry food, so that one capsule provides 1000 daily doses. The best to try in what is essentially a shotgun treatment is chloromycetin (chloramphenicol). It is colorless, apparently tasteless or even nice tasting to fishes, although very bitter to us, does not harm plants, and is rapidly biodegradable. However, the feeding technique can be used with tetracycline or any other antibiotic you care to use, as any adverse qualities they have when added in quantity to the water are not seen with the small amounts involved. If dry food is not taken, the antibiotic can be mixed with chopped frozen or fresh food, even with tubifex, but not with other live foods. As a last resort, it can be added at at least 10 mg per liter to the water, renewed every other

day, but then all the other problems we have tried to avoid crop up—possible effects on filters and plants, cloudy water, and resistant strains of bacteria.

Mouth fungus is so-called because it looks like a fungus, but it is due to a bacterium, *Chondrococcus columnaris*. It is seen around the lips of fishes, rarely spreading elsewhere, and shows at first as a white line around the lips and later as gray or white short tufts sprouting from the mouth like the hyphae of a true fungus. These are filaments composed of rows of the bacteria, hence the name *columnaris*. The toxins produced and the inability of the fish to eat cause its rapid demise unless early treatment is commenced.

As the fishes usually cannot eat, and as the condition is so dangerous, it is felt that this is an occasion when the immediate use of full-scale antibiotic treatment is justified. Luckily, penicillin is effective and should be given at 10,000 units per liter, with a second dose in two days' time. Chloromycetin can also be used, 10 to 20 mg per liter, also repeated in two days. A cure should result in four or five days. Phenoxethol (2-phenoxyethanol) is another drug recommended by some authors. A 1% solution is made up in distilled water and 10 ml per liter of aquarium water to be repeated once only is recommended. Phenoxethol is toxic, and sparingly soluble in water as it is an oily liquid and so has to be made up in large volumes. Its one advantage is that it is also a cure for fungus proper, and so if the aquarist is uncertain which is present, this drug can be used. Otherwise, choose an antibiotic that is less dangerous to the fishes.

Tuberculosis is caused by the bacterium *Mycobacterium piscium*.

A severe fungal infection of the mouth of *Betta macrostoma*, the Brunei beauty.

Microscopic closeup of the mycelia of the fungus *Saprolegnia*.

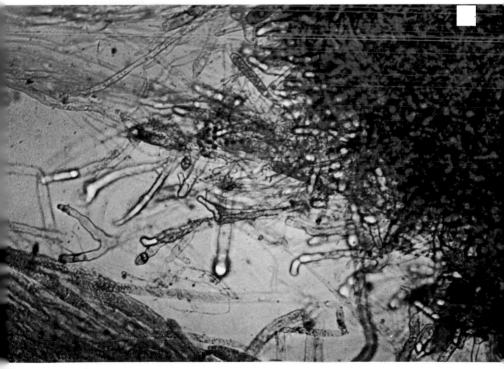

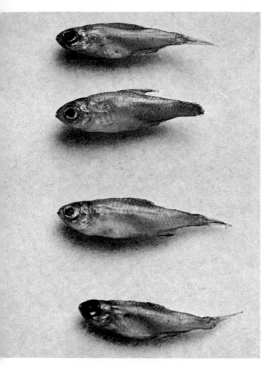

Neon tetras, *Paracheirodon innesi*, that all died from fish tuberculosis. Notice the damage to the fins and the loss of color.

Below: Tuberculosis cysts in the liver of a neon tetra.

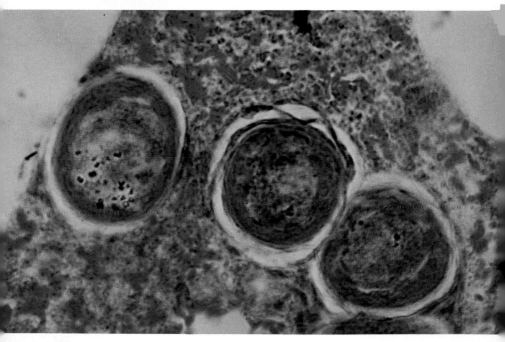

Infected fishes develop a hollow belly, "knife-back" (thinning of the dorsal musculature), become pale, and may show skin ulcers and tattered fins. They do not eat much, which contributes to the condition. The internal organs are spattered with yellowish to darker nodules which may also appear in the eyes or externally elsewhere. No effective treatment has been recorded. The disease, like human tuberculosis, is widespread but only becomes serious when conditions are poor. Infected specimens should be destroyed, to help prevent spread of the disease, and aquarium conditions upgraded as fully as possible. It is apparently possible for humans to become infected with *Mycobacterium piscium*, but only in local lesions.

A dropsical goldfish viewed from above; note the distended scales.

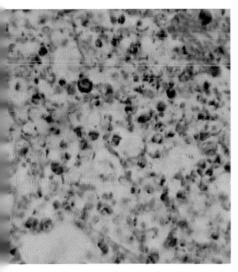

Results of an infection by *Mycobacterium piscium* in the kidney of a fish.

Dropsy in fishes takes two forms, a swelling of the body due to fluid accumulation, eventually causing scale protrusion, and protrusion of the scales without bodily swelling—a kind of false dropsy. True dropsy is caused by bacterial infection of the kidneys and other internal organs, causing the fluid accumulation mentioned, or possibly by simple renal failure. The commonest infective agent is the bacterium *Aeromonas punctata*, again a common inhabitant of the aquarium and its fishes. It only causes trouble to weak fishes, and there appear to be particularly virulent strains that cause dropsy.

Scale protrusion is caused by a variety of bacteria and is essentially an infection of the scales and skin, with swollen reddened areas lifting the scales. *Aeromonas punctata* may cause either dropsy or scale protrusion, but many other organisms can do it.

A cure in both cases should be attempted with chloromycetin or a similar wide-spectrum antibiotic administered in the food as described above, but the success rate does not appear to be high. As with tuberculosis, general aquarium conditions should be improved as far as possible and the infected fishes, if not soon cured, are best destroyed.

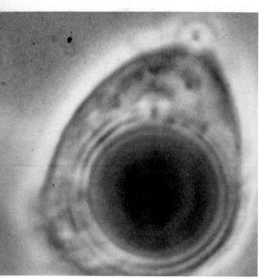

The ripening sporangium of *Oodinoides vastator*.

PROTOZOAL DISEASES

Protozoa, or single-celled animals, can be large enough to be visible, although still consisting of one cell. They are divided into several classes, three of which are important to the aquarist because they contain members parasitic in or on fishes. The Flagellata have one or more whip-like processes by means of which they swim around, the Sporozoa are all parasitic and have spores as a resting stage, but in fact only a few pose problems to the aquarist, while the Ciliata have a surface covered in minute hairs (cilia) by means of which they swim.

Flagellata
Velvet or **rust disease** is perhaps the worst present-day plague of freshwater aquaria. It is caused by a dinoflagellate, classified by some authorities as an alga because it carries chlorophyll, the green pigment of plants. Several species are involved, such as *Oodinium limneticum*, which seems to have originated in the New World, and *Oodinium pillularis*, which seems to have originated in the Old World. All have similar life histories as far as is known.

The free-swimming, infective stage of velvet has a diameter of only about 10u and progresses with the aid of two flagellae, a long one and a short one. It settles down on the gills or skin of the fish, adhering at first by its long flagellum, later putting out pseudopodia, finger-like processes that invade the skin and give it a firmer grip. In the earlier stages, it may move a little while still attached to the skin. It feeds on the host, but the chlorophyll, which enables plants to build up organic substances from gases in the air or water, in *Oodinium* performs a similar function and helps to give it its "rusty" color. Encystment occurs on the fish, and the free-swimming stage is said by some to be produced while the cyst is in the skin, and the cyst is said not to drop off until about 200 young have been released. Others contradict this and describe a free cyst formed on the floor of the tank. Perhaps the life history differs with species. It doesn't make much difference to the aquarist, except that if fishes were removed from a tank and the first account were true, once the free-swimming parasites had died off the tank should be free of infection. Unfortunately, we don't know how long the free-swimming stage lives, so that it is difficult to test the theory.

The appearance of velvet is like a golden or brownish dust over the fins and body which may show the movement described above. Symptoms of irritation, such as glancing off rocks and plants, shortage of

A female killifish (*Nothobranchius kor-thausae*) infected by velvet disease.

Oodinoides vastator shown parasitizing the gills of a fish.

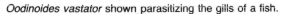

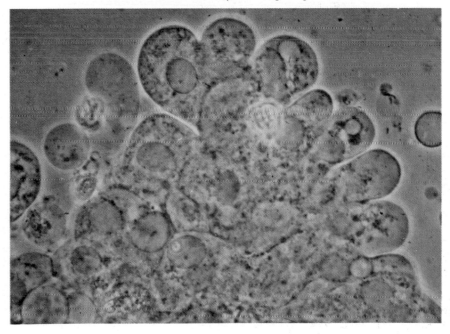

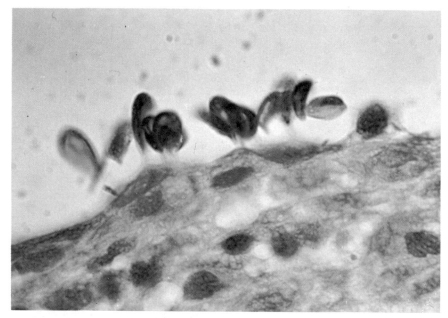

Costia on the skin of an infected fish.

The patches of slimy gray on the sides of this trout have been caused by costiasis.

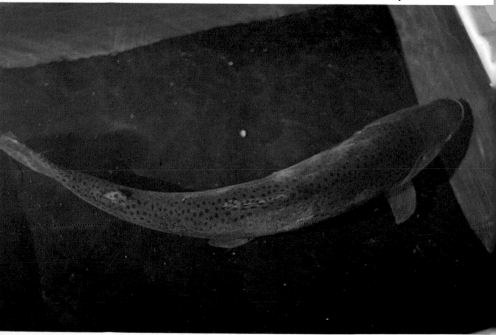

oxygen uptake (rapid respiration), and fin clamping also occur, and the gills will usually be the first affected, followed by the general surface of the fish. Due to its small size, the earlier phases of infestation with the parasite may be hard to see, so take care to examine any suspect carefully, from different angles if possible, and you may be horrified to realize that some of the fishes in a tank carry a heavy infection. The disease affects different species to a surprisingly variable degree. Danios are particularly susceptible, but often show little discomfort even when covered with parasites. However, as the disease is highly contagious and a killer in the end, particularly of young fishes or fry, it should be eradicated as soon as detected.

Treatment is best with copper at a concentration of 0.2 mg per liter, equal to 0.2 ppm, to be repeated once in a few days if necessary. If using blue crystals of copper sulphate, 0.2 mg per liter of copper is contained in 1 mg per liter of crystals, so that a stock solution of copper sulphate crystals should be made in distilled water (not tap water) at a concentration of 0 .5%, and 1 ml per 5 liters added to the aquarium to be treated. The cure is not immediate, but no new velvet parasites should be able to survive and settle on the fish, those already present gradually disappearing. Heat hastens the process and thus helps toward a quicker cure.

Acriflavine (trypaflavine) may be used instead of copper at a strength of 0.2% stock solution adding up to 1 ml per liter. The addition of a teaspoonful of salt per 5 liters may be made, which helps the action of the drug. As acriflavine is said to sterilize fishes if left in contact with them for too

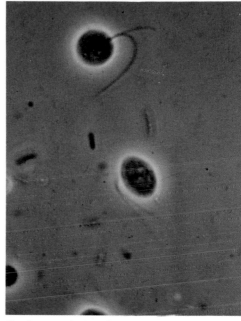

Costia necatrix (also known as *Ichthyobodo necatrix*).

long, the water should be gradually changed after a cure has been effected.

Costia necatrix is a rather rare disease organism in aquaria, causing **skin cloudiness**. It is very like the free-swimming stage of velvet, with two flagellae, and about the same size. However, it does not seem to have a similar life history. Such accounts as are available state that it settles onto the skin, but not by the flagellae, and feeds in an unknown fashion. It multiplies by division on the fish and dies within an hour if separated from it. It is thus a weak parasite but can be a nuisance if untreated. Most fishes can tolerate a temperature of 30-32°C, and this eliminates *Costia*. Otherwise, treatment as for velvet is said to be effective, so if this is true a certain diagnosis is unnecessary.

Hexamita was regarded as causing purely a disease of the intestinal tract until it became associated with **"Hole-in-the-head"** and other lateral line disease symptoms. Another closely related flagellate is *Octomitus*, which may in fact be identical with *Hexamita*. *Hexamita (Octomitus) truttae* is a flagellate with six flagellae in front and two behind that colonizes the gut via ingestion with the food. Infected fishes may become emaciated and may develop sores or ulcerations around the head, sometimes extending down the lateral line. A bad case of hole-in-the-head disease looks as if the head region has been chiselled out here and there. A species said to be found particularly in discus fishes and other large cichlids, *O. symphysodoni*, seems particularly prone to cause this form of the disease. Although the condition is

Hexamita, from the intestines of a fish heavily infected.

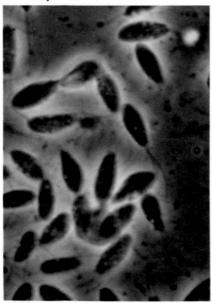

usually associated with *Hexamita*, other causes would seem to exist, but the specific organisms causing it have not been described.

When *Hexamita* is implicated, the drug metronidazole (Flagyl®) is indicated. A combined treatment, in the food (1% in any food the fish will eat) and added to the water (12 mg per liter), is recommended, the latter to be repeated every other day for three treatments. If the fish are not eating, Dylox® can be effective. The drug is available on the market, with directions for use as a bath, not to be placed in the tank. Improvement in general conditions, even without drugs, has been found to help reduce or eradicate hole-in-the-head disease, so that a degree of self-cure is possible.

Trypanoplasma causes **sleeping sickness** of fishes, infecting the blood just as in the corresponding human disease. Infected fishes are drowsy, may swim abnormally, and become emaciated. The disease is seen typically in pond fish brought recently into the aquarium. No cure has been described.

Ciliata

Ichthyophthirius multifiliis (**white spot** or **ich**, pronounced ick) is a large ciliate, up to 1 mm in diameter, spherical in form, and covered by cilia. As an adult, it is embedded in the skin or gills of the fish, causing irritation (with the fish glancing off objects in the tank) and the appearance of small white nodules on skin or gills. Fins and tail may become clamped in the later stages and eventually masses of spots may coalesce and invite ulceration and other infections. In the early stages few spots may be seen, although the gills may be heavily infected and reddened.

In the fish, the parasite penetrates the mucous layer and outer

Ulcerations caused by hole in the head disease on the head of a discus, *Symphysodon.*

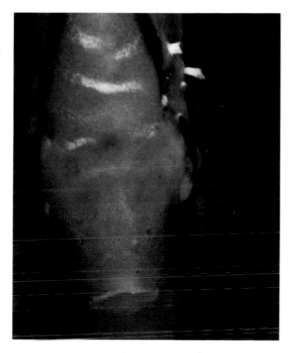

The flagellate *Hexamita,* associated with the disease commonly known as "hole in the head" disease.

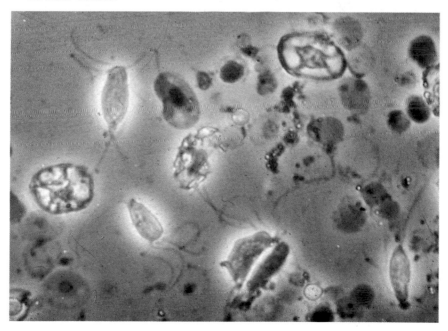

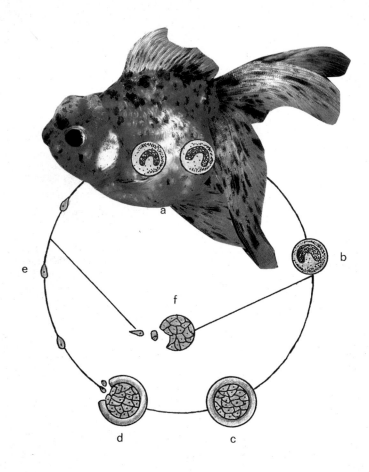

A representation of the life cycle of the parasite *Ichthyophthirius*, with a goldfish as the parasitized species.

a = Infected fish. **b** = closeup of cell. **c** = encysted stage of ich parastite. **d** = eruption of the cyst. **e** parastites in the "swarmer" stage. **f** = direct development on fish.

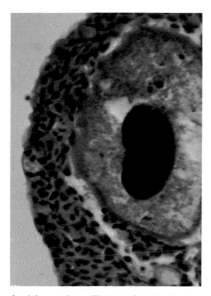

An ich-causing ciliate embedded in the skin of a parasitized fish.

skin layers (outer epidermis) and becomes covered by an epidermal layer, giving rise to a small cyst. This irritates the fish. As the parasite grows it feeds on red blood cells and skin cells. After a few days it is fully grown, bores its way out of the skin, and falls to the bottom of the tank or onto plants or rocks. It then forms a cyst of its own, inside of which rapid cell division results in an average of about 1000 young that swim up into the water seeking a host. The whole cycle takes about four weeks at 20°C but is reduced to about five days at 27°C.

If they do not find a host, the young parasites die within 2-3 days, but unfortunately there appear to be stages in which the adult may remain incompletely developed in the skin of a lightly infected fish and so remain a menace in an apparently healthy specimen. Thus, the tank may be sterilized as far as ich is concerned by removing all fishes and waiting a few days, but complete eradication from the fishes themselves is difficult.

The free-swimming stage is the most readily killed by drugs. In this stage it is very small, about 0.035 mm in diameter, and moves through the water by means of cilia, which row it around by regular beating movements. Because of the filtering effect of the gills and the mass of water passing through them, many of the parasites will be trapped there and become embedded, thence developing into the relatively large, white nodules up to 1.0 mm in size. A few of the free-swimming parasites will also come up against the fins or body, and so at the beginning of an attack of white spot, only a few spots will be seen, most on the fins or tail. The rate at which more become obvious depends on many conditions, but by the time the fishes are heavily infested on fins and body, they will usually be very sick, because their gills will be

This fish is very heavily infested by the parasite *Ichthyophthirius*.

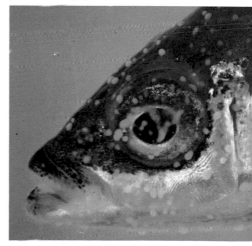

even more heavily laden with the parasites and breathing will be difficult.

Treatment must be external and must be aimed at the free-swimming stage. Hence raising the temperature in tropical tanks hastens development and aids a rapid cure by drugs, but there is a limit to this in coldwater tanks. With certain tropical species, such as labyrinth fishes and many loaches, heat alone may be effective as they can stand temperatures in the 32°C range and the parasite cannot, mainly due to its sensitivity to low oxygen content of the water. With most other fishes, chemical treatment is needed in addition. The drug of choice is quinine hydrochloride at 30 mg per liter (1 in 30,000). Quinine sulphate, which is less soluble, may be used if the hydrochloride is not available. Dissolve the total dose in a liter of water and add it to the tank one third at a time at 12-hour intervals with brisk aeration if possible. At least stir the water well if aeration is not in use. The water may cloud a little, but this will clear, and most plants will not be affected. It will not be necessary to change the water afterwards; just let nature and your periodic partial water changes take care of the residue of the drug.

The cure is not dramatic, as spots on the fish are not much affected. As they fall off in the course of the next few days, the fishes should remain clear thereafter, but any sign of reappearance of spots indicates the need for a further treatment. Do not give this unless necessary, as it can be hard on both plants and fishes. The dose recommended is aimed at eradication of the disease and is near to the tolerance limit of some plants and some fishes too. An acid pH, down to 6.0,

helps in addition, but be sure to make any such adjustment after adding the quinine. Do not remove fishes from the tank for a month after treatment or they may infect another tank, and appear particularly liable to do so. Perhaps quinine helps to cause the resting stage in the skin of the fish mentioned above.

Antibiotics can apparently cure white spot but are still a rather costly method of doing it. Their real advantage is that some are said to effect a cure even on the fish. Thus penicillin is said to clear the condition in a few hours at a concentration of only about 500 units per liter. Other reports would seem to be less optimistic, up to 10,000 units per liter being a more usual dose. Wider spectrum antibiotics are also useful, but some cloud the water, cause frothing, and may discolor the water as they break down. On the whole, antibiotic treatment for protozoal diseases would not be expected to meet with great success, and greater cost plus the danger of causing resistant strains to develop point to their avoidance where possible.

Another frequently recommended cure for white spot is malachite green (zinc-free) at 0.1 ppm, usually cited as 1 drop of a 0.75% solution per 4 liters. It is particularly recommended in commercial use, perhaps for cheapness, but has drawbacks in the aquarium. Firstly, some fishes, particularly tetras, cannot tolerate the drug, and secondly, it stains some plastics and silicone cements. In addition, despite the enthusiasm of its advocates, in the experience of others malachite green does not effect a cure very reliably.

Warning: Note that ich and velvet are not cured by the same drugs, and it is therefore essential

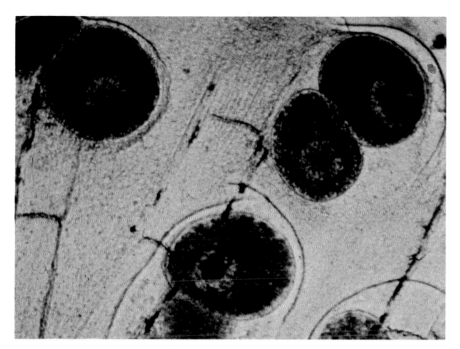

Above: The fins of an infected fish serve just as well as the body as points of attachment for the ich parasite, as shown here. **Below:** A barb that has been heavily infected with ichthyophthiriasis.

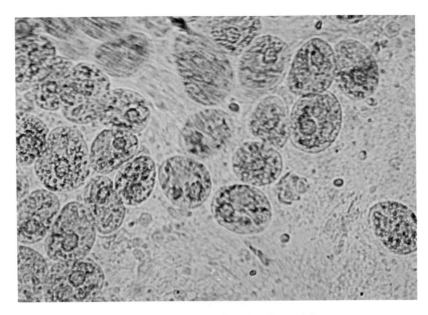

Above and below: Views of the parasite *Chilodonella cyprini*.

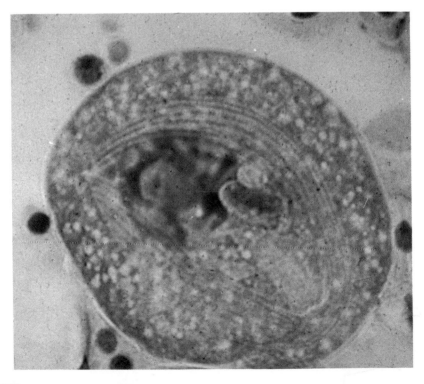

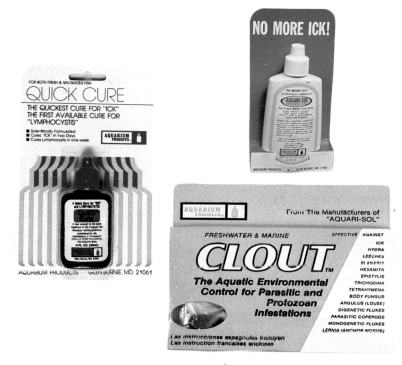

Luckily, ich is fairly easily cured by use of standard remedies sold in pet shops.

to differentiate between them. This is not true of marine white spot, which is caused by a completely different organism (*Cryptocaryon irritans*) which is susceptible to copper treatment, just as is marine velvet. Readers of marine literature might therefore be misled.

Chilodonella cyprini and other species in early stages cause **blue-white cloudiness** of the skin and attack the gills as well. Later the skin may be broken down and the gills destroyed. The ciliate sits on the skin, unlike *Ichthyophthirius* (which bores into it), and can therefore be attacked more readily. The fishes affected behave much as when attacked by any irritating disease that also deprives them of adequate gill function—

glancing off objects, crimped fins, gasping at the surface. Treatment is with acriflavine, as for velvet, but preferably at a stronger concentration, up to 5 ml per liter, with a change of water as soon as possible. It also helps to raise the temperature to 28°C-30°C.

Trichodina, of which there are many species, is rarely found in the aquarium and is famous for its prettiness under the microscope rather than its importance to aquarists. It again resides on the skin and can be treated with acriflavine as above. It causes symptoms similar to *Chilodonella*, so that in amateur practice it is not important to differentiate between them. *Trichodina* rotates constantly on the surface of the host, and with a ring of hooks rather like a circular saw, it eats away at the skin or gills. The life cycles of neither *Trichodina* nor *Chilodonella* appear to have been fully described.

Sporozoa

This is a "class" no longer accepted by systematists, but we shall use it as a convenient dump for spore-forming protozoa that do not progress by flagellae or cilia.

Plistophora hyphessobryconis causes **neon tetra disease**, after the species in which it was first recognized, but it infects other tetras and even other types of fishes. Whitish patches appear as if below the skin surface, very obvious in neons because they obscure or destroy the typical bright blue-green and red stripes along the body. The organisms lie in the muscle tissue in the form of rounded cysts about 30u in diameter which burst and release spores. The spores in turn pene-trate further and form additional cysts. Eventually some spores reach the water, via the skin or perhaps the gut or urinary tract, and are eaten by other fishes in their food. These spores penetrate the gut, migrate to the muscles, and start a new infection. There is no known cure, and infected fishes are best destroyed.

Glugea and *Henneguya*, of each of which there appear to be a number of species, are sporozoans that form large cysts almost anywhere in or on fishes, from which very large numbers of spores are released. When on the surface, the cysts can be confused with lymphocystis, but it doesn't much matter, because in common with it no cure is yet known and infected specimens are best destroyed in the hope that they have not yet passed the disease to others. Luckily, these two sporozoans are not frequently encountered in aquaria, or at any rate recognized.

The spots on the dorsal fin of this *Leporinus* species were caused by *Henneguya*, although they can easily be confused with the spots caused by the ich parasite.

A neon tetra showing evidence of infection by *Plistophora*.

The cysts on the body of this fish were formed by the sporozoan parasite *Glugea*.

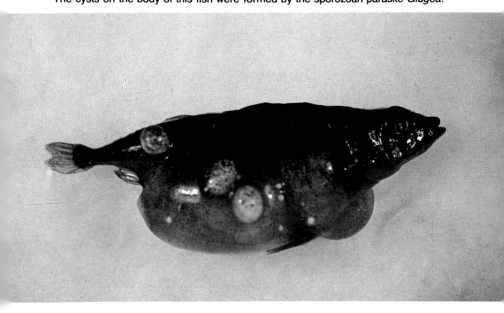

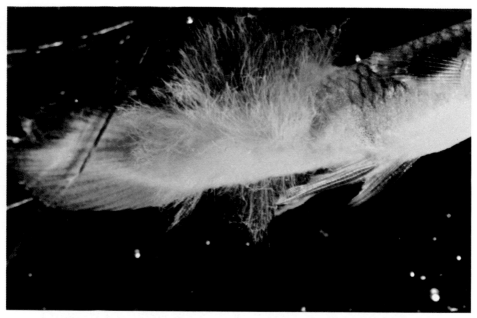

Two different species whose dead flesh has been attacked by the fungus *Saprolegnia*, which has caused the cottony growths. **Above** is an affected guppy; **below** is an affected archer fish.

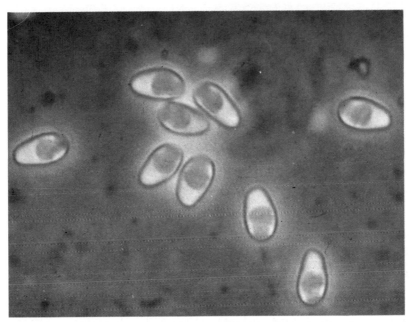

Spores of the sporozoan parasite *Plistophora hyphessobryconis* taken from a neon tetra.

FUNGAL DISEASES

Fungi are colorless plants lacking the chlorophyll characteristic of other plants. They are very diverse in form and life history and have been relatively little studied in fishes. The two following groups of fungi are of importance, but there are no doubt many others.

Saprolegnia and *Achlya* are genera (groups of species) of fungi that attack weakened fishes externally, usually gaining access through damaged skin or gills. They also attack the eggs of fishes. The spores of these fungi are practically universal and enter the aquarium from the air. If only one or two fishes in a tank are affected, it is much better to net them out and to treat each with a fungicidal bath. **Fungus** may attack wounds, damage due to white

spot or other infestations, or even get a hold on undamaged, highly susceptible fishes. Threads of fungus, which eventually form a network below the surface of the skin, spread from a center of infection and eventually produce tufts of external hyphae that may be profuse enough to look like cotton wool. These form spore bodies from which swimming zoospores are eventually freed and infect other fishes, but only if they too are weak or damaged. If left untreated, once it has a hold fungus will spread until it kills the fish, damaging tissues as it does so. Other forms of reproduction also occur, as in many plants.

Symptoms of fungus infection are thus a gray or whitish growth in the skin of the fish, often associated with visible damage, and may

A head-and-tail-light tetra, *Hemigrammus ocellifer*, affected by *Ichthyosporidium*, as evidenced by the mid-body discoloration.

occur anywhere on body or fins. Tufts of external hyphae will eventually give the "cottonwool" appearance. The fish is not distressed, at least at first, unless already showing distress from an untreated precursor such as white spot. It may show loss of areas of fins, tail, or skin, but not the irritation typical of white spot or velvet.

Treatment is with malachite green (zinc-free) or brilliant green in a separate bath for 30 seconds at a strength of approximately 60 mg per liter. Repeat treatments may be given if necessary. The fungus is stained by the dye and killed. Usually it drops off in a few hours. The hyphae below the skin may survive a single treatment, but often seem to be sufficiently affected in any but the heaviest attacks to die off also. It is unwise to treat the whole tank with such

dyes at lower concentrations, as poor or even toxic results have been described.

If a lot of the fishes have fungus, a different approach must be used. This employs phenoxethol at 1% in distilled water. Add 10 ml of this solution per liter of aquarium water, to be repeated once only if necessary. Three treatments within a few days can be dangerous.

Ichthyosporidium hoferi (Ichthyophonus) is a source of great confusion, since biologically *Ichthyosporidium* is a protozoan and *Ichthyophonus* a fungus, but most of the modern literature refers to *Ichthyosporidium* as the fungus and so we shall do so here. This fungal disease is widespread, attacking primarily the liver and kidneys, but it spreads pretty well everywhere. Infection occurs via food, and the parasites invade the bloodstream, settling down to cause cysts of varying size up to 2.5 mm in diameter that are brown in color. Daughter cysts develop from an original one either by budding or inside it, in which case the mother cyst bursts and frees them.

The symptoms are very varied, determined according to the organs infected and the stage of the disease. Fishes may become sluggish, lose balance, show hollow bellies, and eventually external cysts or sores—at which stage the diagnosis becomes fairly obvious, but by then it is usually too late. If only one or two fish are infected it is best to kill them in the hope that the rest may escape the disease, but it is very likely that they are already infected unless the sufferers are newcomers. Unluckily, treatment is difficult. Phenoxethol added to the food as a 1% solution has been advocated and may be combined with addition to the water as for *Saprolegnia*. Chl-

This photo shows sporulation in the fungus *Ichthyosporidium hoferi*.

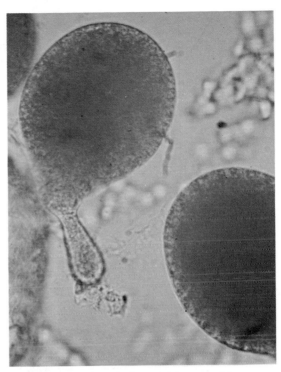

The discolored kidney of the coldwater fish shown here is the grayish mass at the top of the body cavity; the fish was infected with *I. hoferi* at the time of its death.

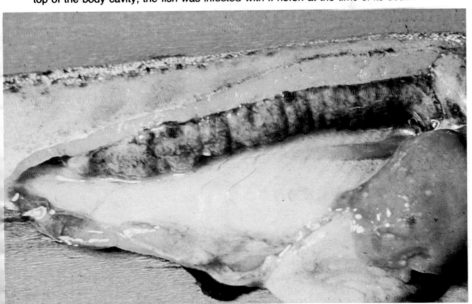

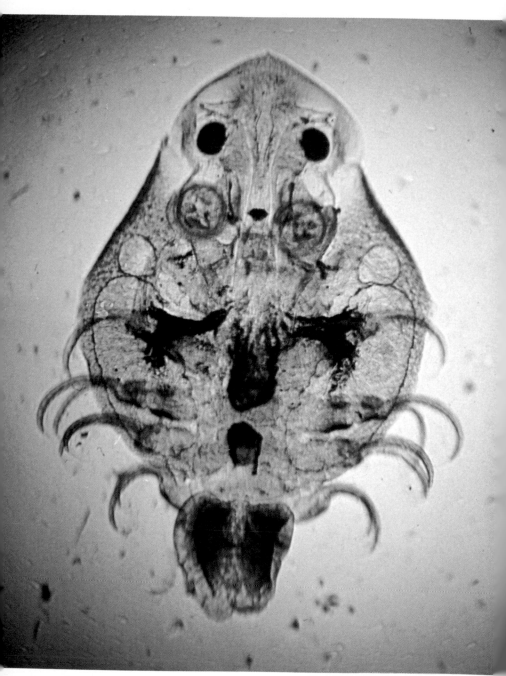

A closeup of *Argulus*, the fish louse; this view, taken from below the animal, clearly shows the attaching mechanisms.

oromycetin added to the food as for bacterial infections has also been recommended. The drug parachlorophenoxethol is apparently a surer cure than its relative but can no longer be recommended as it has proved too toxic.

It is fortunate that with optimal tank conditions infected fishes not yet too badly affected can limit the spread of *Ichthyosporidium* and isolate the cysts within their tissues, no longer allowing it to infect others. This degree of immunity is indeed lucky, since we are dealing with a common infection for which we have only indifferent treatments.

PARASITIC DISEASES

Under this heading, diseases or conditions caused by relatively large creatures will be considered. These are usually grouped under the general heading of parasites, although some of the diseases already dealt with can equally well be described as parasitic.

Argulus, the **fish louse**, a crustacean, may be introduced with live food such as daphnia or on new fishes. There are several species, but only those from the tropics are likely to survive in the tropical tank. All are flattened, mite-like creatures typically about 5 mm in length, that attach themselves to the fish by two large suckers and proceed to feed on its blood. They also have a poison spine between the eyes, are suspected of transmitting diseases, and so should be removed as soon as possible. They irritate the host, which may have clamped fins, become restless, and may even show inflamed areas where the lice have been.

Argulus can be picked off with forceps, but when dealing with small fishes or a heavy infestation this may be impractical. There are

several other treatments. If feasible, a bath of 10 to 30 minutes in 10 mg per liter of potassium permanganate is effective, or the whole tank can be treated with 2 mg per liter, but this is a messy procedure as the drug is deep purple in color and then precipitates out as a brown sludge. A liquid, DFD (difluorodiphenyl-trichloromethylmethane), may be used in a bath at 1 ml per 10 liters for 2-3 minutes but should never be introduced into the tank. Finally, several insecticides have been advocated, but mostly by pondkeepers and for use with coldwater fishes. Extensive aquarium use has not been reported, but if you wish to try them out, the following have been recommended—

The crustacean parasite *Argulus* on a carp. The inverted narrow "V" at the rear end of the parasite is not always so clearly delineated as it is here.

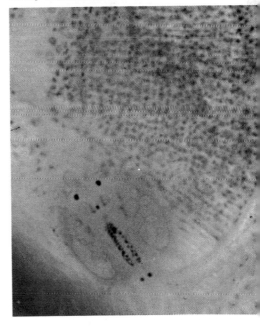

Dibrom or Diptrex at 0.3 ppm (0.3 mg per liter) or lindane at 0.01 ppm (0.01 mg per liter).

Lernaea cyprinacea, the **anchor worm**, is another crustacean and not a worm as the common name suggests. It does, however, look like one as it hangs from a deeply imbedded "anchor" on the skin of the fish, and reaches a length of up to 2 cm. The female is the culprit, as the male does not attack fishes. The young are free-swim-

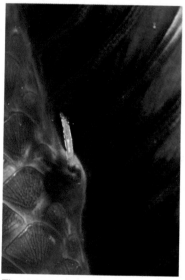

The crustacean parasite anchor worm, *Lernaea*, attached to the body of a goldfish.

ming and penetrate the skin as nauplii (an early developmental stage), go into the muscles and develop for several months before emerging. They release eggs and die, and the holes left behind are ugly and easily infected. Luckily, anchor worms affect mostly coldwater fishes. It is not possible to remove the deeply imbedded worms, and treatments as for *Argulus* must be tried, DFD being the

most recommended.

Ergasilus, another crustacean of which there are several species, attacks the gills of fishes in its nauplius stage, growing to about 2.5 mm. It hangs on by two antennae, modified into hooks, and only leaves when it dies. It does not settle on small fishes, but attacks anything over about 10 cm in length. A bath in DFD as above is recommended.

Flukes (trematodes) are smaller than fish lice or anchor worms, and several genera are found in the aquarium that are parasitic on the fishes. Trematodes may be monogenetic, passing from fish to fish as their only host, or digenetic, passing from fish to another species of animal, such as a bird or mammal, thence via its feces usually to a snail, the commonest intermediate host. Some flukes have as many as five hosts in most complicated cycles. Naturally, the monogenetic flukes are those commonest in aquaria, as the animals necessary to complete the life cycle of digenetic ones aren't going to be available—except for the snails, but these do not usually exchange parasites directly with the fishes.

The commonest genera of monogenetic flukes are *Gyrodactylus*, *Dactylogyrus*, *Neodactylogyrus*, and *Monocoelium*, all flatworms reaching at most 1 mm in length. They infest gills and skin, much like white spot, and can be confused with it, but a lens will show movement of the worms and their typical black eye-spots. The last three genera are predominantly gill parasites and may destroy the gills completely, causing death. *Gyrodactylus* species produce living young, but the others lay eggs that can lie dormant in cold tanks for a long time, but hatch in a few days in a tropical tank. Symptoms of a

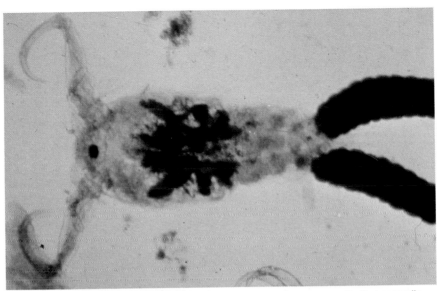

A female (note the egg sacs) *Ergasilus sieboldi*, a crustacean parasite that normally attacks a fish's gills.

A fluke of the genus *Gyrodactylus*.

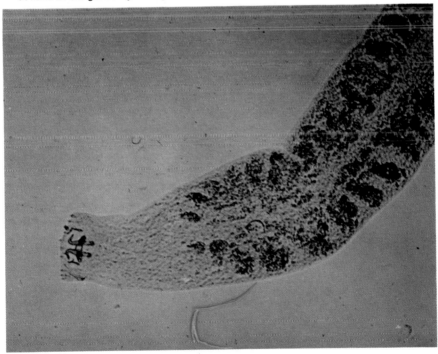

heavy attack are pale fishes with drooping fins, rapid respiration, irritation, and even emaciation.

It is not necessary to try to differentiate between these flukes, as the same treatment applies to all. Treat them as for fish lice, preferably the permanganate bath or aquarium treatment. An alternative is formalin, only as a bath and not in the tank. Two ml of a 40% solution per 10 liters of bath for 45 minutes is adequate. A 20-minute bath in 15 gm per liter of common salt may also prove adequate—this is about half strength sea water.

Diplozoon species are another type of fluke, similarly infesting fish. On the gills, two individuals forming a cross, visible under the hand lens, are normally seen. They are hermaphrodites cross-fertilizing each other. They are about 1.5 mm long. A 20-minute salt bath as described above or the addition of Atabrine (10 mg per liter) or Rivanol (2 mg per liter) to the aquarium has been recommended.

Digenetic flukes do not infest the outside of the fish, and there is no known cure for them. Naturally, they typically occur in newly imported fishes and take two main forms. **Metacercaria disease (blackspot)** is caught from snails that release cercariae, larval forms that penetrate the skin of the fish and encyst as metacercariae in its tissues and may be visible as black or red nodules, especially in the eyes. When, for instance, a bird eats the fish, they develop into adults. **Sanguinicola disease** passes from fish to snail and back, with the adult worms, which are minute, living in the blood of the fish. There they lay eggs that cause obstruction of the blood vessels and may lead to necrosis of various organs, particularly the gills.

To avoid these diseases caused

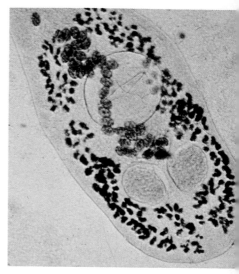

Unlike the monogenetic trematodes, the digenetic trematode shown here has no grasping hooks—but it has suckers that serve efficiently as points of attachment to the victim.

by digenetic flukes, carefully inspect all new fishes before purchase, and never introduce pond snails to the aquarium—only aquarium-bred snails are safe.

Nematodes (threadworms) may infect any part of the body but will usually only be detected when in the gut and seen hanging from the anus. They may be up to 2 cm in length but are usually smaller. A light infestation may not worry the fish, but a heavy one causes emaciation and the fish should preferably be killed. Otherwise, two treatments have been suggested. Soak the food in parachlorometaxylenol and give a bath or treat the tank with 10 ml per liter of the same drug, the bath to last up to several days. Alternatively, Goldstein suggests looking for a pet food containing thiabendazole as a threadworm cure and see if your fish will eat it.

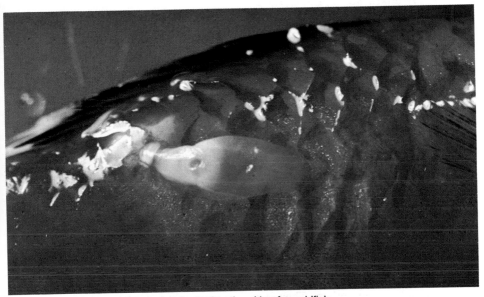

A monogenetic trematode attached to the skin of a goldfish.

In the trematode shown here the holdfast organ can be seen to be supplied with grasping hooks.

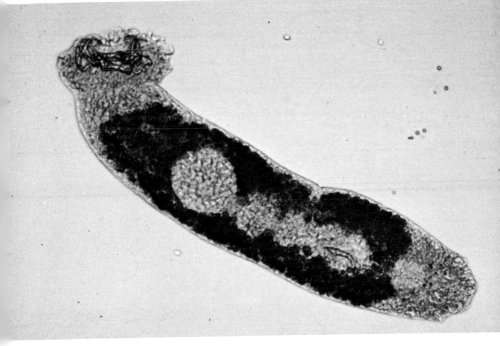

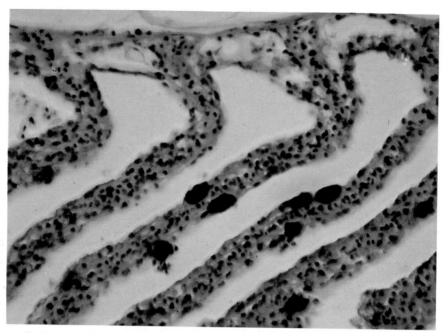

Oodinium shown embedded in the gills of a fish.

The exact cause of the exophthalmic condition of this male *Pelvicahromis pulcher* is not known; the protrusion of the eye is not necessarily the result of an infection.

Cestodes (tapeworms) are not commonly seen in fishes, but those of the genus *Caryophyllaeus* have larvae that live in tubificid worms and can infect fishes. In the gut they become adult worms, not the long type with many segments that gives the cestode its common name, but short worms about 3 mm long. Naturally, such an infestation will only be seen on dissection, but as the condition is rare and not usually dangerous it doesn't much matter. In any case, there is no treatment generally recommended, although there seems no reason why commercial "worming" preparations could not work in fishes.

EXOPHTHALMOS

Exophthalmus, or **pop-eye**, may or may not be caused by infection, and has a number of causes. It is usually found in a single fish, but may occur in many fishes at once if caused by toxic conditions. One or both eyes protrude as in goggle-eyed goldfish, and the condition may proceed to blindness and loss of the eye or eyes. It may be brought on by an excess of copper in the water in marine fishes, but accounts of the same happening in freshwater fishes seem to be lacking. However, if copper treatment has recently been employed, it is worth keeping the possibility in mind. More commonly, it is caused by excess gases in the blood, typically brought about by supersaturation such as when the water comes from high pressure mains. It can occur in association with infections such as *Ichthyosporidium* or dropsy.

Treatment depends on the cause. Look for bubbles in the eye and also look for other symptoms, even in other fishes, of the "bends," as in human divers. These would be signs of nervous upset, distress, paralysis, or just odd movements. If the bends is indicated, lower the temperature as far as possible to increase the solubility of the gas (usually nitrogen), decrease any brisk aeration, and hope for a cure. In a sizeable fish, if large bubbles are seen in the eye it is possible to extract them with a fine hypodermic needle and syringe (best left to a veterinarian).

A final cause of pop-eye is hormonal imbalance, usually an excess of thyrotrophic hormone, which can be shown to cause it experimentally in fishes. There is no feasible cure for the normal aquarist to use, but the condition may spontaneously regress.

NON-INFECTIOUS DISEASES

Tumors may be caused by a virus or by a cancer-producing agent, but many tumors are genetically caused or due to other non-infectious causes. There is a high incidence of tumors in some hybrids

Popeye in a male swordtail.

like swordtail-platy crosses with dark pigmentation, when the pigment-containing cells develop melanosarcomas. Practically all tumors are untreatable, and if a fish is in distress it should be killed. An exception is an occasional thyroid tumor, seen as a throat swelling that may impede feeding, which can be cured by Lugol's solution (a solution of iodine) by adding 0.5 ml per liter to the tank at weekly intervals until a cure is attained or you get tired of trying.

Congenital abnormalities are conditions inherited or caused by teratogenic agents (substances producing disorders of development). Many have been fixed by breeders in domesticated strains of fishes, in which case they are genetic—color, finnage, albino, and other varieties. Others crop up very frequently in goldfish, much less so in tropicals. They include skeletal deformities such as bent spine, missing or misshapen fins, odd-shaped jaws, missing eyes, and swim bladder abnormalities. All are culled out by breeders but still crop up.

Extremes of pH can cause severe trouble, and a suitable pH for one fish may distress another. Fishes such as many tetras can stand a pH down to 5.5 and do poorly above 7.5. Some of the African cichlids live at pH 9.0 and are unhappy at much below it. In general, a low pH for the species causes injury to the gills, cloudy skin due to mucus production, and gasping at the surface. Such symptoms in the absence of signs of infection should indicate the need for an immediate pH check and, if necessary, remedial action. A low pH may be associated with carbon dioxide poisoning.

The congenital abnormality of this male kribensis takes the form of a missing tail; certain other abnormalities—excessively long fins, for example—are deliberately bred for.

A high pH for a species can cause very similar symptoms, but a check will tell which is which. It may also be associated with ammonia poisoning, since the amount of free ammonia in the water, produced by natural processes, increases as the pH rises. Extremes of pH are an exception to the rule given earlier about not making sudden changes, and remedial action should be swift.

Temperature extremes can take the form of prolonged unnoticed exposure to too high or too low a temperature, or of a sudden chilling or overheating. Overheated fishes tend to dash around the tank, gasp at the surface, and try to jump out, whether the overheating is sudden or chronic. Chilled fishes crowd around the heater, if it is still functioning, or stay motionless at the bottom. Sudden chill tends to cause **shimmies**, a slow swimming movement without progression, and, of course, outbreaks of disease. The remedy in all cases is obvious, and again adjusting the temperature to within normal limits in a tropical tank should be done as quickly as possible.

Oxygen shortage and CO$_2$ excess cause similar symptoms—gasping at the surface and irregular respiration. A check of the pH can help to decide which is occurring, as CO$_2$ excess can only happen at a low pH. If O$_2$ shortage is diagnosed (which is the likelier), aeration should be stepped up as fully as possible and a partial change of water given using well aerated aged water if possible. A short period of ozone administration if the equipment is available or the addition of 1 ml per 20 liters of 10%

hydrogen peroxide solution can help. So can methylene blue, but it colors the water too much.

Toxins of various types can cause a great variety of symptoms, and any condition that cannot be put down to one of the above causes should stimulate a thorough check on all possible toxic agents. As an immediate step, make progressive water changes of up to half the tank at a time with aged water if possible, or if necessary with as much tap water at the right temperature as your experience with local supplies dictates. Then investigate the trouble.

Blood patches on skin or fins, cloudy eyes or skin, and listlessness suggest metallic poisoning. Particular culprits are copper pipes, galvanizing (zinc), lead sinkers, and electroplating (cadmium or nickel). If you live in a condominium suspect the pipes and storage tanks, as water from such sources can be very high in copper content. Other possibilities are chlorine or chloramine in tap water, insecticides either direct or via the aerator, tobacco under the fingernails, new paint in the room, ammonia either from the tank itself or from paint, and fungicide sprays or bathroom tile cleaners. Ammonia and nitrite poisoning can damage gills and cause all the troubles associated with the new tank syndrome. Think also of unsuitable plastic in the tank—any plastic with a noticeable smell is suspect. Phenolic compounds that are highly toxic can also be released by tubificid worms, decaying or even living algae, and uneaten food as it decays—all good reasons for keeping a clean tank.

The plants in a nicely planted tank can provide almost as much satisfaction as the fishes—especially for those who enjoy the growing of terrestrial plants.

The Plants

The fishes all belong to one class of the five classes of vertebrates, which in turn belong to one phylum (group with the same basic structure) of animals. This is true of all fishes, whether aquarium species or not. Aquarium plants, in contrast, come from all over the plant kingdom, from the algae to the flowering plants, odd species or genera within families having taken to the water as completely or partially submerged plants. In addition, some plants that normally live out of water can be submerged successfully and have been adapted to the aquarium. It comes as a surprise to many aquarists that most of their favorite centerpieces do not live submerged in nature and indeed were grown submerged only just before they purchased them.

Like fishes, plants do best in water that suits them. Some thrive in soft, acid water, some in hard, alkaline water, with others being fairly indifferent in that regard. Unlike fishes, plants are much more sensitive to light intensity, some growing quite well in poor illumination, while the majority do much better in very bright light. Luckily, there is a vast selection of plants that do well in the usual aquarium lighting. Plants must also be fed, but it is fortunate that most species obtain all their requirements from the excreta of the fishes or its breakdown products already discussed. They do flourish with more carbon dioxide than is usually available, and since fishes can stand CO_2 "aeration" unless very crowded, this has been utilized in attempts to encourage plant growth. It is of more importance, however, in commercial production.

Plants for the aquarium can now be purchased already potted or on special mats that will supply nutriments for months after purchase, a useful fact when starting up a tank. These techniques are an improvement on placing pockets of soil in the sand or gravel, and the pots or mats can be buried or hidden if desired.

In what follows a natural classification will be employed, but in addition, an artificial classification based on that used by J. Stodola in the *Encyclopedia of Water Plants* (TFH Publications) will be used.

Stodola divides water plants into ten types:

Type 1—Small floating plants. (*Azolla, Salvinia,* etc.)

Type 2—Larger floating plants with roots that may sometimes anchor them to the substrate. (*Eichhornia, Pistia,* etc.)

Type 3—Fully submersed (submerged) plants that die out of water. (*Ceratophyllum, Utricularia,* etc.)

Type 4—Submersed plants that flower at the surface and have long thread-like or ribbon-like leaves (*Sagittaria, Vallisneria,* etc.)

Type 5—Plants with leaves usually submersed, but that can sometimes flourish partly out (emersed) or wholly out of water, and always flower above the water. (*Cryptocoryne, Aponogeton,* etc.)

Type 6—Plants that usually send up out of the water leaves that are typically different from the submersed leaves and flower well above the water. (*Echinodorus,* some *Sagittaria,* etc.)

Type 7—Plants rooted in the bottom, but with long petioles (leaf stems) and floating leaves. (*Nymphoides, Nuphar,* etc.)

Vallisneria americana.

Type 8—Similar to Type 7, but the plant-stem itself is long and bears submersed and/or emersed leaves. (*Limnophila*, *Ludwigia*, etc.)

Type 9—The cryptogamous plants (flowerless and with spores other than those in Type 1. (*Nitella*, *Fontinalis*, etc.)

Type 10—Bog or edge of water plants that do not normally have much save their roots in water. (*Sparganum*, *Acorus*, etc.—not usually kept in aquaria.)

The plant kingdom is divided into divisions resembling the phyla of the animal kingdom, thence into the same subgroups of class, order, family, genus, and species as with animals. There is less general agreement about the divisions than about animal phyla, but that need not worry us here. Botanists also denote a change in genus by putting the name of the original classifier in brackets and the later classifier after that—thus *Nitella flexilis* was originally called *Chara flexilis* by Linnaeus and later placed in the genus *Nitella* by Agardh and so we have *Nitella flexilis* (Linnaeus) Agardh. They also use French, so that "Brown jnr" becomes "Brown fils" and "Brown and Jones" becomes "Brown et Jones."

There are about 10 divisions that include the bacteria, fungi, slime molds, and algae—the latter surprisingly falling into many different divisions; green, blue-green, red, brown, etc. It is also not always agreed that bacteria are plants. The algae are of importance mainly as causing diseases or being a nuisance in the tank.

The categories of importance to aquarists are usually agreed to be as follows:

Cryptogamous (Non-flowering) Plants

Division	Chlorophyta	—Green algae
Family	Nitellaceae	—*Nitella* species
Division	Bryophyta	—Liverworts, hornworts, and mosses
Family	Ricciaceae	—*Riccia*, etc.
	Fontinalaceae	—*Fontinalis* species
	Leptodictyaceae	—*Leptodictyum* species
	Hypnaceae	—*Vesicularia* species
	Ceratophyllaceae	—*Ceratophyllum* species
Division	Pterophyta	—Ferns

Seven Families which include Salviniaceae, Azollaceae and Marsiliaceae.

Phanerogamous (Flowering) Plants

Division	Anthophyta	
Class	Monocotyledonae	
Family	Aponogentaceae	—*Aponogeton* species
	Potamogetonaccae	—*Potamogeton* species
	Alismataceae	—*Echinodorus* species
		—*Sagittaria* species, etc.
	Hydrocharitaceae	—*Vallisneria* species
		—*Elodea* species, etc.
	Araceae	—*Cryptocoryne* species
		Acorus species, etc.
	Pontideriaceae	—*Heteranthera* species, etc.

Plus about another 7 families represented in the aquarium by only a few species.

Class	Dicotyledonae	
Family	Nymphaceae	—*Nuphar* species, etc.
	Oenotheraceae	—*Ludwigia* species
	Lythraceae	—*Rotala, Ammania*, etc.
	Yalorhagaceae	—*Myriophyllum* species, etc.
	Scrophulariaceae	—*Bacopa* species, etc.
	Acanthaceae	—*Hygrophila* species, etc.

Plus about another 15 families represented by a few plant species each at most.

From the above it is clear that the flowering plants contribute most of the aquarium species, although it is uncommon to see them in flower. It is also interesting that the monocotyledons (plants with a single seed leaf) contribute more species of importance than the dicotyledons (with two seed leaves), although the latter are represented on land by far more families—some hundred or so compared with about twenty for the monocots. Other land plants fall into divisions that are not represented in the water, such as the Coniferophyta (conifers), the Cycadophyta (cycads), and the Lycophyta (lycopods).

There are many hundreds of species of plants used in aquaria, and more are coming into fashion every year. As with fishes, names change and species come and go—the best one can do is to keep as up to date as possible and make as few mistakes as possible in identification, but it's hard! In what follows we shall discuss about one hundred and fifty popular or semi-popular species, indicating, where appropriate, the ranges of species that have a mention only or are omitted. In a book of this scope, it is impossible to include everything or to discuss some of the plants in adequate detail.

CRYPTOGAMOUS PLANTS
Division Chlorophyta
Family Nitellaceae (Type 9)

This family is represented only by the genus *Nitella* and is the only algal group we shall discuss. In the aquarium *Nitella* reproduces vegetatively and likes hard water and an alkaline pH up to 9. All species are tolerant of cold. *Nitella flexilis* (Linnaeus) Agardh is a green stonewort useful for spawning as it forms dense mats floating in the water. *N. capillaris* and *N. gracilis* are two other species sometimes seen in aquaria, but they usually attach to the substrate and grow less densely than *N. flexilis*. These algae originate in the northern hemisphere.

Division Bryophyta
Family Ricciaaceae (Type 1)

Riccia fluitans Linnaeus, or crystalwort, widely dispersed, is an aquatic liverwort useful, as is *Nitella*, for spawning. More useful, in fact, because it thrives in soft, mildly acid water, in which it forms dense masses floating under the surface and, if left to grow, may even extend to the bottom of the tank if well lit. *Ricciocarpus na-*

Riccia fluitans can form a dense floating carpet, perfect for baby fishes to hide in.

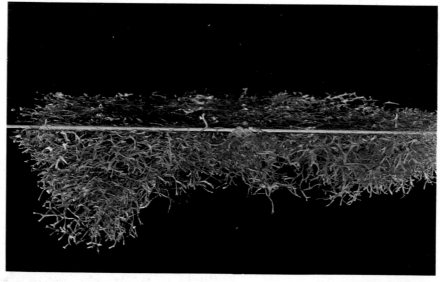

Vesicularia dubyana, Java moss, can form lush thickets.

tans (Linnaeus) Corda is a more terrestrial plant but floats over the surface of the water in an aquarium. Both propagate vegetatively in the aquarium and tolerate temperatures down to 15°C.

Family Fontinalaceae (Type 9)

Fontinalis antipyretic Linnaeus, from northern hemisphere, is the only commonly used plant of the family. It becomes attached to the gravel and develops differently according to pH. In acid water it grows short and dense, but in alkaline water it grows long and with much reduced leaflets. In neutral water it is intermediate in growth. Thus, for aquarium use it should be in neutral to acid water that is also cool—not above 20°C or so. The different varieties of *F. antipyretica* described in the literature are probably reflections of its versatility.

Family Leptodictyaceae (Type 9)

Leptodictyum riparium (Hedw.) Warnst is similar to *Fontinalis* but of a more straggly appearance. It is widely distributed in nature and more adaptable than *Fontinalis*, tolerating poor light and either cold or warm water.

Family Hypnaceae (Type 9)

Vesicularia dubyana (C. Muller) Brotherus, Java moss, comes from the Far East, as its common name suggests. Of over 100 species, *V. dubyana* is the only one commonly utilized. It grows in or out of water, tending to die off if kept fully immersed, but is very useful as a spawning plant. It survives best in soft, acid water and tolerates cool to warm conditions (20°-27°C).

Marsilea quadrifolia

Java fern, *Microsorium pteropus*.

Division Pterophyta
Family Lycopodiaceae (Type 8)

Lycopodium inundatum Linnaeus, club moss, is the only aquarium plant of note in this family. It comes from Europe and North America. A nice, green, bushy plant up to about 10 cm high, it is rather rarely cultivated but worth trying in the cold tank—it likes quite acid, fairly soft water, not warmer than 20°C. It is essentially a bog plant.

Family Isoetaceae (Type 4)

A group of rather rare fern allies with spikey leaves up to 25-30 cm in height, some *Isoetes* species are suitable only to cold water, coming from cold lakes in the northern hemisphere. Of these, *I. echinospora* Durieu does best in the aquarium. There are also species from warmer waters. The Italian *I. malinverniana* Cesti and de Notaris does well up to 25°C, but it is not like the colder water species and has long, fragile, light green spindly leaves up to a meter in length. These curl around the surface of the aquarium and look very interesting as a contrast to other plants.

Family Polypodiaceae (Type 9)

Two ferns of importance in this family are *Microsorium pteropus* (Blume) Ching, the Java fern, and *Bolbitis heudelotii* (Bory ex Fee) Alston, the first from the Far East and the second from Africa. *M. pteropus* is found on land or in water and is a beautiful plant with broad green or brownish leaves up to 25 cm long and 7.5 cm wide. It is tolerant of different water conditions and reproduces by daughter plants that form on the margins of the leaves. Do not plant in sand or gravel, but attach the plant to driftwood or rock and the roots will adhere in time. *B. heudelotii* has more divided (pinnate) leaves up to 40 cm, and is dark green to

Bolbitis heudelotii.

brownish. It also is attached to driftwood or rock and likes soft to medium hard water and a high temperature, not less than 22°C. Other *Bolbitis* species do not seem to have been tried in the aquarium but appear suitable from their descriptions.

Family Parkeriaceae (Types 9 & 2)

There is a single aquarium genus, *Ceratopteris*, in this family of floating or rooted ferns, with six described species, usually all called *C. thalictroides* by aquarists. *C. thalictroides* (Linnaeus) Copel is an annual, up to 80 cm high when rooted, with finely divided emerald green leaves. Floating forms are variable, and give rise to new plants by budding or spores. These ferns are found all over the tropics and thrive in bright light, medium temperatures (20-27°C) and soft, acid water. The trade variety, *javanicus*, which is said to be *C. siliquosa*, is the most decorative.

Family Marsiliaceae (Type 9)

This is another family of amphibious ferns with submersed, floating, and aerial leaves. *Marsilea*, pepperwort, has many species in the genus, of which *M. quadrifolia* Linnaeus is the best known. Also called the four-leaved water clover, it has a creeping rhizome from which two rows of leaves ascend to about 15 cm if the plant is kept shaded, but break the water surface in bright light. The plant is widely distributed. *M. brownii* R. Brown, from Australia, is a small, good aquarium plant that will carpet the bottom, reaching only 5 cm high, but dies off in winter (how does it know in aquarium conditions?).

Water sprite, *Ceratopteris thalicroides*.

Family Salviniaceae (Type 1)

This is a family of floating plants represented by the sole genus *Salvinia*, containing about a dozen species. Fast growers, salvinias are good for shading, especially in ponds, and for spawning surface-breeders such as aphyosemions. *Salvinia auriculata* Aublet is an American species but is now found all over the place. Of the other species, *S. minima* Bak is particularly recommended for aquaria as it survives cold and pH variations.

Family Azollaceae (Type 1)

Another floating family of one genus, *Azolla*, and six species. All are small and can grow on land as well as water if kept moist. *Azolla caroliniana* Wildenow, originally from the Americas, is now found in Europe and Asia. Its leaves are only about 0.5 cm long, green in moderate light, reddish in more intense light. It must have been the inspiration for the puzzle about the plant that doubles its area each day, for that is about what it can do on a pond or tank, particularly in sunlight. It is useful for ponds, not aquaria. *Azolla filiculoides* Lamark, from South America, is a larger plant with leaves up to 2.5 cm, otherwise similar in habits to *A. caroliniana*.

PHANEROGAMOUS (FLOWERING) PLANTS

Division Anthophyta

Class Monocotyledoneae

Family Aponogentaceae (Type 5)

This is a very important family with numerous popular aquarium species. There is one genus, *Aponogeton*, of fully aquatic plants with about 45 species, originating in Africa, Asia, and Australia. In nature, aponogetons are seasonal, and commercially they are grown from seeds, being given seasonal variations in temperature that are not feasible in the tropical tank. However, they survive well in the tropical aquarium and those species forming rhizomes can be subdivided to form new plants. Also, most commercial aquarium apono-

Salvinia auriculata.

Aponogeton echinatus

getons are hybrids, selected over long periods for suitability in the fish tank, and grow well all the year round. This makes detailed consideration of some of the parent species rather pointless, except to distinguish them from the hybrids, often sold under a specific name.

Aponogeton crispus Thunberg comes from Sri Lanka, and the true species is a reddish to red-leaved plant with rather variable strap-like leaves up to 30 cm long and 2.5 cm wide, or wider leaves up to 5 cm in width, both types having wavy edges to the blades. Plants with green leaves are usually *A. crispus* x *A. natans* hybrids sold as *A. crispus*. All tolerate varied water conditions and like a bright light, whereas the more typical *Aponogeton* species like soft water only. Flowers are produced above water if allowed to develop.

Aponogeton elongatus F. Muller, from Australia, has only slightly curved leaf margins, with long petioles and leaves reaching up to 40 cm that are green to brown or reddish in color. The plant also develops floating leaves that are oval, green, and up to 15 cm long. It is not usually hybridized, and can stand temperatures down to 8°C, but hybrids with *A. ulvaceus* are produced which cannot.

Aponogeton madagascariensis (Mirbel) van Bruggen, the Madagascar lace plant, appears to be the only true species having lacy leaves. These are up to 40 cm in length, oval in shape, with the blade up to 20 cm by 7.5 cm. The holes are between the cross-veins, and if kept clear of algae the plant looks most attractive. The plant is, unluckily, very touchy, needing frequent changes of soft, acid water and even then not lasting more than a season. Not for the community tank!

Aponogeton ulvaceus.

Aponogeton rigidifolius

Aponogeton madagascariensis.

Aponogeton undulatus.

A Madagascar lace plant
surrounded by
Cryptocoryne species of
varying sizes.

Aponogeton ulvaceus.

Aponogeton ulvaceus Baker also comes from Madagascar. It has a tuberous rootstock with long, curling light green leaves up to 50 cm on 20-30 cm petioles. A plant needing a large tank, it is otherwise most attractive. Most specimens sold as *A. ulvaceus* are hybrids and may have dark leaves.

Aponogeton undulatus Roxburgh is from Malaya, is also tuberous, and has very crisply crimped leaves, bright green in color, and short petioles, reaching a total length of up to 40 cm. It is a plant to be recommended—resilient and not too big. As usual, most plants resembling it are hybrids sold as *A. undulatus.*

Family Potamogetonaceae (Type 8)

The genus *Potamogeton* contains some 100 species, but only two are really adapted to the aquarium. *Potamogeton gayi* A. Bennet comes from South America and is a rather spindly plant with alternate thin green to reddish leaves, and tough and undemanding with regard to water and temperature. *P. malaianus* Miquel is a rarer but more suitable plant, with much wider leaves that grow in pairs and are quite attractive. Most other potamogetons, some quite handsome, deteriorate in the fish tank.

Family Alismataceae (Type 6)

Two important genera belong to this family—*Echinodorus* and *Sagittaria.* It is the water plantain family, again of some 100 species, including the Amazon sword plants and the arrowheads.

Echinodorus amazonicus (O. Kuntze) Buchenau, the small-leaved

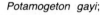
Potamogeton gayi;

Echinodorus longiscapus

Amazon sword plant, from Brazil, naturally, has lanceolate leaves up to about 15 cm long on very short petioles (maximum 5 cm). Although Amazon swords readily flower and produce seeds, in the aquarium they are propagated by runners—dozens of young plants grow at intervals along long stems and take root if weighted down with stones or any suitable device. They can then be separated from the parent. *E. amazonicus* does best in bright light with plenty of room, and in medium-hard water

at not too low a temperature—25°-30°C is best for the plant, if not for all fishes.

Echinodorus argentinensis Rataj is from subtropical and temperate South America. It is a handsome but variable plant, with submersed leaves reaching up to 30 cm in length. The leaves may be either broad, up to 10 cm wide, or narrow, about half that width. The actual leaf blade is only up to 15 cm long, the rest is a long petiole. The color is green, often with reddish veins and reddish brown spots, and the species is resistant to cold.

Echinodorus berteroi (Sprengel) Fassett comes from the southern U.S.A. and Central America and grows in or out of water. Submersed leaves are very variable, ribbon-shaped when young, spear-shaped and heart-shaped as they grow. This is one of the best aquarium plants—hardy, bright

Flower of *Echinodorus argentinensis*.

green, with such variable foliage—but stop it from emerging from the water. It also does best in soft to medium-hard water, in contrast to most Amazon swords.

Echinodorus bleheri Rataj, of unknown origin, is another fine plant, resembling *E. amazonicus* but with broader leaves. It is easy to grow and produces many young plants from runners, being best cultivated as is *E. amazonicus*.

Echinodorus cordifolius (Linnaeus) Grisebach is from the southern U.S. and Central America. A tall, bright green plant with oval leaves on long petioles, its one drawback is a readiness to form emersed leaves, which can be countered by the following technique (applicable to all plants with a similar habit). First, grow it in poor media, offering as little nourishment as possible, then, as the floating leaves begin to develop, pull the plant 1 or 2 cm upward to break part of the root system. This stops development but does not harm the submersed leaves. Also, keep the plant rather poorly illuminated. Otherwise, *E. cordifolius* is a tough plant, standing cool conditions as well as hot ones (15°-30°C).

Echinodorus horizontalis Rataj comes from anywhere in the Amazon region and is a recent import. With broad leaves about 30 cm long when submersed, its name derives from the habit of the leaves to lie horizontally. A difficult plant to cultivate, it requires high temperatures and soft water.

Echinodorus maior (Micheli) Rataj, from Brazil, has light green leaves with lighter veins and is a very handsome plant, often resembling an *Aponogeton* when ill-lit, but with broader and very attractive leaves if given sufficient light. It remains submersed, likes a richer substrate than most *Echinodorus* species, soft to medium-hard water, and a temperature of 20°-25°C.

Echinodorus osiris Rataj, from Brazil, is a very beautiful plant. In nature it is a marsh plant, sending up a floral stalk that eventually bends down and produces leaves and roots. These are transplanted underwater and produce the typical aquarium plant, which has green or red-green 30 cm leaves

844

Echinodorus macrophyllum

Echinodorus osiris.

Echinodorus parviflorus.

Echinodorus tenellus.

Echinodorus paniculatus

Echinodorus cordifolius.

with wavy edges on short petioles. Plants grown in this manner do not become emersed, which is rather extraordinary in view of their origin. They need medium-hard water, a good substrate, and 20°-25°C, but the cooler the plant the redder it becomes. It can be propagated by dividing the rhizome.

Echinodorus parviflorus Rataj from Pacific South America is sold as E. peruensis. It is a relative of E. amazonicus and can be cultivated similarly. It has lance-shaped leaves and dark reddish brown veins that make it very attractive. There may be fifty or so leaves on a mature plant.

Echinodorus quadricostatus Fassett, the dwarf Amazon sword plant, from South America as usual, exists in three varieties, but only one, E. quadricostatus var. xinguensis Rataj, is the aquarium plant. Slender green leaves with very short petioles in the usual rosette are only up to 15 cm long and 1 cm wide. The plant is versatile, indifferent to water quality, and standing temperatures from 15°-30°C, although doing best above 25°C. It reproduces rapidly by runners and will cover the floor of an aquarium in little time.

Echinodorus tenellus (Martius) Buchenau is even smaller than E. quadricostatus, growing to only about 4 cm high, just like grass at the bottom of the tank. It comes from the southern U.S. and Paraguay and can stand cold, growing best at about 20°C, but tolerating up to 30°C. It propagates rapidly by runners and soon carpets the floor. It can do the same on dry land as well! In water or on land, it needs a sandy soil and bright light.

Sagittaria graminea Michaux, called the arrowhead in reference to its emersed leaves, comes from

Sagittaria graminea.

the United States and Canada. Many *Sagittaria* species have been listed for aquarists but few are much good in the aquarium. *S. graminea* var. *graminea* has ribbon-like submerged leaves 1 cm wide and up to 40 cm long, that are green to brownish. It is quite adaptable and can stand temperatures from 15°-30°C soft to medium-hard water, and doesn't emerge too readily from the water. Runners along the gravel reproduce rapidly and a carpet of plants results. *S. graminea* var. *platyphylla* has wider and more decorative leaves, but readily breaks the surface, while *S. graminea* var. *weatherbiana*, the giant arrowhead, has submersed leaves up to 50 cm long and 2.5 cm wide—suitable only for very large tanks.

Sagittaria subulata (Linnaeus) Buchenau, from the eastern U.S., is similar to the above but fully aquatic and can take hard water. In sunlight *S. subulata* becomes very small, with leaves only 5 cm long, but in diffuse light all forms produce longer leaves. Propagation is by runners. *S. subulata* var. *subulata* grows to only about 10 cm, rarely longer, *S. subulata* var. *gracillima* grows 30 to 90 cm high, while *S. subulata* var. *kurziana* is more decorative and grows to 90 cm also, but with wider leaves (0.7 to 1.5 cm as against 0.1 to 0.7 cm in the first two varieties). It is usually sold as *S. japonica*. All *Sagittaria* do best with plenty of light.

Alisma gramineum Gmelin from Europe and the U.S. is the only *Alisma* recommended for aquaria. It has very variable spear-shaped leaves on long petioles and is mentioned since it gives its name to the family.

Family Limnocharitaceae (Type 7)

None of the *Limnocharis* species

that give their name to this family is suitable for aquaria, but one *Hydrocleis* species is a decorative and suitable plant for surface culture.

Hydrocleis nymphoides (Humbolt et Bonpl.) Buchenau has floating leaves and pretty flowers up to 5 cm across that do not rise far into the air and so suit some types of aquarium or vivarium. They are a bright yellow with a red and brown center. The plant comes from tropical South America.

Family Hydrocharitaceae (Types 1, 4, & 8)

This is a family with lots of different genera, each contributing one or more aquarium plants, and of great variety.

Type 1

Limnobium stoloniferum (G.F.W. Meyer) Grisebach is the best of the frogbits, with 2-3 cm leaves that are oval in shape and bright green. It comes from tropical America, needs warm conditions, and flowers readily. Soft to medium-hard water and a neutral pH are required, when the plant will spread too quickly for comfort!

Hydrocharis morsus-ranae Linnaeus is the frogbit that gave its name to the family, but it is not really suitable to any but very large aquaria or vivaria.

Type 4

Various *Blyxa* species such as *B. echinosperma* (Clarke) Hooker fil are recommended to aquarists, but they are touchy annual plants and not for other than specialists.

Vallisneria species, like *Sagittaria*, are excellent background aquarium plants, usually growing in all waters irrespective of hardness or pH. Good lighting is needed for best growth. As with the aponogetons, many of the plants offered are hybrids, selected cultivars, or new species the origin of which is not clear. Four known species are used in aquaria.

Vallisneria americana Michaux,

Vallisneria americana

Vallisneria gigantea

Vallisneria spiralis.

from the U.S., has twisted ribbon-like leaves up to 40 cm long and is exceptional in that it does not do well in hard water. It is often sold as *V. torta* or *V. spiralis*. An even more twisted plant is *V. tortissima*, a horticultural variety of unknown origin that tolerates hard water.

Vallisneria asiatica Miki, from eastern Asia and Japan, also has twisted leaves and is an excellent aquarium plant because it does not grow too high and crowd the top of the tank with masses of leaves as do those of *V. spiralis* and some others.

Vallisneria gigantea Graebner, the giant *Vallisneria*, from the Philippines and New Guinea, has leaves up to 2 meters in length and 3.5 cm wide. It is obviously suited only to very large tanks.

Vallisneria spiralis Linnaeus seems to be native to everywhere, even extending to southern Europe. It is not very spiral (only the older leaves coil a few times), and the name *spiralis* refers to the stem of the female flower, which is tightly coiled. Leaves grow to over a meter.

All species propagate readily by runners, like *Sagittaria*.

Ottelia alismoides (Linnaeus) Persoon is a beautiful annual, not easily cultivated or kept, but worth a try. It is quite widely distributed in Africa, Asia, and Oceania. The first submersed leaves are ribbon-like, but later ones have long petioles and wide blades with embossed-looking veins. All leaves are light green. Yellow flowers float on the water.

Type 8

Egeria densa Planchon is the only plant in the genus kept in aquaria. Originally from South America, it is now found in North America, Europe, Africa, and Japan. It has a long stem of up to 3 meters, branching occasionally, with whorls of bright green narrow leaves 2-3 cm long. In common with other Hydrocharitaceae, it extracts lime from hard water and grows well at all normal temperatures. It has roots but is usually thrust into the substrate in small bunches or even left floating in the water, growing rapidly if well lit.

Elodea canadensis Michaux, the Canadian water weed, is a very similar plant to *Egeria densa*, with which it is often confused. It is not a good tank plant, however, as it needs low temperatures and much light.

Elodea nutalli Planchon, from North America (now found also in Europe), is the usual aquarium species. It is adaptable to warm or cold water and aquarium lighting, has stems only up to 12 cm in length, and whorls of 0.5-1.0 cm leaves that are apt to curl backward and form a very decorative plant. There are 16 other species, but none is used in the aquarium.

Hydrilla verticillata (Linnaeus fil) Royle is widely found in Europe, Asia, Africa, and Australia. It is another plant with long stems (up to several meters) and whorls of leaves up to 2.5 cm long and only 1-2 mm wide. The whorls are widely spaced, and the stem branches frequently, so that a rather straggly mass results. However, it is tolerant of both cold and warm water.

Lagarosiphon major (Ridley) Moss comes from South Africa and is usually sold as *Elodea crispa*, being much like an *Elodea*. It is, however, more attractive, with leaves in close spirals instead of whorls and curling back as *E. nutalli*. It is bright green, must have neutral to alkaline water to flourish, and tolerates cold or warm conditions, doing best at around 20°C. Cultivation is as for *Egeria*. Two other

Egeria densa.

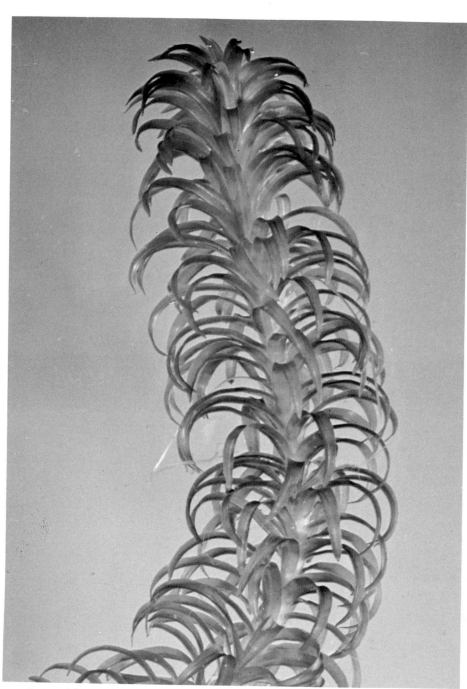

Lagarosiphon major.

species have recently been imported, *L. madagascariensis* and *L. muscoides*, the former needing acid water and the latter alkaline water to remain attractive. They come respectively from Madagascar (surprise!) and Africa.

Family Cyperaceae (Type 4)

The hair grasses (*Eleocharis* species) are among some 200 species of tiny medium-height rushes. The smaller ones are suitable for aquaria as bottom plants forming mats of vegetation. The most suitable aquarium species are:

Eleocharis acicularis (Linnaeus) Roemer et Schultes, found almost universally, has a thin rhizome with runners putting up stalks of grass, each with its roots. The stalks are in tufts, 5 to 10 cm in height. The plant does best in acid

water at any temperature from 10°-25°C.

Eleocharis vivipara Link, *E. parvula* (Roemer et Schultes) Link, and *E. minima* are all warmer water species from various parts of the globe differing very little from each other and from *E. acicularis* except in requiring temperatures over 20°C.

Family Araceae (Types 4 & 5)

Actually, there are Types 2 & 10 water plants in this family, but like *Pistia* (water lettuce) or *Calla* (water arum) they stick up too far above water level to be useful in fish tanks.

Type 4

Acorus gramineus Soland, Japanese rush, is a marsh dweller from Asia that is adaptable to the submersed condition. It has a rhizome

Eleocharis minima

from which 10-15 narrow spikey leaves emerge, fanning out attractively. *A. gramineus* var. *pusillus* (Sieboldt) Engler is a dwarf from China with leaves about 5 cm long, and *A. gramineus* var. *decoratus*, the striped Japanese rush, is a horticultural variety with yellow-striped leaves. All are decorative plants, slow-growing even in rich substrates, that bud off from the rhizome. Their best temperature range is a rather cold 15°–20°C, but they take higher ones.

Type 5

Anubias species are mostly marsh plants, some of which can adapt to underwater life. They are beautiful plants propagated by rhizome division; they come from West Africa. They like shade and a deep substrate. Many are only suitable when young, as they tend to grow large. Their classification is in a mess and certain identification of the plants seen in aquaria is only possible from the flowers, which are rarely produced.

Anubias barteri Engler has arrow-shaped leaves and is in nature an underwater plant coming from Sierra Leone. Two varieties of a somewhat different leaf shape are more common than the parent plant. *A. barteri* var. *nana* (Engler) Crusio has dark green oval leaves about 5 x 10 cm and is a small plant suited to small tanks. *A. barteri* var. *glabra* Brown has spear-shaped leaves up to 25 cm long and 8 cm wide that are also dark green. Both may be propagated by division of the rhizome, but only when it is mature, which takes several years. A few young plants will develop from the dormant buds, hence multiplication is very slow.

Anubias afzelii Schott is also grown submersed. Its origin seems, however, to be unknown. Of medium size, it has green to reddish petioles and dark green leaves and remains small when submersed, but can grow to 25 cm.

Anubias congensis N.E. Brown from West Africa has petioles up to 25 cm long bearing a dark green blade 20 x 10 cm. It requires heat to flourish, 25°C or more, and soft, peaty water. It is not often seen in aquaria.

The genus *Cryptocoryne* offers a wide selection of favorite aquarium plants, yet they are touchy, and success with most of them can only be expected if certain conditions are provided. The water must be slightly acid (pH 6.5), below 100 ppm hardness, and kept clear. The substrate should be of coarse sand with some peat or other leavening agent added, and a layer of detritus is recommended to provide nourishment. The temperature should not fluc-

Acorus gramineus.

Anubias   afzelli

Anubias barteri.

Cryptocoryne hejnyi

Cryptocoryne bullosa.

Cryptocoryne wendtii.

Cryptocoryne affinis.

859

Cryptocoryne beckettii.

tuate and should be between 20°-30°C—not very demanding. Most importantly, illumination should be weak, as these plants come from shady forests or jungles in tropical Asia. Classification of the genus has recently been revised by Rataj, who admits difficulties associated with absence of flowers in some species, so let's hope he's got it right! About 60 species have been listed.

In what follows, only the submersed plant will usually be described, omitting the flower spike, which is normally not seen or wanted by the aquarist.

Cryptocoryne affinis N.E. Brown, from Malaysia, is a very popular species that grows rapidly, particularly for a *Cryptocoryne*. Petioles are about 10-15 cm, as are the leaf blades, which are emerald green on top and purplish on the underside, soft, and spear-shaped. Prop-agated by runners, the plant is capable of spreading quite quickly over the bottom of a tank. It is tough but collapses if not given the right conditions as outlined above. This species often flowers below water, producing the typical lily-like spathe (sheath) of the genus.

Cryptocoryne axelrodii Rataj has also been familiarly known as *C. willisii* and *C. undulata.* It comes from Sri Lanka and can grow large as an emersed plant, but kept submersed it has petioles and leaves both about 10 cm long, with the leaves 1-3 cm wide. The leaves are olive green with reddish undersides to red-brown all over and slightly crinkled at the edges. This is another tough crypt that actually needs medium-hard water.

Cryptocoryne balansae Gagnepain, from Thailand to southern China, is also a plant liking water harder than usual for the genus—

up to 170 ppm in nature. It has fairly short petioles and long, narrow green leaves with an embossed appearance, up to 50 cm in length, but only 1 cm or so wide. In the aquarium it often stays much smaller and is an attractive plant, hardy as long as it is kept warm.

Cryptocoryne becketii Thwaites is from Sri Lanka and is a very popular, tough aquarium plant, standing strong light and hard water and propagating rapidly from rhizome runners. It has long petioles and wide spear-shaped blades that are olive-brown on top and purple to pink beneath and up to 8 cm long on petioles up to twice that length. The stronger the light, the redder the plant.

Cryptocoryne bullosa Beccari, from Borneo, has bright green embossed leaves, sometimes with red petioles. Petioles and leaves are about the same length, up to 15 cm long, the leaves up to 3 cm wide, oval in shape or more elongated, and lighter on the underside.

Cryptocoryne ciliata (Roxburgh) Fischer, from all over the tropical Far East, is an emersed plant in nature that is always cropping up in aquarium books, but only one, var. *latifolia*, tolerates submersed conditions permanently. *C. ciliata* var. *latifolia* Rataj has leaves up to 20 cm long that are leathery and spear-shaped, the green blade being about 10 cm maximum in length and 5 cm wide. It does not propagate by long runners, but either by budding from the rhizome or from very short 1-2 cm runners.

Cryptocoryne cordata Griffith is a variable species from Malaysia to Borneo and Java. It bears long green or red-brown petioles up to 30 cm long, with blades about 10

Cryptocoryne axelrodi.

Cryptocoryne evae

cm x 5 cm wide that are green on the upper surface and green to red below—the more light, the redder. This is a touchy species requiring typical conditions for the genus but with rather more light to keep it red and attractive. *C. cordata* is often sold as *C. griffithii*, but it seems that the latter has not yet been imported.

Cryptocoryne evae Rataj is of unknown origin but very decorative. Its leaves are up to 60 cm long with long petioles and blades up to 22.5 cm x 7.5 cm, lance-shaped, with dark green to olive-brown upper surfaces and shiny red-brown to violet lower surfaces. It is cultivated like *C. cordata* and can stand hard water.

Cryptocoryne hejnyi Rataj is another very attractive plant, probably from Malaya, that is similar to *C. cordata* in appearance and requirements. It is wrongly sold as *C. purpurea*. The leaves have oval or heart-shaped blades that are green with purple, pink, or reddish brown cross stripes, 7 cm x 2.5 cm in size at most, with petioles varying in length.

Cryptocoryne johorensis Engler, from Malaysia and Indonesia, has long petioles and heart-shaped leaf blades up to 7.5 cm long and 5 cm wide, with a total leaf length of up to 20 cm. The leaves are green (reddish in good light), lighter on the undersides. Hardy in the right conditions, the plant is a slow grower, and those on sale are usually imported.

Cryptocoryne nevillii Trimen, from Sri Lanka, is an old favorite often grown by aquarists. It has two leaf forms. The first is a cultivar with deep green oval blades about 7 cm x 2 cm; the second has lance-like blades, also green, up to 10 cm x 1 cm. Both have fairly short petioles, and the leaves are quite stiff and resist injury. They spread rapidly in the aquarium and are to be recommended for toughness and tolerance of wide conditions—even quite hard water and low temperatures.

Cryptocoryne parva de Wit is a dwarf species, probably from Sri Lanka, that is also easily propagated. The leaves are only about 5 cm in total length, with narrow oval blades about 2.5 cm x 0.7 cm that are green and smooth looking. It is a rapidly spreading plant from a strong rhizome.

Cryptocoryne petchii Alston is related to *C. becketii* and, like it, comes from Sri Lanka, but is a smaller plant. Also like *C. becketii*, it is a tough plant, tolerant of hard water and bright light, and easily propagated from a rhizome. Leaves have 8-12 cm blades about 1 cm wide, undulating margins, with olive to brown-red upper surfaces and pink or red under surfaces. The petiole is fairly short.

Cryptocoryne johorensis

Cryptocoryne cordata.

Cryptocoryne tonkinensis Gagnepain, from Vietnam, is usually sold as *C. retrospiralis*, which is not an aquarium plant. It has long reddish brown leaves up to 40 cm long, 0.5 to 1.5 cm wide, with crimped margins. The petioles are fairly short, so that the long blades form the major part of the leaf. The plant is tolerant of hard water and is slow growing but easy to cultivate.

Cryptocoryne usteriana Engler, from the Philippines, is a bright green to brownish plant with leaves up to 70 cm or even longer. Petioles are of variable length, the blades up to 40 cm x 4 cm wide, resembling *Aponogeton*, with a wavy embossed-looking appearance. This is a large plant clearly suited only to deep aquaria.

Cryptocoryne walkeri Schott, from Sri Lanka, comes in three varieties, but as these are virtually indistinguishable submersed, differing only in their emersed forms, this will be ignored. Leaves are up to 25 cm long, with blades

Lemna minor.

up to 10 cm x 4 cm, that are oblong, and green to red-brown. This is a popular and tough plant that can be propagated by runners.

Cryptocoryne wendtii de Wit, also from Sri Lanka, comes in five varieties, but once more the differences are mostly in the emersed plants. For aquarists, the species may be regarded as variable, but usually it has lance- to heart-shaped leaf blades that are brownish green to reddish green on similarly colored petioles. They usually have crimped edges and are up to 10 cm x 4 cm in size. In poor light they become narrow and olive-green. The plant is hardy and grows rapidly, tolerates harder water than most crypts, likes good illumination, and can take temperatures down to 15°C, growing best at the usual 20°-25°C.

Family Lemnaceae (Type 1)

The duckweeds are more of a nuisance in the aquarium than anything else, as they rapidly cover the water surface and are hard to eradicate. There are many species.

Lemna minor Linnaeus is found everywhere and is a minute floating green plant with lobed "leaves" about 3 mm long at most. It flourishes in almost any conditions.

Lemna trisulca Linnaeus, the ivy-leaved duckweed, occurs in branching chains and can be submersed, hanging onto other plants. It is also universal in distribution.

Wolffia arrhiza (Linnaeus) Horkel is worth a mention as the smallest flowering plant, floating on the water as a green disc 0.5-1.5 mm in diameter and without roots.

Family Mayacaceae (Type 8)

This is a family with the single genus, *Mayaca*, with about ten species rarely seen in the aquarium.

Mayaca fluviatilis Aublet has thin stems up to 50 cm long with

Mayaca fluviatilis

narrow green leaves in a spiral. It comes from Brazil and requires very soft, slightly acid water and bright light, yet algae growing on it readily kill it.

Family Pontederiaceae (Types 2 & 8)

Type 2

Eichhornia crassipes (Martius) Solms, the water hyacinth, and *E. azurea* (Swartz) Kunth always seem to be included in aquarium plant lists, but they are large floating plants or rooted with a large emersed portion and are suitable only for ponds or vivaria.

Type 8

Heterianthera zosterifolia Martius, from Brazil, is the most suitable of the genus as an aquarium plant. It has a 40 cm thin stem, that is very fragile, that bears narrow green leaves up to 4 cm long. Floating leaves that are oval may also be produced. Even so, it is a touchy plant requiring soft water, diffuse light, and a fairly high temperature. All told, this is not a very important family of plants to the aquarist.

Class Dicotyledoneae
Family Nymphaceae (Type 7)

Barclaya longifolia Wallich is a touchy but beautiful member of the water lily family with submersed, lance-shaped leaves 30 cm x 4 cm at most. These are green on the upper surface, purplish red below, with wavy margins. It is fragile and easily damaged, needs soft, acid water, a humus-containing substrate, and high temperatures—it dies at 15°C. The plant comes from Thailand and Burma. Most water lilies are, of course, not suited to the aquarium since they produce floating leaves and flowers with little permanent submersed growth, although rooted in the substrate.

Nuphar luteum (Linnaeus) Smith, from Europe and northern Asia and Africa, has submersed leaves as well as emersed ones, and is a suitable and pretty plant that is much tougher than *Barclaya*. Floating leaves can be inhibited by giving the plant the opposite to its natural hard water and bright light, keeping it shaded in soft and

Heteranthera zosterifolia.

Nymphoides aquatica

Barclaya longifolia

Nuphar luteum

slightly acid water. This species can take cold water but does best at 20°-25°C and is propagated from seed.

Nuphar pumilum (Timm) DeCandolle, from Europe and Siberia, is indistinguishable from *N. luteum* except when flowering—it has smaller flowers. It does not flourish in tropical tanks above 20°C.

Nuphar sagittifolium Pursh, from South Carolina, U.S., is a good aquarium plant standing temperatures up to 28°C. It has long arrow-shaped leaves with wavy and light green blades up to 40 cm long on short petioles. It does not produce floating leaves and requires soft, neutral water and bright illumination.

Nymphaea lotus Linnaeus, from Africa and southern Asia, according to Rataj, may or may not be the plant usually sold as var. *japonicus*. It is unusual in that unless well lighted from above it does not produce floating leaves and makes a good aquarium plant. Submersed leaves have rounded blades about 10 cm in diameter and long petioles up to 20 cm. They may be green, red-brown, or spotted. The plant propagates from runners and does well in medium-hard water at around neutral pH and up to 28°C.

Cabomba australis

Cabomba caroliniana.

ing leaves may form in some species.

Cabomba aquatica Aublet has apparently not been imported, although plants are commonly sold under that name.

Cabomba caroliniana A. Gray has in its most typical form leaves up to 7 cm, much segmented and tightly spaced, bright green, and most attractive. It is, however, a brittle plant and easily damaged, liking soft to medium-hard water at over 20°C for growth, but resists cold quite well. Other varieties have reddish stems and leaves and are very attractive, while yet others exist that are quite stringy and unattractive.

Cabomba australis Spengler is a very similar plant but with smaller leaves up to 5 cm long, otherwise indistinguishable from *C. caroliniana.*

Cabomba piauhyensis Gardner when newly imported has bright red or purple stems and leaves, but it deteriorates in the usual fish tank and is difficult to cultivate, demanding good light and very clean conditions. Short days will kill it.

Family Menyanthaceae

Only one plant of note comes from this family.

Nymphoides aquatica (Walter) O. Kuntze is the underwater banana plant from the U.S. It has elongated tubers resembling bunches of bananas, 2 to 4 cm long, and heart-shaped green wavy leaves up to 10 cm long. Kept in the shade, it stays under water, but well lit it forms floating leaves. It likes a neutral pH and medium hard water up to 30°C and can be propagated from cuttings or individual leaves separated from the plant.

Family Cabombaceae

The genus *Cabomba* (the fanworts) is native to the warmer parts of the Americas. It is submersed and produces long branching stems up to several meters in length. The much divided, fan-like leaf blades occur in opposed pairs. Rounded, undivided float-

Family Ceratophyllaceae (Type 3)

Ceratophyllum demersum Linnaeus, hornwort, is universally distributed. It is a submersed plant with a branching stalk up to 2 meters in length and whorls of forked, brittle, thorny leaves. It is suitable more for pools than aquaria and takes cold conditions, doing best in hard water below 18°C. Reproduction is by subdivision or from tiny flowers that form in the hollows of the bracts.

Ceratophyllum submersum Linnaeus is another widespread hornwort differing from *C. demersum* in having three-pronged leaves instead of two-pronged ones. In warm aquaria both species become spindly and non-decorative. However, a new species recently has been imported from Cuba that has dense whorls and retains them in warm water.

Family Brassicaceae (Type 8)

Cardamine lyrata Bunge comes from eastern Asia, Korea, and Japan. Essentially a cold water plant, it also grows on land. However, kept cool and well lit it is a pretty plant. It grows up to 30 cm high and has alternate heart-shaped bright green leaves. Roots develop under the leaves, which makes subdivision easy.

Rorippa aquatica (Eaton) Palmer, from the U.S., is quite beautiful. As a land plant it has rosettes of fleshy divided leaves, but submersed it produces bright green, narrow, finely divided leaves up to 7.5 cm long. Another species, *R. amphibia*, is familiar to us as watercress.

Family Amaranthaceae (Type 8)

Among the many genera in this family, only *Alternanthera* seems to have been used in aquaria, and then only three out of many species.

Alternanthera reineckii Briquet, from Brazil, has erect stems with pairs of strap-like leaves alternating at right angles to each other that are green above and pink below. Flowers form at the base of the leaves, which are up to 3.5 cm long and 1.5 cm wide.

Alternanthera sessilis (Linnaeus) De Candolle is widely distributed in tropical regions and comes to the aquarist in two varieties. *A. sessilis* var. *lilacina* has leaves that are olive green on their upper surface and red or violet below, and are twice the size of *A. reineckii* leaves and more variable in shape. It is a difficult plant to grow and

Cardamine lyrata.

Alternanthera reineckii.

Rorippa aquatica.

prefers old, clean water and a neutral pH. *A. sessilis* var. *rubra* is a bright red plant that is attractive but also touchy. *Alternanthera* species should be planted in groups and broken off and replanted since as they grow the lower leaves degenerate.

Family Crassulaceae (Type 8)

Crassula aquatica (Linnaeus) Schoenland is often quoted as a suitable aquarium plant, but it would seem that only other species, like *Crassula recurva* (Hooker fil.) Ostenfeld from Australia, are actually successful. *C. recurva* produces branching stems up to 20 cm long with pairs of light green leaves about 1.5 cm x 0.2 cm and survives well in aquaria. *C. helmsii* Kirk, from New Zealand, is a similar plant.

Family Elatinaceae (Type 8)

This is an "old-fashioned" family, not so much seen in aquaria today, but one wonders why not. Of about 12 species in the genus *Elatine*, two are good aquarium plants.

Elatine macropoda Gussone is from southern Europe and northern Africa and forms a green carpet on the substrate, with stems lying horizontally and sending up leaves about 2 cm x 0.2 cm. It is a fast grower, flourishing in soft, neutral to slightly acid water at 13° to 25°C.

Elatine hydropiper Linnaeus is a very pretty dwarf plant from similar localities, with rounder, oval leaves even smaller than those of *E. macropoda*, and sends up vertical stems from a main horizontal runner. Oddly, both species are annuals as emersed forms but remain perennial in the aquarium.

Family Onagraceae (Type 8)

Of hundreds of species in this family (from some 20 genera), only *Ludwigia* is used in the aquarium, as none of the others is suitable submersed.

Ludwigia arcuata Walter, from the eastern U.S., is a plant best placed in bunches in a rich substrate for good growth. The reddish stems produce emerald green leaves up to 2.5 cm x 0.5 cm that are lance-shaped. A good light is needed, as well as a temperature between 15° and 25°C. This is another plant that tends to deteriorate at the base, so the tops of the stems should be pinched off at intervals and replanted in the sand or gravel.

Ludwigia repens Forster, from the southern U.S., is a similar plant with broader green leaves about 3 cm x 2 cm. It flourishes at 20°-28°C but can stand colder water

Ludwigia palustris.

and is cultivated as is *L. arcuata* in the aquarium. *L. mullertii* is a redder and somewhat larger horticultural variety of *L. repens*.

Ludwigia palustris (Linnaeus) Elliot, from all over the northern hemisphere, is another species similar to *L. arcuata* but requiring less light. The hybrid *palustris* x *repens* is also a good aquarium plant.

Family Lythraceae (Type 8)

This is a large family of 25 genera and some 500 species in which just the odd plant has been found successful in the fish tank.

Ammania senegalensis Lamark, from Africa, is somewhat like a *Ludwigia* with a thick reddish stem. It comes in three varieties: with green leaves, indicating an unsuitable plant because it will not grow submersed; with oval red leaves 2.5 cm x 1 cm with wavy edges; or with olive to reddish narrow leaves 5 cm x 1 cm, curled backward. The last two varieties do well in water of soft to medium hardness and a good light.

Didiplis diandra (Nuttal) Wood, from the southern U.S. and Mexico, is a very attractive bushy plant when bunched, having dense, narrow leaves that are green but reddish when young. They are about 2 cm x 0.2 cm. It grows in soft to medium hard water in any but very poor light and stands both cold and warm conditions. Growth is slow, but all in all it is a very worthwhile addition to the aquarium.

Rotala rotundifolia (Roxburgh) Koehne, often sold as *R. indica*, comes from India and also resembles *Ludwigia*. Underwater it has oval leaves about 2 cm x 0.5 cm at most, that are olive green above and red-brown below. Another plant that looks best in bunches, it grows well in any type of water and reasonable light at a temperature of 20°-30°C.

Rotala rotundifolia.

Rotala macrantha Koehne is a similar plant with somewhat larger, redder leaves. It prefers shade and grows slowly.

Rotala wallichii (Hook fil.) Koehne is usually sold as *Mayaca* and has small green leaves with red or gold tips that are about 1.2 cm x 0.1 cm. Both *R. macrantha* and *R. wallichii* come from India.

Family Halorhagaceae (Type 8)

This is the family of water milfoils, containing the important genus *Myriophyllum* and little else of aquatic interest. This genus of about 40 species is practically universal. Those used in aquaria multiply vegetatively and never flower. They are best planted in bunches, like many Type 8 plants, and replanted from time to time after cutting off the lower portions. They like hard, alkaline water, about pH 8, plenty of nourishment, and good light. Temperature is less important; anything from 15°C upwards will do.

Myriophyllum aquaticum (Velloso) Verdcourt, often sold as *M. brasiliense*, comes from the southern U.S., Central America, and South America. It is the most popular species of the genus, going under the name of parrot's feathers and now found growing in many parts of the world. The leaves are in whorls, are light green in color, about 3-5 cm long, and finely divided. Above water they become shorter, stiffer, and darker. Stems will grow to 1 or 2

Myriophyllum hippuroides.

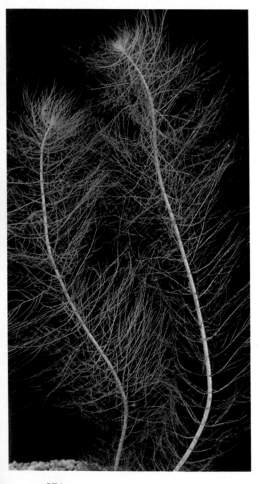

meters if allowed to do so.

Myriophyllum mattogrossense Koehne, from South America, is a similar but very attractive reddish plant, growing somewhat denser than *M. aquaticum*.

Myriophyllum scabratum Michaux is similar in distribution to *M. aquaticum* and has thin green leaves and much branched stems, in contrast to those species above.

Myriophyllum spicatum Linnaeus has reddish stems and green leaves with whorls less densely spaced than in most species. Nevertheless, it is decorative and popular and is widely distributed over the northern hemisphere.

Myriophyllum hippuroides Nuttal, from the U.S. and Mexico, has very finely divided thread-like leaves on a much-branched stem and is another attractive plant, varying from green to yellowish brown to reddish brown.

Myriophyllum ussuriense (Regal) Maxim from eastern Asia is another popular and beautiful species. Its delicate leaves rarely become airborne. It is frequently offered as *M. japonicum*.

Proserpinaca palustris Linnaeus, from North America, is quite like a *Myriophyllum* but with leaves in spirals instead of whorls. The leaves are green and about 6 cm long in the submersed form. The plant likes hard, alkaline water of about pH 8 and grows best when cool (15°-20°C).

Prosperpinaca pectinata Lamark, from the southern U.S., is a coarser plant, with leaves 2-3 cm x 1 cm, and bright green. In contrast to *P. palustris*, it prefers soft to medium-hard water at a pH of 5.5 to 7.0, and grows well at 22°-28°C in bright light.

Family Apiaceae (Type 7)

Hydrocotyle vulgaris Linnaeus, water pennywort, from all over Europe, although normally with

Myriophyllum spicatum.

floating leaves is also found in a submersed form with a long petiole joined to the center of a circular leaf about 4 cm or less in diameter. The leaf is green, notched, and hairy on the underside. Propagation is by cuttings in mildly acid to neutral water.

Hydrocotyle leucopetala Chamisso et Schlechtendahl is from South America, where it can be a floating or a rooted plant. As a rooted plant in the aquarium it has circular leaves like *H. vulgaris*, but the stem joins at a deep cut in the blade so that it is actually at the edge of it. The blade is variable in diameter, from 2.5 cm to 7.5 cm. *H. leucopetala* is fairly indifferent to water and soil conditions but needs plenty of light.

Family Primulaceae (Types 6 & 8)
Type 6

Samolus parviflorus Rafinesque, from the Americas, grows about 10 cm high as a cluster of light green leaves up to 10 cm x 5 cm or nar-

Samolus parviflorus.

rower. It likes medium-hard, but not alkaline, water and plenty of light. It does not flourish over 20°C, so is not suited to the tropical tank. Sometimes it is called the green water rose or underwater rose.

Type 8

Hottonia palustris Linnaeus, the water violet, from central Europe, is an interesting coldwater plant that must be kept under 18°C. The branching stem bears comb-like leaves of variable shape that are colored from green to red-brown. It is said that another species, *H. inflata*, does better submersed and is the preferable aquarium species.

Lysimachia nummularia Linnaeus, the loosestrife, from various parts of the northern hemisphere, is a swamp plant adaptable to underwater growth. Stems with roots at intervals along their length send up long offshoots with pairs of oval green leaves dotted with red. Medium hard water, pH about neutral, and temperatures up to 20°C suffice to cultivate this essentially coldwater plant.

Family Scrophulariaceae (Type 8)

This is an enormous family of 220 genera and 3000 or so species. Seventeen genera have aquatic species, but only four are cultivated and in general use in aquaria—*Bacopa, Hemianthus, Hydrotiche,* and *Limnophila (Ambulia).* The genus *Limosella* is sometimes seen in aquaria.

Bacopa caroliniana (Walter) Robinson (*B. amplexicaulis*), from the southern U.S., is a very handsome plant. Its 10 cm to 20 cm stems carry pairs of green, veined, and somewhat curled leaves up to 3 cm x 1.5 cm. It thrives in medium-hard, moderately acid water at 22°-30°C and rather weak lighting, not liking direct sunlight.

Bacopa monniera (Linnaeus) Pennell is universally in the tropics and subtropics, has strongly branching stems in contrast to *B. caroliniana,* and has smaller, thick flat leaves, at most 2 cm x 0.8 cm. It also likes more light and does poorly if not given it. Otherwise, the same conditions as *B. caroliniana* suit it, but it is not as decorative.

These are only two of many aquatic *Bacopa* species, few of which seem ever to have been tried in aquaria or at least been cultivated.

Hemianthus micranthemoides Nuttall is from the West Indies and the U.S., spreading even to the Arctic. Creeping stems send up branches up to 20 cm high, with masses of light green rounded leaves up to 0.8 cm x 0.3 cm. As may be inferred from its range, the plant doesn't mind what the temperature is, but does best at 18°C to 28°C in fairly soft, acid water.

Hydrotriche hottoniiflora Zucc., from Madagascar, is a recent import and a very nice plant. Creeping stems send up erect portions to the water surface, if not over 50 cm deep, and rarely produce emersed leaves in the aquarium. The submersed leaves are in whorls, are needle-shaped, branching, bright green, and about 5 cm long. The plant needs fairly soft, acid water at 20° to 25°C and bright but not direct sunlight, when it will grow fast.

Family Lentibulariaceae (Type 3)

Utricularia vulgaris Linnaeus is the common northern hemisphere bladderwort. The stem, up to 2 meters in length, is usually in a tangle, with much-branched thin curling green leaves bearing tiny bladders that snap closed, trapping minute water creatures (including fish fry) upon which the

Bacopa monniera.

plant feeds. There are no roots. *U. vulgaris* is adaptable to cool aquaria, liking cold, acid water.

Utricularia exoleta R. Brown, the dwarf bladderwort, is a more tropical species from many Old World areas. This is the usual aquarium species, with very small, more widely spaced leaves on a thin stem and even smaller bladders than *U. vulgaris,* so small that they do not catch fry. While it likes soft, acid water, it is pretty adaptable as long as it is well illuminated and kept at between 18° and 30°C.

Propagation of both species in the aquarium is by subdivision. The dense tangles formed are good for spawning or for livebearer young to hide themselves.

There are many *Utricularia* species, some of which have recently been introduced but not identified. One at least can be pushed under a rock or into the substrate and sends attractive upright stems toward the light; it is much branched and covered by needle-shaped leaves and bladders.

Family Acanthaceae (Type 8)

This is another very large family of some 250 genera, only one of which provides aquarium plants, although it appears that more could well do so. This is the genus *Hygrophila*, all examples of which have an upright, rooted stem with paired oval or lance-shaped leaves. Of the 80 or so known species, the following are good aquarium plants usually planted in bunches.

Hygrophila corymbosa (Blume) Lindau, from Malaysia and elsewhere, roots readily as cuttings if in a rich substrate with any type of water. The bright green leaves are up to 12 cm x 5 cm, lance-shaped, and in pairs. With good light and a temperature of 22°-28°C, growth is rapid. Propagation is by the usual method in bunched plants, breaking pieces from the stem and thrusting them into the gravel.

Hygrophila difformis (Linnaeus fil.) Blume, also from the Far East, is a very different plant, with light green, much divided leaves giving it the common name water wisteria. A beautiful fern-like plant, it requires soft to medium-hard water and not too bright a light. From 20°-25°C it flourishes, growing quickly from portions thrust into the gravel, with leaves up to 12 cm long.

Hygrophila polysperma (Ruxburgh) T. Anders comes from India and has been cultivated for many

Hygrophila corymbosa.

Lobelia cardinalis.

years, but only recently imported specimens produce flowers and are therefore definitely known to be *H. polysperma*—the rest, never having flowered, just look like it! Straight, usually unbranched stems bear light green leaves up to 5 cm x 1.5 cm, the younger ones often reddish in color. In good light the plant grows rapidly if above 20°C, but cool water does not harm it.

Other *Hygrophila* species are becoming popular, including the recently imported *H. lacustris* from Thailand, *H. lancea* from Japan and Taiwan, and *H. stricta* from various parts of southern Asia. The nomenclature of these species seems, however, to be in some doubt—we mention them to show that the three plants described are not the only suitable species.

Family Lobeliaceae (Type 8)

Of ten aquatic genera in this family, out of about 30 in all, only *Lobelia* is so far used in aquaria.

Lobelia cardinalis Linnaeus, from the U.S., lives on land or water. In the submersed form it is an attractive light green plant with oval leaves about 6 cm x 3 cm, best planted in bunches. It prefers a neutral pH, fairly hard water, good light, and a fairly cool tank, although it can take up to 26°C.

Lobelia splendens Willdenau, from Mexico, is a bigger, tougher plant with rosettes of bright green or red leaves up to 10 cm long. It is cultivated as *L. cardinalis*.

Breeding Fishes

Once you become a serious aquarist, it is a challenge few can resist to try your hand at breeding some of the species that grace the tanks you keep. A few fishes, like the livebearers, whose young are dropped into the water already well developed, do it for you. Then it becomes a question of saving and rearing some of their offspring. Others, like the cichlids, may pair off and guard a batch of eggs, but nothing will eventually come of them in a community tank. So it becomes a question of setting up special tanks in which to encourage the fishes to spawn and then to raise as many as possible of the young. These can almost always be sold to your local dealer and help out with the cost of a quite expensive hobby.

Conditioning the Parents
Most species require preparation for reproduction if the best results are to be obtained. If the whole tank in which the parents normally live cannot be specially fed, the chosen pair or pairs should be separated from the rest—and sometimes from each other—and cosseted for a week or two before inducing them to spawn. However, it is usually best to leave them where they are if possible, as other techniques are liable to induce premature spawning unless the sexes are separated.

The main preparation is increased live foods of high quality, which few aquarists find it possible to provide routinely. Despite the excellent freeze-dried, frozen, and canned foods now available, perfectly adequate for normal maintenance, spawning is improved by feeding living or recently killed "meaty" types of food such as chopped earthworms, tubifex, mosquito larvae, and even shredded beef heart or other meat. This is true even of the common guppy. Fed as just outlined, 100 to 200 young per birth were recorded, whereas flakes or even freeze-dried brine shrimp or tubifex gave only 40 to 50 per litter.

Another important conditioning factor is water quality. Look up the requirements of the particular species and see that they are provided. To be realistic, it may be best to turn this particular recommendation around and say that it will probably be useless to try to breed any but very tough species unless their particular requirements are being supplied in the aquarium in which they will eventually spawn, and that should be of the type normal to the species.

A final factor is temperature. This should be normal for the species during the conditioning period, to be raised a few degrees when spawning is to be induced and during the early period of incubation and rearing of the young. Note that a sudden introduction to different water conditions or temperatures should be avoided. Raise the latter only after transfer to the spawning tank.

Suitable Tanks
Aquaria for spawning should preferably be quite large, since although many fishes will perform in a small tank, they usually do best when given plenty of room, and the young will eventually require it. A useful standard size is 40 to 60 liters, larger for prolific species like the bigger gouramis and cichlids, which also need plenty of room for mating procedures. Exceptions are tanks for killifishes, in which a series of quite small tanks is often employed, the parents being moved

Every aquarist is thrilled by his first successful experience at breeding an egglaying species and raising the fry to at least the free-swimming stage. There is a definite sense of accomplishment attending looking into one of your tanks and being able to view a sight such as this adult *Cichlasoma meeki* surrounded by healthy fry.

from one to the other at short intervals so as to get batches of eggs laid at much the same time. Most characins and some barbs can be spawned in 10- to 20-liter tanks, as I myself have advised, but the young will probably have to be moved rather early to a larger tank.

Tanks for livebearers should be clean, planted or at least with a batch of vegetation for the young to hide in, and well lit. They need not be sterile. Tanks for anabantids and cichlids may be similar, although some of the latter tear up plants and are best given bare rock and gravel. Tanks for egg-scatterers such as tetras, barbs, and danios should be newly washed out and preferably disinfected, but at least very clean and free of all parasites. Most egg-scatterers will spawn in a bare tank, but this carries too great a risk of eggs being eaten, so it is usual to provide some plants or spawning material (such as plastic mops) to receive the eggs of those that deposit them on such a site, or to line the base with coarse peat, small pebbles or such to receive nonadhesive eggs from species like zebra danios.

The best way to clean a tank is to raise the temperature to about 50°C, let it cool, then siphon off all the dead debris and replace this water with that of the required conditions. No plants or gravel are

Breeding traps of many different types are obtainable at pet shops. Shown here is a simple net trap, used to segregate a livebearing female (and the babies) from the other fish in the tank in which the net is placed. After the babies are born the mother should be removed from the net, but the babies can be kept in the net until they've gained some size.

This breeding trap can be set up in a number of different ways according to the function its user wants it to perform.

present of course during this phase. Then put in whatever is needed for the actual spawning—usually there is no call for aeration, filtration, etc., at this stage. An alternative method with small, easily handled tanks is to wash them out with a 3 to 6% salt solution and then, after a few minutes, with several rinses of fresh water. Drying for several days is not a good way, as too many pests and diseases can survive this treatment.

Plants can be cleaned by a brisk washing under the faucet, followed by a 15-second dunk in a 3% salt solution (or sea water), then by a further brisk cold wash in fresh water. Plastic mops can be placed in hot water and then anchored at the base of the tank with beads or pebbles, or floated in cork rings at the surface as required. A green color is best for such mops. Never use household disinfectants, as even when thoroughly washed out afterward tanks tend to smell of the product and inhibit spawning. Heat and salt are by far the best.

Sexual Differences
In livebearers, the male possesses a modified anal fin, the gonopodium, which is an organ of copulation. Packets of sperm are introduced into the female or sometimes only shot in her general direction, and these render her fertile for some months without further matings. The male is also smaller than the female in many species, as in the guppy, where he is also more colorful. However, in swordtails, platys, and mollies this size difference is minimal and both sexes are colored, except for *Xiphophorus variatus*, which has drab females. Finally, a pregnant female shows her condition by a swollen abdomen

and at that stage can be separated for dropping her young. In most species she also has a dark spot, the gravid spot, at the rear of her abdomen.

Most egg-scattering fishes have sexual differences in color or pattern, and the ripe female can be distinguished by her swollen, roe-filled belly. Standard texts should be consulted for details about various species, and where there is any doubt, it should be recalled that the male is usually slimmer, more brightly colored, and a little smaller than the female. Characin males usually have characteristic hooks on the lower part of the anal fin that often catch in the net when he is being captured. Cyprinids often have white pearly dots on some part of the body of the male, as in the goldfish, where

they are on the gill covers. Nearly all barbs have sexual color differences, as do most cyprinodonts.

The sexes of the majority of anabantids are easily distinguished, frequently exhibiting color and finnage differences, and in the breeding season the males become brilliantly colored and start building their bubblenests. Brilliantly colored males are also characteristic of most cichlids, but two favorites, angels and discus, present problems. However, cichlids like to select their own mates, so if possible it is best to keep a group of say 6 to 8 in a large tank and allow them to pair off. Then remove each pair to a breeding tank; they can be identified as they keep together, chase off others, and start to clean a spawning site.

Not all other families of fishes

A female livebearer (a guppy) delivering young; this one was born tail first.

are so obliging, and it may be hard to sex loaches and corydoras and other catfishes, for example. Here again, a group system is often the best way to start off, and sometimes, as with some of the loaches, young will appear from "nowhere" if you are lucky. Most times you won't be, as only a few species that do not guard their young fail to eat them.

Mating and Fertilization

Livebearer males fertilize females whenever the opportunity arises, and as they can do this to quite immature young ladies, it is important for the breeder to separate the sexes as soon as possible. Luckily, young males are not functional very early, so it is safe to raise a litter together for a few weeks, but not necessarily until males can be recognized as that may be too late. Various techniques are used by serious breeders who wish to know the pedigrees of their fishes. A mature male of desired stock can be placed with the litter at a suitable stage and will fertilize the females before the immature males can function, but there is still a danger that the immatures may add their quota before being recognized and removed. The only really safe method is to place pairs of young in small tanks or jars and to rely on 50% of known true pairs eventually resulting and progeny-testing those.

Mating in the egg-scatterers takes place when the female is ripe, often with a rise in temperature as a stimulus. It is a useful technique to have tanks with dividers, allowing the two chosen fish to see each other for a day or two, then, when all seems ready, to remove the barrier. About 0.5 cm of well-washed peat at the bottom of the tank produces the right kind

Closeup of the gonopodium of a male livebearer.

of water for most characins and does no harm to others or to barbs, killies, etc. The result should be soft, mildly acid water around pH 6. The peat also helps to hide the eggs if they do not adhere to plants or mops. The fish may spawn immediately or wait for several days, but a watch must be kept to remove them when it is over or too many eggs may be eaten. If nothing happens, try a partial water change with suitable water and raise the temperature by 2° or 3°C. If still nothing happens after, say, 4 days, remove the pair and try others or try again later.

The spawning action varies with species, but usually the male chases the female and they release eggs and milt (sperm) simultaneously over plants or mops, the sperm being very short-lived. Some species have quite interesting habits at the moment of spawning which are repeated for an hour or more as it progresses. The female giant danio (*Danio aequipinnatus*) whirls around several times horizontally, while the female *Rasbora heteromorpha* loops the loop and the glowlight tetra pair (*Hemigrammus erythrozonus*) does a barrel-roll. The bloodfin (*Aphyocharax anisitsi*) leaps out of the water, but the eggs fall back again, whereas *Copella arnoldi* does the same, but the eggs adhere above the water (if given the right environment, such as emersed plants or sanded glass) and are guarded by the male thereafter. He splashes water over them until they hatch, a quite unusual thing for an egg scatterer to do.

The cyprinodonts, or killifishes, do not spawn over a short period, but lay a few adhesive eggs each day for weeks on end or perhaps 10 to 20 eggs each day for a few days and then rest for a few more. These eggs are usually quite large and take anything from a week to several months to hatch, according to species and conditions. The typical fish egg hatches in 1 or 2 days. Some of the long-hatching eggs must dry up before they will hatch, and practically all killifish eggs can be dried if you wish and will hatch on being immersed in water again. When this is done, eggs laid over a period will hatch

A pair of *Copella arnoldi* breaking through the water surface on their way to an exposed leaf to spawn. Note eggs from earlier spawnings attached to leaf.

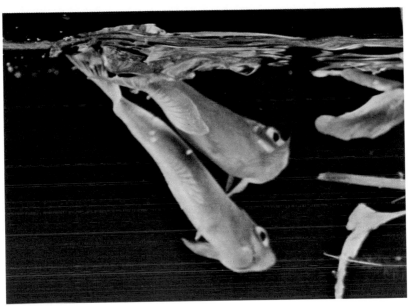

At the height of breeding frenzy a pair of Bengal danios *(Danio devario)* come close to the surface, but spawning takes place elsewhere.

Spawning under the blade of a broad leaf is not unusual for either *Rasbora hengeli,*shown here, or for *R. heteromorpha*. Judging from the size of the abdomen of this female, a good number of eggs can be expected.

A pair of golden pheasants *(Aphyosemion occidentalis)*, are about to start spawning on artificial grass provided.

out together—a great advantage. Most *Aphyosemion* species will stand two weeks of drying, but eggs of other genera, like *Cynolebias*, keep for several months and may require more than one drying period. It is common practice to place a male and two females of many cyprinodonts in a series of small tanks, leaving them in each for a few days, then to dry the eggs, which preferably will be in peat, and later hatch them out as a uniform batch or post them to a colleague in a semi-dry condition. Some cyprinodonts do not lay eggs that will stand drying, *Epiplatys* species, for example, and so must be handled differently, the fry being sorted for size as they hatch out.

Opposite page: Top, the male golden pheasant pressing its body against the back of the female to prevent her escaping. Center, with bodies side by side and with simultaneous tail movements, spawning appears imminent. Bottom, tails and vents close to bottom, the fish spawn; fertilized eggs drop and are caught among the strands of artificial grass, in the wild buried in the soft mud.

Most of the males of *Nothobranchius* are very colorful in comparison to the female. The red tail of this *N. jubbi* coupled with the distinct color pattern of individual scales makes this species appealing to aquarists.

With the parent fish viewed from the front, the red tail of the male is pressed close to the substrate, as he pushes the female's vent closer to the bottom.

Once close to the bottom, he wraps his dorsal fin around the female. If ready, she will not try to swim away.

Driving the female toward the bottom is the objective of this male that is eager to breed.

A pair of tiger barbs *(Capoeta tetrazona)* that are mature, interested in each other, and surveying a possible spawning site.

Butting the female on the side is part of pre-spawning behavior.

Bodies intimately close together, male's tail wrapped around female, violent quivering occurs as eggs and sperm are released simultaneosly.

With spawning over (note the many eggs attached to spawning grass), these tiger barbs will soon start to eat exposed eggs at the bottom.

Selecting a male and a female zebra danio *(Brachydanio rerio)* for breeding is easy. When ready, a female is distinctly filled with eggs and evidently larger than a male.

Courtship includes vigorous chasing in all areas of the tank, culminating in a stage when the partners come very near each other.

When ready to release her eggs, the female stops, expecting the male to position himself beside her, entire length of body in close contact.

Right: With the eggs released and fertilized, the partners separate.

A few egg scatterers do not lay adhesive eggs—the genus *Brachydanio* is a case in point. They scatter their eggs over the bottom of the tank and are very fond of eating them, even as they fall. So these species are spawned in shallow tanks lined with anything that gives them a minimal chance of a feast. Small marbles or pebbles between which the eggs will fall, a grid of glass rods too close for the fish to penetrate, a matt of fine-leaved plants, and even loose peat are all feasible techniques.

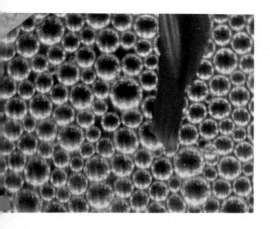

Anabantoid fishes have more of a courtship as well as taking care of the eggs and sometimes the young. The anabantoid male completes his bubblenest, often under a leaf at the surface of the water, and then searches for a female. Often he adopts a fighting stance, and if she doesn't respond with the appropriate submissive attitude he will be likely to attack. If all is well, she accompanies him under the nest, when typically he embraces her after a display of erect fins and they sink downward,

Above: A part of the bubblenest of fighting fish *(Betta splendens)*.
Below: During the spawning embrace this male betta (with long fins) wraps his body around the female in such a way that their genital openings almost lie opposite each other.

Spawning takes place near the bubblenest, usually directly underneath it. During courtship the fins of females are often split apart.

The male betta will deliberately seek and pick up eggs and transfer them to the nest. On the other hand, females often eat them instead. Female bettas are thus transferred elsewhere at the end of spawning.

Above: The bubblenest almost gone, this male betta is still tending to the nest. In time this interest will wane and the fry may be eaten. The yolk sac of the fry are very evident in this photo. **Below:** The same batch of betta fry are older; they will soon swim freely, at which time they'll need an ample supply of food.

releasing eggs and milt as they go. The male then picks up the eggs in his mouth and puffs them into the nest, where they float with the bubbles, which are quite sticky. This goes on at intervals for up to several hours. When it is all over, the female should be removed or she will probably be beaten up. Leave the male with the eggs until they hatch, usually after about 2 days, but, depending upon the species, he must be removed soon afterward as he may eat the young.

Not all *Betta* species build a bubblenest. *Betta unimaculata* and a few others spawn near the bottom and are mouthbrooders. However, their characteristic spawning embrace occurs as usual as seen here, but not near the surface.

A male *B. unimaculata* picking up the fertilized eggs for incubation inside the mouth cavity.

After all the eggs are safely contained in the mouth, the throat area is much larger than at other times in the life cycle of this male.

Cichlid courtship is quite spectacular. The self-chosen pair, sometimes any pair if given no choice, approach each other with erect fins and quivering bodies, then lock jaws and indulge in a vigorous tussle. They roll over and over and look more as if fighting than preparing to mate. Eventually they start cleaning a plant leaf, patch of rock, even the side of a tank, and keep this up for several days. A breeding tube appears on both sexes as spawning is near, and within a day or two the female deposits a few eggs at a time on the chosen spot, followed by the male, who fertilizes them. Up to 2,000 eggs may be laid,

Above: The breeding ritual of most cichlids includes the cleaning of the selected spawning site. Note the smooth appearance of this stone where a pair of flag cichlids (*Aequidens curviceps*) will soon spawn. **Opposite page:** As the male stands aside, the female is in the act of laying a group of eggs, not at random but laid singly one after the other. The eggs are adhesive and will not roll off the smooth stone.

and a constant guard is kept, with frequent fanning and removal of any that are infertile or develop fungus. Sometimes they eat all the eggs for no apparent reason, so

The male flag cichlid after having fertilized the eggs will remain close to the nest. By strong movement of the pectoral fins water currents are produced which increase the supply of oxygen to the incubating eggs. Eggs are mouthed individually to remove any foreign material attached.

The male flag cichlid is seen here watching the fry he transferred by mouth from the nest to a pit that was dug earlier. The swarm of free-swimming fry stays close to the guarding fish for some time; the fry then gradually disperse and stay by themselves.

some aquarists remove them as soon as spawning is over and look after the eggs themselves. However, best results are usually obtained if the parents are left *in situ.* Then, after 3 or 4 days, when the eggs are due to hatch, the parents in many species dig pits in the gravel where the young are deposited as they hatch. They are then moved from pit to pit by mouth as they develop, and after another 3 or 4 days, when they are free-swimming, they are herded together, still by both parents, in a tight swarm. At night they are shepherded into a pit and the parents stand guard over them. This goes on for weeks until the young

Above: An angelfish *(Pterophyllum scalare)* cleaning a leaf in preparation to spawning. If plants are not available, spawning can occur elsewhere, but the sites are always cleaned first. **Opposite page:** The male patiently watches as the female lays an additional batch of eggs to be fertilized next. By alternate oviposition and spraying of milt the nest increases in size.

are quite large and will eventually swim off on their own.

Two very popular cichlids need special mention. The angelfish, *Pterophyllum scalare,* does not dig

Angelfish parents herd their young only for a certain length of time, after which they can possibly devour their own young. Transferring the young to a tank by themselves is a very wise suggestion, if one intends to rear them to maturity.

These are not abnormal angelfish fry; they are from a special strain called golden angel that was much admired when the mutation was first recognized.

In this photo the male angelfish is seen fertilizing the eggs as the female seeks an opportunity to move beside him and lay more eggs. Then the chore of fanning and cleaning the eggs begins.

pits but lays its eggs on a leaf and transfers the young from leaf to leaf, while the young of the various discus fishes, *Symphysodon* sp., must be left with their parents since they feed on a copious mucus produced on the bodies of both parents. Some cichlids are mouthbrooders, which means that one or the other parent retains the eggs and fry in the mouth for several weeks, starving itself meanwhile. The young swim in and out of the mouth, rushing back in

Opposite page: Top, a pair of discus guarding the spawn. Aeration of the eggs is accomplished by rapid fanning movement of the pectoral fins. Debris is removed as usual by mouthing each egg. Bottom, a section of a male discus with fry feeding on the skin secretion only; no skin damage is known to occur.

alarm if threatened, and keep it up until too large for them all to get in.

The breeding behavior of *Symphysodon* is similar to that of angelfish, except for the care of the young. A vertical surface meticulously cleaned earlier is often chosen, like the leaf blade where this female is depositing eggs.

Left: Photographed frontally at the instance of yawning, this African cichlid, *Haplochromis burtoni*, shows the roomy mouth cavity of this mouthbrooding cichlid. **Below:** The eggs of *H. burtoni* are fairly large, but few are produced, just enough for the limited space of the mouth cavity where incubation takes place. This is the female in the process of taking the eggs.

With all the eggs taken into the mouth, the throat is distended, as is evident in this view of a female *H. burtoni*.

After hatching, the fry are free to move back into the mouth cavity of their mother, especially when threatened. The length of stay inside diminishes with age, usually lasting until they are too big to get in.

Corydoras aeneus, the bronze catfish, is one of the most popular armored catfishes found in the hobby. Being bottom feeders, they can be expected to court and breed near the bottom, too.

Seen ventrally, the fairly broad female is almost one and half times as wide as the male. They have already spawned; note eggs attached to plants and on a clump of spawning grass in the surrounding area.

A female bronze catfish with three eggs caught between her cupped pelvic fins. These will be next attached to any place she chooses, possibly on the leaf immediately below. Note the single egg on the leaf above.

915

Corydoras fry, like the adults, feed at the bottom. Fry foods that float are not for them.

Closeup of *Corydoras eggs* attached to the glass wall of a tank. They seem healthy, and if maintained with good aeration, right temperature and ideal water conditions, they should hatch normally. Beside predation, a fungal infection is the main cause of egg loss.

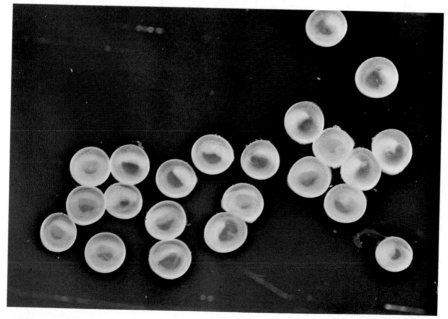

Developing embryo of a characoid, *Metynnis maculatus*. The embryonic membrane is transparent, and one can already see the head and body of the growing fry.

Other than cichlids, there are few species that make safe parents after the first few days. These include the corydoras, which do not look after their young but do not usually eat them, some of the loaches, the medaka (*Oryzias latipes*), the White Cloud Mountain minnow (*Tanichthys albonubes*), and the chocolate gourami (*Sphaerichthys osphromenoides*), which is a mouthbrooder.

Early Development

At 24° to 27°C, most fish eggs hatch out in 24 hours or less. Characin eggs are among the quickest, although the young may not be easily seen until they hang onto the glass sides of the tank, which they may not do for 2 or 3 days. Barbs tend to be a bit later in hatching, up to 36 hours, while danios, pencilfishes (*Nannostomus*), and some others take about 72 hours. The long resting periods of cyprinodont eggs have already been discussed. At lower temperatures the eggs take longer to hatch, and it is

not yet clear how well they could take really low temperatures.

After hatching, the fry carry a yolk sac, looking as if they are stuck onto a ball by the belly, which in fact they are. They absorb this over the course of the next few days—typically 2 to 5 days—and then need to feed actively. It is during the period of attachment to the yolk sac that they first remain at the bottom of the tank, hard to see. They sometimes take flea-like hops into the water, then rise up and hang onto the glass or plants in nearly all species, or onto the surface film of the water. Eventually they are free-swimming, but tend to return to the bottom of the tank at first during periods of illumination and to swim up in the dark. They now require feeding, and it is wise to get an estimate of their numbers so as to gauge how much to give them. This can be done in the hanging stage or by flashlight at night when they are free-swimming. Choose a typical section of the

A guppy, *Poecilia reticulata,* in the process of giving birth. The young guppy has just released itself from an egg membrane and will start to swim immediately.

aquarium and make a careful count, then multiply by the fraction of the whole that it represents.

Livebearer young are relatively advanced, but may sink to the bottom for a short period as they are born folded over head to tail, but soon straighten out. Then they swim toward the light, which is why a good mass of fine-leaved or fine-rooted floating plants is recommended as a cover for them to hide in if parent(s) are still present. Only premature young show a yolk sac; normal young are ready to feed immediately on newly hatched brine shrimp, microworms, baby daphnia, shredded whiteworms, or newly hatched mosquito larvae. These live foods are important for good growth, but a proportion of fine prepared food can be offered as well. This is

available in various commercial preparations. Feed several times a day.

Feeding the Fry

Starting to feed a newly hatched batch of egg-laying fishes used to be a problem. It meant the loss of many batches of fry and a high proportion of others. Messy cultures of infusoria had to be attempted or substituted for by suspensions of yeast, egg yolk, or very finely powdered dry food, none of which were reliable. Today, we have good commercial first foods consisting of fine droplets of a suitable mix suspended in a preservative fluid, but the best first foods are still newly hatched brine shrimp and microworm young. Not all fry can take these live foods immediately, but a surprising

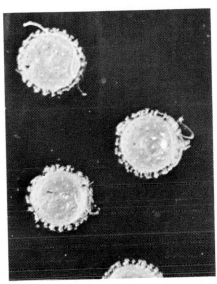 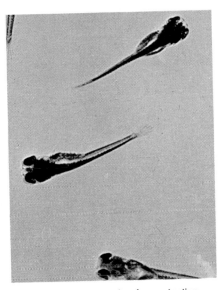

Left: The eggs of an annual fish, *Cynolebias*, have a tough covering for protection during the dormant stage underneath a dry pond in the wild. **Right:** Free-swimming fry of *Cynolebias* ready to accept fry food.

An *Apistogramma amoenus*, a dwarf cichlid, guarding the eggs spawned in the roof of a cave-like spawning site. The nest is usually hidden from view.

number of species can do so, particularly the very tiny young of the microworm, present in large numbers in the cultures. They even eat some of the yeasty culture medium itself. With any preparation but newly hatched brine shrimp, it is best to install mild aeration to keep the food floating around the tank.

Whether the fry of a particular species can take microworms or brine shrimp as a first food depends not only on body size but on their willingness to take a particular food and the size of their mouths. Thus danios, some tetras, such as glowlights (*Hemigrammus erythrozonus*) and head-and-tail lights (*H. ocellifer*), most barbs, and cichlids can take newly hatched brine shrimp straight away, whereas most tetras and many anabantids cannot. If they can't, Grade 1 food, outlined below, must be given. Sometimes part of a

hatch will take a given food, and if it is desired to raise the rest a mixture must be tried.

Grades of Food

Grade 1 is composed of the smallest foods such as one-celled algae, baker's yeast, small infusoria, very fine suspensions of commercial foods, egg yolk, or special preparations for starting egglayer fry. The fry of many gouramis and the Siamese fighting fish (*Betta splendens*) need such a start. The best is green water supplied for the first day or so, but the other materials mentioned can be used. Do not overfeed; just a few drops of a thick suspension of yeast or well shaken egg yolk given several times a day with mild aeration are sufficient. Keep an eye on the fry and see if their bellies are full as the best guide to success.

Grade 2 foods are the newly

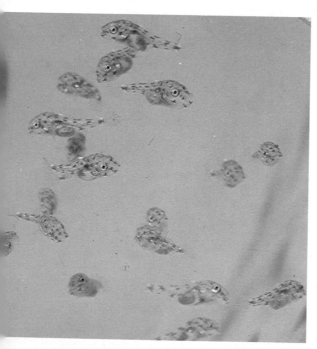

It is of utmost importance to make sure that free-swimming fry are provided with enough food at all times—their bellies should literally be bulging.

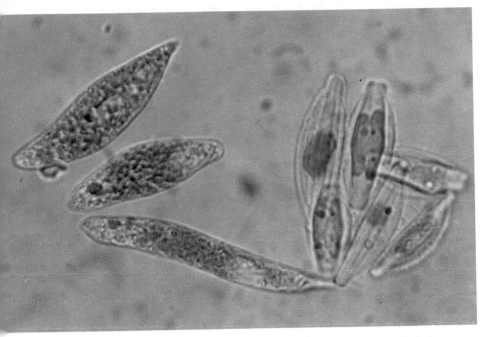

Euglena is easily recognized in a mixture of protozoans. Its green color and single flagellum are very characteristic. Having green pigments, they need sunlight for survival.

hatched brine shrimp and microworms mentioned above, large infusoria such as *Paramecium*, small rotifers, somewhat coarser suspensions of prepared foods, commercial preparations meant for livebearer young, or finely shredded earthworms. See that a top light is supplied when feeding brine shrimp so as to keep them up in the water, otherwise they will stay at the bottom and die. It is also a good idea to introduce small aquarium-bred snails at this stage, to consume uneaten food.

Grade 3 is food for fry a few weeks old or quite recently dropped livebearer young. This is small sifted daphnia, small mos-

quito larvae, large rotifers, Grindal worms, chopped whiteworms, or even coarser suspensions of dry or frozen foods than in Grade 2. Grade 2 foods can still be supplied, but they may be replaced by Grade 3 if desired.

Grade 4 is for well grown fry 2 or 3 cm long, which may be given full-size daphnia, any mosquito larvae, whiteworms, partly grown brine shrimp, and any of the smaller sizes of prepared foods or flakes, but keep up a proportion of live foods for best growth and health.

Infusoria
The older literature frequently prescribed "pond infusoria" for

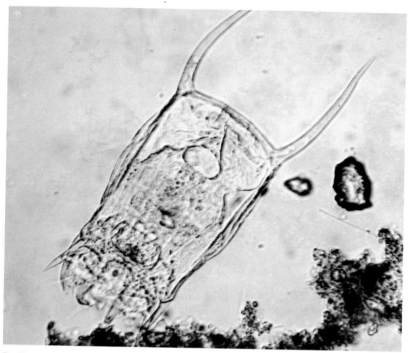

Rotifers can also be raised in pure cultures, if desired.

newly hatched fry, as there was indeed little else then available, however hard it may be to collect much of it. If you wish to use infusorial feeding, it is best to cultivate it free of the diseases and pests that pond life also includes. Infusoria are any small, usually microscopic, creatures that will appear in hordes in any rich culture medium. Make a vegetable infusion by boiling anything from crushed or chopped up leaves, dead flowers, or potato peelings to banana skins in water for a few minutes and leaving it to cool. A fistful per 40 liters is about right. A specific organism can be cultured by keeping the now sterile infusion covered and introducing the desired species either from a purchased culture or by picking some out of pond water or another culture yourself. Otherwise, leave the culture uncovered and let it ripen, aerating it and preferably keeping it at about 15°-20°C and not too brightly lit, or algae will predominate. In a few days, the infusoria should be visible under a microscope or even a hand lens. In fact, anything not seen with a lens is too small to be of use. Make a rough count of visible organisms per drop on a glass slide so that you know the strength of your preparation.

Fry will feed constantly at the

rate of several organisms per minute, say 5 per minute per fry, which is 300 per hour, so 100 fry will need around 30,000 organisms per hour. A good culture may have 100 to 200 organisms per drop, say 100, which gives 2,000 per ml or 2,000,000 per liter. So a tank of 100 fry will need about 70 ml per hour of a 100 per drop culture, or a little under half a liter twice daily, which can be safely dumped into the tank morning and evening, with mild aeration. Alternatively, arrange a drip so that a constant flow into the tank occurs at the desired rate. On the whole, it is best to dump the required amount in several times a day, as drips are not easy to arrange and regulate, also because all the fry get a chance of a good feed, not just those near the drip. Some breeders illuminate their tanks constantly for rapid growth, and this seems to do no harm.

Raising Young Fish

The fry of tropicals can be crowded at around 10 per liter for the first few weeks, so that a 20-liter tank will accommodate a spawning of 200 young fish, but better growth, particularly for prolific fish, is achieved with the larger tanks now recommended. In contrast to goldfish fry, the general run of tropicals develop evenly if well fed, and they breed true. Sometimes abnormalities develop in a spawning, but it is unusual for this to happen. There is therefore no need for severe culling; just throw out obvious runts or abnormals. Most species are not

The arowana, *Osteoglossum bicirrhosum*, is often available as a fry with yolk sac still present, not as an adult fish which is considerable in size in nature.

subject to the rather invidious standards imposed by some associations on goldfish and on some tropicals like the guppy, which at one stage led to colorless fish fulfilling standards set up by people who forgot to include brilliance and color requirements. So keep all the fish you like, select eventually the best for further breeding and sell or give away the rest. Remember that the best are not necessarily the biggest, but those showing alertness, brilliance, and general good condition.

When it becomes desirable to give the young fish more room, be careful about transferring them to a larger tank or series of tanks, taking all the usual precautions against water differences by putting the batch intended for a particular tank in a plastic bag or a jar and gradually making the changeover. Make sure that their new home doesn't differ much in pH, temperature, hardness, etc., from the old one. Select about a dozen of the best if you intend further breeding and raise them in the very best of conditions you can provide—plenty of space, live food, and the most suitable type of water. Depending on species, they will be ready to breed in a few weeks to a few months, at most a year. Then breed them quite early; don't wait for up to 2 years as advocated by some writers, as early breeding with small initial spawnings does good, not harm, and gets fish going. A good pair of characins or barbs will spawn every two weeks for months on end.

Diseases and Pests
In a well managed setup these will be minimal but can happen. Keep an eye open for velvet in particular; it is a killer of fry and should receive immediate treatment if detected. Another more common nuisance is hydra, a small freshwater polyp with long, stinging tentacles liable to be introduced with daphnia or other live foods. It kills young fry and reproduces rapidly and competes later for food with the survivors. The best cure is rather weird in that it consists of the deliberate introduction of ammonium nitrite or sulphate at 100 mg per liter. This is 100 ppm, reputedly toxic to fishes, but fry can usually stand it. Add the appropriate amount of ammonium salt well dissolved in tank water and stir it thoroughly so that it doesn't settle at the bottom and kill fry. Then raise the temperature by 3° to 6°C if possible. The hydra do not die or disappear immediately, but do die off over the next few days. A second treatment is permissible but no more, and a greater than usual series of water changes should follow over the next week, although this is difficult with fry present. The trick is to run the water very slowly into a siphon tube held near the bottom of an illuminated tank into a net sitting over a small container full of water, an excess of which overflows the container into a sink or suitable vessel. The net must, of course, dip under the water surface and be of dense enough material to catch the fry. When enough water has been removed—never more than 20-30% at a time—raise the container plus net and lower them gently into the tank, releasing the fry.

Index

This index covers only the Aquarium Maintenance, Plants and Breeding section (beginning on page 673). Indices for the other sections of this book begin on page 929.

925

INDICES

Codes indicating geographic distribution follow the name (in parens).
AF = Africa; AS = Tropical Asia; AU = Australia and New Guinea;
EA = Eurasia; NA = North America; TA = Tropical America,
including Mexico and the Caribbean.

Scientific Names

A

Abramites hypselonotus,
Headstander (TA), 297, 298

Acanthodoras cataphractus,
Painted Talking Catfish (TA),
394, 395

Acanthodoras spinosissimus,
Talking Catfish (TA), 395

Acanthophthalmus javanicus,
Javanese Loach (AS), 633

Acanthophthalmus kuhli, Kuhli
Loach (AS), 633

Acanthophthalmus myersi, Slimy
Myersi (AS), 634

Acanthophthalmus semicinctus,
Half-banded Loach (AS), 633

Acanthophthalmus shelfordi,
Shelford's Loach (AS), 634

Acanthopsis choirorhynchus, Long-
nosed Loach (AS), 643

Acarichthys geayi, Bandit Cichlid
(TA), 70

Acarichthys heckelii, Thread-
finned Cichlid (TA), 70

Acaronia nassa, Big-eyed Cichlid
(TA), 65

Acestrorhynchus falcatus, Spotted
Cachorro (TA), 333

Acestrorhynchus grandoculis, Big-
eyed Cachorro (TA), 333

Acestrorhynchus isalinae, Isaline's
Cachorro (TA), 334

Acheilognathus lanceolatus, Yari-
tanago (EA), 588

Acheilognathus longipinnis,
Itasenpara (EA), 586

Acheilognathus moriokae, Tanago
(EA), 589

Acheilognathus rhombea,
Kanehira (EA), 589

Acheilognathus tabira, Tabira
(EA), 588, 589

Achirus lineatus, Freshwater
Flounder (TA), 599

Acipenser ruthenus, Sterlet
Sturgeon (EA), 647

Aequidens aff. *dorsigerus*,
Greencheeked Acquidens (TA),
58

Aequidens awani, Gold Aequidens
(TA), 56, 57

Aequidens coeruleopunctatus,
Blue-point Flag Cichlid (TA),
61, 62

Aequidens curviceps, Flag Cichlid
(TA), 55

K

Knodus breviceps, Soap Eater (TA), 346

Kryptopterus bicirrhis, Glass Catfish (AS), 476

L

Labeo cylindricus, Cylindrical Shark (AF), 545

Labeo erythrurus, Rainbow Shark (AS), 572

Labeo frenatus, Red-finned Shark (AS), 573

Labeo rubropunctatus, Red-spotted Shark (AF), 545

Labeo variegatus, Variegated Shark (AF), 545

Labeotropheus fuelleborni, Fuelleborn's Cichlid (AF), 146, 147

Labeotropheus trewavasae, Red-top Trewavasae (AF), 148, 149

Labidochromis exasperatus, Orange-lined Cichlid (AF), 132

Labidochromis joanjohnsonae, Banner Cichlid (AF), 132

Labidochromis textilis, Cloth-of-gold Cichlid (AF), 132

Ladigesia roloffi, Jelly Bean Tetra (AF), 384

Lamprologus attenuatus, Marbled Lamprologus (AF), 173

Lamprologus brevis, Brevis (AF), 173

Lamprologus buscheri, Striped Lamprologus (AF), 174

Lamprologus callipterus, Callipterus (AF), 172

Lamprologus calvus, Pearly Lamprologus (AF), 174

Lamprologus compressiceps, Compressiceps (AF), 172, 175

Lamprologus cunningtoni, Black Lamprologus (AF), 176

Lamprologus elegans, Elegant Lamprologus (AF), 174

Lamprologus fasciatus, Barred Lamprologus (AF), 176

Lamprologus leleupi, Lemon Cichlid (AF), 176

Lamprologus leloupi, Pearlscale Lamprologus (AF), 173

Lamprologus melas, Dusky Lemon Cichlid (AF), 175

Lamprologus sp. "Magarae," Magarae (AF), 172

Lamprologus tretocephalus, Five-bar Cichlid (AF), 177

Lates microlepis, Small-scaled Nile Perch (AF), 624

Lates niloticus, Nile Perch (AF), 624

Lebiasina panamensis, Panama Pencilfish (TA), 285

Lebistes = Poecilia

Lefua costata, Lefua (EA), 639, 641

Leiarius pictus, Sailfin Pimelodid (TA), 410

Leiocassis siamensis, Barred Siamese Catfish (AS), 475

Leiopotherapon unicolor, Jewel Perch (AU), 655

Lepidocephalus thermalis, Lesser Loach (AS), 637, 638

Lepidogalaxias salamandroides, Long-finned Galaxias (AU), 658

Lepomis gibbosus, Pumpkinseed (NA), 649

Lepomis gulosus, Warmouth (NA), 649

Lepomis humilis, Orangespotted Sunfish (NA), 650

Lepomis macrochirus, Bluegill (NA), 650

Lepomis megalotis, Longeared Sunfish (NA), 649

Leporellus vittatus, Leporellus (TA), 291

977

Red Empress, *Haplochromis similis* (AF), 115

Red Leporinus, *Leporinus* cf. *granti* (TA), 296

Red Megalamphodus, *Megalamphodus* sp. "Rubra" (TA), 374

Red Rainbowfish, *Glossolepis incisus* (AU), 663

Red Shiner, *Notropis lutrensis* (NA), 577

Red Snakehead, *Channa micropeltes* (AS), 616

Red Snook, *Petenia splendida* (TA), 54

Red-barred Powder-blue Killie, *Aphyosemion bualanum* (AF), 253

Red-bellied Copella, *Copella compta* (TA), 292

Red-bellied Piranha, *Serrasalmus nattereri* (TA), 323, 324, 329, 330

Red-breasted Cichlid, *Aequidens dorsigerus* (TA), 55, 56

Red-eye Cichlid, *Chaetobranchus flavescens* (TA), 73

Red-eyed Characin, *Arnoldichthys spilopterus* (AF), 382, 383

Red-finned Brycinus, *Brycinus* aff. *imberi* (AF), 380

Red-finned Cichlid, *Crenicara punctulata* (TA), 82

Red-finned Lampeye, *Procatopus nototaenia* (AF), 271

Red-finned Pearl Fish, *Cynolebias antenori* (TA), 226

Red-finned Shark, *Labeo frenatus* (AS), 573

Red-fringed Lyretail, *Aphyosemion schoutedeni* (AF), 252

Red-line Pipefish, *Oostethus brachyurus* (AF/AS/AU), 660

Red-lipped Killie, *Aphyosemion rubrilabiale* (AF), 254

Red-spotted Cichlid, *Cichlasoma bifasciatum* (TA), 33

Red-spotted Copeina, *Copeina guttata* (TA), 289, 290

Red-spotted Gulare, *Aphyosemion gulare* (AF), 258

Red-spotted Killie, *Aphyosemion cognatum* (AF), 251

Red-spotted Panchax, *Epiplatys njalaensis* (AF), 267

Red-spotted Purple Killie, *Aphyosemion riggenbachi* (AF), 243

Red-spotted Pyrrhulina, *Pyrrhulina* sp. "Red-spotted" (TA), 291

Red-spotted Shark, *Labeo rubropunctatus* (AF), 545

Red-spotted Spot-finned Killie, *Rachovia pyropunctata* (TA), 233

Red-streaked Killie, *Aphyosemion labarrei* (AF), 259

Red-striped Xenotilapia, *Xenotilapia ochrogenys* (AF), 156

Red-tailed Dwarf Cichlid, *Apistogramma macmasteri* (TA), 77

Red-tailed Flag Tetra, *Hyphessobrycon agulha* (TA), 360

Red-tailed Goodeid, *Xenotoca eiseni* (TA), 532, 533, 534

Red-tailed Hemiodus, *Hemiodopsis microlepis* (TA), 302

Red-tailed Turquoise Notho, *Nothobranchius patrizii* (AF), 264

Red-top Trewavasae, *Labeotropheus trewavasae* (AF), 148, 149

Red-topped Tetra, *Bryconops affinis* (TA), 356

Redbellied Cichlid, *Aequidens thayeri* (TA), 64

Redbelly Notho, *Nothobranchius kirkii* (AF), 263

Redfin Barb, *Barbodes guirali* (AF), 539

Redfin Black-striped Barb, *Barbodes nicholsi* (AF), 542

Redfin Darter, *Etheostoma whipplei* (NA), 644

Redfin Otocinclus, *Parotocinclus maculicauda* (TA), 450

Redfin Pickerel, *Esox americanus* (NA), 652

Redheaded Cichlid, *Cichlasoma synspilum* (TA), 35

Redhook Metynnis, *Myleus rubripinnis* (TA), 321, 322, 323, 324

Redhump Geophagus, *Geophagus steindachneri* (TA), 69

Redline Rasbora, *Rasbora pauciperforata* (AS), 565

Redspot Callochromis, *Callochromis pleurospilus* (AF), 169

Redtailed Catfish, *Phractocephalus hemiliopterus* (TA), 411

Redtop Green Cichlid, *Aequidens mariae* (TA), 65

Regan's Bishop, *Brachyrhaphis rhabdophora* (TA), 524

Reticulated Cory, *Corydoras reticulatus* (TA), 435

Reticulated Freshwater Stingray, *Potamotrygon reticulatus* (TA), 598

Reticulated Pimelodid, *Perrunichthys perruno* (TA), 406, 409

Reticulated Rivulus, *Rivulus beniensis* (TA), 239

Rhodes's Chilo, *Chilotilapia rhodesii* (AF), 123

Rio Jaguribe Hypostomus, *Hypostomus jaguribensis* (TA), 443

Rio Meta Astyanax, *Astyanax metae* (TA), 348

Rio Meta Pimelodella, *Pimelodella metae* (TA), 405

Rio Napo Rivulus, *Rivulus limoncochae* (TA), 239

Rio Salinas Cory, *Corydoras habrosus* (TA), 422

Rio Xingu Cory, *Corydoras xinguensis* (TA), 432

Rivulichthys, *Trigonectes balzanii* (TA), 232

Roach, *Rutilus rutilus* (EA), 581

Robertson's Cichlid, *Cichlasoma robertsoni* (TA), 49

Robina's Cory, *Corydoras robinae* (TA), 433

Roloff's Killie, *Aphyosemion roloffi* (AF), 247

Roloff's Kribensis, *Pelvicachromis roloffi* (AF), 191

Rose-breasted Tilapia, *Tilapia* sp. "Rose-breasted" (AF), 184

Rosy Barb, *Puntius conchonius* (AS), 552, 553, 554

Rosy Tetra, *Hyphessobrycon bentosi* (TA), 362

Round-banded Barb, *Barbodes pentazona rhomboocellata* (AS), 558

Round-spotted Puffer, *Tetraodon fluviatilis* (AS), 628

Round-tailed Tilapia, *Tilapia ovalis* (AF), 183

Royal Panaque, *Panaque nigrolineatus* (TA), 448, 449, 451

Rudd, *Scardineus erythrophthalmus* (EA), 580, 581

Rummy-nose Tetra, *Hemigrammus rhodostomus* (TA), 369

Rusty Cichlid, *Iodotropheus sprengerae* (AF), 133

S

Saddled Galaxias, *Galaxias tanycephalus* (AU), 658

Sailfin Molly, *Poecilia latipinna* (NA), 519, 520

Sailfin Pimelodid, *Leiarius pictus* (TA), 410

Sailfin Shiner, *Notropis hypselopterus* (NA), 577

Sailfin Tetra, *Crenuchus spilurus* (TA), 279, 280

Sailfinned Prochilodus, *Semaprochilodus squamilentus* (TA), 309

Saiz's Tetra, *Hyphessobrycon saizi* (TA), 359

Salmon Catfish, *Chrysichthys brachynema* (AF), 473

Salvin's Cichlid, *Cichlasoma salvinii* (TA), 36

Sanchez's Cory, *Corydoras sanchesi* (TA), 432

Sanchez's Piranha, *Serrasalmus sanchezi* (TA), 328

Sarawak Betta, *Betta akarensis* (AS), 212

Saw-toothed Micropanchax, *Aplocheilichthys katangae* (AF), 273

Schomburgk's Leaf Fish, *Polycentrus schomburgki* (TA), 609

Schultz's Spot-finned Killie, *Austrofundulus limnaeus* (TA), 234, 235

Schwartz's Cory, *Corydoras schwartzi* (TA), 440

Scissortail, *Rasbora trilineata* (AS), 567, 568

Sepik Rainbowfish, *Glossolepis multisquamatus* (AU), 663

Serpae Tetra, *Hyphessobrycon serpae* (TA), 362

Serrated Piranha, *Serrasalmus serrulatus* (TA), 330

Severum, *Cichlasoma severum* (TA), 52, 53

Sharp-nosed Cory, *Corydoras semiaquilus* (TA), 419

Shelford's Loach, *Acanthophthalmus shelfordi* (AS), 634

Shiny-scaled Curimata, *Curimatopsis macrolepis* (TA), 314

Short-faced Elephantnose, *Mormyrus longirostris* (AF), 615

Short-finned Congo Tetra, *Hemigrammopetersius intermedius* (AF), 383, 384

Short-headed Knife Fish, *Rhabdolichops troscheli* (TA), 607

Short-lined Pyrrhulina, *Pyrrhulina brevis* (TA), 287, 288

Short-lined Pyrrhulina No. 2, *Pyrrhulina* sp. "Short-lined No. 2" (TA), 289

Short-striped Penguin, *Thayeria obliqua* (TA), 372

Short-tailed Trout Tetra, *Brycon brevicauda* (TA), 335

Shovelnose Catfish, *Sorubim lima* (TA), 410

Siamese Tiger Fish, *Datnioides microlepis* (AS), 619

Sickle-band Brycon, *Brycon melanopterus* (TA), 334

Sickle-fin Barb, *Puntius haasianus* (AF), 543

Sicklefin Killie, *Cynolebias dolichopterus* (TA), 229, 230

Silver Bream, *Blicca bjoerkna* (EA), 584

Silver Curimata, *Curimata rhomboides* (TA), 312

Silver Curimata, *Potamorhina latior* (TA), 314

Silver Distichodus, *Distichodus affinis* (AF), 386, 387, 388

Spotline Peacock Cichlid, *Cichla temensis* (TA), 85
Spotted African Lungfish, *Protopterus dolloi* (AF), 603
Spotted Aspidoras, *Aspidoras fuscoguttatus* (TA), 415
Spotted Cachorro, *Acestrorhynchus falcatus* (TA), 333
Spotted Congo Puffer, *Tetraodon schoutedeni* (AF), 630, 631
Spotted Curimata, *Curimata elegans* (TA), 314
Spotted Danio, *Brachydanio nigrofasciatus* (AS), 569
Spotted Elephant, *Marcusensis angolensis* (AF), 613
Spotted Head Peckoltia, *Peckoltia brevis* (TA), 445
Spotted Hoplo, *Hoplosternum pectorale* (TA), 413
Spotted Hypostomus, *Hypostomus punctatus* (TA), 442
Spotted Leporinus, *Leporinus maculatus* (TA), 298
Spotted Mosquitofish, *Gambusia puncticulata* (TA), 525
Spotted Mountain Trout, *Galaxias truttaceus* (AU), 656
Spotted Pike Characin, *Boulengerella maculata* (TA), 279
Spotted Pimelodid, *Pimelodus maculatus* (TA), 407
Spotted Rainbowfish, *Glossolepis maculosus* (AU), 663
Spotted Rasbora, *Rasbora maculata* (AS), 565
Spotted Rivulus, *Rivulus punctatus* (TA), 236, 240
Spotted Sailfin Sucker Catfish, *Pterygoplichthys* cf. *gibbiceps* (TA), 444
Spotted Scat, *Scatophagus argus* (AS/AU, 618

Spotted Snakehead, *Channa argus* (AS), 617
Spotted Synodontis, *Synodontis notatus* (AF), 465, 466
Squarehead Geophagus, *Geophagus gymnogenys* (TA), 66
Stanley Pool Puffer, *Tetraodon duboisi* (AF), 631
Starry Cat, *Parauchenipterus galeatus* (TA), 397
Steel-blue Killie, *Aphyosemion gardneri* (AF), 245, 246
Steindachner's Dwarf Cichlid, *Apistogramma steindachneri* (TA), 79
Sterba's Cory, *Corydoras sterbai* (TA), 440
Sterlet Sturgeon, *Acipenser ruthenus* (EA), 647
Stern's Hemiodus, *Hemiodopsis sterni* (TA), 303, 304
Stippled River Goby, *Awaous grammepomus* (AS/AU), 622
Stone Loach, *Noemacheilus barbatulus* (EA), 639, 640
Straight-finned Black Tetra, *Gymnocorymbus thayeri* (TA), 347
Striped Barb, *Puntius lineatus* (AS), 555, 557
Striped Barb No. 2, *Barbodes fasciatus* (AS), 559
Striped Chela, *Chela fasciata* (AS), 562
Striped Galaxias, *Galaxias nigrostriata* (AU), 657
Striped Goby Cichlid, *Eretmodus cyanostictus* (AF), 157
Striped Headstander, *Anostomus anostomus* (TA), 301
Striped Julie, *Julidochromis regani* (AF), 153
Striped Kribensis, *Pelvicachromis taeniatus* (AF), 190, 191, 192

Wimple Piranha, *Catoprion mento* (TA), 331

Wolterstorff's Pearl Fish, *Cynolebias wolterstorffi* (TA), 226

Y

Yari-tanago, *Acheilognathus lanceolatus* (EA), 588

Yellow Knife Fish, *Distocyclus conirostris* (TA), 606

Yellow Tetra, *Hyphessobrycon* cf. *bifasciatus* (TA), 351

Yellow-banded Moenkhausia, *Moenkhausia sanctaefilomenae* (TA), 355

Yellow-cheeked Dwarf Cichlid, *Apistogramma gibbiceps* (TA), 78

Yellow-faced Lethrinops, *Lethrinops furcicauda* (AF), 124, 125

Yellow-finned Chalceus, *Chalceus erythrurus* (TA), 335

Yellow-finned Hap, *Haplochromis virginalis* (AF), 114

Yellow-finned Xenotilapia, *Xenotilapia flavipinnis* (AF), 155, 156

Yellow-green Killie, *Aphyosemion gabunense* (AF), 252

Yellow-tailed Congo Tetra, *Hemigrammopetersius caudalis* (AF), 384

Yellow-tailed Hemiodus, *Hemiodus unimaculatus* (TA), 302

Yellow-tailed Violet Cichlid, *Gephyrochromis moorii* (AF), 133

Yellow-tipped Ventralis, *Ophthalmochromis ventralis* (AF), 168

Yellowbellied Cichlid, *Astatoreochromis straeleni* (AF), 160

Yucatan Sailfin Molly, *Poecilia velifera* (TA), 520

Z

Zamora Woodcat, *Auchenipterichthys thoracatus* (TA), 397

Zebra, *Pseudotropheus zebra* (AF), 130, 140, 141, 142, 143, 144

Zebra Angelfish, *Pterophyllum scalare* (TA), 94

Zebra Danio, *Brachydanio rerio* (AS), 569

Zebra Killie, *Fundulus heteroclitus* (NA), 242

Zebra Lace Angelfish, *Pterophyllum scalare* (TA), 93

Zenitanago, *Rhodeus suigensis* (EA), 587

Zollinger's Hillstream Loach, *Homaloptera* cf. *zollingeri* (AS), 643

Zygatus, *Corydoras zygatus* (TA), 423